ON THIS DAY...

ON THIS DAY...

by Carl D. Windsor, Ph. D.

Thomas Nelson Publishers
Nashville

Published in Nashville, Tennessee, by Thomas Nelson, Inc., and distributed in Canada by Lawson Falle, Ltd., Cambridge, Ontario.

Printed in the United States of America.

Unless otherwise noted all Scripture quotations are from THE KING JAMES VERSION. Copyright © 1979, 1980, 1982, Thomas Nelson, Inc., Publishers.

Library of Congress Cataloging-in-Publication Data

Windsor, Carl D.
    On this day— / by Carl D. Windsor.
      p. cm.
    ISBN 0-8407-7185–1
    1. Devotional calendars. 2. History—Miscellanea. I. Title.
BV4811.W593   1989
242'.2—dc20   89-38054
                                    CIP

1 2 3 4 5 6 — 93 92 91 90 89

Preface

Throughout history, people have used stories from life to make abstract truths clearer. In *On This Day . . .*, we have used numerous illustrations (what the Bible calls "parables") to demonstrate spiritual principles. It is our hope and prayer that you will enjoy reading these illustrations and might more clearly understand eternal biblical principles.

On This Day . . . lists various significant historical events on the day they occurred. Space limitations have restricted the number of events which could be included. Inclusion of a given event is for information purposes only and does not necessarily imply agreement with the lifestyle or activities of the persons or groups listed. Likewise, exclusion does not necessarily imply disapproval of a given individual, activity, or event.

Efforts have been made to provide a balanced listing between historic and contemporary figures of general interest from such fields as religion, education, entertainment, the arts, politics, athletics, and government.

I hope you will find *On This Day . . .* to provide information, guidance, and, simply, enjoyable reading for years to come.

On This Day...
Daily Inspirational System

★ **BEGIN TODAY**—No matter when you begin reading *On This Day . . . ,* keep at it faithfully for ten minutes each day, and you will complete an entire year's reading on this day next year.

★ **A DEVOTION FOR EVERY DAY** (even leap year)—Take *On This Day . . .* with you when you travel so you won't miss out on God's blessing as you faithfully read his Word every day. You need daily spiritual food just as you need daily physical food.

★ **A DAILY SCRIPTURE READING**—Always read the Scripture passage listed opposite the date. This is God speaking to you through his Word, the Bible.

★ **A SUMMARY OF HISTORIC HIGHLIGHTS ON THIS DAY**— Reflect on how God has guided humankind through good and bad days over the years. Determine that, with God's help, you will make this day the very best you can for him.

★ **BIRTHDAYS OF WELL-KNOWN PEOPLE**—Consider how God has allowed a variety of people to have a place on the world's stage. They, like all of us, will someday give account to God for their lives.

★ **A HISTORIC QUOTATION SETS THE THEME**—Memorable words written or spoken on this day throughout history. (Ask yourself, "What will I say or do today which will stand the test of time?" "Only one life, t'will soon be past; / Only what's done for Christ will last."

★ **DEVOTIONAL EMPHASIS AND ILLUSTRATION**—The heart of *On This Day . . .* is the devotional section, which serves to underscore the spiritual theme with an application from everyday life.

★ **A SUGGESTED PRAYER EMPHASIS**—A different prayer emphasis every day of the year helps to focus your prayer effort on the various needs in your life.

Ways to Use *On This Day...*

★ **FAMILY DEVOTIONS**—Encourage each member of the family to take part by reading the Scripture passage and one or more segments from *On This Day* . . . —great for developing a greater appreciation of our nation's heritage in God's historic plan.

★ **OFFICE/GROUP DEVOTIONS**—Help unite fellow workers around God's Word each day. Reading *On This Day* . . . will develop group cohesiveness and productivity as it focuses on the importance of an individual's daily accomplishments in shaping world events.

★ **IN THE CLASSROOM**—Teach responsibility and proper use of time by beginning each class with a selection from *On This Day* . . . . Help students become more effective as they see the personal side of others who have played important roles in history.

★ **AS A CONTEST FOR TRIVIA LOVERS**—Select and read a quotation, and have others guess who said it. Or guess in what year an event occurred or the year in which a public figure was born.

★ **FIND YOUR SPECIAL DAY**—Discover events that happened on family birthdays, anniversaries, graduation dates, etc. Write these days in the "Our Family Heritage" section (pg. xiii), then look them up in *On This Day* . . . .

★ **INDIVIDUALLY,** as a personal daily quiet time before God (see additional suggestions following).

ALL IN LESS THAN 10 MINUTES A DAY!

Suggestions For a Successful Personal Quiet Time

1. Choose a consistent time and place to be alone and undisturbed with the Lord. For many individuals, early morning hours are best and least interrupted. Others find later in the evening, or some other time during the day, more convenient. In any case *keep at it*. (Research shows you can develop a lifetime habit by repeating an activity daily for 13 weeks. Why not develop a Quiet Time habit that will give you the spiritual strength you need for the work God has given you to do?)

2. Choose a comfortable sitting position which will allow you to be undisturbed and attentive to your communication with God.

3. Have a pen and notebook nearby (along with your Bible and *On This Day* . . .) to jot down what you've learned from God, things to act upon, your praises, prayer requests, etc. (This written record will also serve as an excellent source of encouragement in the future as you review what God has done in *your* life over the years.)

4. Always begin your Quiet Time with prayer, asking the Holy Spirit to interpret the Scriptures as you read God's Word. When reading Scripture, ask yourself: "What is God teaching me in this passage," and "How can I put this knowledge into practice in my daily life?"

5. After reading the Scripture and the devotional message, end your Quiet Time with prayer, considering: "What can I be thankful for which the Lord has done," and "What needs of myself and others should I bring before the Lord?"

"Sin will keep you from this Book or this Book will keep you from sin."

—Dwight L. Moody,
(speaking of the Bible)

OUR FAMILY HERITAGE
Important Dates in Our Family

          Name   *Birthdate*

Grandfather: _____

Grandmother: _____

Father: _____

Mother: _____

Children: _____

_____

_____

Grandchildren: _____

_____

Anniversaries

          Name   *Date*

_____

_____

_____

Other Memorable Dates

_____

_____

_____

_____

_____

_____

To my dear wife, Bev,
whose unfailing encouragement and love
motivated me to become
an author

"Her children arise up,
and call her blessed;
her husband also,
and he praiseth her"
(Prov. 31:28).

Acknowledgments

Credit is due many people who have been an inspiration and encouragement to the author over the years and thus have contributed to this effort, some of whom are acknowledged below:

To my parents, George and Madelyn Guindon, mother-in-law, Jean Margetts, and father-in-law, the late Robert Margetts, who always knew I would succeed.

To my pastor, Dr. Jerry Falwell, for demonstrating the power and impact of the media in communicating the Gospel.

To former pastor Richard Cox, who instilled in me a love for illustrations, and to Christine Barrett, Frieda Taylor, Clyde DePriest, Lowell Wallen, Carl Holwerda, and all those at Bethany who provided godly instruction and exâmple in my early years of life.

To Pastor and Mrs. Winthrop Robinson, for their spiritual nurturance and guidance in the early years of my marriage.

To George Vogt and the many friends at Grace Bible Church, for their fellowship and spiritual enrichment of our family.

To my lifelong friend Mike Blomé, for helping me always to see the brighter side of life.

To the United States Navy, which instilled in me a love for my country.

To Edna Kline, who encouraged me to enroll in college, and who drove me to my first college classes.

To Eva Middleton, for the concept of a devotional book.

To Dr. Harold Willmington, for making the Bible come alive, and for his special encouragement and direction in writing and publication.

To my secretary Linda Burchfield and assistant Manny Laso, who helped with the original manuscript.

To Jerry Edwards, who encouraged me to begin a radio ministry which formed the basis for this book.

To Jim Jensen, who inspired me to embark on a career in mass communications.

To my students, colleagues, and former colleagues who have been an encouragement over the years; among them: Ben Armstrong, Ralph Kennedy, Robert Monaghan, Bill Gribbin, Fred Haas, Jim Pickering, and Steve Troxel.

Most of all to my wonderful wife, Bev, and children Trent, Todd, and Heather, whose understanding and patience with my many projects enabled this book to be completed.

JANUARY

1

Today in History—President Lincoln issues the Emancipation Proclamation, 1863; Ellis Island in New York Harbor becomes reception center for new immigrants, 1892; first religious broadcast, KDKA, 1921; Cuban government collapses under revolt led by Fidel Castro, 1959; U.S. and China formally resume diplomatic relations after nearly thirty years, 1979.

Born Today—Patriot Paul Revere, 1735; first flag maker Betsy Ross, 1752; senator Barry Goldwater, 1909; economist Elliot Janeway, 1913; author J. D. Salinger, 1919; Christian broadcaster David Hocking, 1941.

Today's Quotation—"I am in earnest. I will not equivocate: I will not excuse; I will not retreat a single inch; and I will be heard!"—*William Lloyd Garrison, January 1, 1831*

Freeing the Captives

The greatest freedom is that given by God when he lifts our burden of sin. Years ago, when President Abraham Lincoln prepared to sign the Emancipation Proclamation, he took his pen, moved it to the place for the signature, held it for a moment and then dropped the pen. Upon being questioned, Mr. Lincoln replied, "If my name goes into history, it will be for this act, and if my hand trembles when I sign it, there will be some who will say, 'he hesitated.'" Lincoln then turned to the table, took up the pen again, and slowly, boldly penned his famous signature. As we begin a new year, let us rejoice that as believers, no matter what our background may be, we are no longer enslaved to sin. As John reminds us, "If the Son therefore shall make you free, ye shall be free indeed" (John 8:36). Throughout this new year, let us celebrate our freedom in Christ and tell others of his love.

Prayer Suggestion—That many people would come to know Christ as Savior through our faithful witness this new year.

JANUARY

2

Proverbs 1:7-16

Today in History—First U.S. flag raised by Continental Army, 1776; Manila captured by Japanese, 1942; first successful heart transplant operation, 1968; President Carter seeks delay in arms treaty ratification due to recent Soviet invasion of Afghanistan, 1980.

Born Today—General James Wolfe, 1727; writer Robert Nathan, 1894; composer Michael Tippett, 1905; author Isaac Asimov, 1920, singer Renata Tebaldi, 1922; politician Kay Orr, 1939.

Today's Quotation—"We are not amused."—*Queen Victoria, 1900*

Serious Purpose

A young Christian girl once defended her attendance at some questionable amusements by saying, "I feel a Christian can go anywhere." "That reminds me," said her friend, "of a visit we once took to a coal mine. One young lady had chosen to wear a dainty white dress for the tour, asking the miner, 'Can't I wear a white dress in the mine?' The old miner thought a moment and then replied, 'There is nothing that will keep you from wearing a white dress in the mine, but there will be plenty to keep you from wearing one back.'" How foolish of the girl to think she could be so untouched by the lesser things of this world. It is tragic to see what great lengths some will go to find amusement through immorality, drunkenness, idolatry, or striving for temporal things which cannot satisfy. The believer can say with Queen Victoria, "I am not amused." After all we are not citizens of this world but are "just passing through" much as the weary traveler, spending the night away, anticipates his return home. Why be attracted to the world's amusements?

Prayer Suggestion—That as children of God, he would help us to become more serious in daily carrying out his will for our lives.

18

JANUARY

3

Today in History—General George Washington's troops defeat the British at Princeton, N.J., 1777; March of Dimes campaign begins, 1938; Alaska admitted to the union as forty-ninth state, 1959; U.S. breaks diplomatic relations with Fidel Castro's Cuba, 1961; drug, Laetrile, authorized for trial cancer treatment, 1980; U.S. "family farm" said to be more depressed than in past fifty years, 1987.

Born Today—Roman orator Cicero, 106 B.C.; British statesman Earl Clement Attlee, 1883; actor Ray Milland, 1908; comedian Victor Borge, 1909; consumer advisor Betty Furness, 1916; hockey player Bobby Hull, 1939.

Today's Quotation—"I have nothing to declare, but my genius."— *Oscar Wilde to customs inspectors in New York, January 3, 1882*

Misplaced Confidence

How many people have an inflated view of their accomplishments? It is said that artist Grant Wood often took "artistic license" when painting peaceful scenes of the villages and fields of his native Iowa. Once, after painting a scene of his neighbor's farm, he showed the finished work to the farmer. The farmer said, "Yep, it looks just like it. Thanks for cutting the weeds." While artistic license may be acceptable in paintings, we need to recognize overconfidence in our lives for just what it is: sinful pride. Two ladies were once questioning whether the great pioneer missionary Hudson Taylor was ever tempted to be proud. Later, upon hearing the question, Taylor replied, "I never knew I had done anything." He was right, because it was God who worked through him who had accomplished so much. "To God be the glory great things he hath done!"

Prayer Suggestion—Recognize our "help comes from the Lord who maketh heaven and earth," and "without him I can do nothing."

JANUARY

4

Genesis 11:1-9

Today in History—First State of the Union address given by President George Washington, 1790; first successful appendectomy performed in Davenport, Iowa in 1885; Utah admitted to the union as 45th state, 1896; Ralph J. Bunche first black appointed as State Department official in 1944; Chilean President Augusto Pinochet wins landslide in plebiscite, 1978.

Born Today—Storyteller Jacob Grimm, 1785; creator of blind reading system Louis Braille, 1809; "General Tom Thumb," 1838; writer J. R. R. Tolkien, 1892; boxer Floyd Patterson, 1935.

Today's Quotation—"Time and fire have the same effect."—*Henry David Thoreau, January 4, 1855*

Change

It has been said, "Nothing in life is permanent but death and taxes." Both time and fire are agents of change as are many other factors that affect our lives. But for the believer, change must be in conformity to God's will. The people of Babylon wanted to reach God and thus embarked on an ambitious building project which became known as the Tower of Babel. However, this sinful attempt to reach up to heaven was against God's plan and so he terminated the project. By confounding their language, God ensured the workers could no longer communicate and thus construction came to a halt. Likewise, if our plans run against God's will he can surely stop us. Let us resolve to always *seek* his will and *do* it!

Prayer Suggestion—Be certain we are sensitive to what God wants and that our activities are in accord with his will for us.

JANUARY

5

Today in History—Paris Opera House opens, 1875; Henry Ford announces minimum wage of five dollars for an eight-hour day, 1914; in Wyoming, Nellie Tayloe Ross becomes first woman governor, 1925; U.S. airlines begin baggage inspections of all boarding passengers, 1973.

Born Today—Navy hero Stephen Decatur, 1779; explorer Zebulon Pike, 1779; German leader Konrad Adenauer, 1876; former Vice President Walter Mondale, 1928; Spain's Prince Juan Carlos, 1938.

Today's Quotation—"There can be no divided allegiance here. We have room for but one flag. . . . We have room for but one language. . . . We have room for but one sole loyalty, and that is loyalty to the American people. . . ."—*Theodore Roosevelt, January 5, 1919*

Loyalty

Many distractions are out to influence us in this age. That is why it is so essential that we are loyal followers of the God who knows the way.

Dan Crawford once wrote of a native guide who was leading him along a new trail. Being somewhat uncertain of the direction, he asked his guide just where they were going. "You want to know the way? I am the way!" smiled the native, pointing to his head where the knowledge was stored. Crawford later had an opportunity to share with his guide the One who is the true and living way. If we do not have loyalty to our Lord, how can we expect to find our way through this life?

Prayer Suggestion—The courage to fully trust him who made us, no matter on which path he should lead us in our journey through life.

JANUARY

6

Today in History—Widow Martha Dandridge Custis marries George Washington, 1759; New Mexico admitted to Union as forty-seventh state, 1912; first commercial around-the-world flight completed, 1942; week-long food riots in Tunisia leave seventy-five dead as price of bread doubles, 1984; Texaco buys Getty Oil for record $10 billion, 1984.

Born Today—Joan of Arc, 1412; poet Carl Sandburg, 1878; actress Loretta Young, 1913; entertainer Danny Thomas, 1914; pollster Lou Harris, 1921; football player Howie Long, 1960.

Today's Quotation—"We look forward to a world founded upon four essential human freedoms. The first is freedom of speech and expression . . . everywhere in the world. The second is freedom of every person to worship God in his own way . . . everywhere in the world. The third is freedom from want . . . everywhere in the world. The fourth is freedom from fear . . . anywhere in the world."—*Franklin D. Roosevelt, January 6, 1941*

Freedom

Reading God's Word each day is a privilege many around the world do not have. When the Americans first arrived in the Philippines, many political prisoners were freed. Among the "crimes" some had committed was that of reading the Bible. One day a man came to a missionary and asked quietly if it were true that he could now read his Bible in peace. The missionary pointed to a nearby American flag and said, "So long as you see that flag flying overhead you can read the Bible on the roof of your house and no one can molest you."

Ask yourself the question, "If I were to be arrested for reading God's Word would there be sufficient evidence for a conviction?" Believer, rejoice in the freedom you have in Christ!

Prayer Suggestion—Let us be ever aware of the precious freedom we have to read and enjoy God's Word wherever and whenever we wish.

JANUARY

7

Today in History—First commercial bank in U.S. opens, 1782; George Washington elected as first U.S. president, 1789; President Harry Truman announces U.S. has developed the hydrogen bomb, 1953; Vietnamese troops seize Phnom Penh (Cambodian capital), 1979.

Born Today—President Millard Fillmore, 1800; actor Vincent Gardenia, 1922; broadcast journalist Douglas Kiker, 1930; publisher Jann Wenner, 1947; songwriter Kenny Loggins, 1948.

Today's Quotation—"All men pretend the licentiousness of the press to be a public grievance, but it is much easier to say it is so, than to prove it. . . ."—*Daniel Defoe, January 7, 1704*

Ungodly Influence

It is hard to overestimate the ungodly influence questionable literature has upon an individual. The murderer of Lord Russell said that reading a single vicious romance led him into crime. England's great John Angeli James (of whom it was said "England never produced a better man") said as an old man that he had never gotten over the evil effects of having once read a bad book for fifteen minutes. DeWitt Talmage tells of an incident that occurred in his college days while he was studying for an "honorable profession." One day a friend showed Talmage an ungodly book. Glancing through a few pages, Talmage quickly handed it back to his friend saying, "You had better destroy that book." But his friend ignored the advice, kept the book, and read it again and again. It was not long before this friend gave up religion as "a myth." Today it is the media that has great impact upon society as hour after hour, day after day, they bombard us with such objectionable material as can scarcely be described. Is it any wonder then that our country is wracked by insoluble problems?

Prayer Suggestion—That we, and our families, would turn from evil influences wherever found and cling instead to God and his Word.

JANUARY

8

Psalm 11:1-7

Today in History—Howard University, established as a college for blacks in Washington, D.C., adopts this name, 1867; President Woodrow Wilson outlines peace aims of U.S. in World War I, 1918; Igor Stravinsky makes first public appearance in U.S. as conductor of New York City Philharmonic, 1925; Fidel Castro enters Havana in victory, 1959; Charles de Gaulle inaugurated as president of France, 1959; unmanned Russian space vehicle *(Luna 21)* launched toward moon, 1973; AT&T says it will give up twenty-two local Bell companies in major divestiture, 1982; Arizona Governor Evan Mecham impeached, 1988.

Born Today—Diplomat Nicholas Biddle, 1786; novelist William Collins, 1824; actor Jose Ferrer, 1912; comedian Soupy Sales, 1930; singer Elvis Presley, 1935; actress Yvette Mimieux, 1941.

Today's Quotation—"The day of conquest and aggrandizement is gone by; so is also the day of secret covenants. . . ."—*Woodrow Wilson, January 8, 1918*

Trust

Have you ever noticed the nearly complete trust of young children? Recently our family was watching home movies of my daughter's first steps. At first she would hesitantly start out, walk a step or two, and then collapse in a heap. While such an experience would cause most adults to quit trying, Heather trusted mom or dad to walk along beside her and gave them her trust until she finally mastered the art of walking. We as adults, however, never outgrow our need to trust in God. The Old Testament prophet Abraham is a case in point. Abraham's name meant "Father of Nations," yet he and his wife Sarah were still childless in their nineties. Yet by trusting God to honor his promise of an heir, they did become parents. As Abraham said in faith, "Is anything too hard for God?" (Gen. 18:14) At the end of this first week of the new year we can say, "I don't know what the future holds, but I know who holds the future."

Prayer Suggestion—For God to help us to trust in him and not "run ahead" of his plans or take matters into our own hands.

24

JANUARY

9

Today in History—Connecticut becomes fifth state to enter the Union, 1788; Jean Pierre Blanchard makes first U.S. balloon flight, 1793; General Douglas MacArthur returns to Philippines as he vowed, 1945; United Nations headquarters opens in New York City, 1951; sixty-three persons executed for role in attack on Mecca, 1980.

Born Today—Opera manager Rudolph Bing, 1902; choreographer George Balanchine, 1904; President Richard Nixon, 1913; sportscaster Dick Enberg, 1935; folksinger Joan Baez, 1941.

Today's Quotation—"Where the law ends, tyranny begins."—*William Pitt, the Elder, January 9, 1770*

The Blessed Hope

Most everyone who has read the Bible realizes that Old Testament figures lived under the age of law based on the Ten Commandments. However, after Christ's earthly ministry, he gave us the "blessed hope" of his return for those who have trusted him. In fact, for every prophecy on the first coming of Christ, the Bible contains eight prophecies on his Second Coming. This promise has been called the "blessed hope of all believers." L. T. Talbot tells of leaving Australia some years ago promising his mother, "If God spares me, I will come back to see you." For years she waited expectantly for his personal, visible, actual return. As Talbot said, "If someone had challenged this promise, my mother would have replied, 'He said that he would come back!'" Indeed, Talbot did return some years afterward.

Christians also can expect Christ to keep his word when he promised to return to earth. (To make sure we understood his promise to return, it is referred to 2,163 times in the Scriptures!) Let us long for that day—coming soon—when we can say, "Christ returneth, *Hallelujah!*"

Prayer Suggestion—For Christ to forgive our sins so that we could be a spotless bride for him.

JANUARY

10

Today in History—Thomas Paine publishes *Common Sense*, 1776; oil discovered in Beaumont, Texas, 1901; first photographs taken from an airplane, 1911; League of Nations founded, 1920; Leon Trotsky exiled to Turkestan, 1928; first session of U.N. General Assembly begins in London, 1946; fund drive launched to rescue aging Parthenon in Athens, 1977.

Born Today—Colonial soldier Ethan Allen, 1738; historian Lord Acton, 1834; poet Robinson Jeffers, 1887; singer Gisele Mackenzie, 1910; composer Johnnie Ray, 1927; boxer George Foreman, 1949.

Today's Quotation—"Due attention to the inside of books, and due contempt for the outside, is the proper relation between a man of sense and his books."—*Earl of Chesterfield, January 10, 1749*

The Book of Books

Of all the books ever written, none can compare to the Word of God, the Bible. When Stanley began his pilgrimage across Africa he took with him seventy-three books weighing nearly two hundred pounds! After going three hundred miles on this wearying trek, he decided to lighten the load and throw away some of his baggage. As the journey went on, his library grew smaller and smaller until finally only one book remained—the Bible. Stanley refused to part with this book which he said he read three times during his lengthy trip. How often have you read God's Word? It is the world's only eternal writing. Indeed we are told, "Heaven and earth shall pass away, but my words shall not pass away" (Matt. 24:35). Since it is the only book of everlasting value, shouldn't we be spending more time reading and digesting it each day? Why not resolve to make Bible study an important part of every one of your days?

Prayer Suggestion—That the Bible would become so much a part of our lives that we would allow nothing to interfere with our daily time alone with God.

JANUARY

11

Ephesians 6:1-9

Today in History—Amelia Earhart becomes first woman to fly solo across Pacific, 1935; Surgeon General's report links cigarette smoking and health deficiencies, 1964; three GI's killed in Pershing missile fire in Germany, 1985.

Born Today—Statesman Alexander Hamilton, 1755; university founder Ezra Cornell, 1807; writer William James, 1842; writer Alan Paton, 1903; university administrator Juanita Kreps, 1921; TV executive Grant Tiker, 1926.

Today's Quotation—"A child miseducated is a child lost."—*John F. Kennedy, January 11, 1962*

Obedient Children

One of the most familiar Scripture passages is found in Proverbs 22:6, "Train up a child in the way he should go: and when he is old, he will not depart from it." Studies now show that obedience is healthful. A famed children's specialist was quoted some years ago as saying, "When it comes to a serious illness, the child who has been taught to obey stands four times the chance of recovery that the spoiled and undisciplined child does." When we obey God's Word, we find that life is so much richer in ways we may not have expected. But most important is our response to the question: "Are we obedient to our heavenly Father?" Some day we will give an accounting of all we have done. What will your report be?

Prayer Suggestion—That God would awaken in us an awareness of our need to obey him in all we do and say.

JANUARY

12

Ecclesiastes 5:2-6

Today in History—First museum established in U.S. (in Charleston, S.C.), 1773; Hattie Caraway of Arkansas becomes first woman elected U.S. Senator, 1932; World War II battle of South China Sea, 1945; Biafra surrenders to Nigeria ending Civil War, 1970; mystery writer Agatha Christie dies in London at age 85, 1976; prominent South African black leader Ampie Mayisa found slain hours before meeting with U.S. officials about local conditions, 1986.

Born Today—Colonial governor John Winthrop, 1588; statesman Edmund Burke, 1729; writer Jack London, 1876; civil rights leader James Farmer, 1920; singer Ray Price, 1926; boxer Joe Frazier, 1944.

Today's Quotation—"There are, in every age, new errors to be rectified, and new prejudices to be opposed."—*Samuel Johnson, January 12, 1751*

I Made a Mistake

Anyone who has ever made a mistake can identify with the poor bank janitor who accidentally put a box containing checks worth $840,000 next to the trash shredder. It was not long before the shredder operator dutifully turned thousands of negotiable checks into thin shreds of confetti. Bank officials, realizing the mistake, quickly mobilized fifty employees to reconstruct all 8,000 checks. Imagine the task they faced, a real-life jigsaw puzzle Olympics—all because of an honest mistake. Indeed, "To err is human," but let us be certain that we never consciously err in violation of God's commands!

Prayer Suggestion—That God would forgive past errors and would keep us from making mistakes as we seek to do his will.

28

JANUARY

Today in History—Saar votes to rejoin Germany, 1935; U.S.S.R. begins boycott of U.N. Security Council after failing to unseat Nationalist China, 1950; U.S.S.R. announces arrest of nine doctors on charges of plotting against Stalin regime, 1953; Robert C. Weaver becomes first black U.S. cabinet member (as secretary of Housing and Urban Development), 1966; seventy-eight killed in plane crash in Washington, D.C. blizzard, 1982; McDonald's builder Ray Kroc dies at age 81, 1984; derailment in Ethiopia, worst train wreck in Africa, leaves 392 dead, 1985.

Born Today—Supreme Court Chief Justice Salmon Chase, 1808; entertainer Sophie Tucker, 1884; actor Robert Stack, 1919; actor Charles Nelson Reilly, 1931; broadcast executive Brandon Tartikoff, 1949.

Today's Quotation—" . . . the truth is on the march and nothing will stop it."—*Emile Zola, 1898*

God's Truth

"Small but mighty" aptly describes the shortest chapter in the Bible, Psalm 117, for it is here that we are reminded that "the truth of the LORD endureth forever." What is truth? While preparing to take a comprehensive exam as part of doctoral studies some years ago, my colleagues cautioned that I could expect a challenging line of questioning including the "definition of truth." While the world might find this a challenging concept, every believer's answer should be "(God's) Word is truth" (John 17:17). Just as the child who does not choose to believe a fire is hot until his hand is burned, so millions throughout the ages of time who have not believed in Christ will find out, too late, that indeed God's Word is Truth.

Prayer Suggestion—Ask God to help you realize his Word is Truth and to daily read and memorize it, making it a part of your life.

JANUARY

14

1 Corinthians 15:50–58

Today in History—First written constitution in America adopted, 1639; French President Charles de Gaulle bars British entry into European Common Market, 1963; first docking of two manned spacecraft (Russian *Soyuz 4* and *5*), 1969; William Paley called out of retirement to oversee revitalization of CBS television network, 1986.

Born Today—Patriot William Whipple, 1730; soldier (traitor) Benedict Arnold, 1741; Dr. Albert Schweitzer, 1875; author Hugh Lofting, 1886; pastor Martin Niemoller, 1892; statesman Carlos Romulo, 1899; columnist Andy Rooney, 1919; legislator Julian Bond, 1940.

Today's Quotation—" . . . man is not an annual. He sees the annual plants wither."—*Henry David Thoreau, January 14, 1852*

Eternal Life

A preacher once preached on eternal destiny to several young men who sought to trip him up. The first began by saying, "I believe we have a dispute here sir, and I'd like to settle it." "Okay, what is it?" said the preacher. "Well, you say the wicked will go into eternal punishment and I don't think they will." "Well then," said the preacher wisely, "you don't have a dispute with me, for in Matthew 25:46 you will read, 'And these shall go away into everlasting punishment: but the righteous into life eternal.' Your dispute is with the Lord and I suggest you go and settle it with him."

If spiritual evidence is not enough, space scientist Dr. Wernher von Braun says there are "essentially scientific" reasons for believing in life after death. "Science has found that nothing can disappear without a trace. Nature does not know extinction. If God applies the fundamental principle to the most minute and insignificant parts of the universe, doesn't it make sense to assume that he applies it to the masterpiece of his creation—the human soul? I think it does." Indeed, God has given everyone eternal life, but he has given to each of us the right to decide where we will spend that life. Where will you spend eternity?

Prayer Suggestion—Ask Christ into your heart and life today. As a believer, rededicate your life to serving him.

30

JANUARY

15

Today in History—Queen Elizabeth I crowned in London, 1559; cartoonist Thomas Nast's depiction of the donkey as symbol of the Democratic party first published, 1870; Irish Free State established, 1922; U.S. Defense headquarters (the Pentagon) completed, 1943; commission named to investigate CIA domestic spy operations, 1975.

Born Today—Author Horatio Alger, 1832; industrialist Aristotle Onassis, 1906; physicist Edward Teller, 1908; actor Lloyd Bridges, 1913; Egyptian President Gamal Abdel Nasser, 1918; journalist Rod MacLeish, 1926; civil rights leader Dr. Martin Luther King, Jr., 1929.

Today's Quotation—"Bowed by the weight of centuries he leans/ Upon his hoe and gazes on the ground,/The emptiness of ages in his face,/And on his back the burden of the world."—*Edwin Markham, January 15, 1899*

Life's Burdens

This is an age in which many individuals are depressed, crushed by the burdens of everyday life. Yet there is no need for anyone to feel buried by the weight of life's problems for God has said: "Cast thy burden upon the Lord, and he shall sustain thee . . ." (Ps. 55:22). A teacher, attempting to explain the meaning of the text "My yoke is easy," asked her class, "Who can tell me what a yoke is?" One child said, "A yoke is something they put on the necks of animals." "Good," said the teacher. "What is the yoke God puts on us?" A little girl responded, "It is God putting his arms around our necks." That is the story of God's love for us. When we are beaten down and discouraged by troubles and the problems of life, God reaches down and puts his sustaining arm of strength around us. If you are discouraged and struggling in what seems to be an uphill battle, consider whether you have asked your heavenly Father for help. Remember, there's nothing that will occur today that God and you together cannot handle.

Prayer Suggestion—Ask God for the strength you need to overcome the problems of the day and to see you safely through life's journey.

JANUARY

16

Today in History—U.S. Civil Service established as merit system, 1883; Eighteenth Amendment to U.S. Constitution (prohibiting alcoholic beverages) goes into effect, 1920; General Dwight D. Eisenhower takes command of Allied invasion forces, 1944.

Born Today—Actress Ethel Merman, 1908; baseball player Dizzy Dean, 1911; photographer Francesco Scavullo, 1929; auto racer A. J. Foyt, 1935; opera singer Marilyn Horne, 1943.

Today's Quotation—" . . . were it left to me to decide whether we should have a government without newspapers, or newspapers without a government, I should not hesitate a moment to prefer the latter."— *Thomas Jefferson, January 16, 1787*

Misdirected Communication

It is amazing what can go awry in this age of rapid communication. A department store manager in England wrote a note of congratulations to his employee, Gwen James, who served as clerk at the store's china counter. He put the note in an envelope and addressed it to: "Mrs. James in china." Two months and ten thousand miles later the message finally reached its intended destination. The note had traveled to China, was postmarked in Peking, and stamped, "Return to Sender."

Such confusion isn't, however, limited to the mail. The late President Kennedy told a strange tale of being awakened by the ringing of the emergency hotline phone near his bed. Kennedy answered the phone, "This is the president." A voice at the other end of the line responded timidly, "I'm sorry, I was trying to reach a French laundry," and hung up. White House technicians never were able to discover how the call got misdirected to the president's hotline.

God's "hotline" of prayer operates twenty-four hours a day from all locations, his line is never busy, and we never get a wrong number. How long has it been since you've communicated directly with God?

Prayer Suggestion—Communicate with your Maker today. He is never too busy to listen.

JANUARY

17

1 Timothy 2:1-8

Today in History—General Daniel Morgan's forces rout British at Battle of Cowpens, S.C., 1781; cable car patented, 1871; masked hold-up men take $1.5 million from an armored car in Boston, Mass. (biggest U.S. robbery up to that time), 1950; U.S. Navy submarine *Nautilus* begins first nuclear-powered undersea voyage, 1955; U.S. Air Force plane accidentally drops four unarmed H-bombs on Spain, 1966; Supreme Court rules home videotaping of TV programs is legal, 1984; Civil Rights Commission votes to discontinue racial quotas for promoting minorities, 1984.

Born Today—Statesman Benjamin Franklin, 1706; writer Anton Chekhov, 1860; drama teacher Konstantin Stanislavski, 1863; statesman David Lloyd George, 1863; educator Robert M. Hutchins, 1899; actress Betty White, 1924; actor James Earl Jones, 1931; boxer Muhammad Ali, 1942.

Today's Quotation—"You cannot adopt politics as a profession and remain honest."—*Louis McHenry Howe, January 17, 1933*

Honest Politicians

Just when you thought there was no hope, a Minnesota congressman has proposed a "Truth in Government Act." The law would make it unlawful for federal officials to lie to the public. He pointed out that, "Under current law, it is a crime for a private citizen to lie to a government official, but not for a government official to lie to the people."

Honesty isn't only a problem with U.S. officials. The Japanese government surveyed twenty-five thousand major businesses over a three-year period and discovered that the firms had spent an estimated two hundred thirty-three million dollars for political contributions, payments to secret agents, and outright bribes! It would appear that honesty is not everyone's policy.

As the apostle Paul advised Timothy, we must always pray "For kings, and for all that are in authority; that we might lead a quiet and peaceable life in all godliness and honesty" (1 Tim. 2:2).

Prayer Suggestion—Pray for your elected leaders and let them know they are in your prayers.

JANUARY

18

Romans 12:4-21

Today in History—Lima, Peru founded by Francisco Pizarro, 1535; pilot Eugene Ely lands first airplane on a ship, 1911; England's Captain Robert Scott reaches South Pole a few weeks after Roald Amundsen, 1912; world powers meet to formulate peace treaty after World War I, 1919; gold prices soar to $802 per ounce, 1980.

Born Today—Physician-linguist Peter Roget, 1779; statesman Daniel Webster, 1782; writer A. A. Milne, 1882; comedian Oliver Hardy, 1892; actor Cary Grant, 1904; actor Danny Kaye, 1913; inventor Ray Dolby, 1933.

Today's Quotation—"We should propose that the professors follow no other calling, so that their whole time may be given to their academical functions."—*Thomas Jefferson, January 18, 1800*

Teachers

Teachers have an awesome responsibility. William Alexander says the average high school teacher will have taught approximately five thousand students during his or her lifetime. This means that the result of just one hundred ineffectual high school teachers is fifty thousand citizens who will not receive adequate instruction! Motivation is especially critical in effective teaching. Responding to a comment that he was expecting too much of students, a University of Chicago professor replied, "I aim where their heads ought to be."

Despite being imprisoned in chains, Paul reminded the Colossians to be "teaching every man in all wisdom; that we may present every man perfect in Christ Jesus" (Col. 1:28). Whom are you teaching? What are they learning from you?

Prayer Suggestion—That we would be faithful teachers and examples to those around us, accurately mirroring God's work in our lives.

JANUARY

19

Today in History—Tin canning process for food patented, 1825; first televised presidential press conference conducted by President Dwight D. Eisenhower, 1955; President Nixon nominates Judge G. Harrold Carswell for U.S. Supreme Court, 1970; Egypt readmitted to Islamic National Conference, 1984; Bible translated into Navajo, 1985.

Born Today—Inventor James Watt, 1736; General Robert E. Lee, 1807; writer Edgar Allan Poe, 1809; inventor Henry Bessemer, 1813; artist Paul Cezanne, 1839; actress Jean Stapleton, 1923, singer Phil Everly, 1939.

Today's Quotation—"We shall give generous financial support, and it is understood that Mexico is to reconquer the lost territory in New Mexico, Texas, and Arizona."—*German Foreign Secretary Alfred Zimmerman, in secret note proposing alliance with Mexico, January 19, 1917*

Conquerors

One of the world's most unusual landmarks is a single granite shaft which stands near Wilna on the western boundary of Russia. On opposite sides are two inscriptions. The western side reads, "Napoleon Bonaparte passed this way in 1812 with 410,000 men." On the eastern face is the somber report: "Napoleon Bonaparte passed this way in 1812 with 9,000 men." Napoleon had met his match in this Russian campaign. In the same way, Scripture records that Satan will meet his match when confronted with the judgment of a Holy God in a confrontation that will have no survivors!

Are you a conqueror? The Bible says "we are more than conquerors through him that loved us" (Rom. 8:37). Don't let the world take away your Christian birthright. Realize that you are a child of the King. Go out and act like it today!

Prayer Suggestion—Thank God that believers are the ultimate winners in life's great spiritual battle—because of God's power!

JANUARY

20

Today in History—John Marshall appointed by President John Adams to be Chief Justice of U.S., 1801; U.S. Senate approves treaty with Hawaii to lease Pearl Harbor as U.S. naval base, 1887; first basketball game played, 1892; President Lyndon Johnson signs Medicare Bill, 1966; U.S. threatens to withdraw from Summer Olympics if not moved from Moscow, 1980.

Born Today—Christian pioneer Susannah Wesley, 1669; pianist Josef Hofmann, 1872; violinist Mischa Elman, 1891; comedian George Burns, 1896; film director Frederico Fellini, 1920; astronaut Edwin "Buzz" Aldrin, Jr., 1930; Soviet dissident Anatoly Scharansky, 1948.

Today's Quotation—"The supreme need of our time is for men to learn to live together in peace and harmony."—*Harry S. Truman, January 20, 1949*

Peace

How much peace has the world experienced throughout recorded history? *Christian Victory* has calculated that, since the creation, the world has been entirely at peace only eight percent of the time! In over three thousand one hundred recorded years of history only 286 have been without war. The man who helped create the atomic bomb was once asked if there were any defense against the weapon. "Certainly," he replied. "Peace!"

On this side of eternity, we are told, there will always be "war and rumors of war." Complete world peace will only occur during the thousand-year reign of Christ, following the rapture of the church and the seven-year tribulation. In those days, there will be peace such that "The wolf also shall dwell with the lamb, and the leopard shall lie down with the kid . . . and a little child shall lead them" (Isa. 11:6).

Prayer Suggestion—Pray for peace, not only world peace and the Peace of Jerusalem, but also for God's peace of mind which passes all understanding.

36

JANUARY

21

Today in History—King Louis XVI of France executed, 1793; first Kiwanis Club chartered, 1915; Russian Communist leader Nikoli Lenin dies, 1924; Alger Hiss convicted of perjury, 1950; U.S. Navy submarine *Nautilus* launched, 1954; U.S. Supreme Court legalizes abortion, 1973.

Born Today—Steamboat builder John Fitch, 1743; General Thomas "Stonewall" Jackson, 1824; actor Telly Savalas, 1924; golfer Jack Nicklaus, 1940; singer Placido Domingo, 1941.

Today's Quotation—"No man has a right to fix the boundary of the march of a nation; no man has a right to say to his country—thus far shalt thou go and no further."—*Charles Stewart Parnell, January 21, 1885*

Terrorism

What is the difference between terrorism and violence? Rand Jenkins says, "Terrorists have as their primary goal—getting attention. Coverage of terrorist incidents can intensify the climate of fear and help discredit legitimate political authority. That distinguishes terrorist tactics from muggings and other forms of violent crime."

Speaking of violence today, some of the largest school systems have turned to barbed wire and other security measures in an effort to curb the violence inflicted upon schools. For example, police officers patrol the halls in forty of New York City's schools, while Chicago police patrol two hundred schools, and Los Angeles reports 102 "security agents" armed with revolvers and the authority to arrest. How did all this come about? It is because of the relaxation of spiritual standards in schools. There is never a moral vacuum—sin always rushes in to fill the void because man is born evil.

Prayer Suggestion—That those who have eliminated God from the schools and other areas of society would quickly allow his return.

JANUARY

22

Today in History—An obelisk known as Cleopatra's Needle, a gift from Egypt, placed in Central Park, New York, 1881; Queen Victoria of England dies ending a reign of over sixty years, 1901; in St. Petersburg, Czar's soldiers fire on marching Russian workers, 1905; Allied forces land at Anzio, Italy, in one of the bloodiest engagements of World War II, 1944; Portuguese liner *Santa Maria* hijacked by dissidents at sea, 1961; European Common Market expands to ten nations, 1972; record cold wave severely damages Florida's citrus crop, 1985.

Born Today—Essayist Francis Bacon, 1561; physicist Andre Ampere, 1775; poet George Byron, 1788; architect Richard Upjohn, 1802; writer Beatrice Webb, 1858; statesman U. Thant, 1909; actress Ann Sothern, 1911.

Today's Quotation—"The pleasures of the intellect are permanent, the pleasures of the heart are transitory."—*Henry David Thoreau, January 22, 1852*

Pleasure

Americans are spending ever-increasing amounts each year on pleasure. Homer Duncan cites figures showing that while Americans give $3.5 billion each year to churches, they annually spend over $150 billion on pleasure. This includes $14.5 billion spent on liquor, $5 billion spent for television and radio sets, $3 billion spent on boats, and $1.5 billion spent by young people on records and tapes.

While there is nothing wrong with relaxation and recreation, there is something wrong when the pursuit of pleasure becomes a major obsession. It is easy to get so caught up in the frenzies of this life that we forget that heaven consists of "pleasures forevermore." Why have believers become so concerned with the pleasures in this life when they have forever to enjoy them with other saints in heaven?

Prayer Suggestion—Thank God for the pleasures of life but realize that only by doing Christ's will, can we merit his reward.

JANUARY

23

Today in History—Dr. Elizabeth Blackwell, first woman to receive M.D. degree in U.S., 1849; Netherlands refuses to cancel sanctuary for German ex-Kaiser Wilhelm, 1920; Israel proclaims Jerusalem its capital, 1950; Twenty-fourth Amendment to U.S. Constitution becomes law, 1964; U.S. Navy intelligence ship *Pueblo* captured by Communist North Korea, 1968; court panel rules 18 1/2 minute erasure on tape of key Nixon White House conversation was not accidental, 1974.

Born Today—Statesman John Hancock, 1737; artist Eduard Manet, 1832; writer Edith Wharton, 1862; actor Humphrey Bogart, 1899; actor Randolph Scott, 1903; actress Jeanne Moreau, 1928; Princess Caroline of Monaco, 1957.

Today's Quotation—"I thought what was good for the country was good for General Motors, and vice versa."—*Charles E. Wilson, January 23, 1953*

Good Business

"Human progress has often depended on the courage of a man who dared to be different," says Herbert Prochnow. He cites F. W. Woolworth who conceived the idea of the five-and-ten-cent store. John Wannamaker originated the department store with consistent prices for all customers, while Henry Ford determined to build a light, cheap car for the masses. Ray Kroc discovered that by selling large volumes of carry-out food at a low profit margin, he could have a very profitable business, and the golden arches of McDonald's attest to the accuracy of his hunch.

The Bible addresses the subject of business in a number of passages. The youthful Jesus told his parents " . . . I must be about my Father's business" (Luke 2:49). There is room for both "good business practices" in this life, which can lead to profitability, as well as our "Father's business," the rewards of which will last forever.

Prayer Suggestion—That God would give us wisdom to balance those things which last eternally with the necessary tasks of this life.

JANUARY

24

Today in History—James Marshal discovers gold at Sutter's Mill, 1848; Moldavia and Walachia merge to form Rumania, 1859; Robert Baden-Powell founds first Boy Scout troop, 1908; victorious Russian troops in World War II cross Oder River to make their first entry into Germany, 1948; Sir Winston Churchill dies, 1965; millions in Poland strike in support of Solidarity union, 1981.

Born Today—Lawyer Joseph Choate, 1832; writer Vicki Baum, 1888; sportscaster Jack Brickhouse, 1916; actor Ernest Borgnine, 1917; evangelist Oral Roberts, 1918; singer Neil Diamond, 1941; gymnast Mary Lou Retton, 1968.

Today's Quotation—"The man who makes no mistakes does not usually make anything."—*Edward John Phelps, January 24, 1899*

Mistakes

Even people who should know better still make mistakes. A six-year-old lad once received a note from his teacher suggesting that he be taken out of school because he was "too stupid to learn." That boy was Thomas Edison who earned no less than 1,098 patents during his lifetime (following years of frustrating setbacks and thousands of largely unsuccessful experiments).

It was Lloyd Morris who said, "The only people who never make mistakes are those who never do anything." How true this is! We ponder why we seem to be continually making mistakes while everyone else seems to be doing so well. We should recognize that everyone makes mistakes; everyone has failed—probably many times—before they became successful. Remember, only Jesus never fails!

Prayer Suggestion—Thank God that he never fails and that because of Christ we all are champions, adopted into God's own family!

JANUARY

25

Hebrews 13:17–21

Today in History—Captain Daniel Shays leads vain attack by impoverished farmers on arsenal, 1787; Alexander Graham Bell begins transcontinental telephone service, 1915; widow of Chinese leader Mao Tse Tung, Chiang Ching, given suspended death sentence for crimes against state, 1981; Klaus Barbie, "Butcher of Lyons," arrested in La Paz, Bolivia, 1983; U.S. breaks ties with Libya over continued terrorism, 1986.

Born Today—Poet Robert Burns, 1759; writer W. Somerset Maugham, 1874; actress Mildred Dunnock, 1904; sportscaster Ernie Harwell, 1918; broadcast journalist Edwin Newman, 1919; Philippine leader Corazon Aquino, 1923; actor Dean Jones, 1931.

Today's Quotation—"American reputation in Europe is not such as to be flattering to its citizens."—*Thomas Jefferson, January 25, 1786*

Good Reputation

You can never tell who is watching what you do each day. A young man, called upon to preach on short notice, chose as his text, "Thou shalt not steal." The next day, the man boarded a bus, handed the driver a dollar bill, took his change and walked to the back of the bus. Before taking his seat, the young man paused to count his change and noticed he had been given an extra dime. His first thought was that the company would never miss it. But reflecting further he realized he must return the coin. Going to the front of the bus, the man handed the coin back to the driver, saying that he had been overpaid. It was then that the driver replied, "Yes, it was a dime too much. I gave it to you purposely. You see, I heard your sermon yesterday, and I watched in my mirror as you counted your change. Had you kept the change I would never again have had any confidence in preaching."

What a great influence we have upon this lost and dying world—even when we feel that no one is watching!

Prayer Suggestion—Ask that God would keep us honest, faithful, and consistent, especially when we are certain no one is watching.

JANUARY

26

Today in History—Australia Day marks first British settlement, 1778; Michigan admitted as twenty-sixth state, 1837; Indian Republic Day marks date when nation became self-governing republic, 1950; President Nixon delivers veto message on Health, Education and Welfare appropriation bill, 1970; former Vice President Nelson Rockefeller dies in New York City at age 70, 1979.

Born Today—Author Mary Mapes Dodge, 1831; General Douglas MacArthur, 1880; actor Paul Newman, 1925; director Roger Vadim, 1928; cartoonist Jules Feiffer, 1929; hockey player Wayne Gretzky, 1961.

Today's Quotation—"I wish the Bald Eagle had not been chosen as the Representative of our Country; he is a Bird of bad moral Character. . . .The Turkey is a much more respectable Bird, and withal a true original native of America."—*Benjamin Franklin, January 26, 1784*

Good Character

Warren Wiersbe tells the story of the pious church member who upon visiting the sixth grade Sunday school class asked, "Why do you think people call me a Christian?" There was an embarrassing silence, then a small voice from the back of the class said, "Because they don't know you."

A humbling statement, yet it could be quite true of most of us at one time or another. The term "Christian" (literally "little Christs") was first applied to believers at Antioch, for these people had such great moral fortitude and backbone that in all they did they appeared Christ-like. What a challenge to godly living it is to be called "little Christs." I wonder if our behavior is such that God would be glorified by our character or would he be ashamed of our lifestyle? What a tragedy for a Christian to be considered of poor character!

Prayer Suggestion—Ask God to make us worthy of his name in everything we say and do, both "seen" and "unseen."

JANUARY

27

Ecclesiastes 12:1–7

Today in History—First Greek letter sorority, Kappa Alpha Theta, founded, 1870; Thomas Edison patents his incandescent electric bulb, 1880; National Geographic Society founded, 1888; financier Serge Rubinstein killed, 1955; astronauts Virgil Grissom, Edward White, and Roger Chaffee killed by fire in their *Apollo* spacecraft, 1967; cease-fire ends longest U.S. war (in Vietnam), 1973.

Born Today—Composer Wolfgang Amadeus Mozart, 1756; writer Lewis Carroll (Charles L. Dodgson), 1832; labor leader Samuel Gompers, 1850; composer Jerome Kern, 1885; "Father of the nuclear Navy" Admiral Hyman Rickover, 1900; radio preacher Theodore Epp, 1907; actress Donna Reed, 1921.

Today's Quotation—"The atrocious crime of being a young man . . . I shall neither attempt to palliate or deny."—*William Pitt, the Elder, January 27, 1741*

Youth

The university newspaper ad read: "Sweet little old lady wishes to correspond with six-foot student answering to initials J.D.B.—Signed, His Mother." While this situation might seem familiar to some parents today, history records the fact that many world leaders became active at a very early age. Some examples: playwright Victor Hugo wrote a tragedy at 15; Joan of Arc did all her work and was burned at the stake at age 19; John Calvin joined the Reformation at 21 and wrote *The Institutes* at 27—the same age of Spurgeon when he built the great Metropolitan Tabernacle in London. Martin Luther was just 30 when he began the Reformation. Evangelist Billy Graham was 31 at the time of the Los Angeles crusade. Billy Sunday left baseball for evangelistic work at age 33, while John Wesley began his life's work at 35. Clearly God can use individuals, no matter how young, if their lives are surrendered to him.

Prayer Suggestion—Dedicate your life to fully serve God no matter what your age. You are never too young or too old to serve God!

JANUARY

28

Today in History—Paris surrenders to Germans, 1871; first daily college newspaper, *Yale Daily News,* begins publication, 1878; first commercial telephone switchboard begins operation, 1878; U.S. Coast Guard established, 1915; U.S. spacecraft *Challenger* explodes moments after lift-off, killing seven-member crew, 1986.

Born Today—Evangelist R. A. Torrey, 1856; writer Sidonie Gabrielle Claudine Colette, 1873; pianist Artur Rubinstein, 1887; sculptor Claes Oldenburg, 1929; author Susan Sontag, 1933; actor Alan Alda, 1936

Today's Quotation—"There is nothing stronger than human prejudice."—*Wendell Phillips, January 28, 1852*

Prejudice

In what is reported to be a true story, an old Vermont Republican always seemed to show up at the area Democratic rallies. Intrigued, a party worker asked if he was considering converting to the Democratic cause. He responded, "Oh no, I just come around t'yer meetings to keep my disgust fresh."

Often we tend to judge a particular individual or incident according to how we are taught about such things. The Countess of Blessington was quoted as saying, "Prejudices are the chains forged by ignorance to keep men apart." Another has said, "Prejudice, if not altogether invincible, is perhaps the most difficult of all errors to be eradicated from the human mind; for by disguising itself under the respectable name of firmness it passes through the world without censure, whereas open vice would receive a severe reprimand." Clearly those who carry Christ's name have no business bearing prejudice against anyone!

Prayer Suggestion—Pray that God would help us to remove those remnants of hatred and prejudice that keep us from loving others as God loves us.

JANUARY

29

Proverbs 18:16–24

Today in History—Singapore founded by Sir Stamford Raffles, 1819; Kansas admitted as thirty-fourth state, 1861; Congress establishes a special Electoral Commission to decide the disputed Hayes-Tilden Presidential election, 1876; The American League of Baseball Clubs organized, 1900; Baseball Hall of Fame elects first five players: Ty Cobb, Babe Ruth, Honus Wagner, Christy Mathewson, and Walter Johnson, 1936; six Americans, posing as Canadian diplomats, escape from Iran, 1980.

Born Today—Political essayist Thomas Paine, 1737; President William McKinley, 1843; financier John D. Rockefeller, Jr., 1874; actor Victor Mature, 1916; actor John Forsythe, 1918; actor Tom Selleck, 1945; TV host Oprah Winfrey, 1954; swimmer Greg Louganis, 1960.

Today's Quotation—"Nothing is so fatal to religion as indifference, which is, at least, half infidelity."—*Edmund Burke, January 29, 1795*

Indifference

In many ways today may be called the "Age of Indifference." Historian Arnold Toynbee has found that nineteen of twenty-one civilizations have died from within and not by conquest from without. Dr. Laurence Gould concurs, adding, "I do not believe the greatest threat to our future is from bombs or guided missiles; I don't think our civilization will end that way. I think it will die when we no longer care."

O. A. Newlin once told of a fine community leader who was kind to everybody, with one exception: his mother. It seems he treated everyone else with respect and courtesy but left it to his neighbors to care for his own mother's needs. You say, "who would turn his own mother away?" Newlin says, "One greater than mother is being turned away [by your indifference]. Don't talk to me about being good when you turn Jesus away, treating him worse than you would treat a tramp." Friend, what will *you* do with Jesus? Your eternal destiny rests with your response.

Prayer Suggestion—That we would not be indifferent to God's leading and would willingly surrender fully and completely to him.

JANUARY

30

Today in History—Richard Lawrence tries unsuccessfully to shoot President Andrew Jackson, (first attempt to assassinate a president), 1835; Adolf Hitler ushers in Nazi era in Germany by becoming chancellor, 1933; Mahatma Gandhi, Indian leader and apostle of nonviolence, assassinated, 1948; former aides to President Nixon, James McCord and G. Gordon Liddy convicted in Watergate trial, 1973; Ayatollah Khomeini bars Shah of Iran from returning, 1979.

Born Today—Conductor Walter Damrosch, 1862; President Franklin Delano Roosevelt, 1882; historian Barbara Tuchman, 1912; comedian Dick Martin, 1922; actor Gene Hackman, 1930; actress Vanessa Redgrave, 1937; chess player Boris Spassky, 1937.

Today's Quotation—"A little rebellion now and then is a good thing."—*Thomas Jefferson, January 30, 1787*

Rebellion

When it comes to rebellion against God, the Creator takes a hard-line approach as we read of the Israelites in Deuteronomy 32. Evangelist J. Wilbur Chapman tells a story of a ship which left Boston Harbor in a blinding storm in November 1898 and never returned. Despite all the danger signals which were up when she left (the government agent at the signal office had advised vessels to remain in port; the owners had commanded her to stay docked), she still chose to leave port. Just why she left no one has ever been able to say.

Rebelliousness is caused by pride—an arrogance in thinking that we know more than others or even more than God (as in the Garden of Eden). How dangerous it is to believe we have greater knowledge than God! It is no wonder God considers rebellion to be sin.

Prayer Suggestion—Call upon God to keep your heart tender and open to his leading so that it would never harden into a spirit of sin.

JANUARY

31

Today in History—Guy Fawkes executed for the Gunpowder Plot against the government of England, 1606; President Truman orders development of H-bomb, 1950; U.S. launches its first satellite, *Explorer I*, 1958; Pacific Island of Nauru gains freedom, 1968; U.S. welcomes home 52 American hostages after 444 days in Iranian captivity, 1981; Haiti declares "State of Seige" following national unrest, 1986.

Born Today—Composer Franz Schubert, 1797; western writer Zane Grey, 1872; comedian Eddie Cantor, 1892; writer John O'Hara, 1905; fighter "Jersey Joe" Walcott, 1914; entertainer Gary Moore, 1915; baseball player Jackie Robinson, 1919; author Norman Mailer, 1923; baseball players Ernie Banks, 1931, and Nolan Ryan, 1947.

Today's Quotation—"I have directed the Atomic Energy Commission to continue its work on all forms of atomic weapons, including the so-called hydrogen or super-bomb."—*President Harry S. Truman, January 31, 1950*

The Bomb

In an ironic note, a World War II bomb used for ten years as a blacksmith's anvil in the Philippines exploded when it was moved. A similar fate lay in store for a gigantic weapon of war built in the 16th century. It was a huge cannon with a massive twenty-five-inch bore that could be fired only seven times a day because it took so long to reload. Huge piles of powder were required for each shot. Though the gun could shoot a mile, it could be heard for over twelve miles. In all, 650 men were required to move and operate the gun. But the cannon, first used in the siege of Constantinople, did not last long. After a few days it exploded in a fiery inferno, killing its own creator—a man named Orban. That is why it is known to this day as Orban's Folly.

While the Bible is clear in its support for us to defend our families and property, it never says to trust solely in guns and bombs instead of the God of the universe. For when we begin to lose sight of God's enabling power, fixing our eyes on our own strength, we are bound to fail.

Prayer Suggestion—Relying upon God's mighty protecting arm and not upon the nuclear arms of mankind is the key to survival in this life.

FEBRUARY

1

Today in History—U.S. Supreme Court convenes for first time, 1790; Julia Ward Howe's "Battle Hymn of the Republic" published, 1862; Col. Billy Mitchell, "apostle of air power," resigns from the U.S. Army, 1926; United Nations General Assembly names Red China an aggressor in Korea, 1951; "Roots" mini-series reaches 80 million TV viewers in eight-day sweep, 1977; Ayatollah Khomeini returns from exile in France to the cheers of millions of Iranians, 1979.

Born Today—Composer Victor Herbert, 1859; director John Ford, 1895; actor Clark Gable, 1901; humorist S. J. Perelman, 1904; actor Sherman Hemsley, 1938; director Terry Jones, 1942.

Today's Quotation—"America cannot be an ostrich with its head in the sand."—*Woodrow Wilson, February 1, 1916*

Ignoring Problems

How often have you hoped that by ignoring them, your problems would just go away? There are many people who seem to think that they will be able to escape God's judgment by avoiding church or spiritual issues. In the 1800s the British suspected a small ship near the island of Jamaica of being involved in piracy. But when the vessel was captured and boarded, no incriminating evidence could be found. So the matter was turned over to authorities in Kingston, Jamaica. As the trial date neared, the crew became more and more confident that they would be freed for lack of evidence. However, just as the court convened, a packet of papers which directly linked the ship's crew to illegal activity was presented to the judge. Later it was learned that the packet had been tossed overboard as the ship was about to be boarded and a large shark had swallowed the packet. The crew of a passing ship killed the shark, discovered the packet, and brought the papers to the courtroom just as the trial was to begin! Simply hoping the problem would go away led to their downfall.

Someday all of mankind will be judged by God and in that trial there will be no excuse!

Prayer Suggestion—Ask for increased sensitivity to lost mankind and share God's love with those you meet.

FEBRUARY

2

Today in History—New Amsterdam incorporated as New York City, 1653; Cardiff Giant, a petrified human figure discovered previous year, revealed as a hoax, 1870; baseball's National League formed, 1876; World War II siege of Stalingrad by Nazis ends, 1943; passengers aboard hijacked Portuguese liner *Santa Maria* land in Brazil, 1961; one senator and seven congressmen implicated in FBI Abscam bribery probe, 1980.

Born Today—Writer Havelock Ellis, 1859; violinist Fritz Kreisler, 1875; writer James Joyce, 1882; violinist Jascha Heifetz, 1901; baseball's Al "Red" Schoendienst, 1923; author Liz Smith, 1923; comedian Tom Smothers, 1937; actress Farrah Fawcett, 1947.

Today's Quotation—"Beware of too much confidence in any man."—*Thomas Jefferson, February 2, 1800*

Misplaced Confidence

Do you remember the old television commercial in which the mother, attempting to be helpful, was rebuked by her adult daughter, "Mother, I'd rather do it myself!" I wonder if that might, in some way, describe our relationship with God. If so, we need to recognize our need for God and call upon him for help.

Some time ago there was a young girl who seemed to always have problems understanding her mathematics homework. She discovered a helpful neighbor and often sought his assistance. Her mother, increasingly alarmed at the girl's boldness, went to the neighbor, scientist Albert Einstein, to apologize. Einstein said, "You don't have to apologize. I have learned more from my conversations with the child than she has from me."

Although our omniscient heavenly Father knows what we need before we ask, he nonetheless wants to hear from us and stands ready to assist if we will but call upon him. Don't let your false human pride keep you from God!

Prayer Suggestion—That we would have childlike faith in God and come boldly to him in our time of need rather than "doing it ourself."

FEBRUARY

3

1 Thessalonians 5:1–6

Today in History—First American paper money issued by Massachusetts, 1690; Civil War peace-seeking conference held secretly between President Lincoln and Confederate Vice President Alexander H. Stephens, 1865; U.S. breaks diplomatic relations with Germany (and enters World War I two months later), 1917; western world's largest art museum, the Metropolitan Museum of Art in New York City, opens new wing featuring 20th-century art, 1987.

Born Today—Composer Felix Mendelssohn, 1809; editor Horace Greeley, 1811; inventor Hudson Maxim, 1853; writer Gertrude Stein, 1874; artist Norman Rockwell, 1894; writer James Michener, 1907; conductor Erich Leinsdorf, 1912; actor Joey Bishop, 1918; football player Fran Tarkenton, 1940.

Today's Quotation—"Is peace a rash system? Is it dangerous for nations to live in amity with each other?"—*Charles James Fox, February 3, 1800*

Peace?

In the 1950s a popular chorus sung by Christian youth of the day said, "What though wars may come with marching feet and beat of the drum/ for I have Christ in my heart . . ." Christians have living inside them the peace which passes all understanding. How long has the world been at peace? Since the end of World War I, an average of just two minutes of peace has been recorded worldwide for every year of war! Clearly peace is a much sought-after but elusive goal in this life.

How wonderful then to know the Prince of Peace who is life eternal! We have read the Book and know how it ends—*We Win!* What greater encouragement could we have than the assurance of ultimate victory!

Prayer Suggestion—Thank God for his victory over sin in our life and throughout the universe, and for his everlasting peace.

FEBRUARY

4

1 Corinthians 3:1-9

Today in History—Electoral College elects George Washington as first President of U.S., 1789; Confederate States of America organize, 1861; Philippine insurrection against U.S. rule begins, 1899; first Winter Olympic Games begin, 1932; United Services Organization (USO), founded to entertain U.S. armed forces, 1941; publishing heiress Patty Hearst is kidnapped from her Berkeley, Ca., apartment, 1974; sailor Dennis Connor leads "Stars and Stripes" to four straight wins over Australia to win America's Cup, 1987.

Born Today—Educator Mark Hopkins, 1802; aviator Charles Lindbergh, 1902; feminist Betty Friedan, 1921; comedian David Brenner, 1945; Vice President Dan Quayle, 1947.

Today's Quotation—"Experience makes fools wise."—*Daniel O'Connell, February 4, 1836*

Experience

What a difference a little experience makes! According to the story, the famed pianist Paderewski was walking through a small Connecticut town one day. Suddenly he noticed a sign reading "Miss Jones Piano Lessons—25 cents an hour." Listening, he heard someone inside trying to play one of Chopin's nocturnes, but not doing very well. The great pianist walked up to the door and offered to assist. The delighted piano teacher recognized the famed musician and invited him in to play. After spending about an hour correcting her mistakes, he moved on. A few months later Paderewski was again in town, strolled by the same house, and noticed a new sign which read, "Miss Jones (Pupil of Paderewski) Piano Lessons—$1.00 an hour." The value of experience!

The Bible recognizes varying levels of Christian maturity and even has suggestions on how to gain spiritual strength through added spiritual growth and experience. How experienced a Christian are you?

Prayer Suggestion—Seek, with God's help, to become more mature in faith through added experience in his Word.

FEBRUARY

5

Romans 3:19-24

Today in History—Roger Williams arrives in America, 1531; Mexico adopts constitution, 1917; President Franklin D. Roosevelt proposes plan to enlarge Supreme Court, 1937; highly radioactive debris from defunct Russian satellite located in Canada, 1978; musical manuscript authenticated as Mozart's first symphony composed when he was nine, 1983.

Born Today—Colonial clergyman John Witherspoon, 1723; evangelist D. L. Moody, 1837; statesman Adlai Stevenson, 1900; pastor G. B. Vick, 1901; writer MacKinlay Kantor, 1904; actor Red Buttons, 1919; baseball's Hank Aaron, 1934; football player Roger Stauback, 1942.

Today's Quotation—"Terror is nothing else than justice: prompt, secure, and inflexible!"—*Robespierre, February 5, 1794*

Justice

The administration of justice sometimes takes on unusual forms. There was a loud commotion on a Japanese street one day as one man leaped upon another and beat him furiously. "Confess!" he yelled. "No," gasped his struggling victim, "I didn't do it!" The story was then told of how the attacker had been wrongly imprisoned for 23 years on murder charges—a crime he did not commit. Years later, following his release, the prisoner began looking for the guilty parties, quickly locating one of them. He pressed his search for the other which led to the street battle. Eventually the second criminal confessed his role in the crime leading to a retrial for the prisoner and his exoneration. Yet there was no way he could recover the years he had lost in prison.

Sometimes human justice moves very slowly and sometimes it is simply not just. But God is *always* fair giving not justice but His grace to those who believe on him.

Prayer Suggestion—Thank God for his grace that more than pardons. It justifies, completely wiping clean our debt of sin.

FEBRUARY

6

Today in History—College of William and Mary chartered, 1693; Massachusetts becomes sixth state to ratify U.S. Constitution, 1788; U.S. Senate ratifies Treaty of Paris ending Spanish-American War, 1900; Twentieth Amendment to U.S. Constitution, so-called "Lame Duck Amendment," goes into effect, 1933; King George VI dies and is succeeded by his daughter, Queen Elizabeth II, 1952; former Israeli secret service chief says agents may have executed some Nazi war criminals they did not try, 1985.

Born Today—Queen Anne of England, 1665; actor Sir Henry Irving, 1838; baseball's Babe Ruth, 1895; President Ronald Reagan, 1911; actress Zsa Zsa Gabor, 1919; broadcast journalist Tom Brokaw, 1940; singer Fabian Forte, 1943; singer Natalie Cole, 1950.

Today's Quotation—"It is said that God is always for the big battalions."—*Voltaire, February 6, 1770*

The Underdog

Americans generally have great compassion for the underdog. Years ago in a humble hotel in Philadelphia, an elderly couple approached the night clerk and begged him for a room. It seems a convention was in town and all hotels were booked full for the night. "Are there any rooms left anywhere?" the old man inquired. The clerk thought a moment and then conceded that though the hotel was completely full, his room would be available because he worked the night shift. At breakfast the next morning, the old couple summoned the kindly desk clerk. Without warning the elderly man told the clerk, "You're too good a hotel man for this place. How would you like for me to build a big hotel for you in New York City?" The clerk blurted out, "Why, it sounds wonderful!" The elderly man was none other than John Jacob Astor, who went on to build the famed Waldorf-Astoria Hotel. Because of his faithfulness in little things, that humble night clerk eventually became one of the greatest hotel men in the world.

Christian, God has prepared a wonderful place for you. Don't foolishly trade it away for the temporary, fleeting pleasures of this life!

Prayer Suggestion—Be thankful that you are a child of the King, and that he is now preparing a mansion for your eternal home!

FEBRUARY

7

Exodus 2:1-10

Today in History—John L. Sullivan becomes the last bare-knuckle heavy-weight boxing champion, 1882; flag of the vice president of the U.S. authorized, 1936; U.S. recognizes Saigon government of Vietnam, 1950; Census Bureau says rural areas and small towns are growing faster than cities, 1976; seven missionaries slain in Rhodesian guerilla raid, 1977; two U.S. astronauts embark on space walk, 1984; "Baby Doc" Duvalier flees Haiti after twenty-eight years in power, 1985.

Born Today—Statesman Sir Thomas More, 1478; writer Charles Dickens, 1812; writer Sinclair Lewis, 1885; actor Buster Crabbe, 1907; author Gay Talese, 1932; baseball player Dan Quisenberry, 1953.

Today's Quotation—"No attachments soothe the mind so much as those contracted in early life. . . ."—*Thomas Jefferson, February 7, 1788*

Childhood

What a tremendous responsibility child-rearing is! Today, children are being buffeted by outside forces their predecessors could never even imagine. One highly successful parent of an earlier era was Susanna Wesley (mother of John and Charles Wesley and fifteen others). John Wesley, writing in his journal, recalled several of his mother's rules for children: "When turned a year old (and some before), they were taught to fear the rod and to cry softly to forego further punishment. In order to form the child's mind, their will must first be conquered for by neglecting timely correction, they will contract a stubbornness and obstinacy which is hardly ever after conquered. . . . Self-will is the root of all sin and misery, so whatever cherishes this in children insures their after-wretchedness; whatever checks and mortifies it promotes their future happiness."

Do your children "rise up and call you blessed"? Make sure they are raised to fear God and do what is right!

Prayer Suggestion—Ask yourself, before God, if you are a godly parent, lovingly raising your children by the standards of God's Word.

FEBRUARY

8

Today in History—Mary, Queen of Scots, executed at Castle, England, 1587; Boy Scouts of America chartered, 1910; U.S. breaks diplomatic ties with Nicaragua, 1979; bigamist Giovanni Vigliotto (claims to have married 105 women in thirty-three years) judged guilty, 1983; scientists say new drug, HPA-23, shows promise in inhibiting spread of AIDS virus, 1985; investigation reveals NASA was warned a year earlier of possibility of leaks in solid rocket seals, 1986.

Born Today—Critic John Ruskin, 1819; General William Tecumseh Sherman, 1820; writer Jules Verne, 1828; actress Lana Turner, 1920; actress Audrey Meadows, 1924; actor Jack Lemmon, 1925; actor Nick Nolte, 1934; broadcast journalist Ted Koppel, 1940; actor Gary Coleman, 1968.

Today's Quotation—"The changes between wet and dry are much more frequent and sudden in Europe than America. Though we have double the rain, it falls in half the time."—*Thomas Jefferson, February 8, 1805*

Weather

Sometimes it seems nothing is as changeable as the weather. Indeed many dramatic shifts in weather patterns have been noted in recent years. One confirmation of how the weather can be affected is shown in a 1974 Soviet proposal that called for a ban on (1) creating holes in the ozone layer of the upper atmosphere, (2) setting off a nuclear explosion under the polar ice caps possibly triggering an iceslide that could wipe out whole areas from the face of the globe, and (3) creating acoustic fields on the sea surface to combat naval vessels. According to the Soviet officials, these are not idle concerns but real scientific likelihoods.

The Bible predicts weather patterns will become increasingly erratic as we approach the end. How important it is to trust in an unchanging God in these uncertain times!

Prayer Suggestion—Recognize that, as a believer, your hope is in the Lord who made heaven and earth (including the weather).

FEBRUARY

9

Today in History—John Quincy Adams, son of a former president, elected president by U.S. House of Representatives, 1825; National Weather Service established, 1870; French liner *Normandie*, being converted to a wartime troopship, catches fire at New York pier, 1942; Japanese evacuate Guadalcanal, ending epic World War II battle with U.S. forces, 1943.

Born Today—President William Henry Harrison, 1773; poet Amy Lowell, 1874; statesman Dean Rusk, 1909; actress Kathryn Grayson, 1923; broadcast journalist Roger Mudd, 1928; evangelist Jack Van Impe, 1931; singer Carole King, 1942; actress Mia Farrow, 1945.

Today's Quotation—"Give us the tools and we will finish the job."— *Winston Churchill, February 9, 1941*

God's Provision

How often we worry over nothing, when God wants us to enjoy his bountiful provision! One day evangelist Charles Spurgeon was riding home after a hard day's work, feeling tired and depressed. Suddenly the verse "my grace is sufficient for thee" entered his mind. He then thought of the tiny fish who might be afraid lest they drink the river dry but who hear the reassuring word, "Drink up little fish, my stream is sufficient for thee." Or the mouse who, in Joseph's grain bins in Egypt, worried about depleting the supply of grain only to be reassured, "Cheer up little mouse, my granaries are sufficient for thee." Or a mountain climber fearing lest he exhaust all of the thin oxygen in the atmosphere being reassured, "Breathe away young man and fill thy lungs, for my atmosphere is sufficient for thee." Spurgeon said then that, for the first time, "I experienced the joy that Abraham felt when he rejoiced in God's provision." Friend, whatever your plight, God's resources far outweigh your need. Trust in him today!

Prayer Suggestion—God is your source. Acknowledge him as the origin of all your blessings and you will come to love him anew.

FEBRUARY

10

Isaiah 41:1-10

Today in History—Treaty of Paris ends French and Indian War, 1763; P. T. Barnum's famous midget, General Tom Thumb, marries fellow midget Lavinia Warren, 1862; President McKinley signs peace treaty ending Spanish–American War, 1898; Postal Telegraph Company delivers first singing telegram, 1933; Nazi secret police given free hand to arrest Germans without trial, 1936; liner *Normandie* capsizes at pier in New York, 1942; Twenty-fifth Amendment to U.S. Constitution, Presidential Disability and Succession Act, goes into effect, 1967; Soviet leader Yuri Andropov dies after bout with kidney disease, 1984.

Born Today—Writer Charles Lamb, 1775; editor William Allen White, 1868; comedian Jimmy Durante, 1893; British statesman Harold Macmillan, 1894; opera singer Leontyne Price, 1927; actor Robert Wagner, 1930; singer Roberta Flack, 1939; swimmer Mark Spitz, 1950.

Today's Quotation—"The impersonal hand of government can never replace the helping hand of a neighbor."—*Hubert Humphrey, February 10, 1965*

Neighborliness

Edgar A. Guest used to tell the story of a rich man who was "almost friendless. His life had been one long round of bickering and lawsuits. Friendships apparently meant nothing to him as he was busy making his fortune." Later, Guest recalled, the rich man encountered a man with whom he had had a bitter quarrel many years before. "I don't understand it," the wealthy man said. "You have hundreds of friends while I have almost no one to whom I can turn." The old acquaintance replied, "Sir, I was busy making friends years ago, while you were busy making money."

In this age of "every man for himself," Christians especially need to go the extra mile in showing their neighborliness by offering encouragement and a helping hand to others. As in earlier times, may it be said of us today, "They helped every one his neighbor . . ." (Isa. 41:6).

Prayer Suggestion—Ask God to give you a spirit of love and concern for those around you, then look for ways to help your neighbor.

FEBRUARY

11

Today in History—Governor Eldridge Gerry of Massachusetts devises political redistricting plan known as the "gerrymander," 1812; President-elect Abraham Lincoln leaves Springfield, Ill., for Washington, D.C., inaugural, 1861; Roman Catholic Church and Italian government sign treaties recognizing Vatican City as independent state, 1929; panic buying triggers worst day of energy crisis due to lack of gas, 1974; Margaret Thatcher elected as first woman prime minister of Britain, 1975; Soviet dissident Anatoly Scharansky freed after eight years in prison camps, 1986.

Born Today—Inventor Thomas Alva Edison, 1847; boxer Max Baer, 1909; writer Joseph Mankiewicz, 1909; politician Lloyd Bentsen, 1921; actress Eva Gabor, 1921; actor Burt Reynolds, 1936; band leader Sergio Mendes, 1941.

Today's Quotation—"The people are the masters."—*Edmund Burke, February 11, 1780*

Majority Rule

While the will of the majority is what makes a democracy function, just because the majority is for something does not make it right. In fact, the opposite is sometimes true. Famed lawyer William Jennings Bryan said, "Never be afraid to stand with the minority which is right, for the minority which is right will one day be the majority; always be afraid to stand with the majority which is wrong, for the majority which is wrong will one day be the minority."

Christians need to fearlessly stand up for God regardless of the consequences. Like the sixteen-year-old Russian girl in the Young Communist League newspaper, who, under the caption "The one who has gone astray," was quoted as saying, "I have [young communist] members pass me without greeting. Let them look on me with contempt. My brothers and sisters in God treat me very well. I believe them and I believe God." Who do you believe in—the majority or God?

Prayer Suggestion—Acknowledge God's authority over you and over all areas of your life. Be thankful he alone is the ultimate majority.

FEBRUARY

12

Philippians 4:5-9

Today in History—First around-the-world automobile race begins in New York City, 1908; cornerstone of Lincoln Memorial laid, 1915; Paul Whiteman and his Orchestra, with George Gershwin, present the world premiere of "Rhapsody in Blue," 1924; Yalta agreement of President Franklin D. Roosevelt, Prime Minister Churchill, and Marshal Stalin announced, 1945; computer industry said to be making a comeback in California's Silicon Valley, 1987.

Born Today—Clergyman Cotton Mather, 1663; naturalist Charles Darwin, 1809; President Abraham Lincoln, 1809; labor leader John L. Lewis, 1880; General Omar Bradley, 1893; actor Lorne Greene, 1915; director Franco Zeffirelli, 1923; sportscaster Joe Garagiola, 1926; basketball player Bill Russell, 1934; author Judy Blume, 1938.

Today's Quotation—"That nation has not lived in vain which has given the world Washington and Lincoln, the best great men and the greatest good men whom history can show."—*Henry Cabot Lodge, February 12, 1909*

Integrity

It has been said that integrity describes what we do when we think no one is looking. President Abraham Lincoln was once given a request for 500,000 additional recruits to fight in the Civil War. Political advisors strongly recommended he turn down the request since they thought to do so would prevent his re-election. But Lincoln's decision was firm. "It is not necessary for me to be re-elected," he said, "but it is necessary for the soldiers at the front to be re-enforced by 500,000 men and I shall call for them. If I go down under the act, I will go down with my colors flying."

As God looks down upon earth and looks into your heart, I wonder if he is pleased or saddened by the integrity, or lack of it, he sees deep within your soul?

Prayer Suggestion—Confess your sins and shortcomings to God, asking his forgiveness and become a person of true integrity.

59

FEBRUARY

13

Today in History—Boston Latin School, oldest public school in U.S., founded, 1635; William and Mary proclaimed king and queen of England, 1689; first magazine published in America, 1747; first state university in U.S., University of North Carolina, opens, 1795; American Society of Composers, Authors and Publishers (ASCAP) organized, 1914; new Soviet leader, Konstantin Chernenko, calls for "peaceful coexistence" with U.S., 1972; obesity labeled major killer with at least thirty-four million Americans said to be overweight, 1985.

Born Today—Statesman Talleyrand, 1754; former First Lady Bess Truman, 1885; artist Grant Wood, 1892; singer Tennessee Ernie Ford, 1919; actress Kim Novak, 1933; actor George Segal, 1934; actress Carole Lynley, 1942.

Today's Quotation—"The Revolution was effected before the war commenced. The Revolution was in the hearts and minds of the people. . . .This radical change in the principles, opinions, sentiments and affections of the people, was the real American Revolution."—*John Adams, February 13, 1818*

All Things New

The young woman was being questioned about her salvation experience by the deacon board as she was applying for church membership. Admitting to the group that she still sinned even after becoming a Christian, she was asked, "How has Christ made a difference in your life?" The woman replied, "Sir, it is like this: before I became a Christian, I ran after sin. Now I run from it though sometimes I am still overtaken."

The great man of God George Mueller was known as a drinker and thief while in college, yet after he turned his life over to God he was so radically changed that he was reported as giving over $135,000 to the Lord's work during his lifetime. When he died, all his possessions totaled less than one thousand dollars. Clearly, God had revolutionized Mueller's life. How has God made you anew?

Prayer Suggestion—Commit your life to God. Surrender everything to him and he will revolutionize your entire way of life.

FEBRUARY

14

Today in History—Oregon admitted as thirty-third state, 1859; Arizona forty-eighth state admitted to U.S., 1912; seven gangsters opposed to Al Capone murdered in Chicago in the Valentine's Day Massacre, 1929; first planeload of freed prisoners of war from Vietnam arrives in California, 1973; armed attackers open fire on U.S. embassy in Teheran, trapping diplomats for several hours, 1979; French socialists begin nationalizing banks and industry, 1982; G. M. and Toyota agree to joint production of sub-compact car in California, 1983; State Department says drug crops from Latin America reaching record levels, 1985.

Born Today—Economist Thomas Malthus, 1766; comedian Jack Benny, 1894; broadcaster Hugh Downs, 1921; actress Florence Henderson, 1934; journalist Carl Bernstein, 1944; actor Gregory Hines, 1946.

Today's Quotation—"There are times when the insignificance of the accuser is lost in the magnitude of the accusation."—*Henry Grattan, February 14, 1800*

True Love

Even the most devoted couple will experience a "stormy" bout once in a while. A grandmother, celebrating her golden wedding anniversary, once told the secret of her long and happy marriage. "On my wedding day, I decided to make a list of ten of my husband's faults which, for the sake of our marriage, I would overlook," she said. A guest asked the woman what some of the faults she had chosen to overlook were. The grandmother replied, "To tell you the truth, my dear, I never did get around to listing them. But whenever my husband did something that made me hopping mad, I would say to myself, 'Lucky for him that's one of the ten!'"

Our heavenly Father loves and forgives us, not by overlooking our many faults but choosing instead to do something only he can do; forgive fully our wrongs through his marvelous grace—"grace that is greater than all of our sins!"

Prayer Suggestion—Rejoice at what God has done. He loved us "while we were yet sinners," and saves all those who believe on him.

FEBRUARY

15

Today in History—St. Louis, Mo., established, 1764; first gummed postage stamps introduced, 1842; U.S. battleship *Maine* blown up in Havana harbor, 1898; Chicago Mayor Anton Cermak killed by an assassin aiming at President-elect Franklin D. Roosevelt in Miami, 1933; British surrender Singapore to Japanese in World War II, 1942; four of "Chicago Seven" sentenced of conspiracy to riot during 1968 Democratic Convention begins, 1970; Nobel prize winner Aleksandr Solzhenitsyn arrives in Switzerland after expulsion from U.S.S.R., 1974.

Born Today—Astronomer Galileo Galilei, 1564; inventor Cyrus McCormick, 1809; feminist Susan B. Anthony, 1820; statesman Elihu Root, 1845; actor John Barrymore, 1882; songwriter Harold Arlen, 1905; actor Harvey Korman, 1927.

Today's Quotation—"No people in a great emergency ever found a faithful ally in gold. It is the most cowardly and treacherous of all metals. It makes no treaty that it does not break. It has no friend whom it does not sooner or later betray."—*John J. Ingalls, February 15, 1878*

Gold

There is nothing that so captures the image of beauty and wealth as does pure gold. Robert Ripley tells of a structure built on two underpinnings of solid gold each thirty-five feet square and twelve feet deep! This magnificent foundation, built in 1920, is said to still be standing in Purandhar, India. A total of fifty thousand gold bricks, weighing over 37,500 pounds (and worth well over 240 million dollars today), were used to construct the foundation.

The Bible speaks of our heavenly home in which gold will be so commonplace, it will be used to pave the streets! We can scarcely begin to imagine such grandeur and beauty as this. Yet it belongs to everyone who has put their faith and trust in God. What about you—have you accepted God's priceless gift of salvation?

Prayer Suggestion—Thank God for the beautiful home he is preparing for us in heaven!

FEBRUARY

16

Luke 2:40–52

Today in History—Lieutenant Stephen Decatur with a Navy crew destroys a warship in Tripoli harbor which pirates had captured, 1804; Civil War Brigadier General Ulysses S. Grant, nicknamed "Unconditional Surrender" Grant because he demanded those terms of Fort Donelson, Tenn., 1862; Benevolent and Protective Order of Elks founded, 1868; independence proclaimed for Lithuania, 1918; U.S. forces land on Japanese-held Corregidor island in Manila Bay, 1945; gas prices drop two to three cents a gallon with rapid decrease in crude oil costs, 1982.

Born Today—Writer Henry Adams, 1838; actress Katherine Cornell, 1893; band leader Wayne King, 1901; ventriloquist Edgar Bergen, 1903; labor leader Leonard Woodcock, 1911; actor LeVar Burton, 1957; tennis player John McEnroe, 1959.

Today's Quotation—"While the people should patriotically and cheerfully support their Government, its functions do not include the support of the people."—*Grover Cleveland, February 16, 1887*

Giving Support

Rich or poor, famous or unknown; who doesn't want to be admired? British Prime Minister Lord Melbourne once criticized a London newspaper editor for not supporting him sufficiently. In reply, the editor said he always supported Melbourne's party when he thought it was in the right. Melbourne responded, "We don't want support when we are in the right—what we want is a little support when we are in the wrong!"

Whether we are right or wrong, we all like to be liked. Yet how often do we show kindness to those who most need encouragement, the outcasts of society? Look for someone to encourage today—someone who needs the support only *you* can give.

Prayer Suggestion—Let God lead you to someone who needs encouragement and give them your time, attention, and love.

63

FEBRUARY

17

1 Peter 2:18-25

Today in History—Miles Standish made military captain of the colony of Pilgrims at Plymouth, Mass., 1621; Thomas Jefferson elected president by House of Representatives on thirty-sixth ballot, 1801; Confederate submarine sank Union warship *Housatonic* in Charleston Harbor, S.C., 1864; National Congress of Parents and Teachers established, 1897; Army private flies stolen helicopter within 100 yards of the White House, 1974; General William Westmoreland drops $120 million dollar libel suit against CBS, 1985.

Born Today—Singer Marian Anderson, 1902; businessman Montgomery Ward, 1844; sports announcer Walter L. "Red" Barber, 1908; actor Hal Holbrook, 1925; actor Jim Brown, 1936; basketball player Michael Jordan, 1963.

Today's Quotation—"Religious persecution may shield itself under the guise of a mistaken and overzealous piety."—*Edmund Burke, February 17, 1788*

Persecution

Life leaves us with many scars, only some of which are visible. It is said that when the knights of King Arthur's court returned from battle, they were to bear some scar of the fight. If not, the king would send them back out, telling them, "Go get your scar!"

Do you have any scars as a result of your Christian testimony? A story in *Westminster Quarterly* tells of a harried preacher who was so troubled by his church members and so sharply criticized that he went to his superiors to resign. His bishop thought things over for a moment then asked, "Do your people ever spit in your face?" "No," the preacher replied. "Have they mocked and belittled you?" "No," he said. "Have they stripped and scourged you, crowned you with thorns?" The minister soberly responded, "No sir, and God helping me, I'll carry on until they do."

When we think of what others, including our Savior, have suffered and endured, we are indeed humbled. All of our persecutions seem suddenly insignificant by comparison.

Prayer Suggestion—Have you gotten your scars? Compare them with what Christ bore in your place. Thank God again for his love for you.

FEBRUARY

18

Today in History—John Bunyan's *Pilgrim's Progress* published, 1678; first American opera performed in Charleston, S.C., 1735; Jefferson Davis inaugurated as president of Confederate States of America, 1861; planet Pluto discovered, 1930; British West African colony of Gambia becomes independent, 1965; Chicago jury acquits seven defendants of conspiracy to incite riots at 1968 Democratic Convention (though five of them were convicted on other counts), 1970; U.S. space shuttle makes first flight aboard 747 jet in California, 1977.

Born Today—Philanthropist George Peabody, 1795; politician Wendell Wilkie, 1892; guitarist Andres Segovia, 1894; television's Bill Cullen, 1920; editor Helen Gurley Brown, 1922; actor George Kennedy, 1927; actor John Travolta, 1955.

Today's Quotation—"All we ask is to be left alone."—*Jefferson Davis, February 18, 1861*

Solitary

Ever notice how long some people bear grudges? The village of Town Line, New York, finally ended their eighty-five years of war against the Union in January 1946 when they voted to end hostile relations with the rest of the country. Even then there were twenty-three votes (of ninety cast) against rejoining the Union. It seems that Town Line seceded from the Union in 1861 because of trouble over the system of transporting runaway slaves across their territory into Canada. After nearly 100 years some people still wanted to remain solitary.

The same is true of mankind in our ongoing war against God. Beginning with Adam and Eve's sin in the Garden of Eden, mankind has wanted to be left alone, to be isolated from God and his forgiveness. The end result is death—eternal separation from God and punishment for unbelief. How foolish to wish to be independent from God!

Prayer Suggestion—Tell God how much you love him and the gift of his son, the Lord Jesus Christ.

FEBRUARY

19

Deuteronomy 4:9-14

Today in History—Thomas Edison patents the phonograph, 1878; U.S. Marines land on island of Iwo Jima in bitter battle, 1945; DeLorean car company goes into receivership when British government refuses additional funds, 1982; hundreds riot in Cape Town over announced re-settlement plan for 100,000 blacks, 1985.

Born Today—Astronomer Nicholas Copernicus, 1473; actor David Garrick, 1717; explorer Sven Hedin, 1865; band leader Stan Kenton, 1912; jockey Eddie Arcaro, 1916; actor Lee Marvin, 1924; Britain's Prince Andrew, 1960.

Today's Quotation—"Many college textbooks which were a weari-ness and a stumbling block when studied, I have since read a little in with pleasure and profit."—*Henry David Thoreau, February 19, 1854*

Education

A longtime educator tells of two second-graders who were standing on the playground during recess when a jet fighter flew over. "Look at that," said the first, "it's a BX-50." "No," said the other, "it's a BX-51; you can tell by its wing sweep." "You're right," the first youngster conceded. "It's not going more than 760 miles per hour either, because it didn't break the sound barrier." On that they both agreed. Then the bell sounded, calling the youngsters back into the classroom. The first youngster sighed, "There's that old bell again. Time to go back in and finish stringing beads." Have you ever felt that what you were given to do was meaning-less, that you are up to a greater challenge? Be patient. God often allows us to go through experiences we do not understand at the time, but someday we shall "know as we are known." If we are patient we will fully understand God's system of education.

Prayer Suggestion—Give us patience to understand God's educa-tion for us even when the assignments seem beyond all human under-standing.

FEBRUARY

20

Isaiah 55:1–5

Today in History—Anthony Eden resigns as British Foreign Minister to protest appeasement policies of Prime Minister Neville Chamberlain toward Nazi Germany, 1938; Lt. E. H. O'Hare becomes first World War II naval aviation ace by shooting down five Japanese bombers, 1942; Council of Economic Advisers established to advise president, 1946; new world record for indoor mile set by Irishman Eamon Coghlan (3:50.6), 1981; $7 billion project unveiled to link Britain and France by tunnel, 1986.

Born Today—Actor Joseph Jefferson, 1829; singer Mary Garden, 1877; Russian leader Alexei Kosygin, 1904; designer Gloria Vanderbilt, 1924; actor Sidney Poitier, 1927; singer Nancy Wilson, 1937; actress Sandy Duncan, 1946; actress Jennifer O'Neill, 1948.

Today's Quotation—" . . . there is something radically wrong with so-called 'free enterprise.'"—*Garfield Bromley Oxnam, February 20, 1958*

Free Enterprise

Despite Oxnam's objections, free enterprise has built a number of the most successful businesses in America today. One such example is the young Cincinnati grocer who had $372 and an idea—sell many goods at a small profit each to obtain a large overall profit. Today Bernard H. Kroger's grocery chain operates over two thousand stores in nineteen states. F. W. Woolworth was asked to gather up some assorted items and sell them for whatever he could. Woolworth posted a sign offering any article for just five cents. The items quickly sold, thus giving Woolworth the idea for the first five-and-ten-cent store.

While free enterprise has built America economically, God has his own system of free enterprise in which each and every person is allowed to choose between serving or rejecting him. Which decision have you made in God's free enterprise?

Prayer Suggestion—Be sure you have accepted Christ's forgiveness for your sins, then share your blessings with others you meet today.

FEBRUARY

21

Today in History—Lucy B. Hobbs graduates as first woman dentist from Ohio College of Dental Surgery, 1866; Washington Monument dedicated, 1885; Battle of Verdun began in France, 1916; *The New Yorker* magazine begins publication, 1925; U.S. Army accused Senator Joseph R. McCarthy of Wisconsin of browbeating Army personnel, which leads to his censure by the senate in 1954; President Nixon visits Red China for talks with Mao Tse Tung, 1972; three former top Nixon aides sentenced to two and one-half to 8 years in prison for their role in the Watergate break-in, 1975; election riots in India result in deaths of six hundred Moslems, 1983.

Born Today—John Henry Cardinal Newman, 1801; composer Leo Delibes, 1836; poet W. H. Auden, 1907; author Erma Bombeck, 1927; designer Hubert de Givenchy, 1927; actress Rue McClanahan, 1934; politician Barbara Jordan, 1936.

Today's Quotation—"When angry, count ten before you speak; if very angry, an hundred."—*Thomas Jefferson, February 21, 1825*

Anger

Anger puts a person at a disadvantage in every undertaking. When Sinbad and his crew landed on a tropical island, they spotted coconuts which could quench their thirst and satisfy their hunger. The coconuts were far out of reach of the men, but not a group of chattering apes. Picking up nearby rocks, the men threw them at the apes. To stop the barrage of rocks, the agitated apes began to grab the nearby coconuts and throw them at the men on the ground. The men had gotten the apes so angry the animals had gathered their food for them.

When we lose our temper, we likewise are playing right into the hands of our foes. Don't "fly off the handle" when you get angry; remember, it is the one who is in the wrong who gets the most upset. Practice speaking softly when angry and see how quickly it "turneth away wrath!"

Prayer Suggestion—Promise God that with his help you will not lose control of your emotions and lash out in anger at others.

FEBRUARY

22

Today in History—Indians introduce Pilgrims to popcorn, 1630; Florida ceded to U.S. by Spain, 1819; first five-and-ten-cent store established by F. W. Woolworth, 1879; President Nixon confers with Chinese leader Mao Tse Tung in Peking, 1972.

Born Today—President George Washington, 1732; composer Frederic Chopin, 1810; poet James Russell Lowell, 1819; Boy Scout founder Lord Robert Baden-Powell, 1857; poet Edna St. Vincent Millay, 1892; business executive Nelson Bunker Hunt, 1926.

Today's Quotation—"Few can be induced to labor exclusively for posterity. Posterity has done nothing for us."—*Abraham Lincoln, February 22, 1842*

Descendants

John Mott reports on the family of Andrew Murray of South Africa. Of the eleven children who reached adulthood, five of the sons became ministers and four of the daughters became minister's wives. In the next generation there was an even more striking record as ten grandsons became ministers and thirteen became missionaries. The secret of this unusual dedication to the Christian ministry? The Christian home.

Contrast this with another family about which A. T. Pierson writes. He reports, "a total of twelve hundred descendants have been traced. Four hundred of these were self-wrecked physically, 310 were professional paupers, 130 convicted criminals, sixty were habitual thieves and pickpockets and seven were murderers. Only ten of the twelve hundred were recorded as ever learning a trade on their own."

What a contrast between these two families! Since children become what they see at home, what a grave responsibility this places upon parents!

Prayer Suggestion—May we be worthy examples of Christ before our children so that our descendants would learn to love God.

FEBRUARY

23

Romans 12:16-21

Today in History—Siege of the Alamo begins, 1836; Rotary Clubs founded, 1905; U.S. Marines raise flag at Iwo Jima in World War II, 1945; first mass inoculations with Salk anti-polio serum begin, 1954; captors of Patty Hearst demand $4 million in food for the poor, 1974; buyers line up in China to buy copies of Shakespeare's *Hamlet* now available after cultural ban, 1978; coup attempt in Spanish parliament nets three hundred senators and others, 1981; artist Andy Warhol dies at age 56, 1987.

Born Today—Diarist Samuel Pepys, 1633; composer George Frederick Handel, 1685; educator Emma Hart Willard, 1787; scholar William E. B. DuBois, 1868; writer William Shirer, 1904; actor Peter Fonda, 1939.

Today's Quotation—"I'm as conservative as the Constitution, as liberal as Lincoln, and as progressive as Theodore Roosevelt."—*George Romney, February 23, 1965*

The "Straight and Narrow"

Some say the traditional values of truth and honesty are no longer relevant in this "enlightened" age. However, God's laws have never changed. Dishonesty is just as wrong today as it was in the Garden of Eden, no matter what society may think.

Some years ago, *Liberty* magazine sent out letters containing a one dollar bill to one hundred people selected at random from throughout the U.S. The letter accompanying the dollar stated that the bill was an adjustment of an error which the recipient had complained about. Of the 100 recipients in 1924, twenty-seven returned the dollar, saying it was a mistake. In 1971, *Liberty* repeated the same test, but now only thirteen returned the money.

It appears that honesty doesn't have the importance among some people that once it did. Yet, God's Word has not changed. He still calls dishonesty a sin. If the searchlight were suddenly shining on your life, what would be seen?

Prayer Suggestion—Seek God's help to live your life so that even under the closest scrutiny you would be known for your honesty.

70

FEBRUARY

24

Mark 8:34–38

Today in History—U.S. Supreme Court, for first time, rules an act of Congress unconstitutional, 1803; House of Representatives votes to impeach President Andrew Johnson, 1868; Estonia becomes independent of Russia (only to be absorbed again some twenty years later), 1918; "Voice of America" airs its first broadcast, 1942; Juan Peron elected president of Argentina, 1946; Mrs. Margaret Kienast gives birth to quintuplets—three girls and two boys, 1970; U.S. cuts aid to Argentina, Uruguay, and Ethiopia because of human rights violations, 1977; Dr. Margaret Leakey reports locating humanoid footprints in Africa as many as 3.5 million years old, 1978; U.S. hockey team defeats Russians to win gold medal, 1980; Jean Harris found guilty in Dr. Tarnower murder, 1981; new galaxy twelve billion light years away is sighted, 1987.

Born Today—Storyteller Wilhelm Karl Grimm, 1786; artist Winslow Homer, 1836; lawyer Mark Lane, 1927; composer Michel Legrand, 1932; actor James Farentino, 1938; baseball player Eddie Murray, 1956.

Today's Quotation—"High society is for those who have stopped working and no longer have anything important to do."—*Woodrow Wilson, February 24, 1915*

High Society

Not everyone who makes it to the top of the heap ends up staying there. One such person was George Train. Although a penniless orphan at the age of 3, Train made a fortune in shipping and retired at age 30. He wrote ten books, took two trips around the world, and was even a candidate for U.S. President in 1872. Then his life took a downward spiral. He became a recluse, rarely talking to adults during the last ten years of his life, devoting his time instead to telling stories to children. He died penniless in a three-dollar-a-week New York hotel room in January 1904.

Indeed "what shall it profit a man, if he shall gain the whole world, and lose his own soul?" (Mark 8:36).

Prayer Suggestion—Recognize God as the source of all blessings. Ask that he give you no more wealth and prestige than you can handle.

FEBRUARY

25

Today in History—Hiram H. Revels of Mississippi becomes first black member of U.S. Senate, 1870; Sixteenth Amendment to Constitution authorizing U.S. income tax is ratified, 1913; Czechoslovakia taken over by Communists, 1948; Soviets admit they beam microwaves at U.S. embassy in Moscow, 1975; Ugandan leader Idi Amin detains 240 Americans, 1977; nine alleged Cosa Nostra bosses detained in New York City, 1985.

Born Today—Painter Pièrre August Renoir, 1841; Singer Enrico Caruso, 1873; actor Jim Backus, 1913; tennis player Bobby Riggs, 1918; diplomat Phillip Habib, 1920; musician George Harrison, 1943.

Today's Quotation—"The extensive means of destruction invented by science, the crime against mankind that a nuclear war would constitute, compel us to make peace our first and permanent goal."—*Georges Pompidou, February 25, 1970*

Massive Destruction

No longer is it only governments with the capability to manufacture a major nuclear device. R. W. Mengel says it is now possible for terrorists to make an atomic weapon with about half the power of the Hiroshima bomb. "Assuming a surface burst of about one kiloton, using a truck as the probable means of delivery to the target, the damage in a downtown area of a major city would be more than one hundred thousand immediate fatalities and destruction totaling in the billions of dollars." In this era it may only be a matter of time before someone attempts to hold an entire city hostage in a form of nuclear blackmail. This would be a major tragedy with the prospect of massive destruction.

But the most massive destruction of all time is yet to come: that foretold in the pages of the Bible. Where will you be on that day ". . . in which the heavens shall pass away with a great noise, and the elements shall melt with fervent heat, the earth also and the works that are therein shall be burned up" (2 Peter 3:10)?

Prayer Suggestion—Thank God that you will not be around to be destroyed with the earth on that awful day.

FEBRUARY

26

Today in History—Napoleon escapes from Elba to begin his second war in Europe, 1815; New York's first subway opens in downtown Manhattan, 1870; Twenty-second Amendment to Constitution limiting presidential tenure to two terms is ratified, 1951; last unit of U.S. Marines leaves Beirut, 1984; Robert Penn Warren named Britain's poet laureate, 1986.

Born Today—Writer Victor Hugo, 1802; entertainer William "Buffalo Bill" Cody, 1846; comedian Jackie Gleason, 1916; actor Tony Randall, 1920; actress Betty Hutton, 1921; singer Johnny Cash, 1932.

Today's Quotation—"Justice has nothing to do with expediency."—*Woodrow Wilson, February 26, 1916*

Justice

An example of justice comes from overseas. In the Supreme Court building in Switzerland hangs a huge painting entitled "Justice Instructing the Judges." Various litigants are in the foreground—a wife against a husband, an architect against a builder, while above these stands a group of judges. How will they judge the various litigants? The artist depicts it this way: Justice (usually shown blindfolded with her sword vertical) here is blindfolded with her sword pointing down to a book on which is written "The Word of God."

Yes, God's Word is the basis of not only our system of justice, but also the entire Judeo-Christian ethic by which we work and live. People may not recognize it as such, but God is the very basis for our way of life. May we always give him credit for the great things he has done for us.

Prayer Suggestion—Recognize God's greatness in giving us not only a hope for the future, but a great way to live here and now.

FEBRUARY

27

Today in History—Pacific island of New Britain discovered, 1700; Reichsag (Nazi's headquarters building in Berlin) set on fire, 1933; China launches counterattack against Vietnamese troops along common border, 1979; Wayne Williams sentenced to two life terms on charges stemming from the deaths of twenty-eight black Atlanta youths, 1982; Philippine President Ferdinand Marcos flees his troubled homeland for exile in Hawaii, 1986; Presidential panel urges President Reagan to take responsibility for Iran arms deal, 1987.

Born Today—Poet Henry Wadsworth Longfellow, 1807; actress Dame Ellen Terry, 1847; singer Lotte Lehmann, 1888; broadcasting's David Sarnoff, 1891; writer John Steinbeck, 1902; actress Joanne Woodward, 1930; actress Elizabeth Taylor, 1932; consumer advocate Ralph Nader, 1934.

Today's Quotation—"Let us have faith that right makes might, and in that faith let us to the end dare to do our duty as we understand it."— *Abraham Lincoln, February 27, 1860*

Doing Our Duty

Philip P. Bliss was a songleader for evangelist Dwight L. Moody. Moody told this story of a captain attempting to bring his boat into Cleveland Harbor on a dark, stormy night. "The mighty waves crashed ashore," Moody said, "under a pitch black sky." Finally, the captain of the boat located a single light from the lighthouse. "Are you sure this is the harbor?" he asked the pilot anxiously. "Quite sure, sir," the pilot replied. The captain asked, "Then where are the lower lights?" "Gone out," was the reply. And so, without the guiding lower lights, the ship missed the channel and crashed upon the rocks. Moody concluded his message, "Brethren, the Master will take care of the great lighthouse; but let us be sure to keep the lower lights burning." From this message Bliss went on to write one of his most beloved hymns, "Let the Lower Lights Be Burning."

Prayer Suggestion—Let us call upon God's strength to be faithful in sending forth the Word of life to a lost and dying world.

FEBRUARY

28

Today in History—Baltimore and Ohio Railroad incorporated in Maryland, 1827; two members of President Tyler's Cabinet among five people killed when a gun explodes aboard a ship in the Potomac, 1844; President Nixon concludes historic visit to China, 1972; 250 American Indian Movement members occupy Wounded Knee, S.D., 1973; four mysterious bombs explode in New York's Wall Street area, 1982; Swedish Prime Minister Olafe Palme gunned down on Stockholm Street, 1986.

Born Today—Medical missionary Wilfred Grenfell, 1965; chemist Linus Pauling, 1901; actor Zero Mostel, 1915; actor Gavin MacLeod, 1930; driver Mario Andretti, 1940; football player Bubba Smith, 1945.

Today's Quotation—"Now and then a little difference does not hurt."—*Samuel Pepys, February 28, 1665*

Life's Differences

Many times what draws couples together is not what they have in common but how different, yet complementary, they are. Occasionally this can be carried to an extreme. Such is the story of the man who applied for a marriage license and then waited eleven years before going back to claim the permit. When asked why he and his fiancee had waited so long to get married, he explained, "We had a few disagreements about details."

Though life is marked by its share of differences, some more significant than others, we can still count on an unchanging God to carry us through.

Prayer Suggestion—Rejoice in a God who is the same yesterday, and today, and forever—perfect and unchanging in all his ways.

FEBRUARY

29

Today in History—Britain and U.S. sign treaty on seal hunting in Bering Sea, 1892; Right-wing coup attempted in Finland (defeated in 3 days), 1932; Pakistan proclaims itself an Islamic Republic, 1956; Commission on civil disorders blames black violence on white racism, 1968; Cesar Chavez signs first migrant worker contract in Florida, 1972; report shows worldwide military spending up 45 percent to $300 billion a year since 1961, 1976; Canada's prime minister Pierre Trudeau resigns after fifteen years of leadership, 1984.

Born Today—General Marquis de Montcalm, 1712; Shaker leader Ann Lee, 1736; composer Gioacchino Rossini, 1792.

Today's Quotation—"Our nation is moving toward two societies, one black, one white—separate and unequal."—*President's National Advisory Commission on Civil Disorders, February 29, 1968*

Working Together

The fanner bees provide an excellent example of cooperation for the common good. An old beekeeper was walking down the path to his hives at twilight with his small son. The keeper lit a candle. Suddenly, as he lowered the candle to the entrance of the hive, the flame quickly blew out. The youngster was puzzled. "Why was that, Father?" he inquired. "It's the fanner bees," said the old man. "These tiny insects work together fanning their wings to keep the hive cool. By itself, a single bee can't do much. But by working together, hundreds of bees churn up such a breeze with their wings that it blows a candle out."

If Christians were as willing to work together as the fanner bees, imagine how the world would be changed!

Prayer Suggestion—May we look for ways to assist our fellow believers in doing the work of God.

MARCH

1

Luke 4:31–37

Today in History—U.S. Articles of Confederation adopted, 1781; first United States census begins, 1790; Ohio admitted as seventeenth state, 1803; Napoleon reenters France, 1815; Nebraska becomes thirty-seventh state, 1867; baby Charles Lindbergh, Jr., kidnapped, 1932; Puerto Rican nationalists wound five members of House of Representatives, 1954; Peace Corps established, 1961; Uganda's Idi Amin releases 240 detained Americans, 1977.

Born Today—Sculptor Augustus Saint-Gaudens, 1848; band leader Glenn Miller, 1904; singer Dinah Shore, 1917; sportscaster Harry Caray, 1919; football commissioner Pete Rozelle, 1926; singer Harry Belafonte, 1927; actor Ron Howard, 1954.

Today's Quotation—"I awoke one morning and found myself famous."—*Lord Byron, March 1, 1812*

Fame

Earthly fame is fleeting because it focuses upon the creature rather than the Creator. Ruby Miller tells the story of former President Woodrow Wilson who was quietly getting a haircut one day when it became apparent that another notable person had also entered the room. This gentleman sat in the chair next to Wilson's and soon began talking not about himself, but about the Lord and his love for the barber and others in the world. The man was famed evangelist D. L. Moody. After Moody left the shop, the former president lingered for a moment to watch the barbers' reaction. He observed, "Though they didn't know his name, they knew that something had raised their thoughts. . . . I felt that I had left a place of worship."

Imagine that scene: a famous president and a noted evangelist side by side in a barber shop! Yet the conversation was focused not on either of them but upon God! What a testimony to God's work in a life—that people should not see the small fame we might achieve, but rather would see God's glorious presence reflected by our lives.

Prayer Suggestion—That God would get all the glory in what we say and do today and every day.

Luke 4:31–37

MARCH

2

Romans 10:1-13

Today in History—Texas declares independence from Mexico, 1836; Rutherford B. Hayes declared president by special Electoral Commission, 1877; *Time* magazine first published, 1923; U.S. Air Force superfortress bomber completes first non-stop flight around the world, 1949; U.S. launches *Pioneer 10* spacecraft on twenty-one-month trip to Jupiter, 1972; Soviets call China the "most serious threat to peace in the world," 1979.

Born Today—Statesman Sam Houston, 1793; politician Carl Schurz, 1829; children's author Dr. Seuss (Theodore Geisel), 1904; entertainer Desi Arnaz, 1917; Soviet leader Mikhail Gorbachev, 1931; author John Irving, 1942.

Today's Quotation—"Turn where we may, within, around, the voice of great events is proclaiming to us, Reform, that you may preserve."—*Thomas B. Macaulay, March 2, 1831*

Repentance

Repentance, not reform, has eternal consequences. A nineteen-year-old once held up a bank along with two others. The case was later closed when two convicts, singled out by the bank as being the robbers, were killed in a car wreck. Meanwhile the youth was sure he would never be caught. Time went on and he married, still struggling to reform on his own but with little success. One day he read a gospel tract that said, "Whosoever shall call upon the Lord shall be saved." For the first time the guilty man saw that God had already forgiven his sins if only he would repent, believe, and accept God's pardon. He did so and his whole life became new. But he was still guilty of a serious crime. After some soulsearching and prayer, the man confessed to the crime and offered to repay the bank what he had stolen. However, the statute of limitations had run out, so he was set free. Today he is an outstanding Christian layman not through reform, but through repentance and God's forgiving grace.

Prayer Suggestion—When was the last time you repented and sorrowed over your sins? Turn from your past, "Go and sin no more."

MARCH

3

1 John 5:11–21

Today in History—Florida admitted as twenty-seventh state, 1845; Russia signs World War I peace treaty, 1918; "Star Spangled Banner" adopted as U.S. national anthem, 1931; in Battle of Bismarck, U.S. Navy defeats Japan, 1943; United States and Philippine forces recapture Corregidor in World War II, 1945; parents of Patty Hearst plead for kidnapped daughter's release, 1974; British coal miners call off year-long strike when many unable to feed their families, 1985.

Born Today—Inventor George Pullman, 1831; inventor Alexander Graham Bell, 1847; photographer Arnold Newman, 1918; golfer Julius Boros, 1920; Princess Lee Radziwill, 1933; football player Herschel Walker, 1962.

Today's Quotation—"Three thousand years and the world so little changed!"—*Henry David Thoreau, March 3, 1838*

Eternity

The great warrior Napoleon once saw a painting by Baron Denon and complimented the artist on his beautiful work. The artist boastfully replied, "Yes, it is immortal." Napoleon inquired how long Denon's painting and statue would last. "The painting, five hundred years and the statue, five thousand," was the artist's response. Napoleon exclaimed, "And you call that immortality?"

Just how long is forever? A googol is a one with one hundred zeroes behind it. Then there are googolplexes, googols raised to the googol-th power, which, if written out, would more than cover the entire earth! In fact, such pages would more than fill our galaxy. Yet, even with each page representing one million years, this would represent only a minute of eternity—an eternity that will be spent in heaven with God himself or in the lake of fire which burns forever and ever. We are told "today is the day of salvation." The choice is ours.

Have you settled your eternal destiny with God? Do not put off life's most important decision. Trust God today.

Prayer Suggestion—Remember the millions who are yet unsaved. Pray that God would provide the opportunity to share our faith with someone today before it is eternally too late.

MARCH

4

Today in History—William Penn receives charter for Pennsylvania from England's King Charles II, 1681; United States Constitution goes into effect, 1789; Vermont admitted as fourteenth state, 1791; Chicago city charter approved, 1837; Confederate States of America adopted "Stars and Bars" flag, 1861; New York City's Stage Door Canteen opens in World War II, 1942; Robert Mugabe becomes leader of new African nation of Zimbabwe (formerly Rhodesia), 1980; intoxicated man sets himself on fire in Alabama as TV cameras roll, 1983; Pope John Paul II assails "Liberation Theology" in Nicaraguan visit, 1983; former U.N. ambassador Kurt Waldheim charged with hiding Nazi background, 1986.

Born Today—Patriot Casimir Pulaski, 1748; artist Sir Henry Raeburn, 1756; football coach Knute Rockne, 1888; singer Miriam Makeba, 1932; anthropologist Jane Goodall, 1934; chess player Bobby Fischer, 1943; singer Mary Wilson, 1944.

Today's Quotation—"The only thing we have to fear is fear itself."— *Franklin D. Roosevelt, March 4, 1933*

Fear

Fear is something we never fully overcome. A nationwide survey of over two thousand children ages seven to eleven showed that over two-thirds said they were scared that "something bad" was stalking about their neighborhood. Fully one-fourth were afraid they would be attacked when they went outside and with some reason, since more than 40 percent of them said they have been harassed by older kids or adults while playing. The survey concluded that children who watch over four hours of television a day are twice as likely to be fearful. But it is not only children who are afraid. Doctors say that stress caused by fear is greatly affecting the entire nation's health.

What are you afraid of? If you fear (respect) God, you need not be afraid. As the Bible says, "Be fearful for nothing."

Prayer Suggestion—That God would remove the fear from our lives as we honor him who can see beyond tomorrow and guide us through today.

MARCH

5

Today in History—Boston Massacre occurs, 1770; impeachment of President Andrew Johnson goes before Senate, 1868; President Franklin D. Roosevelt declares national bank holiday, 1933; Soviet Premier Josef Stalin dies, 1953; nuclear nonproliferation treaty goes into effect, 1970; actor John Belushi found dead at age 32, 1982; U.S. Supreme Court rules nativity scenes are allowed in public places, 1984.

Born Today—Mathematician-geographer George Mercator, 1512; composer Hector Villa-Lobos, 1887; actor Rex Harrison, 1908; business executive Lawrence Tisch, 1923; actress Samantha Eggar, 1939.

Today's Quotation—"From Stettin in the Baltic to Trieste in the Adriatic, an Iron Curtain has descended across the Continent."—*Winston Churchill, March 5, 1946*

Communism

Christians must be ever-vigilant against philosophies, such as communism, which deny the existence of God or the deity of Christ. British Prime Minister Winston Churchill was among the first world leaders to recognize the isolation of communist countries from the rest of the world. Lest we become complacent after years of co-existence and detente we should hear closely these words from Gus Hall, head of the U.S. Communist Party: "I dream of the hour when the last Congressman is strangled to death on the guts of the last preacher—and since Christians seem to love to sing about the blood, why not give them a little of it? Slit the throats of their children and drag them over the mourner's bench and the pulpit, and allow them to drown in their own blood; and then see whether they enjoy singing these hymns."

Believers must never forget the deadly battle between the forces of God and the forces of evil for our very souls. Therefore, we must know what we believe and why in order to withstand the onslaughts yet to come.

Prayer Suggestion—For strength in the Christian life and wisdom to know God's way in the spiritual battle for men's souls.

MARCH

6

Today in History—Alamo falls to Mexican forces at San Antonio, Texas, 1836; Supreme Court upholds slavery in Dred Scott case, 1857; National Bank closing "holiday" begins, 1933; Greenwich Village townhouse "bomb factory" explodes, killing several people, 1970; five Moslems sentenced to die in killing of Egyptian president Anwar Sadat, 1982; Soviet spacecraft sends back hundreds of pictures of Halley's comet, 1986; twenty-six dead, two hundred trapped as British ferry capsizes off Belgium, 1987.

Born Today—Artist Michelangelo,1475; poet Elizabeth Barrett Browning, 1806; writer Ring Lardner, 1885; TV personality Ed McMahon, 1923; conductor Sarah Caldwell, 1924; astronaut Gordon Cooper, Jr., 1927; actor-director Rob Reiner, 1945.

Today's Quotation—"I like the system which lets a man quit when he wants to, and wish it might prevail everywhere."—*Abraham Lincoln, March 6, 1860*

Perseverance

You can determine the character of a man by what it takes to make him quit. The father of Cyrus McCormick became the laughingstock of the community when he could not make a grain-cutting device operate properly. So young McCormick rolled up his sleeves, and after years of trial and error, built a successful reaper. But the battle was not over, because opposition prevented it from being used. Finally, after years of persistent effort, and only after McCormick personally guaranteed the reaper would cut grain, was the world able to enjoy the benefits of this machine which mechanized harvesting.

Are you discouraged—close to quitting? Victory lies just ahead if you will only persevere to the end. Are you using all your strength including God's strength working within? If not, you're not using all your strength.

Prayer Suggestion—Ask the eternal God to sustain you when you feel like giving up. Let his Holy Spirit strengthen your resolve to carry on.

MARCH

7

Matthew 22:15–21

Today in History—Telephone patent granted to Alexander Graham Bell, 1876; transatlantic radio-telephone service begins between New York and London, 1926; Hitler orders German troops into Rhineland, 1936; U.S. Ninth Armored Division captures key German bridge speeding World War II victory, 1945; *Voyager I* spacecraft sends photos showing faint ring around planet Jupiter, 1979.

Born Today—Horticulturist Luther Burbank, 1849; statesman Thomas Masaryk, 1850; composer Maurice Ravel, 1875; photographer Anthony Armstrong-Jones (Lord Snowdon), 1930; football player Franco Harris, 1950; tennis player Ivan Lendl, 1960.

Today's Quotation—"We have a great, popular, constitutional government, guarded by law and by judicature, and defended by the affections of the whole people."—*Daniel Webster, March 7, 1850*

Government

God has ordained government to administer the public affairs of mankind. As long as people in government behave in a godly manner, we should give them honor even if it means some discomfort to us. The *Prairie Overcomer* tells of a poor, elderly widow who was sent a tax bill requiring immediate payment. Counting her money she found she had enough to pay the bill and so she set out on foot to settle her obligation. To do so, however, required great effort, for the nearest tax office was some fourteen miles away! Commenting on her faithfulness later, the woman replied matter-of-factly, "We need to take care of our government financially, so that it stays democratic."

How faithful are we in paying our obligations to government, or to the Lord? Will God find you faithful to your government and to him?

Prayer Suggestion—Pray for your government, its elected leaders, and employees. Ask that God would direct the affairs of government so that his Word might continue to go forth to accomplish his will.

MARCH

8

Today in History—Riots in St. Petersburg, Russia, begin country's revolution against monarchy, 1917; Joe Frazier defeats Muhammad Ali (Cassius Clay) in world heavyweight championship, 1971; President Reagan calls Soviet Union "evil empire" in speech before National Association of Evangelicals, 1983; three thousand Polish youths stage mass protest against government decision to remove crucifixes from public classrooms and hospitals, 1984.

Born Today—Supreme Court Justice Oliver Wendell Holmes, 1841; composer Ruggiero Leoncavallo, 1848; economist Stuart Chase, 1888; actress Cyd Charisse, 1923; singer Charlie Pride, 1938; baseball player Jim Rice, 1953.

Today's Quotation—"The First Amendment has erected a wall between Church and State which must be kept high and impregnable."—*Hugo L. Black, March 8, 1948*

Church-State Separation

Separation of church and state should never be confused with separation of God from the state. To do the latter invites disaster. Years ago a group decided to found a community in Missouri so completely separated from God that churches were not even allowed in the town! The community claimed it was the only town of its size in the U.S. "without a priest, a preacher, church, God, Jesus, hell, or devil." What happened in this experiment separating the state and its people from God? One disgruntled citizen leaving the town noted, "An infidel surrounded by Christians may spout his infidelity and the community may be able to stand it, but it will never do to establish a society with infidelity as its basis." So much for the experiment to separate God from society.

God has called Christians to be "salt" here on earth. Apparently without such spiritual preservative, the community quickly began to deteriorate. Are you acting as salt to preserve our Christian freedoms?

Prayer Suggestion—Pray for government and judicial leaders as they make decisions affecting our freedom including the right to worship God as we please.

MARCH

9

Nehemiah 9:7-24

Today in History—Confederate currency authorized, 1861; iron-clad ships *Monitor* and *Merrimac* battle in Civil War, 1862; American B-29 bombers raid Tokyo in World War II, 1945; Soviet spacecraft launched with dog aboard, 1961; Navy divers locate crew compartment of *Challenger* spacecraft with remains of seven astronauts, 1986.

Born Today—Explorer Amerigo Vespucci, 1451; politician Leland Stanford, 1824; architect Edward Stone, 1902; writer Mickey Spillane, 1918; actress Trish Van Devere, 1943; photographer David Kennerly, 1947.

Today's Quotation—"I believe in one God, Creator of the Universe. That He governs it by His Providence. That He ought to be worshipped. That the most acceptable Service we render to Him is doing good to His other Children."—*Benjamin Franklin, March 9, 1790*

God

Do we really believe God answers prayer? The hymn writer so wisely has penned: "Oh, what peace we often forfeit/Oh, what needless pain we bear/all because we do not carry everything to God in prayer." Yet we so often would rather try to do it ourselves.

The story is told of a preacher who was busy in his study while his young son was playing nearby. Needing a book he had left upstairs, the preacher asked the youngster to get it. The boy was gone for a long time when the father heard crying. He went searching for the youngster and found him at the top of the stairs with the large book he could not carry lying at his feet. "Daddy," he cried, "I can't carry it. It's too heavy for me." The father then lovingly stooped down and carried both the boy and the book down to the study below.

Isn't that just like what God does for us? He sees us in our weakness and stands ready to help if only we will cry out to him in our time of need.

Prayer Suggestion—Don't struggle under your burdens; turn them over to God. He will carry you through!

85

MARCH

10

Today in History—Alexander Graham Bell speaks first words over a telephone, 1876; Salvation Army group arrives from England to begin work in the U.S., 1880; anti-communist Czechoslovakian Foreign Minister Jan Masaryk falls (or is pushed) from a window in Prague, 1948; fifteen thousand Iranian women protest restrictions of Islamic rule, 1979.

Born Today—Social worker Lillian Wald, 1867; composer Arthur Honegger, 1892; broadcaster Heywood Hale Broun, 1918; actress Pamela Mason, 1918; playwright David Rabe, 1940; Prince Edward of England, 1964.

Today's Quotation—"Whatever is worth doing at all is worth doing well."—*Earl of Chesterfield, March 10, 1746*

Hard Work

A great orchestra was gathered in rehearsal before the celebrated conductor Sir Michael Costa. Virtually every instrument was playing during one loud crescendo except for the piccolo. The piccolo player was tired and decided that his instrument wouldn't be missed. Suddenly the conductor called for the orchestra to stop playing and asked, "Where's the piccolo?" In the resounding echo of many loud instruments the tiny piccolo was missed!

No matter how insignificant we may feel or how hard the work, we need to be doing God's calling here on earth. Consider the little titmouse who awakens at 3 a.m. and doesn't stop until 9 p.m. during which time he feeds his chicks 417 meals. Or the hard-working thrush who gets up at 2:30 every morning and doesn't stop till around 9:30 at night—a nineteen-hour day! All of a sudden an eight-hour-workday five days a week with three meals a day doesn't seem so bad after all!

God put us on earth to replenish it through hard work. What are you contributing to that effort?

Prayer Suggestion—Pray that God would teach us the rewards of hard work as we go about our daily lives and that we would share this message with our children and co-workers.

MARCH

11

Today in History—Napoleon marries Princess Marie Louise of Austria, 1810; U.S. Lend-Lease Law signed, providing aid to foes of Nazis in World War II, 1941; General Douglas MacArthur leaves for Australia to assume top Pacific war command, 1942; Dr. Herman Tarnower shot to death by headmistress of a prestigious girl's school, 1980; thirty percent unemployment rate sparks exodus of thirty thousand people a year from Ireland, 1987.

Born Today—Sportsman Sir Malcolm Campbell, 1885; band leader Lawrence Welk, 1903; statesman Harold Wilson, 1916; civil rights leader Ralph Abernathy, 1926; publisher Rupert Murdoch, 1931; broadcast journalist Sam Donaldson, 1934; Supreme Court Justice Antonin Scalia, 1936.

Today's Quotation—"There is a higher law than the Constitution."—*William H. Seward, March 11, 1850*

God's Laws

Which laws should we obey, man's or God's? The Bible makes it clear that the only time civil disobedience is allowed is when God's laws run counter to laws passed by man. In Benjamin Franklin's autobiography there is a story of the colonial clergyman who was ordered to read the proclamation issued by King Charles I encouraging the people to participate in sports on Sundays. Much to the amazement of his congregation, the preacher complied and read the edict which many others had refused to do. The preacher then followed the king's edict with these words "Remember the Sabbath Day to keep it holy," adding, "Brethren, I have laid before you the commandment of your king and the commandment of your God. I leave it to you to judge which of the two you ought rather to observe."

When in doubt, check it out—in God's Word, the Bible. When you observe God's laws you will always be right.

Prayer Suggestion—Ask God to guide all judges and legislators that they might write and enforce laws according to God's will. As a citizen, become active in lobbying for laws which honor God.

MARCH

12

Isaiah 29:9-17

Today in History—Carnegie Hero Fund Commission established with five-million-dollar gift from Andrew Carnegie, 1904; first Girl Scout group meets, 1912; President Franklin D. Roosevelt airs first radio fireside chat to the nation, 1933; Nazis occupy Austria, 1938; President Truman proposes anti-Communist aid to Turkey and Greece, 1947; opposition leader Joseph Nkomo flees as Robert Mugabe arrests six hundred in Zimbabwe (Rhodesia), 1983; yuppies said to have largely displaced hippies in San Francisco's Haight-Ashbury section, 1987.

Born Today—Publisher Adolph Ochs, 1858; writer Jack Kerouac, 1922; playwright Edward Albee, 1928; politician Andrew Young, 1932; actress Liza Minelli, 1946; composer James Taylor, 1948; baseball player Darryl Strawberry, 1962.

Today's Quotation—"Curiosity is one of the permanent and certain characteristics of a vigorous mind."—*Samuel Johnson, March 12, 1751*

Curiosity

Have you ever wondered why something is done the way it is? Some of mankind's greatest blessings have been produced through just such a questioning attitude. A department store janitor, Murray Spangler, grew tired of breathing dust when he swept and knew there had to be a better way. His curiosity motivated him to find a way to lift dirt from the floor and into a sealed bag, thus eliminating the dusty broom. The result was a crude but workable vacuum cleaner which he then encouraged his friend, H. W. Hoover, to finance. The rest is history.

Be glad if God has instilled in you a sense of curiosity. Just be sure to channel that curiosity into a greater appreciation of not only God's creation, but also of his Word.

Prayer Suggestion—Thank God for his intricate creation and his allowing us to, in some small way, tame and understand it.

MARCH

13

Jeremiah 17:5-11

Today in History—First Bible printed, 1462; U.S. Senate begins impeachment proceedings against President Andrew Johnson, 1868; world time standard based on Greenwich Mean Time adopted, 1884; "Christ of the Andes," statue between Argentina and Chile, dedicated, 1904; Soviet leader Konstantin Chernenko dies causing third transfer of leadership in U.S.S.R. in thirty months, 1985; inventory of exiled Philippine leader Marcos' savings shows $800 million in foreign bank accounts, 1986.

Born Today—Scientist Joseph Priestley, 1733; astronomer Purcival Lowell, 1855; painter Juan Gris, 1887; publisher Walter Annenberg, 1908; band leader Sammy Kaye, 1913; singer Neil Sedaka, 1939.

Today's Quotation—"Scenery is fine—but human nature is finer."— *John Keats, March 13, 1818*

Human Nature

Despite the sugary veneer mankind displays, the Bible says his heart is "desperately wicked." The ways of deceitful man were clearly underscored by the actions of the game wardens in setting up their check-in station on opening day of hunting season not long ago. The first road sign they erected read, "Check-Station 1,000 yards ahead." Five hundred yards beyond the sign was a convenient side road. The wardens knew from human nature that lawful hunters would continue straight ahead, but over-limit and doubtful hunters were likely to duck down the side road where the check station was located five hundred yards beyond the turn-off.

Left on his own, mankind has no hope. But by acknowledging his helpless condition and accepting God's gift of salvation through Christ's death on the cross, mankind has the strength needed for today and the hope of an eternal future with God in heaven. When God peers down from heaven into your heart what does he see?

Prayer Suggestion—If you have not already done so, ask God's forgiveness for your sins and accept Christ as your Savior. Then as a believer thank God for the hope within you and share it with another today.

MARCH

14

Today in History—Eli Whitney patents cotton gin, 1794; Adolf Hitler arrives in triumph in his native Austria, 1938; Republic of Czechoslovakia dissolved as Nazis move in, 1939; New York City hires a rainmaker, 1950; U.S. budget cut by $13 billion due to effects of inflation on the economy, 1983; OPEC members agree to price cuts for first time in cartel's twenty-five-year history, 1983; Gallaudet, America's only deaf college, gets first hearing-impaired president, 1988.

Born Today—Composer Johann Strauss, 1804; writer Maxim Gorky, 1868; scientist Albert Einstein, 1879; cartoonist Hank Ketcham, 1920; astronaut Frank Borman, 1928; actor Michael Caine, 1933; composer Quincy Jones, 1933; astronaut Eugene Cernan, 1934.

Today's Quotation—"A great obstacle to good education is the inordinate passion prevalent for novels, and the time lost in that reading which should be instructively employed."—*Thomas Jefferson, March 14, 1818*

Use of Time

Much mention is made today of "time management"—planning your day's work and working your plan. How do we spend our time? Evangelist Robert Murray McCheyne, guilt-stricken at having spent an evening too lightly, once wrote in his diary, "My heart must break off from all these things. What right have I to steal and abuse my Master's time? Redeem the time!"

Recent studies have shown that during the average lifetime we will spend 20 years sleeping, 20 years working, 6 years eating, 7 years playing, 5 years dressing, 1 year on the telephone, 2½ years in bed, 3 years waiting for someone, 1½ years in church, 5 months tying our shoes, and 1½ years on other things.

Someday, however, we will all give account of how we have used our time, including how much we have given in service to the Lord. What accounting of your time will you give to God?

Prayer Suggestion—That God would guide us in making wise use of our time, including giving a tithe of our time to him.

MARCH

15

Romans 8:1–8

Today in History—Julius Caesar assassinated in Rome, 44 B.C.; Maine enters U.S. as twenty-third state, 1820; Woodrow Wilson holds first presidential news conference, 1913; Russia's Czar Nicholas II abdicates, 1917; American Legion founded, 1919; President Richard Nixon named coconspirator in Watergate controversy, 1974; Senate votes down voluntary silent prayer in public schools, 1984; Labor Secretary Raymond Donovan resigns following indictment on fraud and larceny charges for which he was later acquitted, 1985.

Born Today—President Andrew Jackson, 1767; trumpeter Harry James, 1916; astronaut Alan Bean, 1932; singer Mike Love, 1941; lawyer Mark Green, 1945; basketball player Terry Cummings, 1961.

Today's Quotation—"Let us then stand by the constitution, as it is, and by our country as it is, one, united, and entire; let it be a truth engraven on our hearts; let it be borne on the flag under which we rally in every exigency, that we have one country, one constitution, one destiny."—*Daniel Webster, March 15, 1837*

Freedom

As free people, we need to be ever vigilant, mindful of the awful price our forefathers paid that we might be free. Visitors to Washington, D.C. often notice high atop the Capitol building dome the "Freedom Lady," a statue nearly twenty feet high. James C. Helley recalls the story of the statue's shipment from Rome. Encountering a fierce storm, the ship's captain ordered some cargo to be thrown overboard. Some of the sailors wanted to jettison the heavy statue but the captain refused, shouting above the howling storm, "No! Never! We'll flounder before we throw 'Freedom' away."

How often do we take our freedom for granted? Yet, if we are not watchful of our leaders as well as our enemies, we may find our freedoms all too quickly gone away. Remember that, "All it takes for evil to triumph is for good men to do nothing."

Prayer Suggestion—Ask God to lead the hearts and minds of our nation's leaders and pray for his protection upon our land and the freedoms we hold dear.

MARCH

16

Today in History—Ferdinand Magellan sights the Philippines, 1521; U.S. Military Academy established at West Point, N.Y., 1802; Federal Trade Commission organized, 1915; Nazi Germany renounces Versailles Treaty, 1935; U.S. defeats Japanese in Battle of Iwo Jima, 1945; U.S. astronauts Neal Armstrong and David Scott successfully dock two spacecraft, 1966.

Born Today—President James Madison, 1751; scientist Georg Ohm, 1787; former First Lady Pat Nixon, 1912; General William Westmoreland, 1914; entertainer Jerry Lewis, 1925; astronaut R. Walter Cunningham, 1932; actor Erik Estrada, 1949.

Today's Quotation—"Every woman is infallibly to be gained by every sort of flattery, and every man by one sort or other."—*Earl of Chesterfield, March 16, 1752*

Flattery

We've all heard the saying "flattery will get you nowhere," yet there is always room for an honest compliment. An example of the lengths some people will go to be flattered is shown by the story of a British telephone company which installed "MOR" (for morale), a service for neglected housewives. Now, when things aren't quite as they should be at home, the lonely Mom can dial a special number to hear a soothing male voice coo, "You're really quite beautiful, you know," and similar words of flattery.

As Christians, and children of God, we should be much more complimentary to our families, our associates, and those we meet. While we should avoid insincere flattery, an honest compliment to those we know can help make their day and make them want to know more about the Lord we love. It was Mark Twain who said, "I can live two months on a good compliment." Compliment someone today!

Prayer Suggestion—That God would point out someone today who is in special need of a sincere compliment, someone for whom Christ died that you might reach out and encourage.

MARCH

17

Today in History—Camp Fire Girls founded, 1910; U.S. midget sub finds missing H-bomb off coast of Spain, 1966; U.S. uses first veto in U.N. Security Council to block censure of Great Britain over Rhodesian issue, 1970; Capital Cities, Inc., buys ABC, Inc., for $3.5 billion, 1985; Iran and Iraq troops clash in fiercest fighting of the five-year war, 1985.

Born Today—Frontiersman Jim Bridger, 1804; golfer Bobby Jones, 1902; civil rights leader Bayard Rustin, 1910; composer Paul Horn, 1930; dancer Rudolph Nureyev, 1938; actor Kurt Russell, 1951.

Today's Quotation—"Let us now forgive and forget. Let each country seek its advancement in its own internal advantages of arts and agriculture, not in retarding or preventing the prosperity of the other."— *Benjamin Franklin, March 17, 1783*

Forgiveness

It is one thing to forgive our friends, but forgiving our enemies takes superhuman strength which only God can give. During the Revolutionary War a pastor named John P. Miller once learned that one of his greatest enemies was to be hanged for his crimes. Upon hearing this, Miller set out on foot sixty miles to visit General George Washington and intercede for the man's life. The general, upon hearing the request, stated that he was sorry but that he could not pardon Miller's friend. "Friend!" said Miller, "that man is my worst enemy." "Well then," said Washington, "that puts matters in a whole new light." Seeing the preacher's forgiveness for his staunchest enemy, the general signed the pardon. Then Miller quickly carried it another fifteen miles to the execution site, arriving just as the condemned man was trudging toward the scaffold.

What forgiveness! Yet Christ did that and more as Scripture reminds us, "While we were yet sinners, Christ died for us" (Rom. 5:8). Look for someone you will forgive today.

Prayer Suggestion—Think of someone who has wronged you and whom you have not yet forgiven. Seek them out and tell them of your forgiveness today. "Forgive as you have been forgiven."

MARCH

18

Today in History—Schick markets first electric razor, 1931; 426 die in New London, Texas, school explosion, 1937; Foreign oil company holdings taken over by Mexico, 1938; North Atlantic Treaty Organization (NATO) formed, 1949; Russian cosmonaut Aleksei Lenov is first man to walk in space, 1965; postal strike in New York spreads across U.S., 1970; U.S. salvage effort unsuccessful in retrieving key parts of sunken Soviet submarine, 1975; psychologist Erich Fromm dies at age 79, 1980.

Born Today—Statesman John C. Calhoun, 1782; President Grover Cleveland, 1837; composer Nikolai Rimsky-Korsakov, 1844; inventory Rudolph Diesel, 1858; author George Plimpton, 1927; actor Peter Graves, 1936.

Today's Quotation—"How the world makes nothing of the memory of a man an hour after he is dead!"—*Samuel Pepys, March 18, 1664*

A Fitting Memorial

It is true that the greatness of many world figures is not fully appreciated until after they are gone. One such individual was Luiz Vaz Camoes, now recognized as one of Portugal's leading poets, though he died virtually unknown and in poverty. Because it could not be determined just where his body had been buried, dust from all the places he was known to have visited was gathered and placed inside an expensive burial vault. In so doing, his friends hoped that at least some of the dust might include a particle of his body.

What will people say of your life when you die? Will you be known as a shining child of God or as something less? While others here on earth may not recognize our passing, our heavenly Father is preparing a place for us to spend eternity with him. Why worry about what mankind thinks of you? Rather, be concerned with what God thinks of you because someday you will account to him for your deeds.

Prayer Suggestion—Ask God to help you so live your life that he will not be displeased when you stand before him in judgment.

MARCH

19

Today in History—U.S. Senate rejects Treaty of Versailles thus defeating League of Nations, 1920; heavily damaged U.S. Navy aircraft carrier *Franklin* (with loss of 832 lives) saved by epic sea-going heroism, 1945; oil embargo lifted resulting in end to ban on Sunday gas sales and other use restrictions, 1974; in worst oil spill thus far, one hundred thousand gallons of crude oil spill ashore over seventy miles off the coast of Brittany, 1978.

Born Today—Puritan leader William Bradford, 1589; missionary doctor David Livingstone, 1813; orator William Jennings Bryan, 1860; former Supreme Court Chief Justice Earl Warren, 1891; Judge John Sirica, 1904; author Irving Wallace, 1916; consultant Brent Scowcroft, 1925.

Today's Quotation—"My fears are as good prophets as my hopes." —*Henry David Thoreau, March 19, 1842*

Hope

It is said, "While there's life, there's hope." This seems to describe the case of the six Navy pilots who left their aircraft carrier on a scouting mission during World War II, searching the seas for enemy submarines believed operating in the area. When they tried to return, they could not find their ship. It seems that while they were gone, the captain had ordered a war-imposed blackout of all lights on the ship. Over and over the frantic pilots radioed, asking for just one light so they could see to land. The pilots were then told of the blackout and that it could not be lifted even for them. After several such appeals and denials of their request, the ship's radio operator finally turned the switch to break radio contact. Rather than risk the lives of thousands on the ship, the pilots were forced to ditch in the cold Atlantic and from there into eternity. The pilots left the ship thinking they would be able to return, but found that this was misplaced hope. In what are you placing your hope?

Prayer Suggestion—Recognize God as your only hope, both for this life and the life hereafter. Praise him for the everlasting hope he provides.

MARCH

20

Deuteronomy 31:3–8

Today in History—King George III succeeds to throne of England, 1751; *Uncle Tom's Cabin* published, 1852; General Federation of Women's Clubs organized, 1890; kidnapped Patty Hearst judged guilty of armed robbery, 1976; conservative Jacques Chirac takes over as prime minister of France from socialist Francois Mitterand, 1986; Jim and Tammy Bakker resign PTL leadership in wake of alleged sexual misconduct, 1986; Jerry Falwell accepts temporary leadership of $100 million dollar-a-year PTL ministry, 1987.

Born Today—Poet Ovid, 43 B.C.; playwright Henrik Ibsen, 1828; psychologist B. F. Skinner, 1904; actor Carl Reiner, 1922; TV personality Fred Rogers, 1928; actor Hal Linden, 1931; Canadian leader Brian Mulroney, 1929; hockey player Bobby Orr, 1948.

Today's Quotation—"A nation is molded by the tests that its peoples meet and master."—*Lyndon B. Johnson, March 20, 1965*

Life's Trials

Over the course of history there are many examples of courageous people who have successfully overcome the hardships and trials of life. Edward Judson said, "Success and suffering are vitally and organically linked. If you succeed without suffering, it is because someone else has suffered before you; if you suffer without succeeding, it is that someone else may succeed after you."

Perhaps you are discouraged by the difficulties you are facing. Maybe you feel that life has shortchanged you and that there's no hope for the future. Recognize that in succeeding you must often first be defeated. According to J. L. Allen, "We spend half our lives fighting for things that would surely destroy us if we got them. A man who has never been defeated is usually a man who has been ruined." Yet there is reason to be optimistic even in the darkest hour when we realize that God is there and can see us through even the darkest hours.

Prayer Suggestion—For God's presence during the trials of life.

96

MARCH

21

Today in History—Yosemite Valley discovered in California, 1851; Rev. Martin Luther King, Jr., leads civil rights march from Selma to Montgomery, Alabama, 1965; after eleven years in office, India's Indira Gandhi suffers resounding election loss, 1977; President Carter says U.S. will boycott Moscow Olympics, 1980.

Born Today—Composer Johann Sebastian Bach, 1685; King James Jesse Strang (ruler of Beaver Island, Michigan), 1813; composer Modest Mussorgsky, 1839; poet Phyllis McGinley, 1905; labor leader Cesar Chavez, 1927.

Today's Quotation—"There is no finer investment for any community than putting milk into babies. Healthy citizens are the greatest asset any country can have."—*Winston Churchill, March 21, 1943*

Hungry Babies

A mother's first instinct is to feed and protect her young. There is a story told of one such mother, a war widow, who had run out of food the week before Christmas. The poor woman entered a small store and asked the grocer for food to feed her small children. She said that she had nothing to pay for the food but a prayer. Unimpressed, the grocer harshly told the woman to "write it on paper," and turned to wait on other customers. Moments later he came back and grabbed the paper with the prayer from the woman, and placed it on his scale. All the while he was muttering to himself, "We shall see just how much food this is worth." Much to his amazement the scale would not go down as he piled on more and more food. Exasperated, he finally tossed the woman a bag, and told her to go ahead and pack up the food. When she had gone, the grocer opened the crumpled note still sitting on his broken scale. It read simply: "Give us this day our daily bread" (Matt. 6:11).

Do you have the faith of this woman for God to supply your needs? He will provide if you ask him in faith.

Prayer Suggestion—Thank God for his meeting your needs on the first day of spring.

MARCH

22

Today in History—Governor John Carver and Chief Massasoit sign nonaggression treaty at Plymouth, Mass., 1621; Naval hero Stephen Decatur killed in duel, 1820; polygamy banned in U.S., 1882; Arab League formed, 1945; Senate passes Equal Rights Amendment, 1972; U.S. and Israel end two days of talks with no sign of compromise in call for Israelis to withdraw from all conquered Arab lands, 1978.

Born Today—Painter Sir Anthony Van Dyck, 1599; actor Karl Malden, 1914; pantomimist Marcel Marceau, 1923; TV evangelist M. G. "Pat" Robertson, 1930; composer Stephen Sondheim, 1930; actor William Shatner, 1931.

Today's Quotation—"All progress has resulted from people who took unpopular positions."—*Adlai E. Stevenson, March 22, 1954*

Progress

In 1870, a bishop speaking before a church gathering stated that, "Man has invented everything that can be invented. He has done all he can do." But the meeting's presiding officer suggested that a great invention would yet be made within the next fifty years. Upon further questioning, the officer replied, "I think man will learn how to fly." The bishop was astonished, saying, "Don't you know that flight is reserved for the angels?" It was just thirty-three years later that the Wright brothers embarked on their first halting flight at Kitty Hawk. Imagine the amazement of Bishop Milton Wright, who had denied the possibility of flight only to later witness his two sons, Orville and Wilbur Wright, become the first humans to fly!

Don't be discouraged if everyone is against you, for that is often the way man's greatest progress has been made.

Prayer Suggestion—Thank God for all he has allowed us to do. Also praise him for spiritual progress in your life.

MARCH
23

Today in History—Patrick Henry delivers famed "Give me Liberty or Give me Death" speech in Richmond, Va., 1775; Tennessee forbids teaching of evolution, 1925; German Reichstag votes dictatorial powers to Nazi regime, 1933; in Miami Anita Bryant, Jackie Gleason, and Kate Smith host thirty thousand at "Rally for Decency" to protest behavior of singer Jim Morrison, earlier arrested on indecency charges, 1969; Florida millionaire gives Oral Roberts $1.3 million when Roberts said he would be "called home" if scholarship fund-raising goal was not met, 1987.

Born Today—Psychologist Erich Fromm, 1900; scientist Wernher von Braun, 1912; track athlete Roger Bannister, 1929; basketball player Moses Malone, 1954.

Today's Quotation—". . . non-cooperation with evil is as much a duty as is cooperation with good."—*Mohandas K. Gandhi, March 23, 1922*

Avoiding Evil

Being vigilant against evil is increasingly important. During colonial days a sentry once stood guard against Indian attack at the entrance to the fort. The soldier had strict orders to fire on any suspicious target. Suddenly he heard a rustling in the leaves, cocked his gun, and found the intruder to be a wild hog. Later another rustling also proved to be a hog rooting under the leaves. From another direction came more movement in the underbrush. The guard cocked his gun then thought, "This could be yet another hog, but to fire and kill it would do no harm. On the other hand, it could be an Indian approaching, covered in hog skin." He aimed and fired. With a loud yell, an Indian sprang from the brush and fell over dead. The sentry had saved the fort.

Likewise in spiritual warfare, if we are in doubt about sin, we should draw the Word of God at every object that approaches. How can we survive in this evil age? By staying in a close walk with the Lord and daily feeding upon his Word, and making sure our families and associates do the same.

Prayer Suggestion—Thank God that he has power over Satan, and that the Holy Spirit living within us gives us victory over all evil.

MARCH

24

Today in History—Tuberculosis bacillus discovered, 1882; construction of the first successful New York City subway begins, 1900; Walter and John Huston became first father and son to receive Oscar awards for "Treasure of Sierra Madre", 1949; British Prime Minister Heath takes steps to quell sectarian violence in Northern Ireland, 1972; five adult members of Rev. Sun Myung Moon's Unification Church allowed by court to be placed into parent's custody for "de-programming," 1977.

Born Today—Financier Andrew Mellon, 1855; escape artist Harry Houdini, 1874; politician Thomas Dewey, 1902; author Lawrence Ferlinghetti, 1919; actor Normal Fell, 1924; actor Steve McQueen, 1930.

Today's Quotation—"All religions united with government are more or less inimical to liberty. All, separated from government, are compatible with liberty."—*Henry Clay, March 24, 1818*

Religious Liberty

Throughout the ages, hundreds of the world's rulers have tried to limit or restrict their citizens' right to worship as they please. One such ruler was King Charles V, who eventually abdicated his throne after failing to compel his subjects to conform to his thinking about religion. Weary after a long reign, Charles retired to a monastery where he amused himself by trying to make a dozen clocks run together. Failing in this, Charles exclaimed, "How foolish I have been to think that I could make all men believe alike about religion when I cannot even make twelve clocks run together."

God has instilled within man a vacuum that only he can fill. Be thankful for the freedom to worship God in the manner you wish, for few in the world today share such good fortune.

Prayer Suggestion—Freedom to worship him as you please. Pray that God will give us the courage to keep our nation strong so that we may always be free.

MARCH

25

James 1:2–5

Today in History—British colonists land in Maryland, 1634; Greek war of independence begins against Turkey, 1821; Palace Theatre opens in New York City as vaudeville showplace, 1913; Sugar Ray Robinson becomes first five-time world middleweight boxing champion, 1958; Saudi Arabia's King Faisal assassinated by deranged nephew, 1975; U.S. embassy in San Salvador struck by grenades and gunfire, 1981; Sandanistas in Nicaragua suspend individual rights for thirty days due to "U.S. plans for aggression," 1982.

Born Today—Conductor Arturo Toscanini, 1867; composer Bela Bartok, 1881; sportscaster Howard Cosell, 1920; actress Simone Signoret, 1921; businessman Tom Monaghan, 1937; singer Anita Bryant, 1940; singer Aretha Franklin, 1942.

Today's Quotation—"How insufficient is all wisdom without love!"—*Henry David Thoreau, March 25, 1842*

Wisdom

Having wisdom and being educated are not necessarily the same thing. Mortimer Adler, former University of Chicago professor, recalls that if he entered the classroom and said, "Good morning," and the students responded, "Good morning," he knew they were undergraduates. But if they took out their notebooks and wrote down his greeting, he knew they were graduate students.

Many of the world's wisest people had little or no education, but they had wisdom. President Lincoln was asked, on the eve of the crucial Battle of Gettysburg, why he was so calm and assured in the nation's hour of peril and darkness. Lincoln calmly replied, "I spent last night in prayer before the Lord and he has given me the assurance that our cause will triumph and that the nation will be preserved." What assurance from a largely uneducated man who, more than one hundred years later, is still considered among the wisest of all our leaders.

Prayer Suggestion—Recognize God as the source of all wisdom and thank him for sharing wisdom with you.

101

MARCH

26

Today in History—Motion picture film first manufactured, 1885; Dr. Jonas Salk announces polio vaccine, 1953; Bangladesh declares itself independent of Pakistan, 1971; Gen. Jorge Videla succeeds ousted Isabel Peron as leader of Argentina, 1976; Carol Burnett wins $1.6 million libel suit against *National Enquirer*, 1981.

Born Today—Author Edward Bellamy, 1850; poet Robert Frost, 1874; Supreme Court Justice Sandra Day O'Connor, 1930; actor Leonard Nimoy, 1931; journalist Bob Woodward, 1943; singer Diana Ross, 1944; actress Vicki Lawrence, 1949.

Today's Quotation—"He who does not borrow trouble does not lend it."—*Henry David Thoreau, March 26, 1842*

Trouble

Though it is difficult for us to understand at the time, it is the troubles of life that help shape us into what God wants us to become. A story is told of a young man who worked hard to establish himself as a fruit grower. His crop blossomed beautifully until a sudden frost wiped it out. Noting that he had stopped coming to church soon after, his pastor decided to pay him a visit. "I am not coming any more," the young man said. "How can I worship a God who allows my entire crop to be destroyed?" Looking at the young man for a moment, the wise old preacher said, "Don't you see, God loves you more than your peaches. While he realizes peaches grow better without frosts, he also knows it is impossible to grow the best men without frosts. God's desire is to grow men, not peaches." Indeed God sees the eternal results while we see only our immediate problem.

The next time trouble comes along (and it is never far away from any of us), ask the Lord, "What would you have me to learn from this?" After all, it is the work of the gritty abrasive that brings out the gem's most glistening shine! Rejoice when God starts polishing you!

Prayer Suggestion—Recognize that sometimes God has to put us flat on our backs before we look up to him.

MARCH

27

Today in History—President Washington signs act to build U.S. Navy, 1794; Marconi sends radio signals across the English Channel, 1899; first Japanese cherry trees planted in Washington, D.C., 1912; Alaskan earthquake kills more than 100, 1964; 123 die as off-shore oil rig collapses off Norwegian coast, 1980; Solidarity union calls nationwide strike in Poland, 1981; Harriet Adams, author of Nancy Drew and Hardy Boys children's mystery series, dies at age 89, 1982.

Born Today—Physicist Wilhelm Roentgen, 1845; photographer Edward Steichen, 1879; composer Ferde Grofe, 1892; actress Gloria Swanson, 1899; singer Sarah Vaughan, 1924; journalist Anthony Lewis, 1927.

Today's Quotation—"There are few ways in which a man can be more innocently employed than in getting money."—*Samuel Johnson, March 27, 1775*

Employed for God

Every believer is in "full-time Christian service" whether he realizes it or not, for being a Christian involves a total commitment. Evangelist John R. Rice tells of a building contractor who was saved in one of his revival campaigns. The contractor was involved in building several houses and had a sizeable crew working for him. The local church had revival meetings scheduled in the mid-morning and the contractor announced to his men that they were all going to go hear the guest preacher. When one man said he planned to remain at work that hour, the builder said they would all receive their wages and go to church on his time. So the work crew attended each day and a number were saved.

How wisely the contractor invested in the lives of his men, giving them something mere wages could never provide—everlasting salvation for their souls! What would happen in America if every businessman took his employees to hear the gospel preached!

Prayer Suggestion—Ask God to show how you can be a witness for him on the job or among your daily contacts. Be salt and light for him.

MARCH

28

Proverbs 23:4-7

Today in History—U.S. Senate votes to censure President Jackson for abuse of his authority, 1834; General Franco captures Madrid in Spanish Civil War, 1939; British commandos raid Nazi-held naval installation in France, 1942; series of accidents at Three Mile Island nuclear power plant near Harrisburg, Pa., 1979; Mt. Saint Helens in Washington begins erupting after 123 years of silence, 1980; despite a recent cease-fire and peace talks, fighting rages on in Beirut, 1984.

Born Today—Statesman Aristide Briand, 1862; pianist Rudolf Serkin, 1903; statesman Edmund Muskie, 1914; consumer advocate Virginia Knauer, 1915; actor Dirk Bogarde, 1921; actor Ken Howard, 1944.

Today's Quotation—"What a man does, compared with what he is, is but a small part."—*Henry David Thoreau, March 28, 1842*

Tough Character

It's been said that character is what you are when you think no one is watching. Character does become more visible when we are caught off-guard.

Such was the story of Roberto DeVincenzo, a tough Argentine golfer, who won a major tournament and was given a check for his winnings on the eighteenth green. After the ceremonies, DeVincenzo walked alone to his car where he met a sad-eyed young lady. Slowly she walked up to him and said, "It's a happy day for you, but the doctors say my baby is dying of an incurable blood disease." Before she could utter another word, the champion golfer took out a pen, endorsed his winning check, and put it in the woman's hand, urging her to "make some good days for the baby." A week later he was told the woman had no sick baby and he had thus been tricked out of his winnings. DeVincenzo, on hearing this, looked up and said, "You mean there is no baby who is dying without hope? Why that's the best news I've heard all week!" What a test of character—seeing the good in a situation even when you have been shamefully wronged!

Prayer Suggestion—Pray that God will so mold our character that he will never be ashamed of something we have done—even in secret!

104

MARCH

29

Today in History—First Swedish settlement in America established, 1638; Dolley Madison's sister, Mrs. Lucy Payne Washington, married in first White House wedding, 1812; Jack Benny makes his broadcasting debut, 1932; Julius and Ethel Rosenberg and Morton Sobel convicted of espionage conspiracy, 1951; Washington, D.C., first allowed to vote in presidential elections, 1961; U.S. troops begin withdrawing from Vietnam as war involvement winds down, 1973; Supreme Court rules states may legally prosecute homosexual acts, 1976; President Carter pushes for more financial assistance to farmers, 1978; Uganda's leader Idi Amin flees from the capital following a three-day siege, 1979.

Born Today—President John Tyler, 1790; politician Eugene McCarthy, 1916; singer Pearl Bailey, 1918; actor Bud Cort, 1950; football player Earl Campbell, 1955; gymnast Kurt Thomas, 1956.

Today's Quotation—"Opinion, and the just maintenance of it, shall never be a crime in my view: nor bring injury on the individual."— *Thomas Jefferson, March 29, 1801*

No Crime

We are uniquely blessed in America with freedom of speech and of religion. Few people in the world enjoy such freedom. Do you exercise your freedoms regularly? Carlisle Castle was a place of imprisonment for many Scotsmen during border wars years ago. A visitor to a prison cell in the castle will notice long grooves worn in the stone. Such grooves came from prisoners frantically clawing at the walls in a vain effort to be free.

I wonder if Christ's love so predominates our lives that it is straining to get out, that is the normal experience of the believer who is right with God. If you were to be tried for your witness for God, would there be enough evidence to convict you? What does he see when he looks down at you?

Prayer Suggestion—Consider your testimony for Christ. What are you doing for Jesus' sake?

MARCH

30

Today in History—Lead pencil with attached eraser patented, 1858; Fifteenth Amendment to Constitution protecting right to vote goes into effect, 1870; President Reagan and three others shot and injured outside Washington, D.C., hotel, 1981; agreement reached with Argentina over $500 million in interest payments owed U.S. banks, 1984; two Marine guards at U.S. embassy in Moscow accused of spying for Russians, 1987.

Born Today—Artist Francisco Jose de Goya, 1746; artist Vincent van Gogh, 1853; singer Frankie Laine, 1913; restauranteur Bob Evans, 1918; TV host Peter Marshall, 1927; actor John Astin, 1930; actor Warren Beatty, 1938.

Today's Quotation—"The right of citizens of the United States to vote shall not be denied or abridged by the United States or by any State on account of race, color, or previous condition of servitude."—*Fifteenth Amendment to U.S. Constitution, March 30, 1870*

One Vote

History is full of examples in which a single vote decided a crucial issue. Oliver Cromwell won control of England in 1645 by just one vote. King Charles was later beheaded on the basis of one vote. But for a single ballot, German would have become America's official language rather than English! In 1845 Texas was granted statehood by just one vote, and the senator who cast the deciding vote had been elected by a single vote. President Andrew Johnson escaped impeachment by one ballot and Rutherford B. Hayes was elected president by a single electoral vote. The course of world history was forever altered in 1923 when, by a single vote, Adolf Hitler was elected head of the tiny Nazi party meeting in Munich.

So never say that one vote doesn't count. Indeed your eternal destiny will be decided by your one vote for or against Christ. "Choose you this day whom ye will serve" (Josh. 24:15).

Prayer Suggestion—Praise God that he has voted for you! Accept his election and live for him today and every day!

MARCH

31

Proverbs 31:10–31

Today in History—First group of New England missionaries arrive in Hawaii, 1820; ten-hour day for government employees established, 1840; U.S. and Japan sign treaty opening Japanese ports to U.S. ships, 1854; Eiffel Tower completed in Paris, 1889; President Lyndon B. Johnson says he will not run for reelection, 1968; first U.S. satellite, *Explorer I,* burns up on reentering Earth's atmosphere after more than twelve years in space, 1970; Three Mile Island nuclear mishap brought under control with no injury or loss of life, 1979.

Born Today—Philosopher Rene Descartes 1596; composer Franz Josef Haydn, 1732; hockey player Gordie Howe, 1928; designer Liz Claiborne, 1929; actress Shirley Jones, 1934; musician Herb Alpert, 1935; actor Richard Chamberlain, 1935.

Today's Quotation—"It is a good time to be a woman because your country, more now than at any time in its history, is utilizing your abilities and intelligence."—*Mrs. Lyndon B. Johnson, March 31, 1964*

The Value of Women

The equality of the sexes is not an issue in the Bible—men and women are equal in God's sight. Yet, the Bible says, wives are to be loved by their husbands as Christ loves the church, that is, treated with deference as if they were superiors. Anthropologist Ashley Montagu goes beyond this by saying women clearly *are* superior in three main ways: "Intellectually, because of their everyday experience which differs from that of men; constitutionally, because they bear and nurture children; and biologically, because they have two X chromosomes." Further, Montagu says, a woman who claims equality with a man has actually taken "a step down." All that from a man!

Whatever society's view on the issue, the Bible clearly holds godly women in the highest esteem.

Prayer Suggestion—Thank God for creating you in his image and making you just as you are. Resolve to serve him in all you say and do.

APRIL

1

Today in History—U.S. House of Representatives begins transacting business in New York, 1789; first wartime conscription law in U.S. goes into effect, 1863; U.S. Tenth Army launches invasion of Okinawa in World War II, 1945; U.S. Bicentennial "Freedom Train" exhibit seen by thirty thousand at first stop, 1975.

Born Today—Statesman Otto von Bismarck, 1815; actress Jane Powell, 1929; football coach Bo Schembechler, 1929; actress Debbie Reynolds, 1932; actress Ali McGraw, 1939; author David Eisenhower, 1947.

Today's Quotation—"Courtesy is as much the mark of a gentleman as courage."—*Theodore Roosevelt, April 1, 1911*

Courtesy

A simple act of kindness is often remembered long after the fact. Years ago, a small congregation in Missouri suffered through a halting sermon delivered by a young preacher who had walked twenty miles to deliver it. Not realizing the distance he had traveled to speak to them, the people grew restless with his floundering presentation and quickly left. Following the sermon, not one person stopped to offer the preacher a meal or lodging. So he dejectedly headed down the long road toward home. As he was leaving, the janitor offered to share his humble meal with the preacher.

Years passed, and the young preacher became world-renowned Bishop Marvin. He was invited to speak at the dedication of a church near the site of his first floundering sermon. People came from miles around to witness this tremendous event. After the service, many offered him lavish hospitality, but the bishop waved them all aside in favor of the old janitor, saying, "When I was here before, I was none too good for you, and I am none too good for you today."

We never can tell to whom we are rendering kindness.

Prayer Suggestion—That God would provide the opportunity to show our Christian love in action today, through a kindness to someone who will never be able to repay our courtesy.

APRIL

2

Today in History—Ponce de Leon lands near what is now St. Augustine, Fla., 1513; Congress authorizes U.S. Mint, 1792; President Wilson asks Congress to declare war on Germany, 1917; Argentine troops seize Falkland Islands after overcoming eighty-four British Marines, 1982.

Born Today—Writer Hans Christian Andersen, 1805; sculptor F. A. Bartholdi, 1834; writer Emile Zola, 1840; pianist Sergei Rachmaninoff, 1873; painter Max Ernst, 1891; actor Buddy Ebsen, 1908; actor Sir Alec Guinness, 1914.

Today's Quotation—"The world must be made safe for democracy."—*Woodrow Wilson, April 2, 1917*

Worldwide Peace

Peace has been the dream of mankind since the dawn of time, yet there have continued to be "wars and rumors of wars" throughout history. President Dwight Eisenhower put the quest for world peace in proper perspective:

> All the world hungers for peace. Military experts tell of the horrible possibility of nuclear war during the foreseeable future and the catastrophic consequences on the human race. This is favorable to Satan's plans as he skillfully weaves his net around the world. Any nation today that could enforce peace could control the world. Satan will have a super man who can do it. He will so overwhelm the world with his talents and abilities that an astonished world will ask, "Who is able to make war with him?"

This is the Antichrist who will seek to deceive many in the end times. Only God can give true peace, "the peace that passeth all understanding," which occurs in the human heart that is right with God.

Prayer Suggestion—Make sure you have made peace with God in your heart, and share that peace with someone else today.

APRIL

3

Romans 14:1-6

Today in History—Bruno Richard Hauptmann executed for kidnap-murder of baby Charles Lindbergh, Jr., 1936; Congress enacts Marshall Plan giving billions of dollars for European recovery, 1948; North Vietnam suggests preliminary discussions to arrange peace talks, 1968; President Nixon says he will pay $425,000 in back taxes, 1974; Arizona governor Evan Mecham convicted and removed from office, 1988.

Born Today—Writer Washington Irving, 1783; actor Marlon Brando, 1924; actress Doris Day, 1924; German leader Helmut Kohl, 1930; singer Wayne Newton, 1942; singer Tony Orlando, 1944.

Today's Quotation—"Increased means and increased leisure are the two civilizers of man."—*Benjamin Disraeli, April 3, 1872*

Leisure

Since the end of World War II, Americans have enjoyed an unprecedented increase in leisure time, but what we have seen thus far may be only the beginning. Social scientists tell us that a "workless world" is just around the corner. Some predict a twenty-hour work week, or a six-month work year as being able to sustain the average American's current standard of living. Author R. F. Norden even goes so far as to predict the eventual establishment of a "Department of Leisure" to balance the present Department of Labor. He says only about two percent of the population can do the work necessary to provide food and goods for the rest of us. (But it is not clear who will decide the two percent who must still work.)

As Christians, we have never been promised a life of leisure on this side of eternity. Rather we are to be busy about the Lord's business, for this is why he has allowed us to remain on earth after we have been saved. Are you "busy about your Father's business"?

Prayer Suggestion—Thank God for leisure time, but realize we will someday have to give account to God for how we have spent all our time.

APRIL

4

Colossians 3:1-17

Today in History—William Henry Harrison dies after thirty-one days as president, 1841; Cecil Rhodes wills $10 million for American scholarship for graduate study in England, 1902; treaty establishing North Atlantic Treaty Organization is signed in Washington, D.C., 1949; Dr. Martin Luther King, Jr., is murdered in Memphis, Tenn., sparking riots in many U.S. cities, 1968.

Born Today—Lock inventor Linus Yale, 1821; photographer William Henry Jackson, 1843; conductor Pierre Monteux, 1875; composer Elmer Bernstein, 1922; author William Manchester, 1922; musician Hugh Masekela, 1939.

Today's Quotation—"I claim not to have controlled events, but confess plainly that events have controlled me."—*Abraham Lincoln, April 4, 1864*

Controlled Events

It has been said that society is made up of people who watch things happen and those who make things happen. An American traveler in Syria was watching as three native shepherds brought their flocks to the same brook. After a while, one shepherd arose and called out, "Men-ah, Men-ah" (Arabic for "follow me") and his sheep followed him. The next shepherd did the same and another flock of sheep went away with him. The traveler asked the remaining shepherd if he could try and see if the sheep would follow his voice. So taking the shepherd's staff and turban, he called out to the flock, "Men-ah, Men-ah," but not a sheep moved. "Will your flock never follow anyone but you?" the traveler asked. "Oh yes; sometimes a sheep gets sick and then he will follow anyone," the seasoned shepherd replied.

How many times have you observed a spiritually weak Christian follow alien voices that have led him astray from God? How close are you following the gentle Shepherd, Jesus Christ, who gave his life for you?

Prayer Suggestion—Surrender your life in full to God today. Don't hold back any secret areas from him, for either he is Lord of all or he is not Lord at all!

111

APRIL

5

Today in History—President Washington exercises first veto, 1792; U.S.S.R. accepts idea of direct emergency communications "hotline" link with U.S., 1963; Nationalist Chinese leader Generalissimo Chiang Kai-shek dies at age 87 in Taiwan, 1975; James Callaghan becomes Britain's new prime minister, 1976; former Pakistani Prime Minister Ali Bhuto reportedly executed, 1979; terrorists bomb Berlin military club wounding fifty-five and killing one American serviceman, 1986.

Born Today—Physician Joseph Lister, 1827; reformer Booker T. Washington, 1856; actor Melvyn Douglas, 1901; conductor Herbert von Karajan, 1908; actor Gregory Peck, 1916; actress Gale Storm, 1922; government official Colin Powell, 1937.

Today's Quotation—"The lament for a golden age is only a lament for golden men."—*Henry David Thoreau, April 5, 1841*

The Gift of Time

When your children leave home, how will they remember you? A successful young attorney recalls the greatest gift he ever received. "It occurred one Christmas when my dad gave me a small box. Inside was a note saying, 'Son, this year I will give you 365 hours, an hour every day after dinner. It's yours. We'll talk about what you want to talk about, we'll go where you want to go, play what you want to play. It will be your hour.' My dad not only kept his promise, but every year he renewed it—it is the greatest gift I ever had in my life. I am the result of his time."

How much time do you share with your children and your spouse? There is nothing we can give someone that will show our love more than the gift of our time and attention. Why not share time with someone you love today and every day?

Prayer Suggestion—Tell God that you are making your family a priority, behind only your time with God himself. Then keep your word. Someday your children will "rise up and call you blessed."

APRIL

6

Romans 14:7-12

Today in History—Joseph Smith organizes first Church of Latter Day Saints, in Seneca County, N.Y., 1830; George Mueller opens orphanage in Bristol, England, 1837; U.S. wins first modern Olympic Games in Athens, Greece, 1896; Robert E. Peary and Matthew Henson reach the North Pole, in epic discovery, 1909; U.S. enters World War I against Germany, 1917; *Early Bird* intercontinental communications satellite is launched at Cape Kennedy, Fla., 1965; U.S. says it will not bar first use of nuclear weapons, 1982.

Born Today—Journalist Lincoln Steffens, 1866; newscaster Lowell Thomas, 1892; composer Andre Previn, 1929; singer Merle Haggard, 1937; business executive John Sculley, 1939.

Today's Quotation—"Taxation is in fact the most difficult function of government."—*Thomas Jefferson, April 6, 1816*

Too Busy for Taxes

One of the growing challenges of this era is that of increasing busy-ness. Some people, including some top government officials, are so busy that they have even been known to forget to pay their taxes. Such was the case of James M. Landis, former dean of the Harvard Law School and chairman of the Securities and Exchange Commission under President Kennedy. Upon being charged with failure to file his income tax return on time for the years 1956 through 1960, Landis said he had been so engrossed with public matters that he neglected personal affairs, including taxes.

May this never be said of us in neglecting the things of God. Imagine our shame at having to admit to God that we were so busy we didn't take time to read his Word and pray! If you haven't already established a daily habit of getting alone with God and his Word, do so today. Encourage your family to do the same, both as individuals and together as a family. Only by making time can you be sure it will happen.

Prayer Suggestion—Pray that you would never be so busy as to forget God and all his blessings to you.

APRIL

7

Judges 21:23–25

Today in History—Henry Ford I dies, 1947; Dag Hammarskjold elected Secretary General of United Nations, 1953; U.S. H-bomb, lost three months earlier in aerial accident over Spain, discovered in ocean off Spanish coast, 1966; neutron bomb production shelved pending Russian arms constraint, 1978; highest price ever paid for a book: $2 million for Gutenburg Bible, 1978; Sudan's president is ousted during visit to the U.S., 1985.

Born Today—Poet William Wordsworth, 1770; columnist Walter Winchell, 1897; musician Percy Faith, 1908; actor James Garner, 1928; television's David Frost, 1939; director Francis Ford Coppola, 1939.

Today's Quotation—"Patriotism is the last refuge of a scoundrel."—*Samuel Johnson, April 7, 1775*

Non-exempt

The Bible speaks of people "who did what was right in their own eyes" apparently feeling they were exempt from the law. Unfortunately this is a growing phenomenon, even in government where one would expect officials to be particularly supportive of the law. During a recent six-year period, statistics show more than one thousand key government officials ranging from county sheriff to the U.S. vice president who have been brought to justice. Federal charges against these officials included those of bribery, kickbacks, and extortion.

Clearly, wrongdoing is not exclusive to any social class or strata but is found at all levels of society. This again proves God's Word true when it says, "The heart is deceitful above all things, and desperately wicked" (Jer. 17:9). When we see dishonesty and corruption occurring all around us, that is even more reason to stay close to the Lord and be sure we don't fall into the same trap.

Prayer Suggestion—That God would continue to convict us of the sin in our life and not allow us to be sidetracked by the evil others may do.

APRIL

8

Today in History—First Jewish congregation in America (Shearith Israel) consecrates its synagogue in New York City, 1730; Seventeenth Amendment to U.S. Constitution requiring direct election of senators ratified, 1913; six Marine Corps recruits drown in a drill exercise at Parris Island, S.C., 1956; U.S. Senate rejects President Nixon's nomination of Judge G. Harrold Carswell for Supreme Court, 1970; Hank Aaron blasts 715th home run to shatter Babe Ruth's longstanding record, 1974.

Born Today—Pathologist William Welch, 1850; actress Mary Pickford, 1893; former First Lady Betty Ford, 1918; basketball player John Havlicek, 1940; football player Mark Clayton, 1961.

Today's Quotation—"This war would never have come unless, under American and modernising pressure, we had driven the Hapsburgs out of Austria and Hungary and the Hohenzollerns out of Germany. By making these vacuums we gave the opening for the Hitlerite monster to crawl out of its sewer on to the vacant thrones. No doubt these views are very unfashionable."—*Winston Churchill, April 8, 1945*

Doing Nothing

It has been wisely said that "all it takes for evil to triumph is for good men to do nothing." Have we as Christians been guilty of ignoring the evil going on around us, hoping it would go away?

Reporting dishonesty is on the decline if action at a major eastern university is any indication. That school has dropped its sixty-one-year-old student honor code in favor of policing students. Cheating had risen to the point that the school felt forced to drop the honor system. That does not speak well of our society, one in which evil is triumphing because good men are doing nothing.

What about that political candidate who is espousing stands counter to those in Scripture? Or that referendum to expand evil influences in your community? Stand up, speak out, and do your part to ensure evil will not triumph where you live.

Prayer Suggestion—Seek God's wisdom in how you can be involved in withstanding the ever-growing threat of evil in society.

APRIL

9

Today in History—Confederate General Robert E. Lee surrenders at Appomattox Court House, Va., ending Civil War, 1865; Nazi Germany invades Norway and Denmark in World War II, 1940; seven members of armed forces are selected as first U.S. astronauts, 1959; Astrodome opens in Houston, Texas, 1965; Federal Communications Commission sets 7:00 to 9:00 p.m. aside for "family viewing time" on television networks, 1975; report shows increased eating out hurts U.S. supermarkets, 1977.

Born Today—Scientist Charles Steinmetz, 1865; impresario Sol Hurok, 1888; singer Paul Robeson, 1898; editor Paul Krassner, 1932; actor Jean-Paul Belmondo, 1933; actress Michael Learned, 1939.

Today's Quotation—"Bataan has fallen, but the spirit that made it stand, a beacon to all liberty-loving people of the world, cannot fall."— *Radio broadcast from Corregidor, April 9, 1942*

Persistence Pays

It is human nature to want to give up when things get difficult, yet this is the very time we need to redouble our efforts and push forward. This may have been the feeling experienced by General Grant's chief of staff who was discouraged after the first day of the battle at Shiloh. Grant's assistant, Brig. Gen. James B. McPherson, reported, "Things look bad, general. We have lost half our artillery and a third of the infantry. Our line is broken and we are pushed back nearly to the river." Grant made no reply and McPherson asked impatiently what he intended to do. General Grant barked back, "Do! Why, reform the lines and attack at daybreak. Won't they be surprised?" The enemy was surprised and they were routed before eight o'clock the next morning.

How many victories were ready to be won but were lost because someone quit at the eleventh hour? Never give up in doing the work of the Lord.

Prayer Suggestion—That God would grant his strength to us in special measure when we are discouraged and ready to quit.

APRIL

10

Today in History—First U.S. patent law approved, 1790; American Society for Prevention of Cruelty to Animals chartered, 1866; Nazi concentration camp at Buchenwald, Germany, liberated at about this time, 1945; Dag Hammarskjold assumes office as Secretary General of United Nations, 1953; U.S. Navy atomic submarine *Thresher* with 129 crewmen aboard, sinks in North Atlantic, 1963; Golda Meir resigns as Israel's Prime Minister in the wake of ongoing criticism of October's war, 1974.

Born Today—Salvation Army founder William Booth, 1829; publisher Joseph Pulitzer, 1847; diplomat Clare Booth Luce, 1903; actor Chuck Connors, 1924; actor Omar Sharif, 1932; sportscaster Don Meredith, 1938.

Today's Quotation—"I wish to preach, not the doctrine of ignoble ease, but the doctrine of the strenuous life."—*Theodore Roosevelt, April 10, 1899*

The Strenuous Life

Few people have ever been reported as dying from overwork. Rather the opposite is true: Many seek a life of ease without the Lord, and in so doing, begin a downward spiral that leads to ruin.

A hard-working young lawyer was struggling with the direction his life was taking. One day he awoke and asked himself what he would do when he finished law school. "Why, make a lot of money," was his silent reply. And after he became rich? "I'll retire," he thought. And then? "I guess, I'll just die," was his response. As a result of these reflections, Charles G. Finney surrendered himself fully to God and was mightily used to further God's kingdom. Such surrender should become a daily habit for all of us.

Shortly after his conversion, evangelist Billy Sunday was advised to follow this simple plan and he would never backslide from the Lord: "Take fifteen minutes each day to listen to God, take fifteen minutes each day to talk to God, and take fifteen minutes each day to talk to others about God."

Are you working as hard for God as you are for gold? What will you do of eternal importance today?

Prayer Suggestion—That through God's help, we will be faithful in putting him first in all areas of our life every day we live.

117

APRIL

11

Today in History—U.S. Navy accepts its first submarine, the *U.S.S. Holland*, 1900; Iowa imposes first state cigarette tax, 1921; Jackie Robinson becomes first black player in major league baseball, 1947; President Truman removes General Douglas MacArthur from command in Korean War, 1951; highest ranking Soviet delegate to U.N. defects to the U.S., 1978; President Reagan leaves hospital twelve days after being shot in the chest, 1981; Albania's leader Enver Hodja is dead after forty-year rule, 1985.

Born Today—Chief Justice Charles Evans Hughes, 1862; statesman Dean Acheson, 1893; chemist Percy Julian, 1899; designer Oleg Cassini, 1913; actor Joel Grey, 1932; actor Bill Irwin, 1950.

Today's Quotation—"Every man will be a poet if he can; otherwise a philosopher or a man of science. This proves the superiority of the poet."—*Henry David Thoreau, April 11, 1852*

Love Poems

A young woman who considered herself a poet once brought her work to a New York magazine. She informed the editor that she had some poems she wanted published in his magazine. "What's the subject?" the editor asked. "Love," she said. "Oh, what kind of love?" "Love as in gazing upon a moonlit lake with an attractive companion. . . ." "Stop, stop," he said. "I'll tell you what love is. Love is getting out of a warm bed at two o'clock in the morning to feed sick children. That's real love. I'm sorry, I don't think we can use your poems."

It is true much of the world today has a starry-eyed view of love: idealistic, all glamour and no pain. But that isn't the way of life, or love, really is. While romantic poetry has its place, we should be as concerned about helping our fellow man as we are in reading someone else's romantic tales. What are you doing for heaven's sake?

Prayer Suggestion—That we would become more motivated to share our love, and God's, with those who are lost and without hope around us.

APRIL

12

Today in History—North Carolina Congress passes declaration urging all British colonies in North America to establish independent governments, 1776; Civil War begins when Confederates fire on Fort Sumter, S.C., 1861; President Franklin D. Roosevelt dies at Warm Springs, Ga., and is succeeded by Vice President Harry S. Truman, 1945; Salk anti-polio vaccine declared safe and effective, 1955; Yuri Gagarin of U.S.S.R. becomes first man to orbit the earth, 1961; Chicago Cubs owner, Philip K. Wrigley, dies at age eighty-two, 1977; British navy sets up blockade around Falkland Islands, 1982; Texaco declares bankruptcy in the wake of $5 billion debt to Pennzoil, 1987.

Born Today—Statesman Henry Clay, 1777; band leader Lionel Hampton, 1913; musician Herbie Hancock, 1940; comedian David Letterman, 1947; actor David Cassidy, 1950.

Today's Quotation—"The only justification of rebellion is success."—*Thomas B. Reed, April 12, 1878*

Loyalty

In going about our daily lives, are we loyal to our calling or rebellious against what we feel is an unfair system? If the latter is the case, we can learn from the story of the two-faced butler. In Yorkshire, England, stands a very unusual sculpture. On the one side is a face that is all smiles and politeness, while on the other side is a face that depicts insolence and rudeness. It seems the sculpture represents a butler who was once employed there and was all smiles and cordiality when his employer was looking. But the moment he thought no one was watching, would stick out his tongue at her and otherwise be impolite. The result was the statue which was erected in a prominent spot both to shame the butler and to warn any other servants who might be tempted to imitate his rebellious behavior.

If such a statue was made of you, how would it appear? Are you loyal to your employer, your church, your God?

Prayer Suggestion—Through God's help, pray that you will be loyal and true to all you love and serve.

APRIL

13

Acts 22:25-30

Today in History—General William Sherman's Civil War march through the South ends, 1865; Metropolitan Museum of Art founded in New York City, 1870; J. C. Penney's first store opens in Kemmerer, Wyo., 1902; President Franklin D. Roosevelt dedicates Jefferson Memorial, 1943; Federal Communications Commission ends four-year freeze on new TV licenses by opening up more channels, 1952; first mass strike in major league baseball settled, 1972; Yusufu K. Lule takes over as head of Uganda's provisional government, 1979; Harold Washington elected first black mayor of Chicago, 1983.

Born Today—President Thomas Jefferson, 1743; businessman F. W. Woolworth, 1852; writer Samuel Beckett, 1906; politician Harold Stassen, 1907; actor Howard Keel, 1919; musician Jack Casady, 1944.

Today's Quotation—"Our Federal Union—it must be preserved!"—*President Andrew Jackson, April 13, 1830*

America

Have you ever stopped to consider what America would be like today if the country had remained divided like it was a century ago? Would a divided America have been able to survive World War I, or Hitler's marauding forces? The freedoms our country enjoys have been pointed out by many stories over the years. But one which appears most unique is the tale of a legendary Moscow resident called Rabinovitch. As the story goes, Rabinovitch left Moscow for a trip through Europe. Along the way he sends back postcards from the various cities he visits: "Greeting from a free Warsaw, Greetings from a free Prague," etc. Finally he arrives outside the Iron Curtain and the last card he sends has this penciled note, "Greetings from a free Rabinovitch."

America is not a perfect nation, but it has been mightily blessed of God and will continue to be blessed as long as it honors the Lord and his chosen people, the Jews.

Prayer Suggestion—Thank God for America and the freedoms all her people enjoy.

APRIL

14

Today in History—President Lincoln shot at Ford's Theatre, Washington, D.C., 1865; *Titanic* strikes Atlantic iceberg on first voyage, 1912; Spain becomes a republic, 1931; world's first reuseable spacecraft, the shuttle *Columbia*, is launched on initial orbital flight, 1981; President Reagan is maintaining compliance with congressional ban on aid to Nicaraguan Contras, 1983; Russian leader Gorbachev proposes banning all missiles from Europe, 1987.

Born Today—Historian A. J. Toynbee, 1889; actor Sir John Gielgud, 1904; actor Rod Steiger, 1925; singer Loretta Lynn, 1935; actor Tony Perkins, 1932; baseball player Pete Rose, 1941.

Today's Quotation—"The insolence of wealth will creep out."—*Samuel Johnson, April 14, 1778*

Wealth

Have you heard the saying, "It is okay to have money if money doesn't have you"? One example of a wealthy man whose priorities were right was Charles M. Schwab. When United States Steel took over the Carnegie Corporation, they inherited Schwab and the contract for his million-dollar annual salary. U.S. Steel head J.P. Morgan was in a quandary—the highest salary next to Schwab's was one for $100,000. Finally he mustered the courage to directly confront Schwab with the issue. Upon asking Schwab about the salary, Schwab reached out took the contract from Morgan and tore it up saying, "I don't care what salary they pay me. . . . I work just for the pleasure I find in work." The wealthy man continued, "I have more money than I need already, and my wife is rich in her own right." An article about Schwab in *Forbes* concluded by saying, "The man who does not work for the love of work, but only for the money, is not likely to make money nor to find much fun in life."

Prayer Suggestion—Be thankful for all your blessings, whether you're rich or poor. Acknowledge that all good things come from God.

APRIL

15

Today in History—President Lincoln dies, 1865; *Titanic* sinks after hitting iceberg, claiming over fifteen hundred lives, 1912; Patty Hearst robs San Francisco bank while a captive, 1974; *Washington Post* reporter returns Pulitzer Prize for fictitious story of eight-year-old heroin addict, 1981; Japanese leader urges citizens to buy foreign goods to ease trade deficit, 1985; U.S. planes sweep across Libya in widespread raids in retaliation for Libyan terrorism, 1986.

Born Today—Artist Leonardo da Vinci, 1452; writer Henry James, 1843; labor leader A. Philip Randolph, 1889; food manufacturer George Cadbury, 1929; singer Roy Clark, 1933; actress Elizabeth Montgomery, 1933; columnist Heloise Cruse Evans, 1951.

Today's Quotation—"God reigns and the government at Washington still lives!"—*James A. Garfield, April 15, 1865*

Feeding the Government

Taxes are the life-blood which keeps all of government functioning. While admitting a need for taxes, have you ever felt it would be nice if the Internal Revenue Service forgot all about you? That happened for many taxpayers shortly after the IRS opened their new computer complex in Louisiana. Without warning part of the gigantic computer's memory went blank. Tax officials discovered that their building was right in the flight path to the New Orleans airport. Stray radar signals from the air field had erased tax records stored on magnetic tape. They had to be retrieved from back-up tapes.

The use of taxes to "feed the government" is nothing new; they were around in Jesus' day and will likely be with us for years to come. Our major concern about taxes should be to maximize government efficiency, keeping it alive and strong so that we might have the continued freedom to worship God as we please.

Prayer Suggestion—As a good citizen, "render to Caesar the things that are Caesar's" (our taxes to the government), and "to God the things that are God's" (our tithes and offerings) (Mark 12:17).

APRIL

16

Matthew 24:6-14

Today in History—Professional company performs first American play, 1787; U.S. Senate ratifies Rush-Bagot agreement providing for un- armed border between U.S. and Canada, 1818; *Apollo 16* launches his- toric moon-walk flight, 1972; runner Bill Rogers sets new record of 2:09:27 in winning Boston Marathon, 1979; Stalin's daughter, Svetlana Alliluyeva, returns to U.S. after two-year stay in U.S.S.R., 1986.

Born Today—Writer Anatole France, 1844; actor Charlie Chaplin, 1889; actor Peter Ustinov, 1921; composer Henry Mancini, 1924; actress Edie Adams, 1931; singer Bobby Vinton, 1935; basketball player Kareem Abdul-Jabbar, 1947.

Today's Quotation—"Let us not be deceived, we are today in the midst of a cold war."—*Bernard Baruch, April 16, 1947*

Cold War?

British Air Chief Marshal Sir Arthur Harris is quoted as having said, "War will go on until there is a change in the human heart, and I see no signs of that." Indeed we are living in an age of "cold war," with heightened inter- national tensions but no open hostilities. In 1960 a research team, in an effort to determine the ways and means of avoiding war, fed a computer with all the data pertaining to World War I. The computer responded by saying the first World War was an impossibility, that it never really hap- pened, that blunders and casualties of such magnitude could only be conjecture and not reality. Of course the first World War did occur at a cost of over $100 billion and an estimated ten million deaths.

The Bible says there will be "wars and rumors of wars . . . but the end is not yet" (Matt. 24:6). It clearly warns us that perilous times will come and that we need to be ready, busy about the work of the Lord, for the time for his return is growing closer every day.

Prayer Suggestion—That we might be faithful in living for the Lord daily, doing his will in all things.

APRIL

17

2 Timothy 3:10-17

Today in History—U.S. invasion of Cuba at Bay of Pigs ends in failure, 1961; Sirhan Sirhan is convicted in murder of Senator Robert Kennedy, 1969; communist-led forces seize control of Phnom Penh, Cambodia, ending five-year civil war, 1975.

Born Today—Supreme Court Justice Samuel Chase, 1741; financier John Pierpont Morgan, 1837; former Russian leader Nikita Khrushchev, 1894; writer Thornton Wilder, 1897; broadcast journalist Harry Reasoner, 1923.

Today's Quotation—"The whole history of Christianity proves that she has little indeed to fear from persecution as a foe, but much to fear from persecution as an ally."—*Thomas B. Macaulay, April 17, 1833*

Persecution

A story in the *Presbyterian Survey* points up the reality of persecution for Christ's sake that we don't often see. The writer reported he had a dream in which he was in heaven and met saints who had been there for nearly two thousand years. The saint said, "I was a Roman Christian who lived in the days of the Apostle Paul. I was burned at the stake by Nero." "How awful," I exclaimed. "Oh, no," he replied, "I was glad to do something for Jesus because he died for me." Then another man spoke. He came from a South Seas island and had been converted because of faithful missionary John Williams. When asked how he had died, the islander said, "I was beaten unconscious, then cooked, and eaten by cannibals." "How terrible," I said. "No, as a Christian I was glad to die because Jesus wore a crown of thorns and was scourged for me." Then these saints asked about me. "How did you suffer for him, or did you sell what you had and use the money to send missionaries like John Williams to tell others about Jesus?" Just then I awoke and with sorrowful eyes lay on my soft bed thinking of the money I had wasted on my own pleasures and not shared with those truly in need.

Have you surrendered *all* to Christ?

Prayer Suggestion—Ask, "Lord what will thou have me do to further your ministry?" Then do it.

APRIL

18

Today in History—Paul Revere's ride warns Boston of pending attack by British, 1775; San Francisco devastated by earthquake and fire, 1906; Lt. Col. James Doolittle leads first U.S. bombing raid on Japan in World War II, 1942; war correspondent Ernie Pyle killed by Japanese sniper, 1945; Republic of Ireland is established, 1949; Albert Einstein dies, 1955; government Environmental Protection Agency says water in seventy-nine U.S. cities is polluted, 1975; President Carter declares war on energy crisis, 1977; author Alex Haley gets special Pulitzer for *Roots*, 1977; Senate ratifies treaty giving canal back to Panama in 1999, 1978; terrorists blamed in bombing of U.S. embassy in Beirut which killed forty persons, 1983.

Born Today—Lawyer Clarence Darrow, 1857; conductor Leopold Stokowski, 1882; grocery heir Huntington Hartford, 1911; labor negotiator Ed Garvey, 1940; physician Joseph Goldstein, 1940; actress Hayley Mills, 1946.

Today's Quotation—"It is neither safe nor honest to act contrary to conscience! Here I stand; I cannot do otherwise, so help me God! Amen."—*Martin Luther, April 18, 1521*

Two Martins

Most everyone has heard of Martin Luther, but there is another Martin who had a similar dramatic conversion. Like Luther, Martin of Basle wrote out his confession but it was hidden in his room for more than a hundred years. About the time it was found, Martin Luther also found salvation in Christ. Luther went on to publicly display his "Ninety-Five Theses" on the church door at Wittenburg and was promptly excommunicated by the Catholic church. But we know much less of what happened to Martin of Basle, a fellow believer in the faith, because he kept his faith secret.

How widely is your witness known? Hundreds of years from now, what will historians record about your faith? Even more important, what will your heavenly Father record about your witness for him?

Prayer Suggestion—Determine, under God, to make a difference in the world as you boldly share your faith wherever you go.

APRIL

19

Today in History—American Revolutionary War begins at Lexington and Concord, Mass., 1775; U.S. abandons gold standard, 1933; Douglas MacArthur delivers his "old soldiers never die" speech to Congress, 1951; Grace Kelly marries Prince Ranier of Monaco, 1956; U.S. prohibits travel to Cuba, 1982.

Born Today—Statesman Roger Sherman, 1721; actor Don Adams, 1927; actor Hugh O'Brian, 1930; composer Dudley Moore, 1935; singer Alan Price, 1942; baseball player Frank Viola, 1960.

Today's Quotation—". . . like the old soldier of that ballad, I now close my military career and just fade away."—*General Douglas MacArthur, April 19, 1951*

Old Age

"You're as old as you feel," or so they say. Here's how General Douglas MacArthur described old age:

> Nobody grows old by merely living a number of years. People grow old only by deserting their ideals. Years may wrinkle the skin but to give up interest wrinkles the soul. Worry, doubt, self-distrust, fear, and despair . . . these are the long, long years that bow the head and turn the growing spirit back to dust. . . . You are as young as your faith, as old as your doubt; as young as your self-confidence, as old as your fear; as young as your hope, as old as your despair.

Whatever your age, realize that your life will never end. The question is, where will you spend your life in the hereafter? In heaven with God, or in the lake of fire which burns forever? Make sure of your eternal destiny and trust Christ today.

Prayer Suggestion—Tell Christ you love him and are looking forward to your eternal home in heaven with him.

APRIL

20

Today in History—Marie and Pierre Curie isolate radium, 1902; head of United Automobile Workers, Walter Reuther wounded by shotgun blast, 1948; exchange of prisoners of war begins in Korean War, 1953; one thousand persons killed by Irish terrorists in five years of violence in Northern Ireland, 1974; Barbara Walters becomes first woman news anchor to gain national prominence, 1976; pianist Vladimir Horowitz gives first recital in Soviet Union after sixty-one years in the West, 1986.

Born Today—Sculptor Daniel French, 1850; Supreme Court Justice John Paul Stevens, 1920; actor Ryan O'Neal, 1941; actress Jessica Lange, 1949; baseball player Don Mattingly, 1962.

Today's Quotation—"Amplification is the vice of modern oratory. Speeches measured by the hour, die with the hour."—*Thomas Jefferson, April 20, 1824*

Speaking Out

There are many stories told of public speakers and their audiences. One such story was told by poet James Whitcomb Riley. It seems he was talking with a fellow writer who asked why Riley's speeches were such a success when his usually fell flat. Riley told the man, "Well Jim, the big reason as I see it is that I talk until I get tired, whereas you talk until the audience gets tired."

Most audiences appreciate a speaker who can state his point simply and briefly and then be done with it. The Bible records the story of one preacher who spoke so long he put a man to sleep and the sleeping man fell to his death from a third story window. But the story had a miraculous ending because the preacher, Paul, brought the victim back to life.

When was the last time you thanked your pastor for his ministry and the way he communicates God's miraculous nature week after week?

Prayer Suggestion—Ask God to bless your pastor, his staff, and all those who minister the gospel around the world.

APRIL

21

Romans 8:14–23

Today in History—San Jacinto Day marks victory of Sam Houston's forces over Mexicans, 1836; Woodville Latham demonstrates projecting motion pictures on a screen, 1895; Russian troops enter Berlin in heavy fighting in World War II, 1945; army takes control of Greece, 1967; U.S. expels three Soviet diplomats on spy charges, 1983; American airstrikes on Libyan leader Khadafy's headquarters draws bipartisan support in Congress, 1986.

Born Today—Educator Friedrich Froebel, 1782; writer Charlotte Bronte, 1816; naturalist John Muir, 1838; actor Anthony Quinn, 1915; England's Queen Elizabeth II, 1926; actress Elaine May, 1932.

Today's Quotation—"Remember, remember always that all of us, and you and I especially, are descended from immigrants and revolutionists."—*Franklin D. Roosevelt, April 21, 1938*

Immigrants

America is unique in all the world in the vast percentage of its citizens who have descended from immigrants. The excitement of coming to America was beautifully captured by Polish immigrant Janina Atkins as she wrote:

> Just six years ago I came with my husband to this country with $2.60 in my purse, some clothes, a few books, a bundle of old letters, and a little pillow. I was an immigrant girl hoping for a new life and happiness in a strange new country. There is something in America that filled my soul with a feeling of freedom and independence which gave me strength. There is no one here to lead you by the hand and order you about. We believed in the future and the future did not disappoint us. Today my husband is studying for his doctorate. We live in a comfortable apartment.

Just as Janina was thankful for her American homeland, Christians should also be thankful that God has adopted us into his family so that we are no longer aliens without a home.

Prayer Suggestion—Thank God for his salvation which gives us eternal hope and a heavenly homeland.

128

APRIL

22

Today in History—Construction of Bastille begins in Paris, 1370; Oklahoma territory opens to homesteaders, 1889; Germans introduce poison gas at World War I Battle of Ypres, Belgium, 1915; televised Senate hearings probing charges against Senator Joseph R. McCarthy begin, 1954.

Born Today—Spain's Queen Isabella I, 1451; philosopher Immanuel Kant, 1724; actor Eddie Albert, 1908; violinist Yehudi Menuhin, 1916; singer Glen Campbell, 1935; actor Jack Nicholson, 1936.

Today's Quotation—"Of all the tasks of government, the most basic is to protect its citizens against violence."—*John Foster Dulles, April 22, 1957*

Violence

One of the most notorious criminals of the 1930s, John Dillinger, was taken to court in his early teens on some minor charge. He was put on probation and began attending Sunday school with his parents. Other parents, disturbed that a youth with a court record was attending the class, went to the teacher and said that if John Dillinger was allowed to attend, they'd keep their children home. The young man never again returned to church. Within twenty years this former Sunday school boy became known as the most dangerous criminal in the country.

Lest anyone say the world is getting better these days, here are some sobering facts: Since World War II ended, serious crimes have risen an average 214 percent. These include murder (up 263 percent), rape (up 100 percent), robbery (up 263 percent), aggravated assault (up 215 percent), auto theft (up 158 percent), burglary (up 290 percent), and larceny (up 192 percent).

As tragic as crime and violence are, they only confirm that "the heart is deceitful above all things, and desperately wicked. . . ." Do not be deceived by those who predict a "heaven on earth"—there are darker days yet to come but, praise God, he will be victorious!

Prayer Suggestion—Praise God that although we live in a violent, sinful world, he has saved us. We are not citizens of this world but will live with him someday.

APRIL

23

Today in History—William Shakespeare dies on his fifty-second birthday, 1616; "Vitascope" process for projecting movies on a theatre screen debuts in New York, 1896; Gambia becomes a Republic, 1970; Ethiopia ousts 330 American government officials and missionaries, probably in response to cut-off in U.S. foreign aid for human rights violations, 1977; after ninety-nine years of success with original formula, Coca-Cola drops it in favor of New Coke, 1985.

Born Today—Writer William Shakespeare, 1564; President James Buchanan, 1791; composer Sergei Prokofiev, 1891; ambassador Shirley Temple Black, 1928; designer Roy Halston (Frowick), 1932; actor Lee Majors, 1940.

Today's Quotation—"People die, but books never die."—*Franklin D. Roosevelt, April 23, 1942*

God's Perfect Book

The Library of Congress houses millions of books, yet the one which is considered the most beautiful and most near perfection is a Bible hand-copied by a sixteenth-century monk. Even the world's best printer could not surpass its matchless perfection. In this 1,000-page Bible is the German text written in black ink and each letter is perfect without a scratch or blot anywhere. There are two columns to a page and even under a magnifying glass, not the slightest irregularity in line, space, or letter formation is detectable. At the beginning of each chapter is a very large initial letter, colorfully drawn in red and blue ink with a scene from the chapter. A priceless book which took a lifetime to copy, it should be admired more for its perfect, God-inspired contents than for the beauty of its appearance.

Think of God's perfection every time you read his book, the Holy Bible.

Prayer Suggestion—Thank God for giving us his Word—the Bible. But don't simply admire it, read its priceless pages every day.

APRIL
24

Today in History—The *Boston Newsletter,* first regularly issued American newspaper, begins publication, 1704; Library of Congress established in Washington, D.C., 1800; Spain declares war on U.S., 1898; Easter Rebellion in Ireland against British rule, April 24–29, 1916; U.S. educated Abel Muzorewa becomes first black Prime Minister of Rhodesia, 1979.

Born Today—Novelist Anthony Trollope, 1815; artist Willem de Kooning, 1904; poet Robert Penn Warren, 1905; actress Barbra Streisand, 1942; basketball player Rudy Tomjanovich, 1948; actor Vince Ferragamo, 1954.

Today's Quotation—"I do not see why there is not greater enthusiasm for planning, except perhaps for this reason: that the word planning does not signify anything very spectacular about it and it takes a good many years to see results from it."—*Franklin D. Roosevelt, April 24, 1934*

Plan Ahead

Many books have recently been written on the importance of planning and time management. Yet this is not a new concept. In describing Napoleon's achievements, George Knox noted the great conqueror "once plotted an entire campaign between the acts, while at the theater . . . . Napoleon conquered all of Europe, because he utilized the time that the rest of the world was letting go to waste." Others have also used their time productively. Thomas Macaulay, for example, was said to have learned German during a long voyage. Robert Fulton and Samuel Morse thought up their inventions during their spare time. During a short thirty years, the apostle Paul preached the gospel and planted churches all over the civilized world!

How well do you use your time? Do you plan ahead and organize your activities to fully utilize your time for God?

Prayer Suggestion—Be thankful for the time God has allowed you today. Utilize each moment to the fullest in service for him.

APRIL

25

Today in History—U.S. declares war on Spain, 1898; Anzac Day marks landing of Australian and New Zealand troops in vain invasion of Gallipoli near Dardanelles in World War I, 1915; U.S. and U.S.S.R. troops in World War II met at the Elbe River in Germany, 1945; conference to form a United Nations Organization opens in San Francisco, 1945; Israel removes last soldiers from Sinai as area reverts to Egypt, 1982.

Born Today—Statesman Oliver Cromwell, 1599; inventor Guglielmo Marconi, 1874; Supreme Court Justice William Brennan, 1906; singer Ella Fitzgerald, 1918; director Paul Mazursky, 1930; actor Al Pacino, 1940.

Today's Quotation—"We believe that the just standing of all nations is the health and security of all."—*Thomas Jefferson, April 25, 1812*

Health and Security

Many things in life can be either helpful or harmful depending on their use. Ordinary table salt, for example, is a blend of two very deadly substances, sodium and chloride. Yet it is essential to human health and, used as a preservative, serves to kill disease organisms. Likewise, cobalt, put in radioactive cylinders, is a versatile substance which has proven to be more powerful than radium in treating various cancers. Yet, when placed with an explosive powder in a bomb, the cobalt becomes a mighty source of death and destruction because its radioactivity settles as fallout over a vast area. In this case, cobalt is useful to enhance security as a strong deterrent to an enemy's aggression.

In the same way, God's Word serves as our spiritual food, giving us security, yet it is a book containing news of death and torment for those who have not believed. What have you done with God's Word in your life?

Prayer Suggestion—Realize that all God has made is good, but that sin has caused his creation to become a means of death as well as nurture.

APRIL

26

Today in History—Associated Press correspondent William Oatis arrested as spy in communist Czechoslovakia, for which he spends two years in prison, 1951; nationwide test of Salk anti-polio vaccine begins in U.S., 1954; Tanganyika and Zanzibar merge in republic later named Tanzania, 1964; education panel concludes "mediocrity is threatening U.S. education," 1983; accident at Chernobyl nuclear plant spreads radiation over a wide area of Russia, 1986. And how much around world

Born Today—Naturalist John James Audubon, 1785; artist Eugene Delacroix, 1798; Korean leader Syngman Rhee, 1875; entertainer Carol Burnett, 1936; musician Duane Eddy, 1938; singer Bobby Rydell, 1942.

Today's Quotation—"I was always, as I still am, trying to fashion a piece of literature out of the life next at hand."—*William Dean Howells, April 26, 1903*

Good Reading

Have you ever heard someone say they "don't get anything out of" reading the Bible? They could learn from Dr. Howard Pope's story of a young lady who after reading a certain book remarked that it was certainly "one of the dullest books" she had read. Soon after that she met and fell in love with a certain young man. Their friendship blossomed and they soon became engaged. One day the woman remarked on a strange coincidence. The book she disliked was written by a man whose name and initials were the same as her fiance. "There's no coincidence," he said. "I wrote that book." Motivated anew, the young lady was said to have gone home and re-read the book straight through with greatly expanded interest because now she knew the author.

In the same way Christians hold the Bible to be so dear as they know the author. In fact they are his adopted children if they've believed and trusted in him as Savior.

Prayer Suggestion—Thank God that as his child you've been adopted into his family with full rights and privileges.

APRIL

27

1 Peter 4:7-11

Today in History—Explorer Ferdinand Magellan is killed in the Philippines, 1521; agreement between U.S. and Canada provides for maintenance of unfortified border, 1817; steamship loaded with Union prisoners explodes in Mississippi River, killing 1,450, 1865; U.S. Social Security System issues first benefit payments, 1937; Charles de Gaulle quits as president of France after defeat of his program in a national referendum, 1969; judge reveals that E. Howard Hunt and G. Gordon Liddy broke into the offices of Daniel Ellsberg and are believed to have stolen "Pentagon Papers" file, 1973; *Apollo 16* space mission ends with Pacific splashdown after eleven-day lunar exploration mission, bringing back some two hundred pounds of moon rocks, 1972.

Born Today—Inventor Samuel F. B. Morse, 1791; philosopher Herbert Spencer, 1820; President Ulysses S. Grant, 1822; lecturer Coretta Scott King, 1927; South African leader Pik Botha, 1932; actress Sandy Dennis, 1937.

Today's Quotation—"If you were to make little fishes talk, they would talk like whales."—*Oliver Goldsmith, April 27, 1773*

Big Talk

Who hasn't smiled at the youngster who admires somebody much bigger and says proudly, "When I grow up I want to be just like you." Even adults sometimes envy those whose voice seems to carry more weight and influence than theirs. Ask anyone to name the largest of all animals alive today and most would say the elephant. In fact, the blue whale is the largest of all animals, ranging in size up to fifty-five feet long and weighing a startling 100 tons—about as much as twenty elephants! No wonder the little fish wanted to talk like a whale.

As believers in Christ, we too should want more—more of God's blessing and fullness to better serve him where ever he has placed us. With God's help we can have as mighty an influence in the world as the great blue whale has in the ocean depths.

Prayer Suggestion—Realize that the same God who created the massive whale has also made us especially to praise and serve him!

APRIL

28

Today in History—Maryland is seventh state to ratify Constitution, 1788; Fletcher Christian leads mutiny against Captain Bligh of *H.M.S. Bounty*, 1789; ex-dictator Benito Mussolini of Italy and his mistress are shot, 1945; U.S. hostage rescue attempt fails as two planes collide in Iranian desert killing eight servicemen, 1980; Secretary of State Cyrus Vance resigns over disagreement with Iranian hostage rescue attempt, 1980.

Born Today—President James Monroe, 1758; actor Lionel Barrymore, 1878; writer Robert Anderson, 1917; politician James Baker, 1930; actress Carolyn Jones, 1932; actress Ann-Margaret, 1941; comedian Jay Leno, 1950.

Today's Quotation—"Preparation for war is a constant stimulus to suspicion and ill will."—*President James Monroe, April 28, 1818*

Make Way for Peace

A boy once asked his father, "Dad, how do wars begin?" The father had just begun to answer the question when his wife interrupted him and corrected his answer. The father then asked pointedly, "Are you answering the questions or am I?" With that the wife stormed from the room and slammed the door dramatically, rattling the dishes in the cupboard. After watching his parents the boy said, "Dad, you don't have to tell me now. I know how wars begin."

Are we looking for ways to make peace? Being a peacemaker is something all of us should work to become in this tumultuous world.

Prayer Suggestion—That God would enable us to be peacemakers among those who are at war.

APRIL

29

Isaiah 45:5-13

Today in History—Jacob Coxey's "army" of unemployed reaches Washington, D.C., 1894; legendary engineer of Illinois Central's Cannonball Express, Casey Jones, rides to his death near Vaughan, Miss., 1900; U.S. troops liberate Nazi concentration camp at Dachau, Germany, 1945; Christian Broadcasting Network begins satellite broadcasting, 1977; filmmaker Alfred Hitchcock dies at eighty, 1980; furor grows over President Reagan's announced plan to visit Nazi cemetery during upcoming trip to Germany, 1985.

Born Today—Publisher William Randolph Hearst, 1863; conductor Sir Thomas Beecham, 1879; scientist Harold Urey, 1893; musician Duke Ellington, 1899; Japanese Emperor Hirohito, 1901; actress Celeste Holm, 1919; poet Rod McKuen, 1933.

Today's Quotation—"The British people do not, as is sometimes thought, go to war for calculation, but for sentiment."—*Winston Churchill, April 29, 1945*

War Costs

What motivates nations to go to war? The reasons are varied but the root cause is greed. And war is not cheap. *Moody Monthly* has calculated that, for the cost of the first atomic bomb (about two billion dollars), ten thousand missionaries could have been sent to the field and supported for a full 100 years! In the same way, the money spent by only the U.S. in World War II would have kept 1.5 million missionaries on the field. The cost of vigilance is indeed high.

As long as we are here on earth, we are in a constant preparation for war—if not against flesh and blood enemies, then against "the rulers of the darkness of this world." If we see ourselves in a continual battle against the forces of evil, we will be better prepared to resist temptation when it comes during a moment of weakness.

Prayer Suggestion—That we might be spiritually and physically strong, and be willing and able to defend our nation.

APRIL

30

Luke 18:18–27

Today in History—George Washington is sworn in as first president of U.S., 1789; Louisiana admitted to U.S. as eighteenth state, 1812; Adolf Hitler believed to have killed himself around this date, 1945; four top Nixon aides resign in the wake of growing Watergate scandal, 1973; Saigon surrenders to communists as last Americans leave Vietnam, 1975; oil well sealed off in North Sea but not before 7.5 million gallons escape, 1977; U.S. sides with Britain in Falkland Island War, 1982; President Reagan signs agreements with China for increased trade, cultural, and scientific exchanges, 1984.

Born Today—Painter Jacques Louis David, 1748; composer Franz Lehar, 1870; actress Eve Arden, 1912; singer Willie Nelson, 1933; actor Gary Collins, 1938; actress Jill Clayburgh, 1944; football player Al Toon, 1963.

Today's Quotation—"There are no such things as incurables; there are only things for which man has not found a cure."—*Bernard M. Baruch, April 30, 1954*

Incurable

Pioneer cancer researcher Charles Kettering objected to use of the term "incurable" in reference to disease, saying an incurable disease is simply "one the doctor doesn't know how to cure." To illustrate his point that the way to overcome defeat is to ignore the possibility of failure, Kettering once assigned a difficult problem to a young research associate. However, he prohibited his assistant from looking at the writings of others on the subject. The researcher went to work and eventually succeeded in his assignment, unaware of the evidence by experts "proving" his accomplishment couldn't be done.

How wonderful it is to know the Great Physician for whom nothing is impossible. Where our strength leaves off, God's power begins. Are you fully utilizing all your strength, relying on God to see you through? He alone can do the impossible.

Prayer Suggestion—Thank God that he gives us all the power we need to do the job he has called us to do, no matter how "impossible."

137

MAY

Today in History—Commodore George Dewey's U.S. fleet decisively defeats Spanish in Battle of Manila Bay, 1898; Empire State Building dedicated as world's tallest building, 1931; "Back to the Bible" broadcast founded, 1939; U.S. reconnaissance plane shot down over U.S.S.R., and pilot Francis Gary Powers is seized for trial, 1960; first hijacking of U.S. airplane to Cuba, 1961; Senator Harrison Williams convicted in Abscam bribery case, 1981; 1.5 million blacks stay off job in biggest strike ever in South Africa, 1986.

Born Today—Essayist Joseph Addison, 1672; architect Benjamin Latrobe, 1764; singer Kate Smith, 1909; actor Glenn Ford, 1916; TV entertainer Jack Paar, 1918; singer Judy Collins, 1939; singer Rita Coolidge, 1945.

Today's Quotation—"There are not enough jails, not enough policemen, not enough courts to enforce a law not supported by the people."— *Hubert H. Humphrey, May 1, 1965*

Man's Laws

In order for a free society to properly function, its citizens agree to be governed by certain laws. But have you ever considered just how many laws there are on the books? If you were to take time to familiarize yourself with just two laws each day, it would take you six thousand years before you qualified as a law-abiding citizen! And modern laws aren't the only ones that are numerous. In ancient Rome, Emperor Justinian ordered all laws to be compiled. It took sixteen assistants three years to collect the Roman laws into two thousand separate volumes!

By comparison, all of God's laws for mankind are contained in just one single volume consisting of sixty-six books. Many people read through God's laws, the Bible, at least once a year. How long has it been since you've read God's laws, or are you more familiar with man's laws than God's?

Prayer Suggestion—That we would get to know God's laws, and through memorizing them, carry them in our hearts for his service.

MAY

2

Today in History—Hudson's Bay Company chartered in England, 1670; Sergei Prokofiev's "Peter and the Wolf" premieres in Moscow, 1936; Berlin surrenders to Russians in World War II, 1945; first British jet plane passenger service begins between London and Johannesburg, South Africa, 1952; Stan Musial of St. Louis Cardinals hits five home runs in one day (in two games), 1954; after forty-eight years as FBI Director J. Edgar Hoover dies at age 77, 1972; twelve thousand demonstrators protest proposed nuclear power plant in Seabrook, N.H., in first protest of nuclear plant, 1977.

Born Today—Russia's Catherine the Great, 1729; Zionism founder Theodore Herzl, 1860; physician Benjamin Spock, 1903; singer Bing Crosby, 1904; singer Theodore Bikel, 1924; singer Larry Gatlin, 1949.

Today's Quotation—"Public office in this country has few attractions."—*Alexander Hamilton, May 2, 1797*

Public Service

It would seem that Marshall Cummings has a better appreciation of laws and lawyers since his conviction on charges of attempted robbery by force. The accused purse snatcher, serving as his own counsel, found things took a sudden turn for the worse when he asked his accuser absent-mindedly, "Did you get a good look at my face when I took your purse?" Following this testimony, Cummings was sentenced to ten years in prison, providing time for him to think over how things might have gone differently.

Sometimes it takes a direct confrontation with the law before we gain a healthy respect, and even grudging support for legal restrictions. When it comes to God's law, as found in the Bible, we are told there will be relatively few who will heed his commands. Yet in no way does that reduce the effect of either God's law or his coming judgment.

Prayer Suggestion—This is not the age of law but of grace. Thank God for his forgiveness despite our sin, and for his immeasurable grace.

MAY

3

Today in History—First U.S. medical school is established at the College of Philadelphia, 1765; Polish Constitution Day commemorates adoption of constitution on this date, 1791; Lord Byron swims the Hellespont, 1810; first air passenger service begins between New York and Atlantic City, N.J., 1919; Margaret Thatcher elected Britain's first woman prime minister, 1979; U.S. Catholic bishops call for elimination of all nuclear weapons and for a ban on nuclear war, 1983.

Born Today—Statesman Niccolo Machiavelli, 1469; Israeli politician Golda Meir, 1898; songwriter Pete Seeger, 1919; boxer Sugar Ray Robinson, 1920; singer Engelbert Humperdinck, 1936; singer Frankie Valli, 1937.

Today's Quotation—"The Constitution is what the judges say it is."—*Charles Evans Hughes, May 3, 1907*

Constitution

Judges who interpret the intent of lawmakers and the writers of the constitution certainly do wield a lot of power and influence—some say more than was ever intended when the documents were written. Speaking to a man who had appeared before him and who was later freed on a technicality, former Supreme Court Justice Gray told him to remember "that one day you will stand before a better and wiser Judge, and there you will be dealt with according to justice and not according to law."

While earthly justice, based as it is on imperfect mankind, will always be flawed, there is coming a perfect Judgment where all will appear and none will escape. But Christians standing before the Almighty have no need to fear, as we are promised Christ will be our advocate; he is the ultimate lawyer who will never lose a case, including yours and mine.

Prayer Suggestion—You have the blessed hope of having Christ as your advocate in the coming judgment. Thank God for his provision.

MAY

4

John 6:35–40

Today in History—Rhode Island declares independence from Great Britain, 1776; Al Capone enters penitentiary, 1932; U.S. defeats Japanese fleet in Battle of Coral Sea in World War II, May 4–8, 1942; Nazi forces at the Elbe River surrender to U.S. and Great Britain in World War II, 1945; four students killed by National Guard at Kent State University, 1970.

Born Today—Educator Horace Mann, 1796; biologist Thomas Huxley, 1825; musician Maynard Ferguson, 1928; actress Audrey Hepburn, 1929; singer Roberta Peters, 1930; columnist George Will, 1941; singer Tammy Wynette, 1942.

Today's Quotation—"The right of every person 'to be left alone' must be placed in the scales with the right of others to communicate."— *Chief Justice Warren E. Burger, May 4, 1970*

Apathy

While citizens expect society to leave them alone, too often in recent years citizens have grown increasingly apathetic to the plight of their fellow man. In New York City, a mailman who had been shot by a sniper is ordered from a building lobby because he is dripping blood. A woman in Oklahoma City unexpectedly gives birth on a city sidewalk while bystanders turn their faces as they walk on by and a taxi driver looks and then speeds away. In Dayton, a woman who accidentally drives her car into the river waves frantically from the car roof, screaming that she can't swim. A dozen people look on indifferently at the woman who later drowns. And the problem has gotten the attention of the media. A Chicago newspaper has established a special "Apathy" file to collect information on this growing indifference.

Yet apathy would never describe our Savior who was known for his loving compassion despite the frequently unreasonable demands of the masses. It was he who said to his overly-protective disciples, "Suffer the little children to come unto me, and forbid them not: for of such is the kingdom of God" (Mark 10:14). Have you come to the compassionate Christ?

Prayer Suggestion—Christ loves you and died for you. Praise him for his love and for reaching down to save the lost human race.

MAY

5

Today in History—Napoleon dies in exile on island of St. Helena, 1821; Cinco de Mayo celebration in Mexico commemorates victory over French, 1862; Carnegie Hall opens in New York City with Tchaikovsky as guest conductor, 1891; Ethiopian Liberation Day marks return of Emperor Haile Selassie to capital, Addis Ababa. City had been occupied on this same date in 1936 by the Italians, 1941; Denmark's Liberation Day marks end of Nazi German occupation, 1945; Federal Republic of Germany becomes free sovereign nation, 1955; despite strong Jewish protest President and Mrs. Reagan visit German cemetery where twenty-five hundred German soldiers are buried, 1985.

Born Today—Philosopher Soren Kierkegaard, 1813; philosopher Karl Marx, 1818; reporter Nellie Bly, 1867; author James Beard, 1903; actress Pat Carroll, 1927; actor Roger Rees, 1944.

Today's Quotation—"Beyond war there is peace."—*Marshal Ferdinand Foch, May 5, 1921*

The Prince of Peace

High atop a mountain between Argentina and Chile stands a massive statue entitled "Christ of the Andes." The statue commemorates the signing of a peace treaty in 1903 which ended a long-smoldering border dispute. In fact, the military cannons which had terrorized the Chileans were melted down and reshaped into the statue. Engraved in Spanish at the base of the towering monument are these words: "Sooner shall these mountains crumble into dust than Argentines and Chileans break the peace sworn at the foot of Christ the Redeemer." This massive statue, towering over both nations, serves as a reminder of Christ who is our Prince of Peace—the hope of the world.

Let us fix our attention on him and not be distracted by the alluring and temporary things of this world.

Prayer Suggestion—In this age of international conflict and tension, thank God that he, our heavenly Father, is still in control.

MAY

6

Psalm 1:1–6

Today in History—First postage stamps are issued by England, 1840; Works Progress Administration for unemployment relief begins operation, 1935; German dirigible Hindenburg explodes and burns while mooring at Lakehurst, N.J., killing thirty-six people, 1937; Liberty Baptist College becomes Liberty University, 1985; leaders of the seven industrialized nations sign anti-terrorism document in Tokyo, 1986.

Born Today—Psychiatrist Sigmund Freud, 1856; explorer Robert Peary, 1856; actor Stewart Granger, 1913; actor Orson Welles, 1915; author Theodore White, 1915; baseball's Willie Mays, 1931; musician Bob Seeger, 1945.

Today's Quotation—"The man with power but without conscience, could, with an eloquent tongue, if he cared for nothing but his own power, put this whole country into a flame."—*Woodrow Wilson, May 6, 1911*

Solid Oak

Perhaps you have heard that the root spread of a tree roughly equals the spread of its branches, with as much as one-tenth of the tree concealed under the ground. The roots, with a combined length of as much as a hundred miles in a large oak, are what gives the tree strength and stability and the power to withstand fearsome storms during its life. Some years ago woodsmen cut down a giant sequoia tree. Upon inspecting its growth rings, they learned that the tree had been a seedling 271 years before Christ and that 516 years later (A.D. 245) the tree was damaged by the first of several fires. It had recovered from all this by the time it was cut down hundreds of years later.

How strong a Christian are you? Will your spiritual maturity measure up to the physical strength of that giant tree?

Prayer Suggestion—When the winds of false doctrine come sweeping around you, pray that God would keep you firm, anchored to the Rock which cannot move.

MAY

7

Today in History—Captain Robert Gray discovers the Columbia River, 1792; British liner *Lusitania* sunk by German submarine in World War I, 1915; Nazis surrender to General Eisenhower in France, thus ending the European phase of World War II, 1945; French forces in Indochina are defeated at Dien Bien Phu in disaster which led to French withdrawal from Asia, 1954.

Born Today—Poet Robert Browning, 1812; composer Johannes Brahms, 1833; composer Peter Ilyich Tchaikovsky, 1840; Archibald MacLeish, 1892; inventor Edwin Land, 1909; actor Darren McGavin, 1922; TV weatherman Willard Scott, 1934.

Today's Quotation—"Why fear death? It is the most beautiful adventure in life."—*Charles Frohman, May 7, 1915*

Fear of Death

Former Soviet dictator Joseph Stalin suffered a "difficult and terrible death" according to his daughter Svetlana. She describes his final moments by saying, "He suddenly opened his eyes and cast a glance at everyone in the room. It was a terrible glance, insane or perhaps angry and full of the fear of death. Then he lifted his left hand as though he were pointing to something above and bringing down a curse on us all. The gesture was full of menace . . . the next moment the spirit wrenched itself free of the flesh."

Yet what hope and peace there is in death for the believer. Speaking before a college audience, former Vice President Alben Barkley gave these last words: "I would rather be a servant in the house of the Lord than sit in the seat of the mighty," and with that, he died.

While it is human nature to fear the unknown, believers can be certain their loving heavenly Father stands ready to carry them safely to the other side, just as a human father tucks his sleeping infant into a snug bed.

Prayer Suggestion—To be absent from the body is to be present with the Lord. Be thankful for the hope that is within you, through Christ.

MAY

8

Today in History—Hernando de Soto discovers the Mississippi River, 1541; VE Day celebrated as Nazi Germany's surrender goes into effect in World War II, 1945; peace demonstrators attacked by hard hat workers on New York's Wall Street, 1970; Yugoslavia's President Joseph Tito dies at age 87 and his funeral is attended by representatives of 115 nations, 1980; Soviets plan to boycott Los Angeles Summer Olympics Games, 1984.

Born Today—President Harry Truman, 1884; religious leader Fulton Sheen, 1895; comedian Don Rickles, 1926; politician James Thompson, 1936; author Peter Benchley, 1940; singer Toni Tennille, 1943.

Today's Quotation—"Men are no more born to speak the truth than they are to fire rifles."—*Henry Ward Beecher, May 8, 1883*

Honest Lips

With ethics taking on added interest these days, it would do well for each of us to review the "Cadet Prayer" repeated during chapel services at the U.S. Military Academy:

> Make us choose the harder right instead of the easier wrong, and never to be contented with half truth when whole truth can be won. Endow us with courage that is born of loyalty to all that is noble and worthy, that scorns to compromise with vice and injustice and knows no fear when right and truth are in jeopardy.

As Abraham Lincoln said, "You can fool some of the people some of the time but not all of the people all of the time." The Bible says, "Be not deceived; God is not mocked: for whatsoever a man soweth, that shall he also reap" (Gal. 6:7). Yes, friend, honesty is still the best, and only, policy.

Prayer Suggestion—That we would always choose the harder right and always be truthful rather than fall into dishonesty.

MAY

9

Today in History—Americans Richard Byrd and Floyd Bennett become first aviators to fly over North Pole, 1926; first eye bank opens at New York Hospital in New York City, 1944; Czechoslovakia liberated by U.S. and U.S.S.R. troops following end of World War II in Europe, 1945; federal judge rules government not responsible for victims of Agent Orange wartime defoliant, 1985.

Born Today—Abolitionist John Brown, 1800; dramatist James Barrie, 1860; broadcast journalist Mike Wallace, 1918; actor Albert Finney, 1936; tennis champion Pancho Gonzalez, 1938; actress Candice Bergen, 1946; singer Billy Joel, 1949.

Today's Quotation—"The history of liberty is a history of the limitations of governmental power, not the increase of it."—*Woodrow Wilson, May 9, 1912*

Limits to Power

The rapid growth of government power is seen in some startling statistics: The steel industry alone is expected to comply with fifty-five hundred separate federal regulations, most of which tell the industry what it must do rather than what it cannot do. And reporting on activities to the government has become a major undertaking. One company was expected to file twenty-seven hundred different kinds of reports (with five hundred thousand copies) to meet all government requirements!

Renowned political theorist Dr. A. D. Lindsay says, "Any big organization is bound to become hierarchical. A community where all organizations are gathered together into one great system cannot give its members equality whether it is theoretically authoritarian or democratic."

Certainly Christians have an obligation to keep their eye on the growth of "big government," and fight with the ballot any attempts to limit religious liberties or permit unscriptural activities.

Prayer Suggestion—Pray for our president, senators, congressmen, judges, and other elected officials that God would guide them.

MAY

10

Luke 12:2-9

Today in History—Fort Ticonderoga, N.Y., is captured in American Revolutionary War, 1775; U.S. transcontinental railroad is completed at Promontory, Utah, 1869; Treaty of Frankfurt ends Franco-Prussian War, 1871; J. Edgar Hoover becomes head of FBI, 1923; Nazis burn books they disapprove of throughout Germany, 1933; Winston Churchill becomes prime minister of Great Britain, 1940; Nazi German leader Rudolf Hess parachutes into England to seek negotiated peace in World War II, 1941; Vietnam peace talks between U.S. and North Vietnam begin in Paris, 1968; Francois Mitterand becomes first French socialist president, 1981.

Born Today—Sportsman Sir Thomas Lipton, 1850; actor-dancer Fred Astaire, 1899; pediatrician T. Berry Brazelton, 1918; actress Nancy Walker, 1921; football coach Ara Parseghian, 1923; actor Gary Owens, 1936; musician Dave Mason, 1946.

Today's Quotation—"There is such a thing as a man being too proud to fight."—*President Woodrow Wilson, May 10, 1915*

Too Proud to Fight

Many a battle has been lost because of traitors who would rather "switch than fight." John Wesley was not one of them. He once said, "Give me a hundred men who fear nothing but sin, and desire nothing but God, and I will shake the world. . . . Such alone will overthrow the kingdom of Satan and build up the kingdom of God on earth."

Henry Ward Beecher once preached a series of sermons on drunkenness and gambling which apparently upset some members of the community who profited from these sins. Once, following these messages, he encountered an assailant who demanded a retraction or he'd shoot. "Shoot away," said Beecher as he walked calmly away. "I don't believe you can hit the mark as well as I did."

Let us have the courage of our convictions and not be too proud to stand up for God.

Prayer Suggestion—Ask for courage and God's power to bravely stand up against the forces of evil which would defeat the work of God.

147

MAY

11

Ephesians 6:10-18

Today in History—Peter Stuyvesant becomes governor of New Amsterdam, 1647; Minnesota admitted to U.S. as 32nd state, 1858; psychiatrist Daniel Elsberg freed of all charges in Pentagon Papers case, 1973; Jose Napoleon Duarte wins presidency of El Salvador with 54 percent of vote, 1984; flash fire kills forty at London soccer match, 1985; three British envoys expelled from Syria following British expulsion of three Syrians, 1986.

Born Today—Inventor Ottmar Mergenthaler, 1854; composer Irving Berlin, 1888; artist Salvador Dali, 1904; entertainer Phil Silvers, 1912; actor Mort Sahl, 1927; writer Stanley Elkin, 1930; physician Robert Jarvik, 1946.

Today's Quotation—"I propose to fight it out on this line if it takes all summer."—*General Ulysses S. Grant, May 11, 1864*

Fearlessness

Sir Alfred Lawrence's memorial in Westminster Abbey consists simply of his name and these words: "He feared man so little because he feared God so much." H. A. Ironside told the story of how he would play "bear" with his little boy. Often he would get down on all fours and chase the toddler into a corner, all the time growling like a bear. Once when the lad was hopelessly cornered, he said boldly, "I'm not a bit afraid—you're not a bear at all, you're my daddy." Dr. Ironside thought to himself how true this was, for in his own life he was once "running away from God, treating him as though he were an enemy . . . but now I thank you for running me down."

Prayer Suggestion—Realize that we are in a deadly spiritual battle and that only those who trust God will triumph. Thank God, he wins!

MAY

12

Romans 8:24-27

Today in History—First Symphony by Dmitri Shostakovich, written when he was nineteen, premieres, 1926; kidnapped baby Charles Lindbergh, Jr., found dead near Hopewell, N.J., 1932; Nazi blitz conquest of France in World War II begins, 1940; Soviet blockade of land routes to West Berlin ends after eleven months, 1949; Irish Republican Army member dies following sixty-six-day prison hunger strike, 1981; Cathleen Webb recants testimony of rape attack thus freeing the accused, Gary Dotson, 1985.

Born Today—Humorist Edward Lear, 1812; nurse Florence Nightingale, 1820; broadcast journalist Howard K. Smith, 1914; baseball manager Yogi Berra, 1925; composer Burt Bacharach, 1929.

Today's Quotation—"The soldier, above all other people, prays for peace, for he must suffer and bear the deepest wounds and scars of war."—*General Douglas MacArthur, May 12, 1962*

Pray for Peace

Radio speaker Wilbur Nelson tells of a tragic irony during the Battle of New Orleans. It seems the peace treaty had already been signed between the British and the Americans; the war was officially over, yet over 2,000 soldiers were needlessly killed. Because of poor communication in the field, the soldiers continued to fight unaware that the war had ended. Perhaps some of them had been praying for peace not knowing that their prayers were already answered.

Has this ever happened to you? You pray earnestly for God's assistance, only to find that he has already answered your prayers. What a great God we have who knows and grants our request even before we ask!

Prayer Suggestion—Ask for God's guidance to determine whether your needs have been met before you ask!

MAY

13

Today in History—Jamestown, Va., founded, 1607; U.S. Congress declares war on Mexico, 1846; noonday prayer meetings begun by D. L. Moody in London, 1867; three children at Fatima, Portugal, report seeing vision of the Virgin Mary, 1917; Pope John Paul II injured in assassination attempt in St. Peter's Square, 1981.

Born Today—Composer Sir Arthur Sullivan, 1842; writer Daphne du Maurier, 1907; boxer Joe Louis, 1914; actress Beatrice Arthur, 1926; critic Clive Barnes, 1927; director Herbert Ross, 1927; singer Mary Wells, 1943.

Today's Quotation—"I have nothing to offer but blood, toil, tears, and sweat."—*Sir Winston Churchill, May 13, 1940*

Hard Work

Under the category "how times have changed" comes this notice which was posted in a Chicago store in 1858:

> The store will be open from 6:00 A.M. to 9:00 P.M. the year 'round. On arrival each morning store must be swept, counters, shelves, and show-cases dusted. Lamps must be trimmed, pens made, a pail of water and bucket of coal brought in before breakfast. After 14 hours of work, leisure hours should be spent in reading. (Speaker's Sourcebook)

Today's employees could learn much from workers in the last century. It seems now that too many people stop looking for work when they get a job.

Christ was well aware of his role in doing the work of his heavenly Father. How much more do we, who call ourselves Christians, need to be doing his work for "the night cometh, when no man can work" (John 9:4).

Prayer Suggestion—For an empowering of God's Holy Spirit so that we would be equipped and motivated to do his will.

MAY

14

Today in History—Paraguay declares freedom from Spain, 1811; Nazi attack destroys Rotterdam in World War II, 1940; U.S. Women's Army Auxiliary Corps (WAAC) founded, 1942; communist East European nations sign Warsaw pact for mutual defense, 1955; President Reagan denies pardon for Watergate criminals Jeb Magruder and E. Howard Hunt, 1983; Soviet leader Mikhail Gorbachev publicly discusses Chernobyl nuclear accident for first time, 1986.

Born Today—Physicist Gabriel Fahrenheit, 1686; painter Thomas Gainsborough, 1727; conductor Otto Klemperer, 1885; singer Patrice Munsel, 1925; musician Jack Bruce, 1943; director George Lucas, 1944; football player Mike Quick, 1959.

Today's Quotation—"America's present need is not heroics but healing. . . ."—*President Warren G. Harding, May 14, 1920*

God's Healing Power

A Christian woman once showed an unforgiving spirit toward another worker. This came to the attention of Rev. E. L. Hamilton who overheard her say, "Well, I'll forgive her but I'll have nothing to do with her again." At this point the preacher stepped in and said, "Is that how you want God to forgive you; by saying he will never have anything more to do with you?" The woman recognized anew God's healing power, how he forgives and forgets our sin.

It is said that while Leonard da Vinci was painting his masterpiece, "The Lord's Supper," he became quite angry with a certain man. Try as he might, he could not forget his anger as he prepared to paint the face of Jesus. Finally he became so perturbed that he sought out the man and asked his forgiveness. He immediately returned to the canvas and went on to give the Master's face the tender, delicate expression he knew it must have.

Have you experienced God's healing power in your life? It will make all things new.

Prayer Suggestion—Be grateful that the Great Physician can still heal all of our heartaches and heartbreaks when we call upon him.

MAY

15

Today in History—Ellen Church becomes first airline stewardess, 1930; nylon stockings first go on sale throughout U.S., 1940; Supreme Court Justice Abe Fortas resigns, 1969; two Jackson State College students killed by National Guardsmen, 1970; eleven die as fire sweeps through sixty-one row houses in Philadelphia following police bombing of radical group headquarters, 1985.

Born Today—Scientist Pierre Curie, 1859; actor Joseph Cotten, 1905; singer Eddy Arnold, 1918; photographer Richard Avedon, 1923; actress Anna Marie Alberghetti, 1936; actor Trini Lopez, 1937; baseball player George Brett, 1953.

Today's Quotation—"The wage paid to the working man must be sufficient for the support of himself and his family."—*Pope Pius XI, May 15, 1931*

Life's Wages

How much are you making? This applies not only to life's wages but to the wages of sin as well. A newly married couple was admiring the wealth of others when the young wife remarked wistfully, "Someday we'll be rich." Taking her hand the husband said gently, "Darling, we are rich. Someday we'll have money."

Indeed wages are far more than just money. In this life we are earning not only wages from our life's work but also, the Bible tells us, wages from sin. According to S. D. Gordon, "Sin pays its wages in kind . . . ," that is, sin against the body affects the body. Sin in contact with other people affects others. Gordon reminds us that "unless the blood of Jesus washes away the stain, sin pays in full," resulting in death of the body, mind, and soul. What a horrible prospect!

How closely are you following God? James 4:8 suggests, "Draw nigh to God, and he will draw nigh to you." That's the best way to avoid sin's deadly wages.

Prayer Suggestion—Have you so followed the Lord in your life that you have earned his reward, or are you collecting the wages of sin?

MAY

16

1 Corinthians 6:15–20

Today in History—Impeachment of President Andrew Johnson fails by one vote in Senate, 1868; first-class postal rate increases to eight cents per ounce, 1971; Helmut Schmidt named new Chancellor of West Germany, 1974; five killed in helicopter mishap atop Pan Am building in New York City, 1977; bloody riots sweep Iran posing strongest challenge to date for Shah Mohahmed Pahlevi, 1978; anti-alcohol drive launched in Russia, with drinking age raised to twenty-one, 1985.

Born Today—Statesman William Seward, 1801; actor Henry Fonda, 1905; band leader Woody Herman, 1913; baseball manager Billy Martin, 1928; author Warren Wiersbe, 1929; singer Lainie Kazan, 1940; actress Debra Winger, 1955.

Today's Quotation—"Some Americans need hyphens in their names because only part of them has come over."—*President Woodrow Wilson, May 16, 1914*

Fully Surrendered

How many people try to "straddle the fence" and still dabble in sin instead of "fully coming over" to God's side as completely surrendered Christians?

A dynamic missionary leader in India was once having dinner with several Navy officers. During the course of the meal one of the officers remarked, "Why don't all these missionaries stay home and mind their own business?" Wisely the missionary leader responded, "Suppose you were ordered to set sail tomorrow, would you choose whether or not to obey?" Quickly an officer replied, "If we are ordered to go, we must go, even if every ship is sunk and every sailor killed." "Quite right," said the missionary. "I have orders from God's divine government: Go and preach the gospel to every creature."

Who do you take your marching orders from: the forces of this world or the eternal God in heaven? Remember that life on earth is fleeting and that only what we accomplish for God will last throughout eternity.

Prayer Suggestion—Let go and let God take control of your life and then you will truly live.

MAY

17

Romans 12:9-18

Today in History—New York Stock Exchange founded, 1792; Conservative Baptist Association formed, 1947; U.S. Supreme Court declares racial segregation in public schools is unconstitutional, 1954; Senate panel begins Watergate hearings, 1973; Continental Illinois Bank receives $7.5 billion rescue loan and is put up for sale, 1984.

Born Today—Scientist Edward Jenner, 1749; Iranian leader Ayatollah Khomeini, 1900; actor Jean Gabin, 1904; actress Maureen O'Sullivan, 1911; lawyer Archibald Cox, 1912; Christian broadcaster Paul Ramseyer, 1927; actor Dennis Hopper, 1936; boxer Sugar Ray Leonard, 1956.

Today's Quotation—"Separate educational facilities are inherently unequal."—*Chief Justice Earl Warren, May 17, 1954*

Equal Education

The "help wanted" announcement in the Pullman *Washington Herald* read, "Wanted: state trooper applicants. Applicants must be six feet tall with a high school education or 5'11" with two years of college." They seemed to have discovered a link between physical size and education.

Apparently in the Army there is only one kind of education. A young man was being questioned by the recruiting sergeant and he was asked if he had gone to grammar school. "Yes, sir," smiled the recruit, "I have also graduated from college, and earned a Ph.D. from Harvard." Satisfied, the sergeant reached for a rubber stamp pad, inked it, and stamped the recruit's application with just one word, "literate."

We should be so filled with Christ's love that we become "kindly affectioned one to another" regardless of the individual's social status, education, or financial condition. With a hurting, dying world all around us, we need to be more like the Lord, full of compassion and understanding whenever he saw human need. As the prophet Isaiah wrote, "In all their affliction, he was afflicted" (Isa. 63:9).

Prayer Suggestion—That God would enable us to have compassion for those less fortunate than we by helping us see the needy as he sees them.

MAY

18

Ephesians 6:10–18

Today in History—Napoleon becomes emperor of France, 1804; Tennessee Valley Authority hydroelectric power system authorized, 1933; United Nations moves into its New York City headquarters, 1951; India triggers nuclear device becoming the sixth nation to do so, 1974; Menachem Begin elected Israel's prime minister, ending 29 years of opposition party rule, 1977; President Reagan undergoes surgery to remove benign intestinal polyp, 1984.

Born Today—Philosopher Bertrand Russell, 1872; director Frank Capra, 1897; musician Meredith Wilson, 1902; singer Perry Como, 1913; ballerina Dame Margot Fonteyn, 1919; baseball player Brooks Robinson, 1937; baseball player Reggie Jackson, 1946.

Today's Quotation—"Not only will we fight for democracy, we will make it more worth fighting for."—*Harold L. Ickes, May 18, 1941*

Fighting for the Right

Many people who are not otherwise militant would quickly become so if a gang of marauders with lighted torches came toward their property looking for them. Yet our greatest enemy, Satan, is roaming constantly, always on the lookout for another Christian whom he "may devour."

How strongly are *you* battling the deceptions of Satan? A father once took his young daughter to the beach, but couldn't convince her to enter the chilly water. Soon he had an idea. Finding some driftwood nearby, he carefully built a little fire and heated a pan of water. When it came to a rolling boil, he took it off the fire and dramatically poured the piping hot water into the ocean. This was sufficient for his young daughter who ran into the surf satisfied that the temperature was "okay." In the same way, Satan can trick us into thinking our "boiling kettle" of good works will dilute an "ocean" of sin and unbelief. Satan delights in trapping the unsuspecting. Be sure you are protected by God's armor to repel the darts of the wicked one.

Prayer Suggestion—That God would make us effective soldiers in his spiritual army and that we would remember to wear our armor every day.

MAY

19

Exodus 32:26–35

Today in History—Second wife of England's Henry VIII and mother of Queen Elizabeth I, Anne Boleyn, beheaded, 1536; Congress establishes national immigration quotas, 1921; Valery Gischard d'Estaing elected French president, 1974; eight dead in eruption of Mt. St. Helens, Wash., which sent ash spewing five hundred miles away, 1980; two Kentucky newspapers sold for $300 million, highest price yet paid for a media property, 1986.

Born Today—Philanthropist Johns Hopkins, 1795; explorer Carl Akeley, 1864; black leader Malcolm X, 1925; journalist James Lehrer, 1934; actor David Hartman, 1937; airline executive Frank Lorenzo, 1940; musician Peter Townshend, 1945.

Today's Quotation—"The ballot is stronger than the bullet."—
Abraham Lincoln, May 19, 1856

Casting Your Vote

One of the cornerstones of civilization is the concept that more is solved through negotiation and discussion than through armed conflict and hostilities. The same is true in the spiritual world. Have you actively surrendered all of your will to God ("voting" for him) or are you still fighting the forces of God?

General William Booth, founder of the Salvation Army, was once asked the secret of his success. He hesitated a moment, then tears came to his eyes as he said, "I'll tell you the secret; God has had all of me there was to have. There may have been men with greater opportunities, but from the day I got the poor on my heart and a vision of what Christ could do, I made up my mind that God would have all there was of William Booth. . . . God has all the adoration of my heart, all the power of my will and all the influence of my life."

Yes, the greatness of man's power is the measure of his surrender. Don't be satisfied with second best. Cast your vote for God and his kingdom today!

Prayer Suggestion—Recognize that the world is watching your every move. Pray that God would help you always to vote for him.

MAY

20

Today in History—Motion pictures shown publicly for first time, 1895; Charles A. Lindbergh begins first solo flight across Atlantic, arriving in Paris following day, 1927; Pan American Airways begins transatlantic passenger service, 1939; German air forces reach English Channel and encircle British, Belgian, and French troops in World War II, 1940; Nazi Germany captures island of Crete in first totally airborne invasion, World War II, 1941.

Born Today—Former First Lady Dolley Madison, 1768; economist John Stuart Mill, 1806; Supreme Court Justice John Marshall Harlan, 1899; actor James Stewart, 1908; Israeli leader Moshe Dayan, 1915; actor George Gobel, 1919; singer Peggy Lee, 1920.

Today's Quotation—"I claim we took a ——— of a beating."— *General Joseph "Vinegar Joe" Stilwell, May 20, 1942*

Self Defense

Many people today are experiencing a fear for their safety. It is not surprising then to see a heightened interest in self-defense. A young man once asked his pastor whether he felt it would be wrong to study self-defense. "Certainly not," said the preacher. "In fact I've learned it myself and found it to be of great value." "Oh really," asked the young man, "which system did you learn?" The pastor replied thoughtfully, "Solomon's system." "Solomon's system?" inquired the youth. "What do you mean?" The preacher said, "You'll find it in the fifteenth chapter of the book of Proverbs, 'A soft answer turneth away wrath.' It is the best system of self-defense I know."

When your spiritual enemy attacks, where will you find your defense? Hide God's Word in your heart now so that you may fend off Satan's deadly blows.

Prayer Suggestion—That we would be ever-vigilant, always on the alert for Satan's attack, and ready to defend what is right.

MAY
21

Today in History—American National Red Cross founded by Clara Barton, 1881; Charles Lindbergh lands in Paris after the first solo flight across Atlantic, 1927; first test explosion of airborne hydrogen bomb conducted by U.S., 1956; Sirhan Sirhan sentenced to death for murder of Senator Robert F. Kennedy, 1969.

Born Today—Spain's King Philip II, 1527; writer Alexander Pope, 1688; reformer Elizabeth Fry, 1780; aviator Glenn Curtiss, 1878; financier Armand Hammer, 1898; actor Raymond Burr, 1917; author Robert Creeley, 1926.

Today's Quotation—"A boy has two jobs. One is just being a boy. The other is growing up to be a man."—*Herbert Hoover, May 21, 1956*

The Boy Becomes a Man

What a transformation occurs before our eyes as a youngster matures from boyhood into manhood. The *Sunday School Times* captured the parent's responsibility in this verse entitled "The Two Prayers":*

> Last night my little boy confessed to me some childish wrong;
> And kneeling at my knee he prayed with tears;
> "Dear God, make me a man like Daddy—wise and strong;
> I know you can."

> Then while he slept I knelt beside his bed,
> Confessed my sins, and prayed with low-bowed head,
> "O God, make me a child like my child here—
> Pure, guileless, trusting Thee with faith sincere."

Prayer Suggestion—That we would raise our youth to become godly men by setting an example before them of Christ at work in our life.

---

*Quoted in *Three Thousand Illustrations for Christian Service*, Walter B. Knight, Grand Rapids, William B. Eerdmans, 1947, p. 110.

MAY

22

Today in History—First life insurance policy in America is issued by Presbyterian group in Philadelphia, 1761; the Truman Doctrine goes into effect with grant of $400 million for aid to Turkey and Greece, 1947; Iraqi missile in Persian Gulf hits *U.S.S. Stark* killing thirty-seven crewmen in resulting explosion and fire, 1987.

Born Today—Composer Richard Wagner, 1813; writer Sir Arthur Conan Doyle, 1859; actor Sir Laurence Olivier, 1907; critic Judith Crist, 1922; actor Richard Benjamin, 1938; actress Susan Strasberg, 1938.

Today's Quotation—"The great society is a place where men are more concerned with the quality of their goals than the quantity of their goods."—*Lyndon B. Johnson, May 22, 1964*

God's Great Society

Nothing in this life begins to compare with the great "heavenly society" God has prepared for those who love him. A poor youngster in London was left in the care of a cruel, drunken woman who forced him to beg. When he didn't bring home enough coins, he was beaten and mistreated. The youngster's greatest joy in life was to look at the many beautiful things displayed in the store windows he passed. But he knew these things were not for him as there was always the window between. Yet the toy soldiers looked so inviting—except for the glass. One day the unfortunate lad was run over by a passing motorist. He was rushed to a hospital where he was placed in a snow-white bed. Following several days in a coma, the lad woke and could see other children recovering nearby. Looking around he could scarcely believe his eyes as he noticed there was a box of toy soldiers there just for him! Slowly, he reached into the box and took out the soldiers one by one, exclaiming, "There's no glass between!"

Imagine the joy we will experience in God's "heavenly society" when we will no longer "see through a glass, darkly, but then face to face."

Prayer Suggestion—Praise God for the glories of heaven!

MAY

23

Matthew 5:3–10

Today in History—South Carolina is eighth state to ratify U.S. Constitution, 1788; New York Public Library dedicated, 1911; U.S. Navy submarine *Squalus* sinks off New England with loss of twenty-six lives, 1939; Israel announces capture of Nazi leader Adolf Eichmann, 1960.

Born Today—Botanist Carolus Linnaeus, 1707; engineer James Buchanan Eads, 1820; painter Marie Cassatt, 1845; musician Artie Shaw, 1910; singer Rosemary Clooney, 1928; inventor Robert Moog, 1934; fighter Marvin Hagler, 1952.

Today's Quotation—"No one can worship God or love his neighbor on an empty stomach."—*Woodrow Wilson, May 23, 1912*

Feed the Hungry

A story was told in the *Methodist Recorder* of former mayor of New York City, Fiorello La Guardia. He was presiding over a police court one day before becoming mayor, when they brought in a troubled old man who was charged with stealing a loaf of bread to feed his starving family. After hearing the case, La Guardia found the man guilty and reluctantly fined him ten dollars. Then, reaching into his own pocket, La Guardia pulled out a ten dollar bill saying, "And I hereby pay the fine in full." But he was not done. The mayor then ordered the bailiff to fine everyone in the courtroom fifty cents for living in a town where a man had to steal in order to survive. After the hat was passed, the grateful old man left the courtroom with forty-seven dollars and fifty cents—more than a week's wage in those days.

How sensitive are we to the plight of the hungry and homeless in our community? Let us never forget that it was with these poor souls that Jesus spent most of his days on earth. Can we love our fellow man any less?

Prayer Suggestion—Ask God to put someone in your heart that you can love to him.

160

MAY

24

2 Corinthians 9:6–10, 15

Today in History—Samuel F. B. Morse sends first telegraph message, 1844; first major league night baseball game in Cincinnati, 1935; world's largest battleship, Britain's *H.M.S. Hood,* sunk by Germans in World War II, 1941; Iran claims biggest victory yet in war with Iraq, 1982; Iran fires on oil tanker, ignoring Arab League warnings, 1984; West Germany launches joint investigation with Israel to find Nazi war criminal Joseph Mengele, 1985.

Born Today—Queen Victoria, 1819; publisher Samuel Newhouse, 1895; politician Coleman Young, 1918; singer Bob Dylan, 1941; puppeteer Frank Oz, 1944; evangelist Jose Reyes, 1945; actress Priscilla Presley, 1946.

Today's Quotation—"What hath God wrought!"—*Samuel F. B. Morse, May 24, 1844*

What God Hath Wrought

Witnessing has been defined as "one beggar telling another beggar where to find bread (the Bread of Life)." A Catholic priest stood before his parishioners one Sunday morning to announce that he was resigning. He then explained, "Last night, I could not get to sleep and so, turning to the New Testament, I saw that salvation is in Jesus Christ, and is in the gift of God's eternal love. Indeed, penance is not salvation, nor is purgatory or absolution." He continued describing his salvation experience for more than an hour. He closed by inviting the congregation to accept God's gift of salvation as he had done. There was a nearly unanimous response as the faithful witness of what God had wrought in his life moved scores to accept Christ as Savior.

God has left us here on earth to be faithful to tell others of him. Believer, how faithful are you in telling others what Christ has done in your life?

Prayer Suggestion—Thank God for his great gift of salvation and life eternal with him in heaven. Share the good news with others.

MAY

25

Acts 4:10-12

Today in History—American Sunday School Union established, 1824; Babe Ruth hit his last home run, 1935; Jordan Independence Day declared, 1946; Shanghai is occupied by Chinese Communist forces, 1949; former labor secretary Raymond Donovan is acquitted of charges of fraud and grand larceny, 1987.

Born Today—Poet Ralph Waldo Emerson, 1803; aviation designer Igor Sikorsky, 1889; Premier Tito of Yugoslavia, 1892; actor Claude Akins, 1918; trumpeter Miles Davis, 1926; singer Beverly Sills, 1929; singer Leslie Uggams, 1943.

Today's Quotation—"There has been entirely too much deliberation and not enough speed."—*Supreme Court Justice Hugo L. Black, May 25, 1964*

Deliberately Lost

A story is told of a godly doctor who once called upon one of his elderly patients who refused to accept Jesus into his life. After examining the patient, the doctor issued some medication for his bronchitis and then turned to leave. The man's wife asked when her husband was to take the medicine. "Well, let's see," said the doctor. "He's not very sick, so maybe he should begin to take it a month from today." Astonished, the woman cried, "A month from today, why he could be dead by then!" "It's not very likely," said the doctor. "Besides if he feels poorly, you'll have the medicine here and he can take it anytime." Overhearing their talk, the man told the doctor, "But sir, I had hoped to begin taking it right away." "Well then, take it now if you wish," said the doctor. "I was simply trying to show you how strange it is to hear you put off taking God's prescription for your sin-sick soul. After all, you could be dead tomorrow."

How many people who thought they'd repent at the eleventh hour, die at ten o'clock? Have you taken God's remedy for sin? If not, do so today.

Prayer Suggestion—Repent of your sin and ask God to forgive you for your unrighteousness. Then share what God has done for you with others.

162

MAY

26

1 John 5:2–10

Today in History—Explosion aboard U.S. Navy aircraft carrier *Bennington* kills more than 100 crewmen, 1954; Iran's Ayatollah Khomeini accuses U.S. of trying to kill top Iranian official, which U.S. denies, 1979; Italy's prime minister and cabinet resign over story of hundreds of government officials being linked to illegal organization, 1981.

Born Today—Singer Al Jolson, 1886; actor John Wayne, 1907; actor James Arness, 1923; sportscaster Brent Musburger, 1939; actress Vickie Lawrence, 1949; singer Hank Williams, Jr., 1949; astronaut Sally Ride, 1951.

Today's Quotation—"The British and American fleets cannot appear on the oceans. . . . The Japanese people can look forward to a triumphal march into London and a victory march in New York."—*Radio Tokyo, May 26, 1942*

Victory

How different the world would be today if the other side had gained the victory in World War II! It was, no doubt, the prayers of thousands of God's people which contributed to the Allied victory. What are you relying on for victory in your life? The *Sunday School Times* once ran the story of an old lady who observed, "Did you ever notice that when the Lord told the discouraged fishermen to cast their nets again, it was right in the middle of the same old place where they had caught nothing?" Have you ever felt, "If only I could be someone else, go somewhere else, or do something else it might not be so difficult to have courage and faith." But for most of us, today will bring us "the same old thing"—the same old faults, the same old temptations to overcome, and the trials and tribulations we have faced before.

Remember it is Christ who helps us win despite life's distressing, heartbreaking failures. Regardless of how you may feel, remember, "We are more than conquerors through him that loved us" (Rom. 8:37).

Prayer Suggestion—That God would renew your determination and strength and help you to see that you are victorious through his grace.

163

MAY

27

Today in History—Achsah Young is hanged as a witch in first recorded execution of this kind in Massachusetts, 1647; Afghanistan Independence Day marks independence from Britain, 1919; German battleship *Bismarck* sunk by British naval force in World War II, 1941; Monaco's Princess Caroline marries French businessman Phillipe Junot, 1978; up to ten thousand feared dead in devastating cyclone in Bangladesh (250,000 are homeless), 1985.

Born Today—Author Julia Ward Howe, 1819; writer Rachel Carson, 1907; former Vice President Hubert Humphrey, 1911; writer Henry Wouk, 1915; political advisor Henry Kissinger, 1923; government official William Sessions, 1930; actor Lou Gossett, Jr., 1936.

Today's Quotation—"The natural progress of things is for liberty to yield and government to gain ground."—*Thomas Jefferson, May 27, 1788*

Christian Liberty

There was once a race car driver who could drive his car at breathtaking speeds. He had won all the great races of Europe and yet was a complete gentleman on the highway. Young men would frequently drive up beside him, revving their engines hoping to lure him into a race, but he never gave in. In fact, if he noticed someone was edging around him to pass, he would deliberately drive beneath the speed limit, sacrificing his pride to be a good example. He could have passed them all in a flash, yet he held his talents in check so that he would not break the laws of humanity.

Likewise all Christians stand before God in Christian liberty; free to do whatever they choose, but bound by a love for God to do only those things which are pleasing to him. Have you surrendered your will fully to him?

Prayer Suggestion—Help us to be as "wise as serpents and harmless as doves," serving our Lord in a spirit of Christian liberty.

MAY

28

Today in History—Japanese fleet defeats Imperial Russian Navy in Russo-Japanese War, 1905; Dionne quintuplets, first to survive, are born, 1934; in period roughly from today to June 4, more than three hundred thousand Allied forces are evacuated from Dunkirk, France, to England in World War II, 1940; Britain's abdicated king, the Duke of Windsor, dies near Paris at age 77, 1972.

Born Today—Statesman William Pitt, 1759; poet Thomas More, 1779; naturalist Jean Louis Agassiz, 1807; athlete Jim Thorpe, 1888; actress Caroll Baker, 1931; Dionne quintuplets, 1934; singer Gladys Knight, 1944; baseball player Kirk Gibson, 1957.

Today's Quotation—"Banking establishments are more dangerous than standing armies. . . ."—*Thomas Jefferson, May 28, 1816*

Banking On It

Shortly after the death of Howard Hughes, someone asked a reporter how much money the multi-millionaire had left behind. "Why, he left it all," was the quick reply. Since we can't take money with us there seems little point in spending so much time in its pursuit.

There's a story told of a man who once walked into a bank and asked to take out a loan for five dollars. When told the bank did not lend such small amounts, the man protested, "Lending money is your business, isn't it?" At last the banker agreed, drew up an agreement, and collected thirty cents in interest. The stranger then turned over his security: government bonds totaling ten thousand dollars! Before the stunned banker could respond, the man said, "Now, this is more like it. At the other bank they wanted ten dollars for a safe deposit box just to keep these things in!" The borrower clearly had a balanced outlook on money. He had it, but it didn't "have" him.

Remember, all that we have or ever will have comes from God who owns all things. We are but temporary managers here on earth of the things he has allowed us to have.

Prayer Suggestion—Praise God for letting us manage his possessions here on earth. May we be good stewards of the blessings he provides.

MAY

29

Today in History—Rhode Island becomes thirteenth state to ratify Constitution, 1790; Wisconsin admitted as thirtieth state, 1848; President Nixon concludes a week-long summit conference in Moscow, 1972; U.S. grounds all DC-10 aircraft following crash four days earlier of DC-10 in Chicago, 1979.

Born Today—Statesman Patrick Henry, 1736; author Gilbert Chesterton, 1874; comedian Bob Hope, 1903; President John F. Kennedy, 1917; biologist Paul Ehrlich, 1932; driver Al Unser, 1939.

Today's Quotation—"Let us have peace."—*Ulysses S. Grant, May 29, 1868*

Personal Peace

What is said to be the oldest comedy in literature, "The Acharnians," centers around the plight of an honest citizen, who, disgusted at the wars going on around him, makes peace with the enemy forces. This leaves him to enjoy the blessings of peace singlehandedly while all around him are at war. That is what happens to the believer who enjoys the blessings of Christ while the world is continuing its downward spiral into the slavery of sin.

In considering the things of this earth it is important that we keep all things in proper perspective. A lady once stopped by the parsonage to see the pastor. While waiting for him she struck up a conversation with his two small sons who were playing joyfully on the floor with some toys. "Tell me, boys, are these your treasures?" she asked pointing to their toys. "Oh no, ma'am," they hastily responded. "These are just our playthings. Our treasures are laid up in heaven." They had life's valuables in the proper perspective.

Whatever love, or kindness, or faith we can give another in Jesus' name, will be among our cherished treasures when we get to heaven, where they will be enjoyed forever.

Prayer Suggestion—Help us to see the things of this life through God's eyes with eternity's values in view.

MAY

30

1 Samuel 3:1-9

Today in History—Joan of Arc burned at the stake in Rouen, France, 1431; House Judiciary Committee warns Richard Nixon that refusal to turn over tapes of White House conversations may be grounds for impeachment, 1974; West German teenager, Mathias Rust, flies unhindered from Germany landing in Moscow's Red Square and the Russian defense minister is fired shortly thereafter, 1987.

Born Today—Tsar Peter the Great, 1672; politician James Farley, 1888; vocal actor Mel Blanc, 1908; musician Benny Goodman, 1909; actor Clint Walker, 1927; football player Gale Sayers, 1940.

Today's Quotation—". . . my voices were of God; my voices have not deceived me."—*Joan of Arc, May 30, 1431*

God's Voice

In helping others, who are we serving? Ourselves or God? There once was a young man who volunteered to teach a class of boys in Sunday school. They enjoyed their teacher's kindness and friendship, but it wasn't long before the young teacher grew tired of the responsibility and vowed to quit. Before his last class he neared the room where he overheard a conversation between two of his students. The first boy said he planned to stop coming to class because the teacher was going to quit soon anyway. The other youth spoke up, "Why, he won't quit the class. He told us that God had sent him to teach us and that God was his boss and he had to do his will—he won't give it up." Needless to say, after hearing this conversation, the young man decided to remain as teacher of the class.

How often are we tempted to just give up despite the knowledge that God has called us to serve him and that he will empower us with the strength we need to do his will. We need merely to be surrendered to him. Are you trusting God to carry you through?

Prayer Suggestion—Ask God to direct your path and lead you on to do his will.

167

MAY

31

Today in History—Johnstown flood kills more than two thousand people near Johnstown, Pa., 1889; British Navy drives the German fleet back from the North Sea, 1916; Nazi leader Adolf Eichmann is hanged by Israel, 1962; Argentine forces are making a final stand in the Falkland Island conflict with Britain after a month-long sea battle, 1982.

Born Today—Poet Walt Whitman, 1819; children's author Elizabeth Coatsworth, 1893; clergyman Norman Vincent Peale, 1898; actor Clint Eastwood, 1930; envoy Terry Waite, 1939; football player Joe Namath, 1943; author Theodore Baehr, 1946.

Today's Quotation—"Here in America we are descended in blood and in spirit from revolutionists and rebels. . . ."—*Dwight D. Eisenhower, May 31, 1954*

Descendants

America is unique among nations in that it has been built largely by immigrants from other nations. Since most of us are descended from this group, we resemble our ancestors not only in rebelling against tyranny but also in seeking a better life. Such identification may extend to our day-to-day relationships as well.

Baron Rothschild was once given a letter of introduction for a young man who was visiting London. The famed banker stated that he regretted not having a position, and walked the man to the door, pointing out various items along the way. But the young man wouldn't be put off so easily. Later that day, he returned to the bank's personnel director to again apply for a job. He was asked, "Weren't you the young man who was walking with the baron this morning?" The youth agreed that he was. "Well, then," said the banker, "you were in good company. We'll consider that a sufficient recommendation."

In the same way all believers know that they are descendants of God, through adoption into his heavenly family. Are you a child of God? If not, believe that Christ died for you and trust him today as your personal Savior.

Prayer Suggestion—Thank God for your heritage as a child of God, realizing you are truly a child of the King of kings!

JUNE

1

Today in History—Kentucky admitted to U.S. as fifteenth state, 1792; Tennessee admitted to U.S. as sixteenth state, 1792; Irish force invades Canada from U.S. and seizes Fort Erie and then surrenders next day to U.S. forces, 1866; British star Leslie Howard killed when German aircraft downed his transport plane en route from Lisbon to London in World War II, 1943; Tunisia National Day marks signing of that nation's constitution, 1959; Cuban refugees riot over conditions at Ft. Chaffee, Ark., 1980; inventor of TV ratings, Charles Nielsen, dies at age 83, 1980.

Born Today—Explorer Pere Marquette, 1637; poet laureate John Masefield, 1878; playwright John Drinkwater, 1882; actor Andy Griffith, 1926; singer Pat Boone, 1934; actor Cleavon Little, 1939.

Today's Quotation—"Don't give up the ship!"—*Captain James Lawrence, June 1, 1813*

Persistence

The late evangelist John R. Rice told the story of how a group in Texas once warned him that if he did not give up a certain ministry activity his name would be blacklisted in their churches. Feeling that the Lord could take care of his own, the great preacher went on about his ministry, unfazed by the criticism of these good, but misguided men. "Thank God," Dr. Rice would later say, "more doors have opened, wider usefulness has come my way, as I disregarded men and tried to be true to Jesus Christ."

Are you discouraged by the criticism of other, well-meaning people and ready to give in because of the pressure? Heed the words of the apostle Paul, "And let us not be weary in well doing: for in due season we shall reap, if we faint not" (Gal. 6:9).

Prayer Suggestion—May God give us the strength to persist in spite of all of life's obstacles.

JUNE

2

John 19:25-27

Today in History—Great Britain awards first radio patent to Guglielmo Marconi, 1896; Battle of Warsaw Ghetto ends, 1943; Italy Republic Day commemorates vote to form republic, 1946; Elizabeth II crowned Queen of Great Britain, 1953; final report of assassination commission backs plot theory against John F. Kennedy's life, 1979; Alan Greenspan named to replace Paul Volker as head of Federal Reserve Board, 1987.

Born Today—Writer Thomas Hardy, 1840; composer Sir Edward Elgar, 1857; swimmer Johnny Weissmuller, 1904; astronaut Charles Conrad, Jr., 1930; actress Sally Kellerman, 1936; composer Marvin Hamlisch, 1944; actor Jerry Mathers, 1948.

Today's Quotation—"Is there a free nation that would restrict the right of its citizens to migrate in search of greater opportunities?"— *Alexander B. Trowbridge, June 2, 1967*

Homing Instincts

Though many a young man has ventured out on his own in search of the better life, it is most often home where the memories are fondest. The writer of the song "Home Sweet Home," John Howard Payne, once related how he came to write those words. He was a drifter walking the exclusive neighborhoods of London as the words came to him. Years later, after the song became well known, Payne again found himself walking the London streets. Many a time he heard the words of his song come wafting from a luxurious townhouse window, while he, cold and lonely, had no bed to call his own.

It is not only humans who are attracted to thoughts of home, for the same principle applies throughout much of the animal kingdom as well. A bee taken from its hive knows its way home. Migrating birds instinctively return to their homelands every year. Dogs and cats taken from their homes will often return to their place of birth sometimes hundreds of miles away.

God has placed within each of us a special "homing instinct" that calls us back to our family and home. Spiritually as well, God lovingly beckons us to him. Are you following his lead and returning to him?

Prayer Suggestion—May we so live our lives that we feel at home with the people of God and feel loved when standing in his presence.

JUNE

3

John 13:13-20

Today in History—Dutch West India Company receives patent to what is now New York, 1621; Reserve Officers Training Corps established by act of Congress, 1916; Duke of Windsor marries Mrs. Wallis Simpson, for whom he had abdicated British throne, 1937; U.S. routs Japanese fleet in Battle of Midway, 1942; Italy ratifies agreement with Vatican ending Roman Catholicism as state religion, 1985.

Born Today—Author William Hone, 1780; Confederate President Jefferson Davis, 1808; physician Charles Drew, 1904; actor Tony Curtis, 1925; actress Colleen Dewhurst, 1926; poet Allen Ginsberg, 1926.

Today's Quotation—"I pledge you, I pledge myself, to a new deal for the American people."—*Franklin D. Roosevelt, June 3, 1932*

A New Deal from God

Often God lets us exhaust all human resources before coming to our aid. Captain Edward Rickenbacker tells of just such supernatural provision as he describes his twenty-one days adrift at sea. In bailing out of their crippled plane, the eight men managed to take with them only four small oranges as their sole source of food. These soon disappeared and the men sought help from God through prayer. Within an hour of one prayer meeting, a seagull landed near one of the life boats. Before long the bird was carved up, cooked, and devoured by the hungry crew. Fashioning crude fish hooks with the gull's remains, they were able to catch two fish. Later, they caught some rain water which provided two sips of water per man each day. Finally, after a grueling three weeks of drifting, a passing airplane rescued the stranded airmen.

Why did God allow them to remain adrift for so long, waiting three long weeks before allowing their rescue? It might be for no other reason than that we might recognize his assistance and providence as a result of reading about it today.

Prayer Suggestion—Tell God how much you love him for his bountiful provision and goodness in first loving us.

171

JUNE

4

Today in History—Roquefort cheese discovered near Roquefort, France, 1070; Rome liberated from Nazis in World War II by U.S. and British forces, 1944; Tonga becomes independent nation in British Commonwealth, 1970; Anne Morrow Lindbergh arrives in Paris for fiftieth anniversary of husband's epic flight, 1977; Supreme Court strikes down Alabama law permitting a "moment of silence" in public schools, 1985.

Born Today—Britain's King George III, 1738; Finland's Field Marshal Manneheim, 1867; opera singer Robert Merrill, 1919; actor Dennis Weaver, 1924; tennis player Andrea Jaeger, 1965.

Today's Quotation—"Why doesn't somebody do something? A voice from my subconscious answered: You are that somebody."—*Elreta Alexander, June 4, 1976*

Doing Something for God

A little boy was having problems with falling out of bed. It seemed that no matter what his parents tried, the little fellow would roll out onto the floor in the middle of the night. One night an uncle came to visit and asked the youngster why he fell out so frequently. The lad thought a moment and then replied, "I don't know unless it is that I stay too close to where I get in."

That describes the problem with many Christians today. Yes, they are believers, but they are staying so close to where they got in that they are doing little for him. Industrialist Charles F. Kettering was once quoted as saying: "I don't want any fellow 'who has a job' working for me." Rather Kettering sought "a fellow whom a job has."

The distinction is important, especially in service for God. Rather than being content to simply put in our time as a Christian, we need to be so consumed with doing something for him that it becomes the driving force in our life day after day.

Prayer Suggestion—That others would see Christ reflected from our lifestyle of actively serving him.

JUNE

5

Daniel 16:4–27

Today in History—First hot-air balloon flight lasts ten minutes, rising a distance of about seventy-five hundred feet in Annonay, France, 1783; Danish Constitution Day marks adoption of that country's basic law, 1849; Marshall Plan proposed to aid Europe, 1947; Israel defeats Egypt, Syria, and Jordan in six-day war, June 5–10, 1967; Senator Robert Kennedy is shot in Los Angeles, 1968; Suez Canal opens for first time since 1967 Arab-Israeli War, 1975; Queen Elizabeth II celebrates twenty-five years as British monarch, 1977.

Born Today—Economist Adam Smith, 1723; economist John Maynard Keynes, 1883; director Tony Richardson, 1928; actor Robert Lansing, 1929; journalist Bill Moyers, 1934.

Today's Quotation—"If nominated, I will not accept; if elected, I will not serve."—*General William T. Sherman, June 5, 1884*

Steadfast Determination

In politics, as in religion, it is necessary to state what we believe and to stand firm on that belief despite the opposition. A traveler was once treading a lonely jungle path in the darkness of night when he was confronted by a man coming from the opposite direction. "Do you know the bridge is gone?" the man asked. "No," the traveler answered, "why do you think it so?" "I heard a report to that effect this afternoon, though I am not really sure it is true," said the man halfheartedly. Unconvinced, the traveler proceeded on toward the gorge and the rushing river below. Just as he neared the canyon he encountered a second man who exclaimed, "Sir, the bridge is out. I was just there and barely escaped with my life!" Convinced by the urgency of his cry and his earnest gestures the traveler turned back and was saved.

What had made the difference? The steadfast determination of the second man who was unshakable in his knowledge of the missing bridge.

When we represent the Lord how determined are we? Are we known for our unyielding stand for God and right?

Prayer Suggestion—May God help us to so live that others will always see Christ reflected in our lifestyle and actions.

JUNE

6

Psalm 37:35–40

Today in History—Y.M.C.A. (Young Men's Christian Association) founded in London, 1844; first U.S. victory over Germans in World War I, Battle of Belleau Wood, fought June 6–25, 1918; Securities and Exchange Commission established, 1934; D-Day: Allies begin World War II invasion of Normandy, 1944; Senator Robert Kennedy dies of assassin's bullet in Los Angeles, 1968; Proposition 13 approved in California (will trim $7 billion from property tax revenues), 1978.

Born Today—Patriot Nathan Hale, 1755; writer Thomas Mann, 1875; physician Paul White, 1896; composer Aram Khachaturian, 1903; politician George Deukmejian, 1928; tennis player Bjorn Borg, 1956.

Today's Quotation—"Every bullet has its billet."—*Attributed to William III by John Wesley, June 6, 1765*

God's Invisible Shield

In order to win the battle, the bullet must reach its intended target. Likewise, if Satan is to defeat the Christian he must strike with deadly accuracy at the believer's weakest point. Fortunately God protects us. Often we do not fully know how much he has shielded us from harm.

The offering had just been taken and the prayer of dedication given at a church when a robber came forward and took it. Church officials followed the man and a scuffle broke out. Suddenly the robber pulled a gun on the ushers and pulled the trigger. Miraculously the gun did not fire! Checking the gun later, police discovered it was loaded and there was no reason for it not to shoot. Perhaps it was God's "invisible shield" serving as a barrier to protect his people from harm.

That brings to mind the story of Daniel in the den of lions. He had been faithful to God and God honored him in his hour of need and kept the lions' mouths sealed. God hasn't changed; he stands ready to meet our needs and carry us through the day's trials if we just trust in him.

Prayer Suggestion—Call upon God for his strength to carry you through the burdens you are facing today. God has power to help!

JUNE

7

Daniel 1:8-20

Today in History—Daniel Boone begins exploring Kentucky, 1769; Japan occupies Alaska's Attu and Kiska islands in World War II, 1942; Eduard Benes, president of Czechoslovakia, refuses to sign communist constitution, 1948; Israeli planes demolish Iraqi nuclear reactor, 1981; U.S. closes six Nicaraguan consulates and expels twenty-one of their diplomats in response to their expulsion of U.S. personnel, 1983.

Born Today—Fashion's Beau Brummell, 1778; artist Paul Gauguin, 1848; conductor George Szell, 1897; author Robert Cook, 1912; poet Gwendolyn Brooks, 1917; boxer Rocky Graziano, 1922; Christian broadcaster Paul Holling, 1935; poet Nikki Giovanni, 1943.

Today's Quotation—"Man stands to revere, he kneels to pray."— *Henry David Thoreau, June 7, 1841*

A Servant of God

A southern gentleman once asked how he could recognize George Washington at a meeting of the Continental Congress. The gentleman was told, "General Washington is the man who kneels when the Continental Congress stops for prayer." What a fine way to be remembered—as the person who kneels to pray!

Another man of humble spirit was the great missionary Hudson Taylor, who was introduced at a crowded meeting as "our illustrious guest." After the applause subsided, Taylor slowly rose, the light of Christ shining in his face, and said, "Dear friends, I am only the little servant of an illustrious Master."

It often does us well to consider our humble roots, lest pride overtake us. Visitors to the famed Thomas Road Baptist Church are often amazed to discover that the congregation, now numbering in the tens of thousands, began with just thirty-five people meeting in a defunct bottling plant. So that no one would forget the church's humble beginnings, a plaque has been placed on the tiny building, still standing, from which this great church began. Lest we become proud, let us recall where we were when God rescued us from the depths of sin.

Prayer Suggestion—May we be known as people of prayer, those who humble themselves in service to God and man.

JUNE

8

1 John 5:1–5

Today in History—Britain's George VI and Elizabeth first British monarchs to visit U.S., 1939; U.S. forces authorized to go into combat against Vietcong in South Vietnam, 1965; James Earl Ray arrested for murder of Dr. Martin Luther King, Jr., 1968; Polish leaders warned by Soviets to "toughen stance" against rebels, 1981; President Reagan gives first presidential address to British Parliament, 1982.

Born Today—Composer Robert Schumann, 1810; architect Frank Lloyd Wright, 1867; Supreme Court Justice Byron White, 1917; First Lady Barbara Bush, 1925; singer James Darren, 1936; actress Nancy Sinatra, 1940.

Today's Quotation—"Our best protection against bigger government in Washington is better government in the states."—*Dwight D. Eisenhower, June 8, 1964*

Self-control

Just as in a maturing democracy, where power is transferred to local authorities, so too as individuals mature into adulthood, they rely more on self-control and less on outside authority. This is especially true in spiritual matters.

A missionary asked a young man who had recently been converted to describe how he felt. The man replied, tapping himself on the chest, "Two dogs are always fighting inside there. The one is a good dog, the other is a bad dog, and they fight all the time." The missionary explained that believers still have the old sin nature to deal with after they become saved and so he asked the convert, "Which dog wins when they fight?" The young convert replied, "The one I say, 'Sic 'em' to."

Yes, a Christian can live in victory over daily sins, but he must realize he still has to grapple with the old sin nature. However, with God's help we can have victory over sin. The decision as to which nature will dominate is up to us. We are the ones who determine which side will triumph. Which side are you saying "Sic 'em" to?

Prayer Suggestion—Help us to live and do what is right through God's strength.

JUNE

9

Today in History—President Eisenhower undergoes operation on his small intestine, 1956; U.S. Navy's first ballistic missile submarine, the *George Washington*, is launched, 1959; Senate confirms appointment of Warren Burger as chief justice, 1969; Mormons move to allow black men into the priesthood, 1978; Margaret Thatcher elected decisively to second five-year term as Britain's prime minister, 1983; presidential commission says *Challenger* disaster was caused by failure of a joint on the solid rocket, 1986; Lt. Col. Oliver North's secretary tells how she helped her boss in the Contra aid endeavor, 1987.

Born Today—Playwright John Howard Payne, 1791; composer Cole Porter, 1893; conductor Fred Waring, 1900; actor Robert Cummings, 1910; musician Les Paul, 1916; writer George Axelrod, 1922; broadcast journalist Marvin Kalb, 1930; actor Michael J. Fox, 1961.

Today's Quotation—"Oh promise me that someday you and I. . . ."— *song lyric by Clement Scott, June 9, 1891*

A Godly Love

The words of this romantic song of bygone years recall to mind the story of the poor young farmer who had little of this world's wealth. He had almost no education and his influence was unlikely to ever extend much beyond the local community. Yet this man was blessed with a godly, loving wife "radiant in face and beautiful in form . . . who loved her husband with a great outpouring of service, admiration and delight." Reflecting on this story, Dr. John R. Rice said, "I thought to myself how blessed he is. No king on the throne could have healthier, happier, more beautiful children, nor be better taught or better mannered. That young farmer was not poor. He was rich beyond expression. God had flooded his life with 'loving-kindness and tender mercies.' "

What a blessing from God—a loving spouse and family which only he could bring together!

Prayer Suggestion—Thank God for his great love in allowing us to have a taste of heaven here on earth within godly, loving families.

JUNE

10

Today in History—Italy attacks France as Nazis crush that nation in World War II, 1940; Nazis destroy town of Lidice, Czechoslovakia, in retaliation for Czech killing of Gestapo leader Reinhard Heydrich, 1942; Italy formally becomes a republic, 1946; Socialists and Social Democrats each win twenty-five percent in first-ever direct vote for seats in European Parliament, 1979; Pope John Paul II says mass for over one million Poles in his former homeland, 1979; Israelis begin withdrawing from Lebanon after three years of fighting, 1985.

Born Today—Actor Sessue Hayakawa, 1890; composer Frederick Loewe, 1904; England's Prince Philip, 1921; singer Judy Garland, 1922; lawyer F. Lee Bailey, 1933; author Jeff Greenfield, 1943.

Today's Quotation—". . . the hand that held the dagger has stuck it into the back of its neighbor."—*President Franklin D. Roosevelt, June 10, 1940*

Trust

We all like someone we can trust, someone whose life consistently reflects what they say with their lips. An American was once hired to teach in a Japanese school. As part of the arrangement, the man, a godly believer, had to agree not to mention Christianity during the school day and the man kept his word. However so consistent was his life and so Christlike his example that unknown to him, forty of his students publicly denounced their idolatry.

We never know who may be influenced by observing our life. Preacher Robert Murray McCheyne received a letter from one of his converts which read, "It was nothing you said which made me wish to be a Christian; rather it was the beauty of holiness I saw in your face." McCheyne had reached the goal, for his conduct was consistent with his creed. He reflected the love of Christ in his every move.

Be thankful we have an unchanging God in whom we can always trust.

Prayer Suggestion—Trust Christ to be your Savior and forgive your sins today, then your life will be transformed, consistent, and new.

JUNE

11

Matthew 6:19–21

Today in History—First U.S. Distinguished Flying Cross given to Charles Lindbergh, 1927; actor John Wayne dies of cancer at age 72, 1979; Lt. Col. Oliver North testifies that Iranian arms sale and diversion of funds to the Nicaraguan Contras was directed by officials inside the White House, 1987.

Born Today—Artist John Constable, 1776; composer Richard Strauss, 1864; writer William Styron, 1925; actor Chad Everett, 1936; driver Jackie Stewart, 1939; actor Gene Wilder, 1939; football player Joe Montana, 1956.

Today's Quotation—"Prosperity is only an instrument to be used, not a deity to be worshipped."—*Calvin Coolidge, June 11, 1928*

Prosperity

In what do you put your trust? Henry Ford's mansion in Dearborn, Michigan, built in 1917 at a cost of over one million dollars, stands as a monument to the great industrialist's prosperity. It had fifty-three rooms and thirty-one thousand square feet on three floors overlooking the meandering Rouge River. The home was powered by its own generators providing current to 550 switches for light at the flick of a finger. The generators operated continuously from when the home was completed until one rainy night in April 1947. Torrential rains had caused the nearby river to flood, extinguishing the fire in the boilers and causing the steam-powered generators to stop. In the mansion lay the dying Henry Ford. Surrounded by engineering marvels, he left this life in the same manner in which he had entered it nearly ninety years before—in a cold, dark house lit only by candles.

Where is your prosperity—in this temporal life on earth or in the eternal life to come?

Prayer Suggestion—Give us God's vision of how to lay up eternal treasures which will not rust or fade away.

JUNE

12

Psalm 86:1-17

Today in History—Philippines declare independence from Spain, 1898; Baseball Hall of Fame opens in Cooperstown, N.Y., 1939; black leader Medgar Evers killed by a sniper in Jackson, Miss., 1963; Supreme Court rules Nazis may demonstrate in heavily Jewish Skokie, Ill., 1978; eight hundred thousand demonstrators protest nuclear proliferation in New York City march, 1982; Margaret Thatcher wins third straight term as Britain's prime minister, 1987.

Born Today—Engineer John Augustus Roebling, 1806; author Charles Kingsley, 1819; statesman Anthony Eden, 1897; actor Jim Nabors, 1912; financier David Rockefeller, 1915; President George Bush, 1924; singer Vic Damone, 1928.

Today's Quotation—"A vile race of quislings—to use the new word—which will carry the scorn of mankind down the centuries."—*Winston Churchill, June 12, 1941*

The Scorn of Mankind

We don't need to look far today to become disturbed at the activities of various leaders today. Madame Tussaud's famous wax museum in London surveyed thirty-five hundred visitors in the early 1970s. Asked to name the ten most hated public figures of all time, those polled listed Adolf Hitler first, followed by Mao Tse-Tung, Richard Nixon, Edward Heath, and Spiro Agnew.

This dim view of mankind was echoed by famed film actress of the 1950s and '60s, Brigette Bardot, who is quoted as stating: "I hate humanity, I am allergic to it, I see no one. I don't go out. I am disgusted with everything. Men are beasts and even beasts don't behave like them." This, following her "sun-kissed life on the French Riviera," and a series of lovers. While the source of the scorn reflects a variety of causes, the feeling of hatred is real nonetheless.

While the believer should hate sin and those who revel in it, he should never hate the sinner for whom Christ died.

Prayer Suggestion—In some small way, may we have the ability to see the world as God sees it and lovingly draw it to him.

JUNE

13

Psalm 116:1–19

Today in History—Four Nazi saboteurs land on Long Island, N.Y., 1942; missile age begins as German flying bombs strike England in World War II, 1944; Supreme Court hands down Miranda Decision requiring "warnings before valid statements could be taken by police," 1966; Thurgood Marshall nominated as first black Supreme Court justice, 1967.

Born Today—Poet William Butler Yeats, 1865; football player Harold "Red" Grange, 1903; inventor Luis Alverez, 1911; actor Malcolm McDowell, 1943; actor Richard Thomas, 1951; tennis player Bettina Bunge, 1963.

Today's Quotation—"Can anything be imagined more abhorrent to every sentiment of generosity or justice than the law which arms the rich with the legal right to fix the wages of the poor?"—*William Cullen Bryant, June 13, 1836*

Fixed Wages

Some of the greatest heroes in God's eyes are those whose earthly wages are the lowest. A medical missionary, having just completed surgery on a penniless native, was asked what he would have earned had he performed the operation in the States. "Several thousand dollars," was his reply. "And what will you receive for doing the surgery here?" The missionary quickly replied, "My payment will simply be the gratitude of this man, and there can be no greater payment than that."

The Bible doesn't record any wages being paid to Jesus Christ when he was on earth, and he was God's own beloved son! Have you ever thanked the Lord for the price he paid to forgive your sins? Would he feel that he paid too much? We recall the haunting words: "After all he's done for me, / how can I do less than give him my best and live for him completely?" No matter what wages you may make here on earth, what of eternal importance have you done for God?

Prayer Suggestion—Acknowledge the debt you have to God for his forgiveness of your sins. Put him in *first place* in your life!

JUNE

14

Today in History—Copenhagen, Denmark, founded, 1167; U.S. Army becomes first military service, 1775; California established independent of Mexico, 1846; first nonstop transatlantic flight (from Newfoundland to Ireland), 1919; Nazi Germany occupies Paris in World War II, 1940; world's first commercial computer, "Univac," unveiled in Philadelphia, 1951; Heimlech Maneuver, an anti-choking, life-saving technique, introduced by Dr. Henry Heimlech, 1974.

Born Today—Writer Harriet Beecher Stowe, 1811; editor John Bartlett, 1820; actor Burl Ives, 1909; pathologist Alois Alzheimer, 1864; actress Dorothy McGuire, 1918; journalist Pierre Salinger, 1925; speed skater Eric Heiden, 1958.

Today's Quotation—"The flag is the embodiment, not of sentiment but of history. It represents the experiences made by men and women, the experiences of those who died and live under that flag."—*Woodrow Wilson, June 14, 1915*

The Flag

Looking at your lifestyle, whose banner do you fly? The title for the world's oldest national flag goes to Denmark for its banner: a white cross on a red ground. It has not changed since the thirteenth century! The story behind the flag says that in 1219 King Waldemar saw a cross in the sky while leading his troops into battle. Taking this as a sign of victory, the cross design was later incorporated into the nation's flag.

What is our banner? Bitten by poisonous serpents in the wilderness, the Israelites were required to look upon the golden serpent on the pole in order to be healed. Sinners today may look to the cross of Christ as their banner—a symbol of the salvation Christ earned for us there. What is your flag?

Prayer Suggestion—That we will recognize Christ's death upon the cross, the place of his eternal victory over sin as being our "flag."

JUNE

15

Revelation 20:12–15

Today in History—Magna Carta signed, 1215; Arkansas admitted to U.S. as twenty-fifth state, 1836; Idaho Pioneer Day marking first permanent settlement in Idaho, 1860; U.S. invades Japanese-held Marianas Islands in World War II, 1944; Spain holds first free elections in forty-one years under new King Juan Carlos, 1977.

Born Today—England's Prince Edward, "The Black Prince," 1330; composer Edvard Grieg, 1843; sculptor Malvina Hoffman, 1887; psychologist Erik Erikson, 1902; politician Mario Cuomo, 1932.

Today's Quotation—"No free man shall be taken or imprisoned or dispossessed, or outlawed, or banished, or in any way destroyed, nor will we go upon him, nor send upon him, except by the legal judgement of his peers or by the law of the land."—*Magna Carta, June 15, 1215*

The Law of God

Except for Christ, a perfect man—one who has never broken a law—has never lived. It appeared, however, that one had been located in a western state some years ago. Testifying in a court proceeding the man said he neither "smoked nor chewed, drank nor swore." Attempting to clarify the point, the lawyer then asked the witness, "You admit, then, that you are a perfect man?" The man responded, "I do; as perfect as a man can be." Of course, the witness lost any claim to perfection when he qualified his testimony with the words "as perfect as a man can be," for there is no such thing as partial perfection.

While we might find such a story humorous, there are doubtless those who believe they have fully obeyed the law of God. But the Bible tells us, "There is none righteous, no, not one"; "for all have sinned, and come short of the glory of God" (Rom. 3:10, 23). When we hear, "I'm doing the best I can," there is a complete misunderstanding of the sovereignty of God and of how short we all fall in measuring up to his standards of perfection.

Prayer Suggestion—Thank God that through trusting in Christ's sacrifice on the cross, we are able to fulfill God's absolute law.

183

JUNE

16

Today in History—Marshal Henri Petain becomes premier of Nazi-conquered France, 1940; Washington (D.C.) National Airport opens, 1941; Soviet leader Leonid Brehznev arrives in U.S. for nine-day visit, 1973; rocket scientist Wernher von Braun dies of cancer at age 85, 1977; Supreme Court ruling allows new life forms to be patented, 1980; John Turner elected to replace Pierre Trudeau as Canada's prime minister, 1984.

Born Today—Comedian Stan Laurel, 1895; opera singer Helen Traubel, 1903; publisher Katherine Graham, 1917; author Erich Segal, 1937; author Joyce Carol Oates, 1938; basketball player Wayne Rollins, 1955.

Today's Quotation—"A house divided against itself cannot stand."—*Abraham Lincoln, June 16, 1858*

United at Home

It has been said that if you really want to get to know someone, visit them in their home. Bible teacher C. I. Schofield once wrote a friend, "I like to be able to think of people who deeply interest me in their homes. Downtown we are all pretty much alike, but at home we are just ourselves. . . . At home we are at ease; we throw off care; we are understood, and loved, and welcome."

We should never lose sight of the fact that our outlook on the world is in large part determined by what we have learned at home. Such basic concepts as sharing, recognizing the abilities of others, politeness, and putting others' interests ahead of our own are first learned at home. Think of how many disputes, wars, and dissensions could be prevented simply by remembering these fundamental principles learned at home!

Prayer Suggestion—Help us not to live in a house divided; rather may our families be united as one through the bonds of Christ.

JUNE

17

Today in History—Battle of Bunker Hill, Mass., fought, 1775; four Nazi German agents land at Ponte Vedra Beach, Fla., in World War II, 1942; televised hearings on Army dispute with Senator Joseph McCarthy of Wisconsin end, 1954; people of East Berlin rebel briefly against communist regime, 1958; U.S. Supreme Court bans prayer and Bible reading in public schools, 1963; five arrested in connection with break-in at Democratic Party headquarters in the Watergate, 1972; fourteen thousand Argentinians captured by British in Falkland Islands War, 1982.

Born Today—Composer Charles Francois Gounod, 1818; composer Igor Stravinsky, 1882; actor Ralph Bellamy, 1905; author John Hersey, 1914; singer Dean Martin, 1917; singer Barry Manilow, 1946.

Today's Quotation—". . . how little do my countrymen know what precious blessings they are in possession of, and which no other people on earth enjoy."—*Thomas Jefferson, June 17, 1785*

Blessings of Liberty

Hanging near the platform at Boston's historic Faneuil Hall is a large painting of Webster debating Hayne. It bears the following inscription: "Union and Liberty, one and inseparable, now and forever." William Boothe, founder of the Salvation Army, was once in Faneuil Hall to make an address. Referring to the imposing painting nearby, he said, "Union and Liberty—union with Christ and liberty from sin, one and inseparable now and forever. . . . There is no spiritual liberty apart from this union."

As great as the freedoms we enjoy here on earth are, much greater is the eternal freedom from the consequence of sin we enjoy as believers. Recall these ringing words of Paul describing our spiritual freedom, "There is therefore now no condemnation to them which are in Christ Jesus, who walk not after the flesh, but after the Spirit. For the law of the Spirit of life in Christ Jesus hath made me free from the law of sin and death" (Rom. 8:1–2). And this ironclad guarantee: "If the Son therefore shall make you free, ye shall be free indeed" (John 8:36).

Prayer Suggestion—Be thankful for our God-given freedoms both in this life and in the life to come.

JUNE

18

Today in History—U.S. Congress declares war on Great Britain, 1812; Winston Churchill rallies the people of England to "their finest hour" against Nazi Germany in World War II, 1940; General Eisenhower returns to Washington, D.C. from Europe, 1945; President Carter and Soviet leader Leonid Brezhnev sign SALT II agreement limiting spread of nuclear arms, in Vienna, 1979.

Born Today—Actor E. G. Marshall, 1910; journalist Sylvia Porter, 1913; educator Donald Keene, 1922; columnist Tom Wicker, 1926; critic Roger Ebert, 1942; singer Paul McCartney, 1942.

Today's Quotation—"Millions for defense but not a cent for tribute."—*Robert Goodloe Harper, June 18, 1798*

The Joy of Giving

Have you ever stopped to think that we have nothing of our own to give God?

Many years ago, the finance committee of a small church was calling on its members to seek donations for the church fund drive. Eventually, they visited a widow's meager home. The poor woman had to take in washing to make ends meet and the visitors were embarrassed even to ask her to give. However, the woman surprised the group by going into another room and bringing back a five-dollar bill which was a larger gift than many wealthier church members had given. The leader of the committee sought to return the gift to the woman saying kindly, "Why, you cannot afford to give so much. We couldn't take your money!" Suddenly the woman broke down and wept. "You want to take away my blessing," she cried. "I love the Lord and my church as much as the rest of you and I want to do my part, but you want to take away my joy." Humbled by the woman's sincerity, the men departed with her gift. Clearly this woman had experienced the blessings and joy received from giving to the Lord.

Prayer Suggestion—May we be as joyful in giving to God as we are in receiving from God.

JUNE

19

1 John 5:6–15

Today in History—Emperor Maximilian executed by Mexico, 1867; Statue of Liberty arrives at Bedloe's Island in New York Harbor, 1855; Julius and Ethel Rosenberg executed for wartime espionage, 1953; worst racial violence in fifteen years sweeps through township near Johannesburg, South Africa, 1976; University of Maryland basketball standout, Len Bias, dies of cocaine overdose, 1986.

Born Today—Writer Blaise Pascal, 1623; conductor Guy Lombardo, 1902; baseball player Lou Gehrig, 1903; Supreme Court Justice Abe Fortas, 1910; critic Pauline Kael, 1919; architect Charles Gwathmey, 1938; actress Phylicia Rashad, 1948.

Today's Quotation—"Weakness cannot cooperate with anything. Only strength can cooperate."—*Dwight D. Eisenhower, June 19, 1945*

Strength to Win

A construction foreman who was recently saved acknowledged that he was having difficulty kicking the cigarette habit. He said that as long as he was with the preacher he did all right, but that when the preacher left, he could hardly keep away from the habit. He was then given this sound advice: "If you can go one hour without smoking, you should go to the Lord each hour in prayer, confessing your weakness, and asking again for God's help." The man gladly followed the advice and soon experienced the power of God in breaking a firmly entrenched habit.

On another occasion a severely burned man admitted to his pastor that he had been drinking a glass or two of beer each night to help ease the nightmares of his tragic car accident. Together they called on God's power and God honored the request. Later, the man testified that never again did he have another nightmare, nor was he again tempted to drink the beer. He had tapped into God's unlimited supply of power.

Problems? Take them to the Lord in prayer!

Prayer Suggestion—Admit your failures. Let go and let God have his way in your life—then watch his power work things out for you.

JUNE
20
Ephesians 4:2–13

Today in History—First U.S. steamship to cross Atlantic reaches Liverpool, England, 1819; West Virginia admitted to U.S. as thirty-fifth state, 1863; 263 Americans evacuated from Beirut in wake of ongoing civil war, 1976; trans-Alaskan pipeline opens across some eight hundred miles of Alaskan wilderness, 1977; four off-duty Marines killed in blast of gunfire at outdoor cafe in San Salvador, 1985; police in Seoul, Korea, are overrun by students in climax of ten days of violence, 1987.

Born Today—Composer Jacques Offenbach, 1819; playwright Lillian Hellman, 1905; actor Errol Flynn, 1909; guitarist Chet Atkins, 1924; songwriter Brian Wilson, 1942; singer Anne Murray, 1945; pianist Andre Watts, 1946; singer Lionel Richie, 1949.

Today's Quotation—"E Pluribus Unum" (From many, one)—*Great Seal of U.S., legend adopted by Congress, June 20, 1782*

One in Christ

A missionary to China tells of a new Christian who said he could no longer worship his ancestors after trusting in Christ. A fellow believer, knowing the first man would be beaten with a thousand stripes for his faith, went to visit the head of the local tribe to plead mercy. He told the tribal leader, "As a believer in Christ, this man is the same as my brother. I cannot stand by and do nothing while he is beaten. This is what we are going to do: we will get all the believers from nearby tribes to join us and share those stripes with him." Knowing there would be trouble if members of another tribe were beaten by them, the leader sent his apologies, saying he did not understand the oneness of the Christian religion. Thus, noted the *Sunday School Times*, the "unity of the Christians was stronger than the heathen powers and the Lord was glorified."

Scripture tells us that when we are saved, we are adopted into God's family and as such we have countless brothers and sisters, both here on earth as well as in heaven, all one in Christ.

Prayer Suggestion—Rejoice in the unity that we have with other believers—one in the family and one in the Lord.

188

JUNE

21

Today in History—New Hampshire's ratification as ninth state puts U.S. Constitution into effect, 1788; U.S. forces complete conquest of Okinawa in World War II, 1945; CBS demonstrates long-playing record, 1948; Thomas Road Baptist Church begun in Lynchburg, Va., 1956; Chief Justice Earl Warren resigns, 1968; Supreme Court rules states should set obscenity standards, 1973; John W. Hinckley, Jr., would-be assassin of President Reagan, ruled not guilty by reason of insanity, 1982; body found in Brazil believed to be that of Nazi Joseph Mengele, 1985.

Born Today—Illustrator Rockwell Kent, 1882; actress Jane Russell, 1921; actor Bernie Kopell, 1933; actress Meredith Baxter-Birney, 1947; baseball player Rick Sutcliffe, 1956; Prince William (son of Britain's Prince Charles), 1982.

Today's Quotation—"We was robbed!"—*Joe Jacobs, June 21, 1932*

Avoiding the Robber

It is no secret that Satan would love to rob you of your salvation. Failing in that (see Rom. 8:38–39), he will try to make you ineffective and discouraged.

A little girl was shown a painting of a stormy sea in which there was a rock with a cross on it. Upon the rock was a woman who had just been rescued from the raging sea. The girl was told the painting meant that we must "cling to Jesus." "Then that can't be my Jesus," the girl said, "for he holds me!"

Henry Bosch notes that "while in ourselves we may not have sufficient strength to withstand temptation, there is one who 'is able to keep you from falling'" (Jude 1:24). When you become a child of God you are held firmly in his grasp, and Satan, and all of his forces combined cannot remove you from the hand of God.

Prayer Suggestion—God's salvation is permanent. It cannot be lost or stolen, for it is he who holds us and not we who cling to him.

JUNE

22

Ephesians 6:10-18

Today in History—D. L. Moody's first service in England, 1873; France surrenders to Germany in World War II, 1940; Germany invades U.S.S.R., 1941; three civil rights workers disappear in Mississippi (later found slain), 1964; law giving eighteen-year-olds the right to vote in U.S. elections signed, 1970; Sikhs blamed for Air India 747 crash off England killing all 329 aboard, 1985.

Born Today—Biologist-writer Julian Huxley, 1887; director Billy Wilder, 1906; author Anne Morrow Lindbergh, 1907; broadcast journalist Ed Bradley, 1941; actress Lindsay Wagner, 1949.

Today's Quotation—"We will never negotiate with Hitler or any of his gang. We shall fight him by land; we shall fight him by sea; we shall fight him in the air, until, with God's help, we have rid the earth of his shadow and liberated its people from his yoke."—*Winston Churchill, June 22, 1941*

Fight the Good Fight

William Law has warned that "the world is now a greater enemy of the Christian than it was in Christ's time." Robert Lauer reports this is the case because the world now has "greater power over Christians by its favors, riches, honors, rewards, and protection than it had by the torture and enslavement by its persecutors." It is a more dangerous enemy by having lost its threatening appearance. Certainly it is more difficult to fight an enemy you like and feel comfortable with. The Bible says Satan goes about "as a roaring lion seeking whom he may devour." Christians must recognize that even attractive enticements can be used by Satan to further his diabolical purposes.

Prayer Suggestion—For Christians to awake and realize they are surrounded on every hand in this world by the enemy of their souls.

JUNE

23

Today in History—Principality of Luxemburg founded, 963; Taft-Hartley Act becomes law, 1947; treaty for scientific cooperation and peaceful use of Antarctic signed, 1961; Warren Burger takes office as chief justice of Supreme Court, 1969; President Carter meets with heads of other industrialized nations to discuss ways to reduce Western oil dependence, 1980; French President Mitterand names four communists to his cabinet, 1981.

Born Today—Humorist Irvin Cobb, 1876; England's Edward VIII, Duke of Windsor, 1894; director Bob Fosse, 1927; singer June Carter Cash, 1929; astronaut Donn Eisele, 1930; track athlete Wilma Rudolph, 1940; conductor James Levine, 1943.

Today's Quotation—"The beginning of all is to have done with falsity—to eschew falsity as death eternal."—*Thomas Carlyle, June 23, 1870*

Be Done with Falsehood

There was a trust department in a certain bank in which several young men were being considered for promotion. After reviewing their qualifications, one was selected. It was decided that the candidate would be notified of his selection later that day. At noon the candidate went to the cafeteria to eat. Several others were behind him, followed by a director of the bank. As the young man went through the line he put a pat of butter on his plate and then flipped some slices of bread on top to conceal the butter from the cashier. The bank officer saw him. That afternoon he was summoned to the board room, but instead of receiving a promotion, he was dismissed. The bank officers felt they could not tolerate someone who was dishonest in their trust department.

Yes, honesty is the best policy in both natural and spiritual things.

Prayer Suggestion—May God remind you to treat each activity as if he was intently watching you—for he is!

JUNE

24

Psalm 91:1–16

Today in History—John and Sebastian Cabot land in Newfound-land, 1497; Soviets begin blockade of land and water routes to Berlin leading two days later to beginning of great airlift, 1948; physicist Sally Ride returns from six-day Challenger mission as first U.S. woman to travel in space, 1983; hundreds of thousands of demonstrators in Paris protest the socialist government's attempt to regulate private schools, 1984.

Born Today—Industrialist E. I. Du Pont, 1771; preacher-orator Henry Ward Beecher, 1813; fighter Jack Dempsey, 1895; editor Norman Cousins, 1912; actress Michelle Lee, 1942; sports announcer Phyllis George, 1949.

Today's Quotation—"All eyes are opened, or opening, to the rights of man."—*Thomas Jefferson, June 24, 1826*

Our Rights

Although the U.S. constitution guarantees citizens certain human rights, the Bible says that spiritually we have no rights. We are slaves, to either God or Satan. Rather than having more rights, believers need to recognize their responsibilities before God. Two young men were caught red-handed in a hold-up attempt. One, from a wealthy family, was represented by several high-powered lawyers and the other, who had spent two years in prison, had a court-appointed attorney. What was surprising were the sentences—only three years in prison for the repeat offender, compared with ten years for the wealthy lad. In explaining the sentences, the judge said the wealthy youth had been given tremendous opportunities, yet had not lived up to them.

Whatever our feelings in the matter, the judgment follows God's standard, "For to whom much is given, of him shall much be required" (Luke 12:48). As God's children, he expects more from us. The more you have, the more God expects. We would all do well to recognize our God-given responsibilities in this life before having to give account before God in the life to come.

Prayer Suggestion—Recognize your responsibilities before God and ask for his guidance in making you more faithful in doing his will.

JUNE

25

Ephesians 5:22–33

Today in History—Virginia is tenth state to ratify Constitution, 1788; Custer's Last Stand in Montana, 1876; North Korea invades South Korea thus beginning Korean War, 1950; former White House Counsel John Dean tells Senate committee that the eight-month coverup of Watergate activities has become a "cancer on the presidency," 1973; Alexander Haig resigns as Secretary of State in policy disagreement and is replaced by George Shultz, 1982; in major policy shift, Congress approves $100 million aid package for Nicaraguan Contras, 1986; Soviet leader Gorbachev proposes new reforms in the structuring of the Soviet economy, 1987.

Born Today—Composer Gustave Charpentier, 1860; playwright George Abbott, 1887; Admiral Louis Mountbatten, 1900; actress June Lockhart, 1925; basketball player Willis Reed, 1942; singer Carly Simon, 1945.

Today's Quotation—"It is the man and woman united that makes the complete human being. . . . A single man . . . is an incomplete animal. He resembles the odd half of a pair of scissors."—*Benjamin Franklin, June 25, 1745*

Holy Matrimony

One of the reasons so many marriages are falling apart today is because husbands are not following the advice of Scripture to "love your wives, even as Christ also loved the church, and gave himself for it" (Eph. 5:25). Husbands, do you love your wife as Christ loved the church? Do you live to please your wife and not yourself? Does your wife feel that you are giving her dignity and importance? (See 1 Pet. 3:7.) It is love which gives dignity to a faithful wife and mother. Do you tell your wife that you love her? Do you tell her she's beautiful? (It will not make her vain.) Do you remember your anniversary and other important dates? The honeymoon is never ended for true lovers!

Prayer Suggestion—Thank God for a loving spouse and family.

JUNE

26

Today in History—First U.S. troops land in France in World War I, 1917; *New York Daily News* publishes its first issue, 1919; charter of United Nations is signed in San Francisco, 1945; U.S. and British aircraft begin Berlin Airlift to Soviet-blockaded West Berlin, 1948; court charges Indira Gandhi with corrupt election practices and invalidates her election victory, 1975; Rev. Jesse Jackson concludes talks with Cuba's Fidel Castro, 1984.

Born Today—Baseball's Abner Doubleday, 1819; writer Pearl Buck, 1892; athlete "Babe" Didrikson Zaharias, 1914; children's author Charlotte Zolotow, 1915; actress Eleanor Parker, 1922; politician Charles Robb, 1939.

Today's Quotation—"The highest condition of art is artlessness."— *Henry David Thoreau, June 26, 1840*

Beauty

Thanks to Margaret K. Fraser for the following beautiful poem:

> God could have made the sun to rise, without such splendor in the
> skies;
> He could have made the sun to set, without a glory greater yet. . . .
> He could have made the ocean roll without such music for the soul
> The mighty anthem, loud and strong—the birds without their clear,
> sweet song.
> The charm of kittens' dainty grace, the dimples in a baby's face—
> All these are extras from His hand, whose love we cannot
> understand,
> The God who fashioned flow'rs and trees, delights to give us things
> that please.
> And all his handiwork so fair His glory and His love declare.
> Yes, He who made the earth and skies gave "extras" for our ears
> and eyes.
> And while my heart with rapture sings, I thank Him for the "extra
> things."

Prayer Suggestion—Beauty is God's creation. Acknowledge his part in creating all that is bright and beautiful.

JUNE

27

Today in History—Mormon leaders Joseph and Hyrum Smith are killed by a mob in Carthage, Ill., 1844; FBI announces capture of eight World War II Nazi saboteurs, 1942; U.S. troops aid South Korea in Korean War, 1950; third summit meeting between President Nixon and Soviet leader Brezhnev begins in Moscow, 1974; angry California motorists are involved in nine separate freeway shooting incidents since June 18, 1987.

Born Today—Statesman Charles Parnell, 1846; poet Paul Lawrence Dunbar, 1872; blind-deaf author-lecturer Helen Keller, 1880; television's Bob Keeshan (Captain Kangaroo), 1927; philanthropist H. Ross Perot, 1930; opera singer Anna Moffo, 1934.

Today's Quotation—"Older men declare war. But it is youth that must fight and die."—*Herbert Hoover, June 27, 1944*

War Deaths

War is certainly a tragedy and the death rate is regrettable. Yet few may realize that ten thousand persons are murdered each year in the United States alone! It works out to more than one person per hour every day. This is in contrast to all the wars in America's history in which a total of 530,000 have been killed. Things have gotten to the point where a baby born in the 1970s was more likely to be murdered than an American soldier in World War II was to die in combat, according to Dr. Arnold Bennett of Massachusetts Institute of Technology! Donald T. Lunde of Stanford says it is American youths who are most likely to become victims (and perpetrators) of murder with a 19 percent increase in the death rate of young adults.

Life is not certain for one of any age. We therefore must always be ready for we know not when this life will end and eternity will begin for us.

Prayer Suggestion—God's assurances of salvation comfort us as we face an uncertain future. Thank him that we can know we are saved.

JUNE

28

Today in History—Unfinished Panama Canal bought from France by U.S., 1902; Archduke Ferdinand's assassination triggers World War I, 1914; Treaty of Versailles ends World War I, 1919; three-day revolt against communist Poland flares, 1956; U.S. to Europe commercial telephone service begins via satellite, 1965; first women enroll as cadets at U.S. Air Force Academy, 1976; Supreme Court affirms the right of college admissions officers to favor minorities to correct past racial imbalance, 1978; Soviet leader Gorbachev proposes new policies of glasnost (openness) and perestroika (economic revamping) for his country's economy, 1988.

Born Today—England's King Henry VIII, 1491; theologian John Wesley, 1703; author Esther Forbes, 1891; composer Richard Rodgers, 1902; musician Lester Flatt, 1914; actor Mel Brooks, 1928; football player John Elway, 1960.

Today's Quotation—"All the world over, I will back the masses against the classes."—*William E. Gladstone, June 28, 1886*

The Masses

How God must grieve at the masses of people who have never heard of his saving love. How large is this population? According to figures cited by *Christian Victory*, missionaries throughout the world are reaching about two million unchurched every year. However that contrasts with a sixty-five million annual increase in world population. United Nations figures show a net gain of 178,200 in the world population each and every day!

With these figures in mind we may begin to see why God has seen fit to save the development of the mass media until it became impossible to reach these vast masses of humanity with the gospel in any other way. How great is God! His timing is perfect, yet he still commands us to "Go" and "Tell." Have you shared your faith with someone? Do so today!

Prayer Suggestion—Ask God to make you faithful in fulfilling the Great Commission where you are and support others doing the same.

JUNE

29

Proverbs 22:1-6

Today in History—Townshend Act passed leading to American Revolution, 1767; Jewish and Arab Jerusalem becomes single city under Israeli administration, 1967; Supreme Court rules death penalty in existing law is unconstitutional, 1972; Israel launches major invasion into Lebanon trapping some PLO leaders, 1982.

Born Today—Artist Peter Paul Rubens, 1577; surgeon William Mayo, 1861; army engineer George Washington Geothals, 1858; astronomer George Hale, 1868; composer LeRoy Anderson, 1909; politician Elizabeth Dole, 1936.

Today's Quotation—"Self-government is our right, a thing born in us at birth; a thing no more to be doled out to us or withheld from us by another than the right to life itself.—*Roger Casement, June 29, 1916*

A Christian Birthright

A young man was recovering from very serious injuries when his doctor noted his rapid progress. In answer to a question, the patient said, "Oh, yes, all my family is religious but I don't take much stock in that sort of thing myself." "You have inherited stock in it, young man," the doctor replied. "Do you know why you are recovering so rapidly from your accident? It is because your family has given you a strong physical makeup. You have also been given a strong spiritual heritage which you have the responsibility of passing on to your children."

This may be thought of as our "Christian birthright." A young mother held her baby in her lap while reading aloud from the Bible. When asked whether she thought her baby understood what she was reading, the mother replied, "I'm sure he does not understand now, but I want his earliest memories to be that of hearing God's Word." What a testimony of establishing God's birthright in the infant's life—not leaving it up to chance how he or she will grow up. What have your children learned about God from watching and listening to your?

Prayer Suggestion—May I be a good example to my children and early lead them to the Savior. May I not lose a single one to Satan's grasp!

JUNE

30

Deuteronomy 15:2-12

Today in History—Socialist leader Eugene Debs arrested for interfering with World War I military recruiting, 1918; eighteen-year-olds given right to vote by ratification of Twenty-sixth Amendment to U.S. Constitution, 1971; Nuclear Regulatory Commission votes to halt construction of the controversial power plant at Seabrook, N.H., 1978; one U.S. serviceman killed and thirty-nine others released unharmed after seventeen-day drama aboard at TWA flight hijacked to Beirut, 1985.

Born Today—Actor Walter Hampden, 1879; East German leader Walter Ulbricht, 1893; singer Lena Horne, 1917; author Ben Bagdikian, 1920; actress Nancy Dussault, 1936; boxer Mike Tyson, 1966.

Today's Quotation—"A lover of Nature is pre-eminently a lover of man. If I have no friend, what is Nature to me?"—*Henry David Thoreau, June 30, 1852*

Brotherly Love

Two brothers were fighting side by side in a battle in France, when one of them fell in battle. The survivor requested permission to go out and rescue his brother from the line of fire. "Aw, he's probably already dead," he was told. "Why risk your life just to bring back the body?" But the soldier persisted and was finally given permission to go to his brother's side. Just as the soldier returned with his brother over his shoulder, the injured man died. "You see," his office cried, "you risked your life for nothing!" "No," said the brave soldier, "I did what was expected and I have my reward. Just as I crept up to him, he looked me in the eye and said, 'I knew you would come for me. I was sure you would come.'"

The bond of brotherly love is described in the Bible as it says, ". . . and there is a friend that sticketh closer than a brother" (Prov. 18:24). Have you found that friend whom to know is life eternal?

Prayer Suggestion—Praise God for his eternal love and friendship and for his promise "never to leave us nor forsake us."

JULY

1

Today in History—Battle of Gettysburg, July 1–3, 1863; Dominion Day marks Canada's becoming self-governing, 1867; Battle of San Juan Hill in Spanish-American War, 1898; N.Y. Governor Franklin D. Roosevelt nominated for president, 1932; first post-war atom bomb test conducted in Pacific, 1946; five-cent subway fare ends in New York City, 1948; Somalia Independence Day marks African nation's becoming republic, 1960; Rwanda and Burundi, former Belgian territories, become independent, 1962; Medicare goes into effect, 1966; John Mitchell resigns as Nixon re-election committee head to be with wife, 1972; Argentina's leader Juan Peron dies, wife Isabel succeeds him, 1974.

Born Today—Mathematician Gottfried Leibnitz, 1646; Revolutionary War General Comte Rochambeau, 1725; aviator Louis Bleriot, 1872; actress Olivia DeHavilland, 1916; actress Leslie Caron, 1931; Britain's Princess Diana, 1961.

Today's Quotation—"Peace is indivisible."—*Maxim Litvinov, July 1, 1936*

Peace

A story is told of a woman who lay dying with but a few hours to live. A preacher was summoned who attempted to counsel her in her remaining hours. He kindly asked the woman, "Have you made your peace with God?" She replied, "No, and I don't intend to, either." Surprised, he asked, "You're not afraid to die then?" "No." "And you realize that within a few hours you will be standing in God's presence?" "Yes, and I have perfect peace."

Intrigued by her response he questioned, "How's that?" "Why I am resting in the peace which Christ made for me in his death for me on the cross. You see, I don't have to make peace with God; I am resting in the peace Jesus Christ has already made for me."

Are you resting in the peace that only God can give? Trust him today and you too will receive "the peace of God which passeth all understanding" (Phil. 4:7).

Prayer Suggestion—Recognize God's peace is with all those who have trusted in Christ and the debt he has paid for their sin.

JULY

2

1 Corinthians 1:26–31

Today in History—Continental Congress in Philadelphia adopts resolution stating that colonies "are, and of a right ought to be, free and independent States," 1776; President James Garfield shot in Washington, D.C., 1881; aviator Amelia Earhart vanishes in Pacific on round-the-world flight, 1937; President Lyndon B. Johnson signs Civil Rights Act, 1964; Supreme Court rules a minor may have an abortion without parental consent, 1979; President Carter signs into law a measure which requires all males to register for the draft at age eighteen, 1980.

Born Today—Writer Hermann Hesse, 1877; Supreme Court Justice Thurgood Marshall, 1908; politician John Sununu, 1939; actress Cheryl Ladd, 1952; basketball player Jose Canseco, 1964.

Today's Quotation—"The State, in choosing men to faithfully serve it, takes no notice of their opinions. If they be willing to serve it, that satisfies."—*Oliver Cromwell, July 2, 1644*

Serving the King

Philadelphia businessman John Wanamaker once was asked, "How do you find time to run a Sunday school for four thousand students, in addition to operating your stores, serving as postmaster general, and all your other commitments?" Wanamaker responded, "Why, the Sunday school *is* my business! All other things are just *things*. I determined years ago to follow God's sure promise, 'Seek ye first the kingdom of God and His righteousness and all these things shall be added unto you' (Matt. 6:33), and he has not failed me yet."

You say you are not talented and could not do what Wanamaker did? The apostle Paul describes five things God uses: "the weak things, the foolish things, the base things, the despised things, and the things which are not." Are you not blessed with great ability? Rejoice, for God's Word says you are fully qualified to serve the King.

Prayer Suggestion—Make yourself available to God, no matter what your ability may be.

JULY

3

Acts 16:25–31

Today in History—General George Washington takes command of the Continental Army in Cambridge, Mass., 1775; Idaho admitted to U.S. as forty-third state, 1890; U.S. and North Korean troops meet in battle for first time in Korean War, 1950; State Department asks White House to allow immigration into U.S. of fifteen thousand Indochina refugees, 1977; *USS Vincennes*, on patrol in the Persian Gulf, mistakenly fires on approaching Iranian jetliner killing all 290 aboard, 1988.

Born Today—Explorer Samuel de Champlain, 1567; artist John Singleton Copley, 1737; composer George Cohan, 1878; shipping magnate Stavros Niarchos, 1909; musician Pete Fountain, 1930; actor Tom Cruise, 1962.

Today's Quotation—"Yesterday the greatest question was decided which ever was debated in America; and a greater perhaps never was, nor will be, decided among men."—*John Adams, referring to resolution which preceded Declaration of Independence, July 3, 1776*

Life's Greatest Question

What must I do to be saved? These probing words point up life's greatest question.

A food processing company once thought they had a great idea for a timesaver housewives were sure to love—a cake mix so simple all you had to do was add water. The mix produced a creamy batter and a fine cake but there was just one problem: It would not sell. Amazed, the company hired researchers who found out that the mix was just too simple! The public wanted a product that required something more from them. So the company changed the formula to require adding an egg in addition to the water, and the cake mix became an immediate success.

This sounds like many people today. They want to go to heaven but don't want to believe the Bible's formula because it sounds too simple. Rather, they think they can get to heaven through something they can do. How tragic to miss salvation for all eternity because of feeling God's plan is just too simple!

Prayer Suggestion—Acknowledge that the way of salvation is so simple that even a child can understand it, yet so profound it amazes the genius.

201

JULY

4

Today in History—Construction of Erie Canal linking Hudson River and Great Lakes begins in New York State, 1817; Henry David Thoreau goes to live in rustic hut near Walden Pond, Mass., 1845; Statue of Liberty presented to U.S. as gift from France, 1884; Philippine Republic becomes independent nation, 1946; Lynchburg Baptist College becomes Liberty Baptist College, 1975; U.S. observes its two hundredth birthday with numerous festivities nationwide, 1976; Israel rescues 105 hostages held in Uganda, 1976; restored Statue of Liberty celebrates one hundredth birthday, 1986.

Born Today—Writer Nathaniel Hawthorne, 1804; songwriter Stephen Foster, 1826; President Calvin Coolidge, 1872; trumpeter Louis Armstrong, 1900; advice columnists Ann Landers (Esther Lederer) and Abigail Van Buren (Pauline Friedman), 1918; playwright Neil Simon, 1927; television host Geraldo Rivera, 1943.

Today's Quotation—"What we seek is the reign of law, based upon the consent of the governed and sustained by the organized opinion of mankind."—*Woodrow Wilson, July 4, 1918*

The Reign of Law

It was a gloomy atmosphere which greeted the delegates gathered in the old Statehouse in Philadelphia. They had come from all thirteen colonies to act upon the troubled conditions which plagued the New World. Should a new nation be considered or not? American patriot and elder statesman Benjamin Franklin spoke: ". . . the longer I live, the more convincing proofs I see of this truth, that God governs the affairs of men. And if a sparrow cannot fall to the ground without his will, is it possible for an empire to rise without his notice? . . . except the Lord build the house, they labour in vain that build it. I firmly believe this." This statement, from Psalm 127, was followed by a time of prayer from which came the singleness of purpose which gave birth to America on July 4, 1776.

Prayer Suggestion—Recognize that America was founded upon a rock—the rock of prayer and the Word of God.

JULY

5

Today in History—Venezuela Independence Day marks freedom from Spanish rule, 1811; U.S. National Labor Relations Board established, 1935; free health care for everyone in England begins, 1948; Pakistan leader Ali Bhutto ousted by Army officers in bloodless coup, 1977; Isle of Man celebrates one thousand years as world's oldest parliament, 1979; evidence reveals herbicide Dioxin was sold for years after it was known to cause serious health problems, 1983.

Born Today—Admiral David Farragut, 1801; circus showman P. T. Barnum, 1810; statesman Cecil Rhodes, 1853; playwright Jean Cocteau, 1889; statesman Georges Pompidou, 1911; baseball player Richard "Goose" Gossage, 1951.

Today's Quotation—"Women ought not to be treated the same as men."—*Winston Churchill, July 5, 1945*

Ladies First

A country boy was hoping to attract the attention of a beautiful young lady at his church. She was lovely in form, face, and character. After several dates, he phoned to invite her out once again, but she announced she was busy. Repeated requests met with the same response. Finally, he got her to say why she wasn't willing to see him again. "Your fingernails were dirty, you slurped your soup, and you didn't even open the car door for me," she told him. "Please, just give me a chance," he pleaded. "I know I've been poorly raised, but I will learn good manners if you will just be patient with me." After two years they were married. For, in waiting on her, he learned to please her, and he grew into the kind of companion she wanted.

In the same way the young Christian waits upon God. He begins to read the Bible to discover what God wants. Then, little by little, the rough edges are smoothed off and he becomes more and more like Christ. How much like Christ are you today?

Prayer Suggestion—Let me so live that all can see I am a child of God and joint heir with Christ.

JULY

6

John 1:22-29

Today in History—First all-star National League vs. American League baseball game, Chicago (American League wins 5–2), 1933; Truman Memorial Library dedicated in Independence, Mo., 1957; former Argentine leader Isabel Peron freed after five-year house arrest, 1981; President Reagan agrees to contribute U.S. troops to Beirut peacekeeping effort, 1982.

Born Today—Naval hero John Paul Jones, 1747; Mexican Emperor Maximilian, 1832; former First Lady Nancy Reagan, 1921; television's Merv Griffin, 1925; actress Janet Leigh, 1927; actor Sylvester Stallone, 1946.

Today's Quotation—"Our cause is just. Our nation is perfect. . . . The arms we have been compelled by our enemies to assume we will, in defiance of every hazard, with unabating firmness and perseverance, employ for the preservation of our liberties, being with one mind resolved to die free men rather than live slaves."—*Thomas Jefferson, July 6, 1775*

A Just Cause

The weather was uncomfortable and the mud was deep that day in November 1918. Citizen-soldiers—recruited to fight for a just cause and uprooted from their families and jobs—were waiting to go home on Armistice Day. Little by little the news trickled back to camp: "Peace was at hand!" What excitement there was! The long, bloody war which had covered half the globe had at last come to an end. Bells rang from church towers, guns fired, soldiers yelled and sang; it was a time for rejoicing for the just cause had triumphed and the soldiers would soon be going home!

Yet all this rejoicing was nothing compared to that night long ago when the angel appeared to the shepherds in the rolling fields outside Bethlehem. The angels sang glad tidings for the newborn Savior who was God's own son, the Prince of Peace!

Prayer Suggestion—Praise God, the Savior has come to take away the sins of the world and his cause is always just!

JULY

7

Today in History—Commodore John Sloat proclaims annexation of California, 1846; U.S. annexation of Hawaiian Islands authorized, 1898; U.S. forces set up Iceland station as World War II measure, 1941; first solar-powered plane crosses English Channel at speed of thirty m.p.h. and at eleven thousand feet, 1981; Sandra Day O'Connor nominated by President Reagan to become first woman Supreme Court justice, 1981.

Born Today—Composer Gustav Mahler, 1860; artist Marc Chagall, 1887; designer Pierre Cardin, 1922; composer Doc Severinsen, 1927; actress Shelley Duvall, 1949; basketball player Ralph Sampson, 1960.

Today's Quotation—"It is fatal to enter any war without the will to win it."—*General Douglas MacArthur, July 7, 1952*

The Will to Win

A young college student was bedridden with a deadly disease, but his attitude was always bright and cheerful. One day a friend came to visit him and remarked, "With such a serious illness, how on earth can you be so happy?" "It's simple," the young man replied, "you see, it hasn't touched my heart." He had grasped the will to win.

Years ago Samuel Chadwick described the new life in this way: "There came into my soul a deep peace, and a new sense of power. There was a new sense of vitality and exhilaration come over me. Things began to happen. What we had earlier attempted through our own strength, now came to pass without labor." Now Chadwick had gained not only the will to win, but God's power to achieve the victory. "I can do all things through Christ which strengtheneth me" (Phil. 4:13). Do you have the will to win? With God's help you can!

Prayer Suggestion—Realize that there is no problem so big that you cannot handle it with God's help!

JULY

8

James 1:5-11

Today in History—Liberty Bell cracks in Philadelphia, 1835; William Jennings Bryan speech electrifies Democratic National Convention, 1896; John L. Sullivan won last bare-knuckle heavyweight boxing championship in seventy-fifth round, 1899; U.S. captures Saipan from Japanese in World War II, 1944; lightning strike may have contributed to crash of Pan Am 747 jetliner shortly after takeoff from New Orleans killing 145, 1982; "Classic" Coca-Cola re-introduced after sales of "New" Coke drop after only ten weeks, 1986.

Born Today—Inventor Ferdinand von Zeppelin, 1838; financier John D. Rockefeller, 1839; politician George Romney, 1907; former Vice President Nelson Rockefeller, 1908; critic Walter Kerr, 1913; TV producer Roone Arledge, 1931; singer Steve Lawrence, 1935.

Today's Quotation—"States have no rights—only people have rights. States have responsibilities."—*George Romney, July 8, 1964*

Our Responsibilities

An Arab leader once gave a banquet for all his friends. To help with the expense, he asked each guest to bring a beverage to share at the feast. The day arrived and one by one each guest lined up to empty his wineskin into a bowl. But much to the embarrassment of the host, each of the wineskins contained not a festive beverage but only water. Each guest had neglected his responsibility, assuming the others would provide the beverage and that his small contribution wouldn't be missed.

This is a temptation all believers face—thinking that our service for the Lord is insignificant, that no one will know the difference if we don't take part. While your part may seem small, never underestimate the value of your contribution in the work of the Lord.

Prayer Suggestion—Ask God to help you fulfill your responsibility as a Christian in service to him.

JULY

9

Luke 16:1-13

Today in History—Argentine Independence Day marks independence from Spain, 1816; President Zachary Taylor dies in the White House and is succeeded by Millard Fillmore, 1850; Henry Kissinger begins secret trip to Red China to arrange visit by President Nixon, 1971; former Chief Justice Earl Warren dies at age 83, 1974; police arrest seventy-two protestors in Chicago Nazi rally, 1978; Britain's Queen Elizabeth finds intruder in her bedroom; she summons police and is unhurt in embarrassing lapse of security, 1982; M. Ali Agca, convicted attacker of Pope John Paul II, says Soviet secret police took part in plot against pope's life, 1983.

Born Today—Novelist Ann Ward Radcliffe, 1764; inventor Elias Howe, 1819; electrical engineer Nikola Tesla, 1856; Prime Minister Edward Heath, 1916; football player O. J. Simpson, 1947; actor Tom Hanks, 1956.

Today's Quotation—"I have endeavored to do my duty."—*President Zachary Taylor's last words, July 9, 1850*

Doing Our Duty

Have you seen the plaque sometimes seen hanging over a kitchen sink which reads, "Divine service conducted here three times daily"? This recognizes so well how all our duties, no matter how small they may seem to us, are honorable if done in God's name.

Psychologist William James recommended that everyone perform an unpleasant task daily just to "keep in moral trim." He wisely realized that our moral "muscles" grow with exercise and use. Therefore we should help to strengthen them by using them to resist life's ever-recurring "small" temptations.

Prayer Suggestion—That God would empower us with the ability to go about our duty each day and do it as unto him, no matter how small.

JULY

10

Revelation 21:10—22:7

Today in History—Wyoming admitted to U.S. as forty-fourth state, 1890; smaller-size paper money goes into use in U.S., 1929; U.S. and Britain invade Sicily in World War II, 1943; President Jimmy Carter meets with Chinese leaders to solidify stand against Soviet threat, 1980.

Born Today—Theologian John Calvin, 1509; artist James Whistler, 1834; author Marcel Proust, 1871; educator Mary Bethune, 1875; broadcast journalist David Brinkley, 1920; author Jean Kerr, 1923; actor Fred Gwynne, 1926; tennis player Arthur Ashe, 1943.

Today's Quotation—"Every monopoly and all exclusive privileges are granted at the expense of the public, which ought to receive a fair equivalent."—*Andrew Jackson, July 10, 1832*

Exclusive Privileges

What are the most exclusive privileges available for someone in this life? Whatever they are, all earthly "perks" will pale beside the truly exclusive privilege of every believer—that of being adopted into God's family and living with him forever! D. L. Moody spoke of his "homegoing" this way: "Someday you will read in the papers that D. L. Moody is dead. Don't you believe a word of it. At that moment, I shall be more alive than I am now. I shall have gone higher, that is all—out of this old clay tenement into a house that is immortal. . . . That which is born of the Spirit will live forever."

It has been said that death for the believer is a bit like exchanging money at the bank. For, as we bring a crumpled paper note to the bank to obtain a silver dollar in exchange, so it is when we depart this life; we exchange a frail body which we cannot retain and receive instead eternal privileges—treasures, liberty, victory, and knowledge! What benefits there are in trusting Christ—all of this and heaven too!

Prayer Suggestion—Be thankful for the exclusive privileges you enjoy as a Christian, a believer in Christ.

JULY

11

Hebrews 12:3–11

Today in History—Aaron Burr fatally wounds Alexander Hamilton in a duel, 1804; Triborough Bridge in New York City opens, 1936; U.S. Air Force Academy begins operation at Lowry Air Force Base (moves to Colorado Springs three years later), 1955; Chinese uncover remarkable burial mound with six thousand statues of warriors believed to be several thousand years old, 1975; truck mishap near campground in Spain kills two hundred in resulting explosions and fire, 1978.

Born Today—King Robert Bruce (who freed Scotland from England), 1274; editor Thomas Bowdler, 1754; President John Quincy Adams, 1767; merchant John Wanamaker, 1838; critic Harold Bloom, 1930; fighter Leon Spinks, 1953.

Today's Quotation—"Idleness and pride tax with a heavier hand than kings and parliaments."—*Benjamin Franklin, July 11, 1765*

Idleness

It has been wisely said that doing nothing is about the most tiresome work in the world because you cannot stop and rest. The Chinese tell the story of a merchant who had a son who loved to sleep late. Despite repeated warnings from his father against laziness, the youth still would not rise until midday. In desperation, the father thought of another idea: he would use the profit incentive to motivate his son toward early rising. "Want to make some money?" he asked. "You know the saying, 'Get up early in the morning, pick up a pot of lost gold!'" "In that case," answered his son, "the one who lost the gold must have gotten up even earlier."

While life has no guarantee of success, it is certain success will never come from laziness.

Prayer Suggestion—For strength to do the work God has called us to do and the determination to carry on despite discouragement.

JULY

12

Proverbs 3:1–10

Today in History—Orangemen's Day marks Protestantism's victory in Ireland, 1689; U.S. Congressional Medal of Honor authorized, 1862; U.S. establishes minimum wage of forty cents an hour, 1933; Democratic presidential candidate Walter Mondale announces Congresswoman Geraldine Ferraro from Queens, N.Y. as his choice for running mate in the presidential race, 1984.

Born Today—Pottery manufacturer Josiah Wedgewood, 1730; writer Henry David Thoreau, 1817; inventor George Eastman, 1854; lyricist Oscar Hammerstein II, 1895; entertainer Milton Berle, 1908; artist Andrew Wyeth, 1917; actor Bill Cosby, 1938.

Today's Quotation—"Next in importance to freedom and justice is popular education, without which neither freedom nor justice can be permanently maintained."—*James A. Garfield, July 12, 1880*

Education

Years ago, when Woodrow Wilson was president of Princeton, he faced the parents of a new student who were concerned about the quality of education their only child would receive at the school. Confronting Wilson they declared, "We want to be sure our only son is getting the very best education. Can you assure us that he will do well here?" Anticipating their question, Wilson responded mildly, "Madam, we guarantee satisfaction or we return the boy."

There are some people who become professional students, worshipping education as an end in itself. How foolish, for schools only serve to get you ready for examination. It is life that gives the finals.

Prayer Suggestion—That God would give us the education that will last forever through belief in the Lord Jesus Christ.

JULY

13

Today in History—U.S. Northwest Territory established, 1787; draft riots in New York City, July 13–16, in Civil War, 1863; John F. Kennedy nominated for president, 1960; politician Adlai Stevenson dies in London, 1965; Israeli planes, under fire from Arab rockets, raid largest Palestinian refugee camp in Lebanon, 1975; "Live Aid" benefit concert draws ninety thousand in Philadelphia while thousands of others gather at a similar event in London, 1985; President Reagan undergoes surgery to remove cancerous polyp, 1985.

Born Today—Economist Sidney Webb, 1859; educator Mary Emma Woolley, 1863; playwright David Storey, 1933; actor Robert Forster, 1941; actor Harrison Ford, 1942; inventor Erno Rubik, 1944.

Today's Quotation—"Washington is not a place to live in. The rents are high, the food is bad, the dust is disgusting, and the morals are deplorable."—*Horace Greeley, July 13, 1865*

Deplorable Morals

An Army corporal, writing in *Moody Monthly*, tells of his experience some years ago on a train enroute to New York. As he was riding along, a black Army officer came and sat beside him. They struck up a conversation and soon learned of each other's faith in Christ. The soldier asked the officer if the latter had had many opportunities to witness back at camp. He replied, "Well the first night in the tent most of the troops were swearing and telling filthy stories." Finally, having had enough of the filth, the officer told the soldiers, "I've heard your rough talk but now I am going to talk to God and, out of respect to him, I ask you to please be quiet." The tent grew suddenly silent and the officer never again had to contend with immoral talk.

It is amazing how the world will respect the Christian who unashamedly takes a stand for that which is right!

Prayer Suggestion—Help us to have the courage to be God's light shining forth in a world of darkness.

JULY

14

Luke 6:27–35

Today in History—Bastille Day (French national holiday), 1789; William Bonney, "Billy the Kid" killed in Fort Sumner, N.M., 1881; Iraq overthrows monarchy, 1958; Gallup poll shows Americans more concerned about inflation than anything else, 1974; three Soviet dissidents receive long prison terms, 1978.

Born Today—Writer Irving Stone, 1903; folksinger Woody Guthrie, 1912; President Gerald Ford, 1913; director Ingmar Bergman, 1918; broadcast journalist John Chancellor, 1927; actress Polly Bergen, 1930.

Today's Quotation—"I come . . . from the West where we have always seen the backs of our enemies."—*General John Pope, July 14, 1862*

Our Enemies

Have you ever felt how nice it would be if you were able to see the backs of your enemies—as they walked away in defeat? While God may give us the victory over our challengers, many times he lets us continue the struggle to further his will and to strengthen our trust in him.

R. C. Campbell tells of two men who owned farms on opposite sides of a river. One day, the neighbor's cows got out of the field and damaged about half an acre of corn before they were corralled by the second farmer and locked in his barn. Rather than return the herd, the second farmer demanded a significant ransom. Later, his hogs escaped and began rooting up potatoes in the first neighbor's field. Rounding up the hogs, he herded them across the river back to where they belonged. The hogs' owner saw his neighbor returning with the herd and, suspecting the worst, got out his gun. When he saw that his neighbor had no intention of harming him or his hogs, he said, "You must be a Christian." Indeed, later that night both the unsaved man and his wife accepted Christ as Savior.

The Bible reminds us to "be an example of the believers." Do others see the love of Christ when they look at you, or do they see your back turned to them in impatience and disgust?

Prayer Suggestion—Do you have enemies? Pray for them and ask God to let you see them through his eyes.

JULY

15

Today in History—President Eisenhower sends U.S. troops into Lebanon, 1958; President Nixon announces plans to visit Red China, 1971; Democrats pick former Georgia Governor Jimmy Carter and Senator Walter Mondale of Minnesota to head their presidential ticket, 1976; in massive ceremony, 4,150 followers of Korea's Sun Myung Moon are married in New York's Madison Square Garden, 1982.

Born Today—Architect Inigo Jones, 1573; artist Rembrandt van Rijn, 1606; author Clement Moore, 1779; musician Julian Bream, 1933; football player Alex Karras, 1935; actor Ken Kercheval, 1935; singer Linda Ronstadt, 1946.

Today's Quotation—"If every nation will employ itself in what it is fittest to produce, a greater quantity will be raised of the things contributing to human happiness, than if every nation attempts to raise everything it wants within itself. . . ."—*Thomas Jefferson, July 15, 1808*

Human Happiness

Preacher Donald Gray Barnhouse used to tell the story of how he often sent gifts home to his mother from Europe during World War I. "Imagine if I included a note that read, 'I am sending these gifts so that you will love me,'" he said. "Why, her response would be that she loved me before I was born, and that her love had no bearing on whether or not I sent her gifts. I did, however, write notes saying I was sending the gifts because I loved her, thus adding to both her joy and mine. This is the example of true Christian giving, motivated by the love of Christ to do for others as he has done for us."

A little old deaf woman sat by the mission hall door in London day after day. Once asked what her ministry was, she replied, "Oh, I smile them in and then I smile them out again." It was evident God had given her a radiant, contagious happiness. Are you living victoriously like a child of the King? If not, begin enjoying life today!

Prayer Suggestion—Realize that with all God has done for you it is impossible not to be happy.

JULY

16

Matthew 28:18–20

Today in History—District of Columbia established, 1790; first U.S. atom-bomb test explosion, 1945; *Apollo II* astronauts Neil Armstrong, Edwin Aldrin, Jr., and Michael Collins blast off from Cape Kennedy, Fla., on first voyage to land on moon, 1969; seven New Jersey teenage computer "hackers" accused of accessing confidential computer data, including Pentagon files, 1985.

Born Today—Artist Sir Joshua Reynolds, 1723; explorer Roald Amundsen, 1872; actress Barbara Stanwyck, 1907, actress Ginger Rogers, 1911; tennis player Margaret Court, 1942.

Today's Quotation—"I would remind you that extremism in the defense of liberty is no vice. And let me remind you also that moderation in the pursuit of justice is no virtue!"—*Barry M. Goldwater, July 16, 1964*

Extremism

How motivated are Christians in proclaiming God's Word? Here are some interesting comparisons: Fuller Brush Company sales representatives get into one of every seven homes called on, with a sale made in one of every six homes entered. In contrast, Mormon missionaries are said to succeed in entering one in every seven homes visited and spend five hundred hours dealing with an individual before he or she is converted.

Vance Havner once told of a meeting in Indianapolis many years ago on "How to Reach the Masses." One day, during the meeting, a young preacher stood on a street corner and began to preach. Soon such a huge crowd had gathered that they had to move indoors where they soon filled the main floor. Yet their service had to be shortened to make way for the convention on "How to Reach the Masses." Havner pointed out, "While the convention was discussing how to reach the masses, D. L. Moody was out there doing it!"

Are we discussers or doers of God's command to "preach the gospel to every creature"? (Mark 16:15)

Prayer Suggestion—Give us the zeal of D. L. Moody to reach our generation all around the world with the gospel.

JULY

17

Proverbs 22:1-6

Today in History—First issue of *Punch* published in London, 1841; Douglas "Wrong Way" Corrigan begins flight from New York to California, 1938; Potsdam Conference of Truman, Stalin, and Churchill begins in Germany, 1945; Methodist minister Marjorie Matthews becomes first woman bishop of an American church, 1980; Ronald Reagan chooses rival George Bush as his running mate on the Republican presidential ticket, 1980; two aerial walkways collapse onto lobby of Hyatt Regency Hotel in Kansas City, Mo., killing 111 people and injuring 188 more, 1981.

Born Today—Hymn writer Isaac Watts, 1674; merchant John Jacob Astor, 1763; writer Erle Stanley Gardner, 1889; actor James Cagney, 1904; entertainer Art Linkletter, 1912; actress Phyllis Diller, 1917; singer Diahann Carroll, 1935.

Today's Quotation—"I was born an American; I will live an American; I shall die an American."—*Daniel Webster, July 17, 1850*

Free Born

It is how we were raised that governs our eternal destiny. Much of the blame for the decline in America's moral life can be placed squarely at the door of Christian parents who insisted on providing their children's physical needs but who then left spiritual choices for the kids to decide.

Evangelist John R. Rice told of a revival campaign in which he met with the mother of a bright eleven-year-old girl. The mother told Rice that she wanted "the girl to make up her mind for herself" about spiritual things. The evangelist asked thoughtfully, "If she wanted to drink poison, would you let her make up her mind about that? Why does God give a mother influence over a child if not to use it to get the child to heaven?" The next service both mother and daughter came forward weeping; the girl trusting Christ at her mother's insistence.

Will your family circle be unbroken in the life to come with all members present in heaven? Do your utmost to persuade each one to trust Christ as Savior while there is still time to decide for him.

Prayer Suggestion—Ask for God's help to raise your children to love and serve him.

JULY

18

Philippians 4:6–13

Today in History—Douglas "Wrong Way" Corrigan lands at Dublin, Ireland, 1938; Allied forces capture key Nazi-held town of St. Lo in western France in World War II, 1944; Mary Jo Kopechne dies when car driven by Senator Edward M. Kennedy plunges off bridge at Chappaquiddick Island, Mass., 1969; unemployed security guard goes on shooting rampage at San Diego area McDonald's restaurant killing twenty and wounding sixteen others, 1984.

Born Today—Naturalist Gilbert White, 1720; writer William Thackeray, 1811; comedian Red Skelton, 1913; astronaut John Glenn, 1921; singer Dion Di Mucci, 1939; singer Martha Reeves, 1941.

Today's Quotation—"Great men are they who see that spiritual is stronger than material force, that thoughts rule the world."—*Ralph Waldo Emerson, July 18, 1876*

Spiritual Strength

According to *Truth for Youth* a certain society in Africa once wrote to David Livingstone: "Have you found a good road to where you are? If so, we want to know how to send other men to join you." Livingstone replied, "If you have men who will come *only* if they know there is a good road, I don't want them. I want men who will come if there is *no road at all!*"

A little boy once stated that he loved his mother with "all his strength." Asked to explain, the youth said, "Well, we live on the fourth floor of this tenement house with no elevator. The coal is kept in the basement. Mother is not very strong so I see to it that the coal shuttle is never empty. It takes all my strength to get the coal up the four flights of stairs. Now, isn't that loving my mother with all my strength?"

Are we demonstrating our love for Christ through developing greater spiritual strength?

Prayer Suggestion—Help me to set priorities in my life so that I will gain the spiritual strength I need to serve God daily.

JULY

19

1 Peter 5:6-11

Today in History—British Prime Minister Churchill introduces World War II "V for Victory" theme, 1941; Spain's Prince Juan Carlos succeeds his father Generalissimo Francisco Franco as Spanish ruler, 1974; U. S. spacecraft docks with Soviet counterpart for two days in epic international space mission, 1975; Summer Olympics open in Moscow without U.S. or West German teams represented, 1980; Walter Mondale and Geraldine Ferraro are nominated by the Democratic Party to head its presidential ticket, 1984.

Born Today—Inventor Samuel Colt, 1814; artist Edgar Degas, 1834; surgeon Charles Mayo, 1865; politician George McGovern, 1922; football player Roosevelt "Rosey" Grier, 1932; singer Vikki Carr, 1941.

Today's Quotation—"Man cannot fulfill his destiny alone. . . ."— *Elizabeth Cady Stanton, July 19, 1848*

Man's Destiny

The magazine advertisement seemed to jump from the page with its bold headline: "You have 24 hours to live," followed, in smaller print, by the single word: "today."

A good example of the importance of doing things which must be done day by day was a man who once had an open sore break out on his face. Some of his friends felt that it might be cancer and that he should seek immediate treatment, but the man read an ad for a salve which promised to cure cancer. He bought the salve, applied it, and boasted that he had been able to save the cost of the doctor's visit and the pain of possible surgery by using it regularly. Indeed on the surface the sore did seem to heal, but underneath lay the deadly cancer which eventually claimed the man's life. Though he had a desperate need, he refused the source of healing.

How many people in the world today are just like this man? They struggle to get by on their own strength, fully ignoring God's all-encompassing cure for their need. They need to simply let go and let God have his way in their life, accepting his guaranteed, everlasting cure for sin.

Prayer Suggestion—Acknowledge your weakness and dependency upon God. Cast all your burdens upon him who has promised to forgive.

JULY

20

Today in History—"Riot Act" in England makes gatherings of twelve or more people illegal, 1715; German Army officers plant a bomb in Adolf Hitler's quarters but miss killing Hitler, 1944; U.S. invades Japanese-occupied Guam in World War II, 1944; astronaut Neil Armstrong becomes first man to set foot on the moon, 1969; after an eleven-month journey, *Viking* spacecraft sends detailed photos of Mars, 1976.

Born Today—Poet Petrarch, 1304; explorer Sir Edmund Hillary, 1919; business executive Mike Ilitch, 1929; basketball coach Chuck Daly, 1933; publisher Nelson Doubleday, 1933; singer Sally Ann Howes, 1934.

Today's Quotation—"That's one small step for a man, one giant leap for mankind."—*Neil Armstrong, on the moon, July 20, 1969*

One Small Step

Few who saw it will ever forget the sight of Neil Armstrong setting foot on the moon; a small but greatly historic step. Sometimes we take steps in this life which God may use to do his will.

Some time ago, the British Press Association reported the story of a submarine which lay disabled on the ocean floor. All hope of her rescue was abandoned. The commanding officer told the crew they did not have long to live and led them in singing "Abide with Me." Following the song, the sailors awaited their seemingly inevitable fate. Suddenly, one of the men collapsed and fell against a control panel, setting in motion the jammed surfacing mechanism. Slowly the craft began to rise and eventually made it safely back to port. What some might term a freak stroke of fate, the sailors knew was God at work on their behalf. God may even allow an accident to be the small step he uses to fulfill his will.

Prayer Suggestion—Remember, no matter how bleak things may be for the moment, "we know that all things work together for good to them that love God" (Rom. 8:28).

JULY

21

Today in History—U.S. Veterans Administration established, 1930; President Franklin D. Roosevelt nominated by Democrats for fourth term, 1944; agreement partitioning Indochina and removing French authority signed, 1954; leaders of the seven western industrialized nations meeting in Ottawa agree unemployment and inflation must be contained, 1981; after nineteen months, martial law is set to end in Poland with little change expected for the Polish people, 1983.

Born Today—Writer Ernest Hemingway, 1899; author Marshall McLuhan, 1911; violinist Isaac Stern, 1920; actor Don Knotts, 1924; producer Norman Jewison, 1926; actor Robin Williams, 1952.

Today's Quotation—"Remember that Time is Money. . . .Waste neither Time nor Money, but make the best Use of both."—*Benjamin Franklin, July 21, 1748*

Wasted Years

Sometimes what we feel is totally useless service for the Lord may, in his eyes, really be some of the best. Such was the case with an old Scottish woman who was lamenting her many "wasted years" spent raising children and keeping a busy household clean and neat. "I so wanted to serve Jesus," she sorrowfully told her pastor, "and all these years I have only had time to take care of my family." "Where is your family now?" the preacher asked. The woman explained that all four were either in full-time missionary service or in training for the Lord's work. The wise old preacher straightened up and said, "And you think you've wasted your life? Why with all you are accomplishing through them, your heavenly mansion will be right next to the throne!" It was her faithful example, day after day at home, that helped all her children surrender their lives to the Lord's service.

Never feel your years are wasted if you are doing what God has provided for you to do!

Prayer Suggestion—Resolve to use every moment God has given you, in some way, to further his kingdom—even by serving at home.

JULY

22

1 Peter 4:12-19

Today in History—Pilgrims leave from Holland bound for the New World, 1620; Cleveland, Ohio, founded, 1796; explosion at San Francisco parade kills ten people, 1916; public enemy John Dillinger shot in Chicago, 1934; conference of forty-four nations at Bretton Woods, N.H., establishes International Monetary Fund, 1944.

Born Today—Scientist Gregor Mendel, 1822; sculptor Alexander Calder, 1898; poet Stephen Vincent Benet, 1898; politician Robert Dole, 1923; designer Oscar de la Renta, 1932; singer Bobby Sherman, 1945.

Today's Quotation—"I would not be my natural self if I did not utter my consciousness of my limited ability to meet your full expectation. . . ."—*Warren G. Harding, accepting Republican Presidential nomination, July 22, 1920*

Limited Abilities

Our Daily Bread tells of the mother of a handicapped, brain-injured child who once wrote that her daughter's handicap could have become the greatest tragedy of their lives if it had not been for the fact that through it they came to know the Lord much better. The mother wrote, "How disappointed we were when our little girl failed to experience normal mental development—perhaps like the Savior feels when his children do not spiritually mature."

He knows that it is these trials and heartaches that enrich our lives in such a way that could not happen otherwise. Then, fortified anew, we come through life's trials stronger and more effective Christians with a new and brighter testimony. Are you going through some difficult times? Perhaps you have sensed your limited human abilities. Admit to God your limitations and ask him to carry you through the rough straits of life.

Prayer Suggestion—Thank God for life's trials, which help us to develop spiritual strength and become more effective Christians.

JULY

23

Today in History—U.S. forces invade Tinian Island in World War II, 1944; Marshal Petain goes on trial for treason, 1945; Bedloe's Island, site of Statue of Liberty, renamed Liberty Island, 1956; Miss America, Vanessa Williams, resigns following discovery of published indecent photos, 1984; England's Prince Andrew marries Sarah Ferguson in ceremonies seen by an estimated three hundred million persons worldwide, 1986.

Born Today—Actress Charlotte Cushman, 1816; writer Raymond Chandler, 1888; Ethiopian leader Haile Selassie, 1891; psychiatrist Karl Menninger, 1893; actress Gloria De Haven, 1925; sportscaster Don Drysdale, 1936.

Today's Quotation—"If I treated with the enemy it was to save you."—*Marshal Henri Petain, July 23, 1945*

A Deadly Enemy

It has been noted that certain deadly poisons look perfectly clear—like crystal spring water. A glass containing poison and a glass of clear water may both look the same, but one contains death; the other, life. Many seemingly innocent pleasures, amusements, or activities may appear innocent. Satan is a deadly enemy who is just waiting to see whom he may devour. Don't let it be you!

An ancient king once became jealous of the town blacksmith. The king asked the blacksmith to make a chain that "no man can break" and so the smith set to work, carefully putting together the chain, link by link. Finally, the blacksmith declared he had made a chain so strong that "if it had an elephant on each end pulling, they couldn't break it," and with that he presented the chain to the king. The king then commanded his guards to "bind him with it," and they wrapped the sturdy chain around the hapless blacksmith.

Many in this world are bound by chains of sin which bind and enslave them. But, praise God, "he breaks the power of sin, he sets the captive free!" Have you experienced the freedom found only in Christ's forgiveness?

Prayer Suggestion—Christ has broken the power of sin in our lives and it no longer has dominion over us. Praise his name!

JULY

24

Today in History—Vice President Richard M. Nixon and U.S.S.R. Premier Nikita Khruschev engage in a spontaneous "kitchen" debate in Moscow, 1959; *New York Times* reporter is jailed for refusing to turn over notes sought in a murder trial, 1978; Iraq charges U.S. with giving weapons to Iranians in Iran-Iraq war, 1983.

Born Today—Patriot Simon Bolivar, 1783; playwright Alexandre Dumas, 1802; aviator Amelia Earhart, 1898; actress Ruth Buzzi, 1936; musician Peter Serkin, 1947; actress Lynda Carter, 1951.

Today's Quotation—"The most important thing in the Olympic Games is not winning but taking part . . . the essential thing in life is not conquering but fighting well."—*Baron Pierre de Coubertin, July 24, 1908*

Taking Part

The husband was vainly protesting having to dry the dishes by saying, "This isn't a man's job." But his wife was prepared. "Oh yes, it is," she said, quoting 2 Kings 21:13, "I will wipe Jerusalem as a man wipeth a dish, wiping it, and turning it upside down." No matter how boring the task may be, the believer who is serving God will find it a blessing to participate as part of God's family. As the English poet and clergyman John Donne wrote some four hundred years ago:

> No man is an island, entire of itself;
> every man is a piece of the continent, a part of the main;
> Any man's death diminishes me, because I am involved in
>   mankind;
> and therefore never send to know for whom the bell tolls;
> it tolls for thee.

When asked to do a job you feel is beneath your abilities, rejoice that you may serve the Lord in yet another way. Keep a good attitude in the little things, then watch God bless you with increasingly greater responsibilities for him.

Prayer Suggestion—Recognize that when we are saved we must then part in furthering the work of God in whatever way he provides.

JULY

25

1 Corinthians 15:51–58

Today in History—France's Louis Bleriot makes first airplane flight across English Channel, 1909; Italian liner *Andrea Doria* collides with Swedish liner off Nantucket and sinks early next day, 1956; Louise Brown, world's first test tube baby (from egg inseminated outside the womb), is born normally in Great Britain, 1978; Nicaragua's President Somoza resigns under pressure, thus ending forty-six-year family dynasty, 1979.

Born Today—Artist Thomas Eakins, 1844; statesman Arthur Balfour, 1848; painter Maxfield Parrish, 1870; actor Walter Brennan, 1894; philosopher Eric Hoffer, 1902; football player Walter Payton, 1954.

Today's Quotation—"Inconsistencies of opinion, arising from changes of circumstances, are often justifiable."—*Daniel Webster, July 25, 1846*

Inconsistencies

Family Weekly reported a man from Brooklyn had his name changed from Kelly to Feinberg and then a year later from Feinberg to Garibaldi. Appearing before the judge, the man was asked the reason for yet another switch of names. His reply, "My neighborhood keeps changing."

Consistency seems to be a dying virtue in many areas these days. There's at least one agency known for its consistency, right or wrong, and that is the federal government. Seven times now, the Veterans Administration has sent Ronald Vest's check to Cany Postlethwaite. Despite valiant efforts to return the check, it keeps being mis-delivered time after time. To make matters worse, the recipient is not allowed to simply destroy it since it is government property. Thus much time and energy is wasted in simply attempting to get the check to the rightful owner.

Indeed it is one thing to be consistent, but we can be consistently wrong. Thank God that he is not only perfect, but consistently so in our ever-changing world.

Prayer Suggestion—Ask God to make us consistent Christians in all we do and say each day of our lives!

JULY

26

Today in History—New York becomes eleventh state to ratify U.S. Constitution, 1788; Federal Bureau of Investigation established, 1908; U.S. Department of Defense established by Armed Forces Unification Act, 1947; Egypt seizes and nationalizes Suez Canal, 1956; Israel's Menachem Begin approves Jewish settlements on conquered West Bank of the Jordan River, 1977; Rev. Sun Myung Moon under investigation for tax evasion, 1981.

Born Today—Writer George Bernard Shaw, 1856; conductor Serge Koussevitzky, 1874; psychologist Carl Jung, 1875; producer Blake Edwards, 1922; actor Jason Robards, 1922; director Stanley Kubrick, 1928.

Today's Quotation—"There are no gains without pains."—*Adlai Stevenson, July 26, 1952*

No Pain—No Gain

A preacher was having a hard time getting through to a grizzled old miner about God's salvation being a free gift. When asked what he thought of the plan of salvation the miner replied, "I can't believe in a religion such as that. If there's no pain, then there can be no gain." Changing the subject momentarily, the preacher asked how the miner got out of the mine at the end of the day. "In an elevator, of course," came the response. "Well," said the preacher, "that sounds too simple to me. Isn't there *something* you have to do to help raise yourself?" "No, of course not," he responded. "Was it very expensive to drill the eighteen hundred foot mine shaft?" "Why, yes, but it was necessary, so we could get out of the mine." "Well, the same is true of salvation."

The work of Christ on the cross has already been completed at a tremendous cost—the best that heaven had—so that we might be saved. All we need to do is to believe. "How shall we escape, if we neglect so great salvation?" (Heb. 2:3).

Prayer Suggestion—Thank God that though free, our salvation is not cheap. It cost the best that heaven had to give, the Lord Jesus Christ.

JULY

27

Today in History—Army Medical Service established, 1775; Atlantic telegraph cable between England and U.S. completed, 1866; Korean War armistice signed ending the fighting, 1953; exiled Shah of Iran dies in Egyptian military hospital a year-and-a-half after being ousted from power, 1980; Britain's Margaret Thatcher submits package of new proposals to battle unemployment, 1981; Israeli jets bomb West Beirut killing 120 and wounding 252 in first raid on a civilian area, 1982; pollster George Gallup, Sr., 82, dies in Switzerland, 1984.

Born Today—French novelist Alexandre Dumas, 1824; baseball manager Leo Durocher, 1906; actor Kennan Wynn, 1916; producer Norman Lear, 1922; songwriter Bobby Gentry, 1942; figure skater Peggy Fleming, 1948.

Today's Quotation—"One with the law is a majority."—*Calvin Coolidge, July 27, 1920*

One Alone

We should be faithful in the little things of life, for the power they wield is often tremendous. For example, a single seemingly insignificant rudder controls the movement of a massive ocean liner. And a single life dedicated to God can move a multitude.

A lady was once preparing a box to send to missionaries when a little girl came to her door with a penny to send along. With this one penny, the woman bought a gospel tract and included it in the box. The tract was read by a tribal chief who accepted Christ as Savior. He was influential in reaching many of his friends with the gospel. Eventually, as a result of that little girl's one-penny gift, more than fifteen hundred natives were saved from the hopelessness of sin!

Never underestimate the little things of life, for God uses the little things to confound the wise.

Prayer Suggestion—Recognize that God can use every believer for his service—all are equally loved and important to him.

JULY

28

Today in History—Peru declares freedom from Spain, 1821; Fourteenth Amendment to U.S. Constitution ratified, 1868; World War I begins as Austria and Hungary declare war on Serbia, 1914; "Bonus Army" of World War I veterans disperses in Washington, D.C., 1932; Army bomber crashes into the Empire State Building killing 13 people, 1945; brush-fire near Santa Barbara, Ca., destroys 185 homes and causes evacuation of three thousand people, 1977; Latin American nations call for removal of all foreign bases and forces from Central America; meanwhile, U.S. House votes to cancel all covert aid to the Nicaraguan Contras, 1983.

Born Today—Author Beatrix Potter, 1866; singer Rudy Vallee, 1901; explorer Jacques Piccard, 1922; former First Lady Jacqueline Kennedy Onassis, 1929; actor Darryl Hickman, 1931; actress Sally Struthers, 1948.

Today's Quotation—"Democracy will never solve its problems at the end of a billy club."—*Lyndon B. Johnson, July 28, 1964*

Carrying a Big Stick

In this age of mass destruction there is a tendency to rely upon our weapons rather than God for strength. This is a misplaced confidence. A UPI news story tells of a remarkable catch made some time ago by a French fishing trawler. After reporting an "enormous pulling" in its nets, the crew of the Lorraine-Bretagne discovered they had caught a 382-foot-long submarine, the *USS Robert E. Lee.* After five hours the submarine, which suffered no major damage, finally came untangled from the trawler's nets. All the might of sixteen Polaris missiles and a crew of 112 sailors were for naught as their boat lay entrapped by a simple fishing net.

In what do you place your trust? In the "big stick" of human weapons and defenses or in the almighty power of God?

Prayer Suggestion—May we be honest before all men and especially before a holy God who knows our hearts and sees all things.

JULY

29

Today in History—English forces rout the Spanish Armada, 1588; Vincent van Gogh dies in France, 1890; thousands die in China as it is rocked by strongest earthquake in years, 1976; Britain's Prince Charles marries Lady Diana in lavish London wedding seen by millions, 1981; Senate opens confirmation hearings on Chief Justice nominee William Rehnquist, 1986.

Born Today—Writer Booth Tarkington, 1869; explorer William Beebe, 1877; composer Sigmund Romberg, 1887; actor William Powell, 1892; lawyer Melvin Belli, 1907; broadcast journalist Peter Jennings, 1938.

Today's Quotation—"No personal considerations should stand in the way of performing a public duty."—*Ulysses S. Grant, July 29, 1875*

Grant's Surrender

Though much has been written about Ulysses S. Grant as public servant, less is known of his conversion experience. Walter B. Knight describes Grant's surrender to God in the waning days of his life. Calling for a minister, the general was told of his need to sincerely seek God's face and that he would forgive his sins. God opened the general's heart to respond, and Grant was saved. On hearing Grant's prayer, the minister excitedly said, "God's kingdom has gained greatly in your conversion, general." Grant, showing great maturity in his first response as a believer, replied, "God does not need great men, but great men need God." Later the general said he had but one remaining wish, that he could live one more year in order that he might share with others his new-found faith in God.

Prayer Suggestion—Thank God that he loves you and that he has allowed you the opportunity to tell others of his redeeming love.

JULY

30

Psalm 119:10-20

Today in History—Virginia General Assembly, first in America, meets in Jamestown, Va., 1619; WAVES (Women's Unit of U.S. Navy) created, 1942; Dan Mitrione of U.S. Agency for International Development kidnapped in Uruguay by terrorists (found dead on August 10, 1970); H. R. Haldeman says secret White House tapes fail to show his or President Nixon's involvement in Watergate crisis, 1973; Supreme Court rules President Nixon must turn over all tapes sought by the special prosecutor. House committee votes twenty-seven to eleven for impeachment, 1974.

Born Today—Industrialist Henry Ford, 1863; sculptor Henry Moore, 1898; producer Peter Bogdanovich, 1939; singer Paul Anka, 1941; actor Arnold Schwarzenegger, 1947; basketball player Bill Cartwright, 1957.

Today's Quotation—"The man who cannot live on bread and water is not fit to live. . . ."—*Henry Ward Beecher, July 30, 1877*

Bread and Water

All priests and nuns take a vow of poverty upon their acceptance into the clergy. However, this policy was challenged recently by two priests on the law school faculty of a Catholic institution in the Washington, D.C. area. The two, whose pay may be as little as half what other professors make, have filed separate suits against their administration seeking parity with other law professors. The priests contend the university had promised an end to their discounted salaries but that nothing was ever done.

In the spiritual realm, what kind of sacrifice are we willing to make for Christ? "Not just a part nor half of my heart, I will give *all* to thee!"

Prayer Suggestion—Recognize that God wants all of our heart, not just a "bread and water" existence on the edge of our lives.

JULY

31

Hebrews 9:24-28

Today in History—Cornerstone laid for U.S. Mint, 1792; Charles de Gaulle named to head the Committee of National Defense of the Free French, 1943; presidential candidate George McGovern drops Senator Tom Eagleton as running mate following revelations that Eagleton had undergone treatment for an emotional ailment, 1972; Chrysler asks for record one billion dollars in loan guarantees, 1979; South Africa declares a state of emergency and bans mass funerals for victims of black unrest, 1985.

Born Today—Legal scholar James Kent, 1763; engineer John Ericsson, 1803; economist Milton Friedman, 1912; sports commentator Curt Gowdy, 1919; black leader Whitney Young, Jr., 1921; tennis player Evonne Goolagong, 1951.

Today's Quotation—"Only those are fit to live who are not afraid to die."—*General Douglas MacArthur, July 31, 1941*

Afraid to Die

The Prussian "manufacturer of death," Alfred Krupp, was said to be so afraid of death himself that he never forgave anyone who talked about death around him. Under threat of being fired, all of his employees were strictly barred from speaking of death when he was around. Once a relative who was visiting him suddenly died, driving Krupp out of the house in terror. Later, when his wife chided him for his action, Krupp forsook her and never lived with her again. Finally, nearing death himself, Krupp offered his physician the equivalent of one million dollars to prolong his life for ten years. The doctor was, of course, unable to do this and eventually Krupp died.

The Bible says, "It is appointed unto men once to die" (Heb. 9:27). We can be sure that, if we have trusted in Christ for salvation, we will have nothing to fear. "Oh death, where is thy sting?" (1 Cor. 15:55).

Prayer Suggestion—Through the darkest valley, God will go with us and carry us safely over if we but trust in him.

AUGUST

1

Today in History—Republic of Switzerland founded, 1291; Bank of England opens in London, 1694; compilation of first U.S. census begins, 1790; Colorado admitted to U.S. as thirty-eighth state, 1876; Heaven and Home Hour begins, 1933; U.S. Atomic Energy Commission established, 1946; Far East Broadcasting begins transmitting to Russia, 1949; President Ford and leaders of thirty-three other countries sign Helsinki agreement recognizing sovereignty of European nations, 1975; Manville Corporation pays $2.5 billion in asbestos-related claims, 1985.

Born Today—Composer Francis Scott Key, 1779; editor Richard Dana, 1815; astronomer Maria Mitchell, 1818; writer Herman Melville, 1819; conductor William Steinberg, 1899; comedian Dom DeLuise, 1933.

Today's Quotation—"I like the dreams of the future better than the history of the past."—*Thomas Jefferson, August 1, 1816*

Past History

Many years ago, the manager of Baltimore's largest hotel, not wanting to discredit his establishment, refused lodging to a man dressed as a humble farmer. The man left and found a room elsewhere. It was not long before the manager discovered, much to his horror, that he had just rejected none other than the vice president of the United States, Thomas Jefferson. He tried to remedy his mistake by sending an urgent message to the famed patriot inviting him to be his guest. Jefferson responded with this reply: "Tell him I have already engaged a room elsewhere . . . if he has no room for a dirty American farmer, he also has none for the vice president of the United States."

Clearly the innkeeper would have liked to repeat history, but, as he discovered, the past is past and cannot be redone. Thank God he gives us a second chance, forgiving and forgetting our past sinful history.

Prayer Suggestion—Accept God's forgiveness and thank him for rewriting your history to forgive and forget all your sins.

AUGUST

2

Romans 1:16–25

Today in History—Wild Bill Hickok dies in ambush at Deadwood, S.D., 1876; U.S. War Department buys first military airplane from Wilbur and Orville Wright, 1909; President Warren G. Harding dies in San Francisco and is succeeded by Vice President Calvin Coolidge, 1923; President Coolidge refuses to run for another term, 1927; Adolf Hitler proclaims himself leader of Germany on death of President Hindenburg, 1934; Hatch Act, restricting campaign contributions by civil servants, is signed into law by President Franklin Roosevelt, 1939; Albert Einstein writes to President Roosevelt to urge atomic energy research, 1939; President Nixon's aides John Dean and John Ehrlichman sentenced to jail for Watergate crimes, 1974; Delta jet crashes on landing in Dallas thunderstorm, all but twenty-one of the 161 aboard are killed, 1985.

Born Today—Architect Pierre L'Enfant, 1754; painter John Sloan, 1871; writer John Kieran, 1892; actress Myrna Loy, 1905; writer James Baldwin, 1924; actor Carroll O'Connor, 1924; actor Peter O'Toole, 1933.

Today's Quotation—"It is my living sentiment, and by the blessing of God it shall be my dying sentiment—Independence forever."—*Daniel Webster, August 2, 1826*

Independence Forever

One of the greatest blessings of being born again is the independence forever from the bondage of sin. Someone has likened the bonds of sin to a chained dog asleep in the back yard. While he is sleeping he isn't aware of the chain and later, when he eats from his dish near his kennel, he still feels free. But when his master calls and he runs the length of the chain, he abruptly realizes his plight.

That is the way it is with sin; for a time it gives an appearance of independence, but when you try to get free, you suddenly find you're trapped with no way out.

Prayer Suggestion—Thank God that he overcomes the power of sin and sets us free; otherwise we would still be dead in sin.

AUGUST

3

John 1:1–14

Today in History—Christopher Columbus sails from Spain, seeking route to India, 1492; confessed ex-communist Whittaker Chambers accuses Alger Hiss of being a communist operative, 1948; U.S. Military Academy dismisses ninety cadets for cheating, 1951; first black female to occupy a cabinet position, Patricia Harris, becomes the new secretary of Health, Education and Welfare, 1979.

Born Today—Poet Rupert Brooke, 1887; journalist Ernie Pyle, 1900; activist Maggie Kuhn, 1905; composer Richard Adler, 1921; author Leon Uris, 1924; singer Tony Bennett, 1926; actor Martin Sheen, 1940.

Today's Quotation—"The lamps are going out all over Europe; we shall not see them lit again in our lifetime."—*Viscount Grey, August 3, 1914*

Light the Lamp

What a sobering thought to realize that God has entrusted to believers the eternal destiny of mankind. He has left us on this earth to light the lamp of salvation so that others might see the way.

An evangelist was once consoling two discouraged women who had been faithfully witnessing all day and had only seen one soul accept Christ. "If you won just one soul every half day all year, in a year's time that would amount to over seven hundred souls kept out of hell!" he said. "You shouldn't feel bad about that. No, you cannot win everybody, but, thank God, you can win somebody!"

Whatever you do, be faithful and don't quit. Think of how you came to Christ. Are you thankful others didn't get discouraged and give up before they witnessed to you? Then be faithful in your witness every day. Light the lamp for others walking in the darkness of sin.

Prayer Suggestion—May we be found faithful in sharing the gospel with thousands who are dying without Christ every day.

AUGUST

4

Today in History—Editor John Peter Zenger is acquitted of libel and sedition charges in New York City, 1735; Coast Guard founded, 1790; plans for city of Chicago completed by surveyor James Thompson, 1830; U.S. buys Virgin Islands from Denmark, 1916; Soviets announce new policy of decentralized economic decision-making, 1985.

Born Today—Poet Percy Bysshe Shelley, 1792; financier Russell Sage, 1816; writer Knut Hamsun, 1859; singer Harry Lauder, 1870; Britain's Queen Mother Elizabeth, 1900; journalist Helen Thomas, 1920; baseball player Roger Clemens, 1962.

Today's Quotation—" . . . just for a scrap of paper, Great Britain is going to make war on a kindred nation who desires nothing better than to be friends with her."—*German Chancellor Theobald von Bethmann-Hollweg, August 4, 1914*

Worth Defending

You can tell what kind of person a man is by what he is willing to fight to defend.

Dr. Dale Ingles tells a story of the Duke of Wellington who met a challenge he was unable to overcome. It seems farmers were tired of huntsmen galloping over their fields and so they locked the gate and posted some boys there to stand guard. Time went by and eventually the Duke of Wellington's hunting party arrived at the entrance and asked the lad to open the gate. "I must not," said the boy, faithful to his charge. It was now up to the duke himself to intervene. The duke asked, "Do you know who I am?" The boy said nervously, "I believe you are the Duke of Wellington, sir." "Won't you open the gate for me?" "My master told me not to open the gate to *anyone*," claimed the lad. The duke was so pleased at the youth's faithfulness that he handed him a reward, the equivalent of a five-dollar bill. The lad was thrilled and sat on the gatepost waving his cap in victory at the departing huntsmen. He had done what Napoleon and his army could not do—held back the advance of the Duke of Wellington.

Prayer Suggestion—Call upon God for strength and courage to be true and faithful in the face of hardship, regardless of what others do.

AUGUST

5

1 Corinthians 6:15-20

Today in History—Benedict Arnold, already dealing treasonously with the British, is put in command of West Point Fort in American Revolutionary War, 1780; cornerstone of Statue of Liberty laid at Bedloe's Island, 1884; Marilyn Monroe dies in Hollywood, 1962; George McGovern names Sargent Shriver as his running mate in Democratic race for president, 1972; President Nixon admits he ordered coverup of Watergate events for political as well as national security reasons, 1974; actor Richard Burton dies of stroke in Switzerland, 1984; painter Andrew Wyeth sells 240 long-hidden paintings and drawings never before seen by the public, 1986.

Born Today—Bible translator for American Indians John Eliot, 1604; author Ruth Sawyer, 1880; director John Huston, 1906; astronaut Neil Armstrong, 1930; actress Loni Anderson, 1946; basketball player Patrick Ewing, 1962.

Today's Quotation—"I look upon it that he who minds his belly will hardly mind anything else."—*Samuel Johnson, August 5, 1763*

Caring for the Temple

It has been said that the liquor dealer is one businessman who is ashamed of his best customer. While the gunman wants "your money or your life," the tavern-keeper takes both.

In this permissive age, many people who call themselves Christians knowingly partake of things which are harmful to their bodies. The Bible says our bodies are the "temple of the Holy Ghost," and that "ye are not your own for ye are bought with a price" (1 Cor. 6:19–20). This dictates care for our bodies including proper nutrition, recreation, and exercise. How well are you maintaining God's temple?

Prayer Suggestion—Help us never to put anything into our bodies that we wouldn't want to be seen taking into God's house.

AUGUST

6

Matthew 21:18-22

Today in History—Warner Brothers begins era of talking pictures with world premier of Vitaphone films, 1926; New York Supreme Court Judge Joseph F. Crater disappears in a case that was never solved, 1930; atomic age begins when U.S. bombs Hiroshima, Japan, in World War II, 1945; President Reagan fires twelve thousand federal air traffic controllers following illegal strike, 1981; longest-living heart recipient to date, William Schroeder, dies after 620 days with artificial heart implant, 1986.

Born Today—Patriot Daniel O'Connell, 1775; writer Alfred Lord Tennyson, 1809; penicillin discoverer Sir Alexander Fleming, 1881; actress Lucille Ball, 1911; actor Robert Mitchum, 1917; airline executive Freddie Laker, 1922.

Today's Quotation—"The force from which the sun draws its power has been loosed."—*President Harry S. Truman, August 6, 1945*

Irresistible Force

New York's Wall Street is known as the financial center of the world, but it was also the scene in which Evangelist D. L. Moody was empowered by God's irresistible force. It seems Moody had gone to Wall Street to raise funds for one of his schools when suddenly, God's power swept down upon him in a mighty way. Moody had to beg God to stop "or I will die." After this, though Moody used the same Scripture, the same outlines, and the same sermons, he began to see hundreds coming to be saved rather than the handful who had been making the decision before. The difference was God's anointing power.

That same power, from God's Holy Spirit, lies within each and every one who has believed on the Lord Jesus Christ and put their trust in him. Do you have this irresistible force in your life? Remember: Little Prayer—Little Power; Some Prayer—Some Power; Much Prayer—Much Power!

Prayer Suggestion—Be faithful in prayer then stand back and see God go to work!

235

AUGUST

7

Today in History—Military Order of Purple Heart founded, 1782; Whiskey Rebellion protesting new tax leads President Washington to call out the troops, 1794; Battle of Guadalcanal begins as U.S. Marines land against Japanese, 1942; Congress adopts Gulf of Tonkin Resolution, giving president broad powers to use armed forces, 1964; families begin to leave Love Canal area of Niagara Falls, N.Y., due to seepage from abandoned chemical dump, 1978; Cable TV's Ted Turner abandons plans to buy CBS network and buys film company MGM/UA for $1.5 billion cash instead, 1985.

Born Today—Revolutionary War General Nathanael Greene, 1742; scientist Louis Leakey, 1903; statesman Ralph Bunche, 1904; satirist Stan Freburg, 1926; radio producer Garrison Keillor, 1942; singer B. J. Thomas, 1942; actress Lana Cantrell, 1943; marathon runner Alberto Salazar, 1957.

Today's Quotation—"There is no indispensable man."—*Woodrow Wilson accepting presidential nomination, August 7, 1912*

I Am Nothing

Have you noticed how God seems to allow his greatest work to be accomplished by those with the greatest humility? Francis of Assisi was once asked why he was able to accomplish so much for God. His humility was evident as he said, "God was looking for the weakest, smallest, most insignificant man there is, when he found me. Then God said, 'I will work through him, and he won't be proud for he will see that I am only using him for his smallness and insignificance.'" What a testimony of surrender to the will of God!

Dr. F. B. Meyer once wrote that he had always assumed that God saved his best gifts on a high shelf for those who showed greater Christian maturity and accomplishment. Later in life he came to realize that just the opposite is true: God has stored his best gifts on the lowest shelves for those who are willing to stoop to find them. Have you realized that, in the Christian life as well as in the world, there really is no "indispensable man"?

Prayer Suggestion—Recognize that we are nothing aside from God and what he has done in our life.

AUGUST

8

Today in History—Battle of Britain begins in World War II as Germany launches aerial attacks, 1940; U.S.S.R. announces it has a hydrogen bomb, 1953; bandits take $7 million from a train thirty-five miles from London, in the biggest haul in train robbing history, 1963; Vice President Spiro Agnew being investigated for bribery, extortion, tax fraud, and other charges, 1973; President Nixon resigns from office becoming first president ever to do so, 1974; five Central American countries sign peace accord with regional cease-fire, 1987.

Born Today—Architect Charles Bulfinch, 1763; editor Charles Dana, 1819; poet Sara Teasdale, 1884; producer Dino DeLaurentis, 1919; actress Esther Williams, 1923; artist Andy Warhol, 1931; singer Mel Tillis, 1932; actor Dustin Hoffman, 1937; actor Keith Carradine, 1950.

Today's Quotation—". . . mighty proud I am (and ought to be thankful to God Almighty) that I am able to have a spare bed for my friends."— *Samuel Pepys, August 8, 1950*

A Thankful Heart

Have you ever stopped to consider that thinking precedes thanking? Somewhere in our minds should be thoughts of God. When Paul charts the downward course of mankind, he begins by saying that men, "when they knew God, they glorified him not as God, neither were thankful" (Rom. 1:21).

Why are we not more thankful? It is probably because we do not stop to think. Thanksgiving is really the result of careful cultivation. It is the fruit of a deliberate resolve to think about God, ourselves, and our privileges and responsibilities. In giving thanks we demonstrate the fact that our lives are not dictated by the material things of life.

Prayer Suggestion—Give gratitude where it is due—to God for the blessings he has seen fit to provide in our lives.

AUGUST

9

Today in History—Jesse Owens becomes the first man to win four gold medals in the Olympic Games in Germany, 1936; U.S. drops atom bomb on Nagasaki, Japan, in World War II, 1945; Vice President Gerald Ford sworn in as president upon resignation of Richard Nixon, 1974; William and Emily Harris found guilty of 1974 kidnapping of newspaper heiress Patty Hearst, 1976.

Born Today—Author Izaak Walton, 1593; writer John Dryden, 1631; physician William Morton, 1819; violinist Zino Francescatti, 1905; basketball's Bob Cousy, 1928; tennis player Rod Laver, 1938; actress Jill St. John, 1940.

Today's Quotation—"Free Soil, Free Speech, Free Labor and Free Man."—*Motto of Free Soil Party, August 9, 1848*

Free Salvation

What a difference God's free salvation makes in a life! Evangelist John R. Rice tells of a man who came to him one Saturday night. That morning he had tried to kill himself but was rescued just in time. In the evening he came to Brother Rice totally distraught at the many problems in his life: His wife had left him, he had no home or job, his health was broken, and he was suffering from an incurable disease. He then knelt and trusted Christ as Savior. Suddenly he got up and said, "Isn't that strange. A moment ago I was so worried I thought I wouldn't live; couldn't face another day. Now all that is gone and I feel so peaceful and happy. I haven't a care in the world. Isn't that strange?" Dr. Rice replied, "No, that isn't strange. Jesus said, 'Come unto me, all ye that labor and are heavy laden, and I will give you rest. Take my yoke upon you, and learn of me; for I am meek and lowly in heart: and ye shall find rest unto your souls' (Matt. 11:28–29). Friend, you have found rest for your soul."

If you haven't done so, accept God's priceless yet free salvation today!

Prayer Suggestion—Thank God for his unspeakable gift of salvation that gives mankind a blessed hope and a reason for living.

AUGUST

10

Revelation 5:7-14

Today in History—Missouri admitted to U.S. as twenty-fourth state, 1821; Smithsonian Institution established, 1846; body of kidnapped U.S. police advisor found in Uruguay, 1970; Soviet composer Dimitri Shostakovich dies at age 68, 1975.

Born Today—Composer Alexander Glazunov, 1865; President Herbert Hoover, 1874; actress Rhonda Fleming, 1923; police administrator Benjamin Ward, 1926; singer Jimmy Dean, 1928; singer Eddie Fisher, 1928.

Today's Quotation—"Our one desire—our one determination—is that the people of Southeast Asia be left in peace to work out their own destinies in their own way."—*Lyndon B. Johnson, August 10, 1964*

Our Destiny

A man once overheard the following conversation: "You know, it is unfair for God to judge me because I was born a sinner. After all, I could not help how I was born." Then an elderly saint leaned over and exclaimed, "The Bible does not condemn anyone for being born a sinner. Rather we are condemned if we reject the Savior God has provided as our way of escape."

It's as if a man was trapped in a burning building. A passerby sees the fire and awakens the occupants from their sleep. Though most quickly heed the warning and flee from danger, one stubborn occupant states wearily, "I didn't see this building afire and so I am going to stay here."

"How shall we escape if we neglect so great a salvation?" (Hebrews 2:3). Have you accepted God's offer of escape? Do so today.

Prayer Suggestion—Praise be to God who sacrificed his only Son, the Lord Jesus Christ, to provide our escape from certain judgment.

AUGUST

11

Today in History—First radioed S.O.S. sent by ship off the Carolina coast, 1909; French begin withdrawal from Vietnam, 1954; six days of rioting begin in Watts District of Los Angeles, 1965; last U.S. ground unit is deactivated in Vietnam, 1972.

Born Today—Composer Carrie Jacobs Bond, 1892; actor Lloyd Nolan, 1902; author Alex Haley, 1921; TV host Mike Douglas, 1925; journalist Carl Rowan, 1925; pastor Jerry Falwell, 1933.

Today's Quotation—"We in America today are nearer the final triumph over poverty than ever before in the history of any land."—*Herbert Hoover, August 11, 1928*

Poverty

Historians tell us that in the entire history of man, there have been only about one hundred thousand truly great achievers. Of that number an estimated eighty thousand or more have come from humble backgrounds. While no one wishes to live in poverty, those who have experienced it often become notable successes.

J. H. Bomberger has compiled a list of some of these achievers. Christopher Columbus begged for bread as a boy and died in poverty, but he discovered a new continent. Preacher Jonathan Edwards' wife and daughters helped support the family while he produced perhaps the most profound book written on this continent. American businessman John Wanamaker began work at a salary of just $1.25 a week, and industrialist Andrew Carnegie was not much better paid at three dollars a week to start. Abraham Lincoln was a miserably poor farmer's son. The greatest man of all time, Jesus Christ, had neither gold nor silver in this life and later was to suffer and die between two thieves—yet his words today still ring with priceless truth.

Never be ashamed of your roots; rather, work to become all that God intended you to be regardless of your beginnings.

Prayer Suggestion—Give God praise for life. Dedicate yourself to serving him in whatever area of service he directs.

AUGUST

12

Today in History—First great American-Indian War ends, 1676; Spanish-American War ends with signing of terms for peace treaty, 1898; Hawaii annexed by U.S., 1898; air mail service begins between Washington D.C. and New York City, 1918; Russian schoolteacher jumps from window to escape being returned to Russia, 1948; U.S.S.R. explodes a hydrogen bomb in secret tests, 1953; *Echo I* communications satellite sent into orbit by U.S., 1960; East Germany erects wall overnight to seal off East Berlin from West Berlin, 1961; actor Henry Fonda dies at age 77, 1982.

Born Today—Historian Robert Southey, 1774; actor Cantinflas, 1911; poet Katharine Lee Bates, 1859; philanthropist Julius Rosenwald, 1862; director Cecil B. De Mille, 1881; actor George Hamilton, 1939.

Today's Quotation—"If heaven had looked upon riches to be a valuable thing, it would not have given them to such a scoundrel."—*English satirist Jonathan Swift, August 12, 1720*

God's Riches

You don't need to be a believer for long before God's riches become evident in your life. Seldom, however, does God respond as quickly as he did to a Baptist pastor years ago. During his morning devotions the preacher called upon the Lord to provide ten dollars for license plates so he could drive to the prison to preach the next Sunday. In a prayer of belief the pastor told God that if he wanted him to preach he would have to supply the money for the plates. While he was still praying, his wife, who was cleaning, called up the steps, "Are you praying for ten dollars?" she cried. "Yes," the preacher responded. "Well, you can quit praying now," she said. "Someone has just shoved a ten dollar bill through the mail slot in the door." God had answered his prayer even while he was still praying!

Prayer Suggestion—Praise God that he is the source of all good things in your life.

AUGUST

13

Today in History—Spanish rule of Manila ends, 1898; first motorized taxis begin operating in New York City, 1907; *Apollo II* astronauts Armstrong, Aldrin, and Collins attend civic ceremonies in New York, Chicago, and Los Angeles, 1969; according to Israeli report, Russians agree to let thirty-five thousand Jews annually emigrate to Israel, 1972; crash of Japanese Airlines plane into mountain range kills 517 in second major air disaster this month, 1985.

Born Today—Sharpshooter Annie Oakley, 1860; director Alfred Hitchcock, 1899; golfer Ben Hogan, 1912; TV evangelist Rex Humbard, 1919; Cuban leader Fidel Castro, 1927; composer Dan Fogelberg, 1951.

Today's Quotation—"Preach, my dear Sir, a crusade against ignorance; establish and improve the law for educating the common people."—*Thomas Jefferson, August 13, 1786*

Educate the People

Someone has wisely said, "You cannot lift your children to a higher level than that on which you live yourself." Along that vein, professor Sidney Hook has said that both intelligence and courage are essential outcomes of education. Stated Hook, "There are human beings who have intelligence but who do not have the moral courage to act on it. On the other hand, moral courage without intelligence is dangerous, for it leads to fanaticism." "Intelligence alone," noted Hook, "is not enough."

God has given us our "gray matter" but what we do to develop it he leaves up to us. When you are asked to give account of what you have done with your talents, what will be your report?

Prayer Suggestion—Seek God's wisdom and guidance as you consider what he would have you to do with your abilities.

AUGUST

14

2 Corinthians 7: 1-10

Today in History—International force enters Peking to smash Boxer Rebellion, 1900; U.S. Social Security Law enacted, 1935; President Franklin D. Roosevelt and Prime Minister Winston Churchill issue Atlantic Charter, 1941; VJ Day, when Japan surrenders, ends World War II, 1945; Benazir Bhutto, 33, daughter of slain Pakistani leader Ali Bhutto, is jailed for addressing a protest rally against the new prime minister, 1986.

Born Today—Artist Ernest Thompson Seton, 1860; writer John Galsworthy, 1867; circus operator John Ringling North, 1903; food authority Julia Child, 1912; basketball player Earvin "Magic" Johnson, 1959.

Today's Quotation—"Sudden converts are superficial and transitory. . . ."—*Charles Lamb, August 14, 1801*

Sudden Converts

Over the years some preachers have used high pressure tactics to gain immediate converts, but the practice frequently results in temporary decisions. Too often the sinner doesn't really believe he is lost. A story in *Wonderful Word* relates how a mother and her daughter once attended a service in a large auditorium and somehow the little girl slipped away. The mother sent a note up to the podium seeking to locate her. It read, "If there is a little girl in the audience who is lost, will she please raise her hand so her mother can find her?" No hands were raised. Finally, when mother and daughter were reunited, the mother sternly asked the daughter, "Didn't you hear the message being read? Why didn't you raise your hand?" "Why mother," said the girl, "it couldn't have been for me because I wasn't lost!"

While we may smile at this story, the way some sinners feel God's message is not for them is deadly serious. To their eternal sorrow, they resolve not to be sudden converts until it is finally too late to repent.

Prayer Suggestion—Recognize that today is the day of salvation and don't put off deciding life's most urgent decision one minute longer.

AUGUST

15

Psalm 139:1-12

Today in History—National Education Association given its name, 1870; wartime gasoline rationing ends, 1945; President Nixon announces ninety-day freeze on wages and prices, 1971; wreckage of the luxury liner *Titantic* believed found in twelve thousand feet of water off of Newfoundland, 1980.

Born Today—Emperor Napoleon Bonaparte, 1769; writer Sir Walter Scott, 1771; actress Ethel Barrymore, 1879; writer Edna Ferber, 1887; author Phyllis Schlafly, 1924; civil rights leader Vernon Jordan, Jr., 1935; Britain's Princess Anne, 1950.

Today's Quotation—"What a happy thing it would be if when we are in our graves (as Shakespeare resembles it) we could dream . . . that we should not need to be so fearful of death."—*Samuel Pepys, August 15, 1665*

Dream

How many people today, distressed or fearful of death, rely on medication to help them sleep? Under such conditions, it is doubtful whether or not they dream. God, however, sometimes uses dreams to impart spiritual lessons. Theologian Dr. A. J. Gordon was once preparing his sermon when he fell asleep and began to dream. He dreamed he was in his pulpit preaching when a stranger walked in and sat down. The stranger's manner was so commanding and attentive Dr. Gordon resolved to speak with him after the service. As the congregation filed out, the pastor searched in vain for the stranger. "Do you know him?" Dr. Gordon asked a deacon. "Why yes," said the deacon, "He is Jesus Christ. It's all right pastor," the deacon went on, "He'll be back next Sunday." At this point Dr. Gordon awoke with the realization that Christ is always present, hearing every word.

Remember that an all-knowing God is observing everything you do and goes with you everywhere you go. Will he be ashamed to be seen with you?

Prayer Suggestion—As the unseen companion in all you do, and the unseen guest at every meal, make sure you include God in all you do.

AUGUST

16

1 Corinthians 10:21-33

Today in History—Bennington Battle Day marks victory over British in Vermont, 1777; gold discovered in Alaska, 1896; Cyprus Independence Day, 1960; Turkish invaders split Cyprus in two in battle against Greek Cypriots, 1974; singer Elvis Presley dies in Memphis at age 42, 1977; former Canadian Prime Minister John Diefenbaker dies of heart attack at age 83, 1979; "Butcher of Lyons," Klaus Barbie, spied for the U.S. in World War II, according to testimony today, 1983.

Born Today—Labor leader George Meany, 1894; actor Robert Culp, 1930; sportscaster Frank Gifford, 1930; singer Eydie Gorme, 1932; actress Julie Newmar, 1935; actor Timothy Hutton, 1960.

Today's Quotation—"This world is a comedy to those that think, a tragedy to those that feel."—*Horace Walpole, August 16, 1776*

Those Who Think

One must be more than just a good thinker to get through school. Consider these brilliant men who nearly didn't make it! Thomas Alva Edison was judged "too stupid to learn." Sir Isaac Newton was next to the lowest in his class and failed geometry because he didn't do the problems according to the book. Even space scientist Wernher von Braun was reported to have failed math and physics in his teens.

Sound familiar? Even if you weren't the greatest student, there's still hope. Christ loves you just as you are and has a wonderful plan for your life. Regardless of the past, seek his lead for a new beginning in your life.

Prayer Suggestion—No matter what the world may think of you, remember that God loves you. You matter to him! Ask for his guidance.

AUGUST

17

Ephesians 5:24-27

Today in History—Robert Fulton's steamboat sets out from New York, 1807; Alger Hiss denies being a communist agent, 1948; Dr. Philip Blaiberg dies after surviving 19½ months with a heart transplant, 1969; Soviet nuclear icebreaker becomes first surface ship to reach the North Pole, 1977; Iraq strikes blow against Iran's strategic Kharg Island where ninety percent of all Iranian oil passes, 1985; last of Hitler's colleagues, Rudolf Hess, dies in West German prison at age 93, 1987.

Born Today—Frontiersman Davy Crockett, 1786; actress Maureen O'Hara, 1920; artist Larry Rivers, 1923; pilot Francis Gary Powers, 1929; actor Robert De Niro, 1943.

Today's Quotation—"It is generally and historically true that tyrannies do pass away in time, that doctrines are always diluted by realities, that any church militant tends to become, with prosperity, the established church."—*Eric Sevareid, August 17, 1963*

The Church Militant

God has called his people to be both salt and light in this sin-darkened world. A look at the early Christians shows a heightened commitment that believers should follow today. Early believers were dedicated. H. A. Ironside reported that the early church met in the dead of night or in the early morning. (How many pastors today could get their congregations to meet at these times?) Their worship consisted of the singing of hymns to Christ, readings from the Scriptures, and the partaking of a simple meal of bread and diluted wine.

Early believers were loyal. Ironside reported the early church encouraged one another to be subject to the government and to pray for all men. The church today could do well to learn from the example of the early Christians lest it become "with prosperity, the established church," ineffectual for God.

Prayer Suggestion—Pray that as members of the church today we would be as faithful in our Christian love and witness as was the early church.

AUGUST

18

John 17:14-23

Today in History—The last Indians leave Chicago, 1835; Adolph Ochs takes control of *The New York Times*, 1896; President Nixon nominates Judge Clement Haynsworth, Jr. for U.S. Supreme Court (later rejected by Senate), 1969; sixty-five thousand cheering fans welcome singer Bruce Springsteen back to his home state of New Jersey, 1985.

Born Today—First colonial child born in America (Virginia Dare), 1587; explorer Meriwether Lewis, 1774; merchant Marshall Field, 1835; actress Shelley Winters, 1922; former First Lady Rosalynn Carter, 1927; actor Robert Redford, 1937.

Today's Quotation—"The first law of history is not to dare to utter falsehood; the second is not to fear to speak the truth."—*Pope Leo XIII, August 18, 1883*

Speak the Truth

How important it is to always speak the truth. Writer Dr. John Todd says he was a young boy when his critically ill father sent him to the druggist for medicine. He was unwilling to go and made up a story that the druggist did not have the needed medicine. Later, as his father's condition worsened, Todd was again sent to get the medicine, but it was too late. Upon his return Todd found his father nearly dead. Faintly, his father told his son, "Love me and always speak the truth for the eye of God is always upon you." Imagine Todd's regret at being untruthful with his father and for not having gone for help the first time!

Prayer Suggestion—That we would be true in all things.

AUGUST

19

Today in History—*U.S.S. Constitution* sinks British frigate, 1812; kidnappers release Samuel Bronfman, II, after nine days in captivity, 1975; bloody fight breaks out in the Demilitarized Zone between North and South Korea; two are killed and nine injured in the battle, 1976; former head of Cambodia, Pol Pot, is sentenced to death, 1979; two U.S. Navy F-14's shoot down two Libyan planes about sixty miles off the Libyan coast in the Gulf of Sidra, 1981.

Born Today—Clockmaker Seth Thomas, 1785; statesman Bernard Baruch, 1870; aviator Orville Wright, 1871; poet Ogden Nash, 1902; author Ring Lardner, Jr., 1915; publisher Malcolm Forbes, 1919; jockey Willie Shoemaker, 1931.

Today's Quotation—"Books have had their day—the theatres have had their day—the temple of religion has had its day."—*James Gordon Bennett, August 19, 1836*

Better Days

A Baptist deacon in a small country church once told evangelist Dr. John R. Rice, "I am afraid the preachers around here are not called to preach. They have no tears when they preach. Nobody is ever converted. There seems to be no burden for souls and no power to win them." Dr. Rice responded, "Oh, they are probably called, but perhaps they have not been anointed to preach. One needs not only divine instruction . . . but he also needs a holy empowering to melt his heart, give him compassion and power to win souls."

Maybe one reason churches today aren't what they once were is because some of them have lost their first love of Christ. Are you concerned about the eternal destiny of those you meet each day—your neighbors, acquaintances, fellow workers, friends? Ask God to give you a new concern for the lost you meet each day.

Prayer Suggestion—Ask God's empowering strength to infuse your pastor and give him the holy boldness to preach against sin.

AUGUST

20

Today in History—Vitus Bering discovers Alaska for Russia, 1741; exiled Russian leader Leon Trotsky attacked and dies the following day, 1940; U.S.S.R. troops occupy Czechoslovakia, 1968; former New York governor Nelson Rockefeller nominated by President Ford to be the forty-first vice president, 1974; cease-fire is called in Iran-Iraq War after more than one million killed in eight years of fighting, 1988.

Born Today—Chilean independence leader Bernardo O'Higgins, 1776; President Benjamin Harrison, 1833; politician George Mitchell, 1933; musician Isaac Hayes, 1942; baseball player Greg Nettles, 1944; broadcast journalist Connie Chung, 1946.

Today's Quotation—"Never in the field of human conflict was so much owed by so many to so few."—*Winston Churchill, August 20, 1940*

Indebtedness

It took sixty years and eleven presidents before the U.S. had spent its first billion dollars. Now the government spends that much every four hours (a total of more than 400 billion dollars per year!). And people are making money on other people's debt. A Dallas firm was reportedly charging fifty-eight percent interest annually to its indigent customers. One victim borrowed $20.00 for a medical bill and was still paying it off nine years later! By then the interest had mushroomed to $1,053—plus the $20!

While we need to be cautious in assuming needless financial debt, God has promised to provide our legitimate needs through his bountiful riches in heaven. "But my God shall supply all you need according to his riches in glory by Christ Jesus" (Phil. 4:19).

Prayer Suggestion—Acknowledge God as the source of your need. Seek his face and he will supply according to his will.

AUGUST
21

Today in History—Slave rebellion in Virginia results in 160 deaths, 1833; U.S.S.R. and Nazi Germany announce ten-year non-aggression treaty, 1939; U.S., United Kingdom, and U.S.S.R. conference lays groundwork for United Nations, 1944; U.S. orders construction of first nuclear-powered submarine, 1951; Hawaii admitted to U.S. as fiftieth state, 1959; exiled Philippine leader Benigno Aquino shot and killed upon arrival at Manila airport, 1983; Geraldine Ferraro denies financial wrongdoing in connection with a loan her husband received from a client, 1984.

Born Today—Illustrator Aubrey Beardsley, 1872; musician Count Basie, 1904; Britain's Princess Margaret, 1930; basketball player Wilt Chamberlain, 1936; singer Kenny Rogers, 1938; football player Jim McMahon, 1959.

Today's Quotation—"That certainly is the best government where the inhabitants are least reminded of the government."—*Henry David Thoreau, August 21, 1851*

Invisible Government

While the government keeps society functioning, what is the "invisible government" that keeps individuals under control? For Christians, it is the Holy Spirit who governs us. J. A. Clarke tells of a time when the young Charles Spurgeon encountered a busy-body who proceeded to assail him with a flood of verbal abuse. When she was done, Spurgeon smiled and said, "Yes, thank you. I am quite well. I hope you are the same." Then came another verbal blast after which the preacher said, "Yes, it does look as if it might rain. I think I had better be getting on." "Bless the man," the woman said, "he's as deaf as a post." And she never attempted her criticism again.

Spurgeon's "invisible government" had kept his temper under control. Gaining control over self is a lifelong struggle which every believer must win daily in order to be effective for God.

Prayer Suggestion—That God would give us the victory over our inner being so that we would be effective servants for him.

AUGUST

22

Today in History—King Richard III of England dies in battle, 1485; Secretary of State William Rogers resigns: National Security Advisor Henry Kissinger named to fill the position, 1973; Philippine President Ferdinand Marcos denies rumors of his involvement in shooting of Benigno Aquino, 1983; Ronald Reagan and George Bush win nomination to head the Republican presidential ticket, 1984.

Born Today—Composer Claude Debussy, 1862; author Dorothy Parker, 1893; photographer Henri Cartier-Bresson, 1908; author Ray Bradbury, 1920; baseball player Carl Yastrzemski, 1939; actress Valerie Harper, 1941.

Today's Quotation—"The time has come for the National and American Leagues to organize a World Series."—*Barney Dreyfuss, August 22, 1903*

Getting Organized

Everyone experiences a point in life when he must get organized and decide who or what will determine his lifestyle and behavior. Failing to decide is to let Satan take control.

Early in the 1800s an artist, who was also an avid chess player, created a picture showing a young man in a chess game with Satan. For years it appeared as if Satan was making the winning move. No one challenged that view until an undefeated chess champion was brought in to see the painting and give his interpretation. He studied the work in awe, and in his mind, played and replayed every move. Suddenly the chess master shouted, "Young man, make *that* move." The veteran chess champion saw a combination that even the creating artist had overlooked. Now it became clear that the young man was defeating the devil!

Is Satan being defeated in your life, or is he making inroads in areas where you know he shouldn't be? Call upon God's Holy Spirit now to defeat Satan before he tries to defeat you.

Prayer Suggestion—Ask God to make you sensitive to areas of your life under Satan's influence and call upon him to defeat your foe.

AUGUST

23

2 Timothy 4:1-5

Today in History—Romantic film star Rudolph Valentino dies in New York City, 1926; Japanese forces land at Shangai in prelude to World War II, 1937; World Council of Churches is established in Amsterdam, 1948; two defense lawyers arrested in violence stemming from trial of American Indian leaders involved in occupation at Wounded Knee, 1974; Communist Pathet Lao takes over control of Laos, 1975; first man-powered flight (of one mile) made by Bryan Allen at Schafter, Ca., 1977; Israel forces one thousand Palestinian guerrillas to leave Lebanon, 1982.

Born Today—Commodore Oliver Perry, 1785; biographer Edgar Lee Masters, 1869, actor Gene Kelly, 1912; actress Vera Miles, 1930; comedian Mark Russell, 1932; actress Barbara Eden, 1934; singer Rick Springfield, 1949.

Today's Quotation—"Cultivators of the earth are the most valuable citizens."—*Thomas Jefferson, August 23, 1785*

Back to Basics

There is a growing sentiment in this country to get "back to basics" in all areas of life: education, politics and religion. *Gospel Herald* tells of a Dr. Baldwin, a godly man who had faithfully served as pastor of a church, who had this to say about the gospel through the years: "At age thirty, after looking at all the other philosophies and religions of the world, I thought that nothing was better than the Gospel of Christ. At forty when the burdens began to press heavily I felt nothing is as good as the Gospel. At fifty when there were empty chairs at home, it was that there is nothing to be compared with the Gospel. At age sixty when I saw through the vanities and delusions of earthly things, I decided there is nothing but the gospel, and at age seventy, I'll bind the Gospel to my heart."

In the same way, we as believers need to get back to the basics of our faith—the death, burial, and resurrection of Christ which is the gospel—God's good news for mankind.

Prayer Suggestion—May we ever keep our eyes upon the gospel of Christ, never letting modern techniques alter the facts of God's unchanging message of love for the world!

AUGUST

24

1 Peter 2:9-10

Today in History—British capture and burn Washington, D.C., in War of 1812, 1814; Nazi-Soviet non-aggression treaty formally signed, 1939; Russians blow up own dam to stop Nazi onslaught in World War II, 1941; bomb blast at Army math research center at the University of Wisconsin kills one, 1970; Hamilton Jordan, on staff of President Carter, denies drug use, 1979.

Born Today—Statesman William Wilberforce, 1759; artist Aubrey Beardsley, 1872; pianist Louis Teicher, 1924; composer Mason Williams, 1938; baseball player Cal Ripken, Jr., 1960.

Today's Quotation—"Man looks back eastward upon his steps till they are lost in obscurity, and westward still makes his way till the completion of his destiny."—*Henry David Thoreau, August 24, 1840*

Our Destiny

The skeptic was taunting the Christian by saying, "Tell me, George, what will you do if, when you die, you find out there wasn't such a place as heaven after all?" The confident believer replied, "Well, I've had a fine time getting there anyway." Then he rephrased the question for the challenger, asking him, "Fred, what will you say if, when you die, you find there is such a place as hell after all?"

A refugee from Hitler's Europe once said a sad farewell to his family as he left for a new life in America. So convinced was his mother of this better life that she told her son, "You are going home while I am staying in a foreign land." When our loved ones in Christ pass on before us, that should be the sincere cry of the believer's heart. As the hymn writer has so beautifully written: "This world is not my home, I'm just a passing through, / My treasures are laid up somewhere beyond the blue." Where is your eternal home?

Prayer Suggestion—Believers know their destiny where God has prepared a glorious, eternal home in heaven with him.

AUGUST

25

Today in History—National Park Service established, 1916; Paris freed from Nazi occupation in World War II, 1944; China exercises first United Nations veto, barring Bangladesh from membership, 1972; French cargo ship carrying load of uranium sinks after collision in the North Sea; no radioactivity detected, 1984; toxic gas cloud escapes from lake bed in Cameroon killing twelve hundred, 1986; bull market on Wall Street now five years old as high stock prices continue to prevail, 1987.

Born Today—Writer Bret Harte, 1836; actor Mel Ferrer, 1917; conductor Leonard Bernstein, 1918; former Governor George Wallace (Alabama), 1919; TV host Monty Hall, 1923; tennis player Althea Gibson, 1927.

Today's Quotation—"The making of a good living does not necessarily blind a man to a critical period which he is passing through. Such people, in fact, may feel a special insecurity and anxiety. They seek a moral solution in a world of moral confusion."—*Whittaker Chambers, August 25, 1948*

A Moral Solution

This is an era in which integrity seems to be more and more lacking. It is in this world that God has called believers to be both salt and light. Abraham Lincoln recognized this when he stated, "My desire is to so conduct the affairs of this administration that if at the end, when I come to lay down the reins of power, I have lost every other friend on earth, I shall have at last one friend left—the friend deep down inside of me . . . . I do the very best I know how; the very best I can; and I mean to keep on doing it to the end. If the end brings me out all right, what is said against me will not amount to anything. If the end brings me out all wrong, then a legion of angels swearing I was right will make no difference." What a vivid example of integrity from one of the world's greatest leaders!

Prayer Suggestion—That we would always trust God for the wisdom needed to make the correct moral decisions of life.

AUGUST

26

Acts 10:34–43

Today in History—British defeat French at Battle of Crecy, 1346; volcano in Netherlands' East Indies erupts creating tidal waves which kill more than 35,000 people, 1883; women win the right to vote in the U.S. as nineteenth Amendment is ratified, 1920; mysterious flu-like disease kills twenty-eight persons mostly conventioneers at American Legion convention in Philadelphia, 1976; Netherlands Prince Bernhard resigns from key positions in the wake of Lockheed bribery probe, 1976; Pope Paul VI dies in Italy; John Paul I is new pontiff, 1978.

Born Today—Radio inventor Lee De Forest, 1873; writer Jules Romains, 1885; General Maxwell Taylor, 1901; microbiologist Albert Sabin, 1906; journalist Benjamin Bradlee, 1921; politician Geraldine Ferraro, 1935.

Today's Quotation—"The right of citizens of the United States to vote shall not be denied or abridged by the United States or by any state on account of sex."—*Nineteenth Amendment, August 26, 1920*

Equality

The drive for the right of women to vote was long with quite a few struggles. A debate was held in Kansas in 1920 on the question of the women's suffrage amendment. Those opposed to women having the right to vote stated that women could not be relied upon to exercise good judgment in voting because they change their minds too often. A young woman won the debate, however, by stating, "I would like to ask my honorable opponent if he ever tried to change a woman's mind once it was made up." End of debate.

God is no respecter of persons, but loves all of us equally, regardless of racial, social, financial, or gender concerns. What a loving God we have! Do we love him?

Prayer Suggestion—That our love for God would equal his love for us and enable us to love others as he loves us.

AUGUST

27

Psalm 46:1–11

Today in History—First U.S. oil well begins operation at Titusville, Pa., 1859; Kellogg-Briand Pact outlawing war is signed, 1928; European commission on human rights accuses Britain of torture in Northern Ireland, 1976; continued racial unrest in South Africa results in the rand dropping in value to just thirty-five cents, the lowest rate ever, 1985; divers locate safe from sunken passenger ship the *Andrea Dorea*, 1981.

Born Today—Educator Margaretha Schurz, 1833; writer Theodore Dreiser, 1871; producer Sam Goldwyn, 1882; novelist C. S. Forester, 1899; President Lyndon Johnson, 1908; entertainer Martha Raye, 1916; singer Tommy Sands, 1937.

Today's Quotation—"In war, moral considerations account for three-quarters, the balance of actual forces only for the other quarter."— *Napoleon Bonaparte, August 27, 1808*

A Holy War

Throughout history there have been numerous instances in which nations declared "holy wars" to preserve what they saw as the truth. The Reformation was one such era, and it was in this setting that Luther came to write his beloved hymn, based on Psalm 46, "A Mighty Fortress Is Our God."

It was this psalm that Sergius used to give him courage and strength to fight the invading forces which were overrunning his country in the fourteenth century.

As Edward Elson notes, "Throughout the ages men have been stirred by the realization that the eternal God is available to them and that nothing, literally nothing, can overwhelm or destroy a man when he lives this faith." On what do you base your faith?

Prayer Suggestion—God, give us the faith of our fathers in trusting you through all of life's situations and lead us home to heaven at last.

AUGUST

28

Today in History—Henry Hudson discovers Delaware Bay, 1609; over 200,000 people stage peaceful civil rights march in Washington, D.C., 1963; demonstrators clash with police in efforts to disrupt Democratic National Convention in Chicago, 1968; after nine years of trying, M.I.T. biologist has synthesized the functioning of a gene, 1976; convicted spy Jerry Whitworth sentenced to 365 years in prison for involvement in spy ring, 1986.

Born Today—Writer Johann von Goethe, 1749; actor Charles Boyer, 1889; opera singer Richard Tucker, 1914; actor Donald O'Connor, 1925; actor Ben Gazzara, 1930; baseball player Ron Guidry, 1950.

Today's Quotation—"Positively, the best thing a man can have to do is nothing, and next to that perhaps, good works."—*Charles Lamb, August 28, 1827*

Doing Nothing but Good Works

How many people will recognize, too late, that it is not good works which qualifies them for eternal forgiveness? To believe in good works alone is to go through life attempting to buy forgiveness on credit when God has already paid our sin-debt in full!

Bill Gold, writing in the *Washington Post*, tells of a little girl who had saved up enough money to buy her father a present for Father's Day, but she had one concern. "I can't be going downtown every month to make payments," she said to her mother. "Is there a store where they'll let you pay the whole thing at once?"

God has done just that for us through the sinless sacrifice of Christ on the cross. He has pre-paid our sin-debt in full and thus he has no need for our feeble good works. "For man looketh on the outward appearance, but the Lord looketh on the heart" (1 Sam. 16:7). Have you accepted God's payment for your sins or are you still struggling to earn what has already been paid?

Prayer Suggestion—Take God at his word. Confess your sins to him, repent, and ask him to stamp your sin-debt "paid in full."

AUGUST

29

Today in History—First U.S. abolitionist newspaper published in Ohio, 1817; chop suey introduced in New York, 1896; U.S. Marine Corps Reserve established, 1916; two airlines announce plans to examine passenger's baggage to thwart hijackers, 1972; professional basketball player Moses Malone becomes highest paid teenage athlete in U.S. (total earnings could exceed $3 million), 1974; Philippine military quells armed revolt against President Aquino, 1987.

Born Today—Statesman Jean Baptiste Colbert, 1619; Oliver Wendell Holmes, 1809; actress Ingrid Bergman, 1915; actor Elliott Gould, 1938; Indian leader Rajiv Gandi, 1944.

Today's Quotation—"It is a great consolation to the well, and still greater to the sick, that they find themselves not neglected; and I know that you will be desirous of giving comfort, even when you have no great hope of giving help."—*Samuel Johnson, August 29, 1783*

Giving Comfort

Charles Dickens masterfully captured the story of sacrificial love in his epic work *A Tale of Two Cities*. In this story, a young Frenchman with a wife and child is condemned to die at the guillotine. His friend, an Englishman who has wasted his livelihood in riotous living, vows to save his friend. The night before the execution, he creeps into the dungeon, pausing as he goes to look up at the light in the window of the condemned man's daughter. Then, with renewed resolve, he enters the prison where he exchanges garments with the condemned man and from there goes to his death at the guillotine.

What an illustration of Christ's love. "Greater love hath no man than this, that a man lay down his life for his friends" (John 15:13).

Prayer Suggestion—That we would love others and seek to comfort them as Christ has loved and comforted us.

AUGUST

30

Today in History—U.S. occupying forces arrive in Japan after World War II, 1945; "hot line" communications link between White House and Kremlin installed, 1963; Thurgood Marshall confirmed as first black associate justice of U.S. Supreme Court, 1967; hundreds of hostages seized in raid on national palace in Nicaragua, 1978; Polish shipyard workers end seventeen day strike after getting government approval to unionize, 1980.

Born Today—Physicist Ernest Rutherford, 1871; politician Huey Long, 1893; actor Raymond Massey, 1896; civil rights leader Roy Wilkins, 1901; actor Fred McMurray, 1908; baseball player Ted Williams, 1918; singer Kitty Wells, 1919; skier Jean Claude Killy, 1943.

Today's Quotation—"The enemy makes a wilderness and calls it war."—*Richard Harding Davis, August 30, 1914*

Making War

The U.S. Marines had a slogan some time ago which said, "No one wants to fight, but somebody has to know how." Consider the price of keeping the peace. Worldwide spending for military arms each year is said to total more than $300 billion (of which the U.S. and Soviets account for about 60 percent). This represents about 10 percent of the world's total production of goods and services. The United Nations reported that the world's nuclear arsenals contain enough explosives to blast every man, woman, and child from the face of the earth. No wonder the apostle John reports the world "melting with a fervent heart" at the end of the age. Now is the time to be sure you are ready for the coming judgment day when we will all be measured according to God's perfect law. Only those who have Christ as their advocate, through accepting his gift of salvation on earth, will survive.

Prayer Suggestion—That we would have our spiritual house in order so that we will constantly be ready for Christ's return.

AUGUST

31

Today in History—Lewis and Clark begin exploring western America, 1803; Thomas Edison patents motion picture kinetoscope, 1887; Polish police move to break up rally for Solidarity union in Warsaw, 1982; opening is delayed in one hundred New Jersey schools which have not yet removed asbestos from classrooms, 1984; Yale president A. Bartlett Giamatti says politicians are afraid to face up to Moral Majority which played a key role in President Reagan's election, 1981.

Born Today—Educator Maria Montessori, 1870; entertainer Arthur Godfrey, 1903; writer William Saroyan, 1908; broadcast journalist Daniel Schorr, 1916; composer Alan Jay Lerner, 1918; comedian Buddy Hackett, 1924; actor James Coburn, 1928; violinist Itzhak Perlman, 1945.

Today's Quotation—"Answer violence with violence."—*Juan Peron, August 31, 1955*

Violence

The United States is becoming a nation of growing violence. Our capital city, Washington, D.C., has been labeled "the murder capital" for its growing drug-related crimes. Just how violent is our land? Since World War II, serious crimes have risen over 214 percent with murder gaining over 263 percent! As a result, Americans are arming themselves in record numbers. Private citizens today own far more guns (over 90 million weapons according to the FBI) than do all of the U.S. armed forces combined (which have 4.6 million guns and small arms). In such an atmosphere of violence there are increasing calls for peace. But earthly peace is not the answer. Instead, the world longs for inner peace from the Prince of Peace, God's son, who has "come that they might have life, and that they might have it more abundantly" (John 10:10). Have you accepted God's inner peace or is sin's violence still warring against your soul?

Prayer Suggestion—That God would stop the violence in our souls as we repent and confess our sins to him.

SEPTEMBER

1

Romans 14:7–13

Today in History—Aaron Burr is acquitted of treason, 1807; French defeat leads to downfall of the Second French Empire, 1870; James Walker resigns as mayor of New York following investigation, 1932; World War II begins with Nazi Germany's invasion of Poland, 1939; U.S. pilot James Sullivan flies from New York to London in less than two hours (1:55:42), 1974; Soviets believed to have shot down Korean jetliner off U.S.S.R. coast killing 269, 1983; wreckage of ocean liner *Titanic* found in twelve hundred feet of water off coast of Newfoundland seventy-three years after sinking, 1985.

Born Today—Author Lydia Sigourney, 1791; journalist James Gordon Bennett, 1795; writer Edgar Rice Burroughs, 1875; labor leader Walter Reuther, 1907; actress Lily Tomlin, 1939; singer Barry Gibb, 1946.

Today's Quotation—"Necessity hath no law."—*Oliver Cromwell, September 1, 1654*

Above the Law

Pranksters thought it funny when they removed the stop sign from a busy rural intersection, but it wasn't long before they became aware of the magnitude of their crime. A speeding car neared the intersection unaware of an approaching vehicle which was not warned to stop. Following the grinding crash, the toll became grimly clear: the driver of the first vehicle was killed instantly and his wife hospitalized with broken legs. The children and driver of the approaching car were also injured. All because of someone who felt above the law!

While some may escape unpunished from the laws of man, we may be certain that the laws of God will never be violated. As the Bible says, "Whatsoever a man soweth, that shall he also reap" (Gal. 6:7).

Prayer Suggestion—While we should obey all earthly laws, how much greater should be our obedience of God's eternal laws!

SEPTEMBER

2

Proverbs 15:1-10

Today in History—Great London fire destroys center of British capital, 1666; U.S. Treasury Department established, 1789; Japan formally surrenders in World War II, 1945; North Vietnam established by communists, 1945; three thousand blacks clash with police in Cape Town, South Africa, 1976; Yitzhak Shamir is elected to succeed Menachem Begin as party leader and new prime minister of Israel, 1983.

Born Today—Economist Henry George, 1839; writer Eugene Field, 1850; violinist Albert Spalding, 1850; author Cleveland Amory, 1917; actor Mark Harmon, 1951; tennis player Jimmy Connors, 1952.

Today's Quotation—"Speak softly and carry a big stick."—*Theodore Roosevelt, September 2, 1901*

Speak Softly

Teddy Roosevelt had the right idea: Don't antagonize others but keep your defenses ready in case challenges should arise. Could you withstand the following challenge? The missionary candidate arrived for his scheduled interview but his interviewer did not arrive until five hours later. The interviewer asked the candidate to spell "flavor." Following this request, the candidate was asked, "How much is three plus five?" After another correct answer, the interviewer announced, "Very good, you have passed the test. I will recommend that you be appointed for missionary service."

Later, the interviewer explained the tests the candidate had passed: Punctuality—he arrived for the interview on time; Patience—he waited over five hours to be interviewed and never questioned the delay; Temper—no sign of anger despite the frustrating setting; Humility—he gladly answered questions a six-year-old could get right without taking offense. In short, he was not antagonized by his "trial" and was therefore considered emotionally qualified for missionary service!

Prayer Suggestion—Thank God for the Holy Spirit who gives us the control over our temperament and helps us to be Christ-like.

SEPTEMBER

3

2 Corinthians 12:9-15

Today in History—Treaty of Paris signed (ending Revolutionary War), 1783; U.S. Navy dirigible crashes in Ohio killing fourteen, 1925; Britain and France declare war on Germany for attacking Poland, 1939; Italy surrenders to Allies, 1943; Nicaraguan President Somoza rescinds charter of nation's top political group, 1978.

Born Today—Author Sarah Orne Jewett, 1849; architect Louis Henry Sullivan, 1856; merchant Edward Filene, 1860; physician Macfarlane Burnet, 1899; actress Kitty Carlisle, 1915; cartoonist Mort Walker, 1923.

Today's Quotation—"Nuclear energy is one of the great hopes of all those nations which do not have any national resources of their own."— *Willy Brandt, September 3, 1968.*

Natural Resources

How futile it is for someone to try to please God through his own natural resources. Ezra Roth tells a story of the difference made by the margin of power. He says when his family first crossed the Rocky Mountains, it was in a vintage car, which huffed and puffed and had a radiator that often boiled over. All the beauties of the mountain scenery went unnoticed due to the continued problems with the car, which was struggling on its own natural resources; there was no margin of power. Some years later they made the trip again. This time they traveled in a modern car with the margin of power needed to conquer even the tallest mountain peaks. The family was able to stop and enjoy the scenery—without concern over their lack of power.

Likewise, with God's power, Christians are able to take on "impossible" tasks knowing that God will supply all the power needed to carry out his will. Do you have God's power or are you still struggling under your own strength?

Prayer Suggestion—May we draw on God's power to complete the job he has called us to do.

SEPTEMBER

4

Matthew 10:5–15

Today in History—Los Angeles, Ca., founded, 1781; electric power first supplied to customers in New York City, 1882; Geronimo, leader of the Apache Indians, surrenders, 1886; George Eastman patents first roll-film (Kodak) camera, 1888; first coast-to-coast live television service in U.S. begins with President Truman's speech in San Francisco, 1951; U.S. claims Russian spy plane was flying in area of downed Korean jetliner, 1983; Canada's Brian Mulroney chalks up big win over John Turner in prime minister's race, 1984.

Born Today—Pioneer missionary Marcus Whitman, 1802; composer Anton Bruckner, 1824; author Richard Wright, 1908; broadcaster Paul Harvey, 1918; business executive Donald Peterson, 1926.

Today's Quotation—"No matter what happens, England will be destroyed, one way or another."—*Adolf Hitler, September 4, 1940*

Coming Destruction

While Hitler's warning was designed to intimidate England into surrender, almighty God has forecast eternal destruction for all those who reject his salvation. Evangelist John R. Rice tells of a revival campaign he held in a large northeastern city. Although many were saved, the local ministerial association publicly ridiculed the revival meetings. When Dr. Rice likened the city's attitude to that of Sodom and Gomorrah, the local police contacted other law enforcement officials to see if there were any charges pending against him. At the end of the five-week crusade, the evangelist paused to shake the dust from his feet upon leaving the city, and asked God to hold it accountable for rejecting the gospel. Sure enough, in less than twenty-four hours, a great thaw melted the accumulated snow that had gathered, triggering massive flooding and some loss of life.

Those who reject God's message today will experience his coming destruction tomorrow!

Prayer Suggestion—May my heart always be warm and open to the gospel message that God has for me and my fellow man.

SEPTEMBER

5

Today in History—Sam Houston elected president of Republic of Texas, 1836; three Catholic universities, St. John's in Long Island, Loyola in Chicago, and Canisius in Buffalo, founded, 1870; first Labor Day parade held in New York City, 1882; Baptist Bible College founded in Springfield, Mo., 1950; Arab terrorists kill eleven Israeli olympic athletes in Munich, 1972; U.S. space shuttle *Discovery* returns after successful six-day maiden voyage, 1984; invading forces from nearby Chad destroy major Libyan base, 1987.

Born Today—Researcher Arthur Nielsen, 1897; producer Darryl Zanuck, 1902; composer John Cage, 1912; comedian Bob Newhart, 1929; actress Raquel Welch, 1942; cartoonist Cathy Lee Guisewite, 1950.

Today's Quotation—"A man of sense only trifles with them, humors and flatters them, as he does with a sprightly and forward child; but he neither consults them about, nor trusts them with serious matters."—*Lord Chesterfield, about women, September 5, 1748*

God's Woman

The cigarette advertisement says, "You've come a long way, baby!" While we may decry this terminology, it is true that motivated women have contributed much to the heritage of this nation.

One such individual was Sarah Hale. As a magazine editor, Mrs. Hale began campaigning for restoration of a national Thanksgiving Day. She tirelessly wrote letters and contacted national leaders in an effort to persuade them to approve quickly. Thirty-five years after she began her crusade, President Lincoln declared the fourth Thursday of November to be observed as the official "National Thanksgiving Day." All because of one dedicated woman who would not be discouraged nor defeated in a cause that was right!

Prayer Suggestion—Let us be thankful for God's blessings throughout the year and for the godly women who have contributed greatly to our nation's spiritual heritage.

SEPTEMBER

6

Today in History—President William McKinley shot in Buffalo, N.Y., 1901; nationwide stage strike by Actors Equity ends, 1919; Arab guerrillas hijack three U.S.-bound airplanes, 1970; two Arab gunmen open fire in Istanbul synagogue, killing twenty-one worshippers, 1986.

Born Today—Statesman Marquis de Lafayette, 1757; social worker Jane Addams, 1860; financier Joseph P. Kennedy, 1888; producer Billy Rose, 1899; comedienne JoAnne Worley, 1937; actress Jane Curtin, 1947.

Today's Quotation—*"A hungry man is not a free man."—Adlai Stevenson, September 6, 1952*

Hungry Man

Some churches have sponsored "starvation banquets" to underscore the problem of world-wide hunger. Typically each banquet guest is served a half cup of soup, a half slice of plain bread, and a cup of black tea. Following the banquet an offering is taken up for world missions. One such project at a major university netted over $12,000 during a single semester of once-a-week rice lunches. The money was used for famine relief.

Rats are one of the causes of severe hunger. In India alone there are estimated to be some three billion rats which annually consume 1.25 million tons of grain (about $740 million dollars worth)! No wonder there's a lack of food!

Believers must be conscious of the plight of the physically hungry and do what they can to assist if they hope to reach those who are spiritually hungry.

Prayer Suggestion—May we be sensitive to the needs of mankind and be willing to share our blessings with those less fortunate.

SEPTEMBER

7

Today in History—Brazil Independence Day marks nation's becoming monarchy, independent of Portugal, 1822; cruise ship *Morro Castle* catches fire off New Jersey coast and sinks following morning with the loss of 137 lives, 1934; Boulder Dam (later renamed Hoover Dam) goes into use, 1936; President Carter signs treaty giving Panama Canal to Panama in 1999, 1977.

Born Today—England's Queen Elizabeth I, 1533; artist "Grandma" Moses, 1860; financier J. Pierpont Morgan, Jr., 1867; surgeon Michael DeBakey, 1908; director Elia Kazan, 1909; pianist Arthur Ferrante, 1921.

Today's Quotation—"The Communist Party cannot be neutral toward religion. It stands for science, and all religion is opposed to science."—*Josef Stalin, September 7, 1927*

Religion and Science

Stalin's opinions notwithstanding, there is no conflict between the Bible and science, though a conflict between the two is sometimes perceived. The issue of science and the Bible was underscored by Dr. Joseph A. Parker who said to an audience, "In comparing science and the Bible, let us see what science has to say about the poor widow woman who has lost her only son." There was silence. "Does existence end with death?" Still no response. "Then we must turn to Scripture." Opening the Bible he read, "The dead shall arise. . . . For this corruptible must put on incorruption, and this mortal must put on immortality. O death, where is thy sting?" (1 Cor. 15:52–53, 55).

God's Word speaks where science is silent—on the life hereafter. We know God's Word is always true, even when it may appear to disagree with science!

Prayer Suggestion—Rejoice that we may know that God is alive and that we shall live again because the Bible tells us so.

SEPTEMBER

8

Today in History—U.S. Senator Huey P. Long of Louisiana is shot and dies two days later, 1935; Nazi forces begin siege of Warsaw, 1939; Nazis encircle Leningrad, beginning lengthy siege that ended in crushing defeat for Germans, 1941; Japanese Peace Treaty signed by forty-nine nations in San Francisco, 1951; John F. Kennedy Center for Performing Arts opens, Washington D.C., 1971; three Lutheran denominations vote to merge to become third largest Protestant group in U.S., 1982; Nicaraguan Contras have raised over $10 million from private sources in past six months, 1984.

Born Today—Composer Antonin Dvorak, 1841; comedian Sid Caesar, 1922; government official Samuel Pierce, Jr., 1922; actor Peter Sellers, 1925; journalist Barbara Frum, 1937; opera singer Marilyn Mims, 1954.

Today's Quotation—"There is no patent recipe for getting good citizenship."—*Theodore Roosevelt, September 8, 1906*

Good Citizens

Is it possible for a Christian to be a good citizen? And is it possible to fight as a soldier and still live for God? Let us turn to the Bible for the answer. Were not David, Joshua, Joseph, and Moses all soldiers while at the same time good citizens and children of God? In more modern times, what about Abraham Lincoln, Commander-in-Chief of the army during the Civil War? Both Stonewall Jackson and Robert E. Lee have reputations as strong Christians and valiant warriors which exist to this day. What about the father of our country, George Washington, whose heartfelt prayer in the snows of Valley Forge is still a model for us? All of these were Christian citizens whose lives demonstrated what they believed. Can others say the same about you?

Prayer Suggestion—Help us to "render to Caesar the things that are Caesar's and to God the things that are God's" (Mark 12:17).

SEPTEMBER

9

Today in History—California admitted into Union as thirty-first state, 1850; Boston police go on strike September 9–12 (giving Governor Calvin Coolidge a national reputation from handling the crisis), 1919; Salerno Day marks Allied landing at Salerno, Italy, against Nazi strong points, 1943.

Born Today—Statesman Cardinal Richelieu, 1585; Admiral William Bligh, 1754; writer Count Leo Tolstoy, 1828; politician Alf Landon, 1887; actor Cliff Robertson, 1925; football player Joe Theisman, 1949.

Today's Quotation—"I have observed that a Letter is never more acceptable than when received upon a rainy day. . . ."—*Charles Lamb, September 9, 1826*

An Application Letter

Have you noticed how a friendly letter is more warmly received when times are rough? Imagine then the reception of a letter like the following:

> I understand your pulpit is currently vacant. Allow me to state my credentials. I have been a good leader in most of the places where I have been and am generally considered to be a good preacher. Although I have done some writing, I am over fifty and not in the best of health. I have never preached in one place for more than three years and it has usually been in small churches. I had to leave some places when riots broke out. I have been threatened several times and have gone to jail for witnessing. Does your church want to hire me?
>
> (signed)
> Paul, of Tarsus.

While it is hard to imagine any present-day congregation welcoming that application, it was from similar humble beginnings that today's church was born. Without those early limitations, think what the church of today can do with all the modern resources God has provided for his work.

Prayer Suggestion—That believers would look to God for strength and guidance to perform the work that he has called us to do.

SEPTEMBER

10

Today in History—Commodore Oliver Hazard Perry's U.S. ships defeat the British in Battle of Lake Erie in War of 1812, 1813; in epic civic celebration, New York City welcomes home General John J. Pershing and the Army's First Division after World War I, 1919; Alaska awards $900 million worth of oil leases, 1969; Egypt bans Moslem Brotherhood in purge of radical elements, 1981; eleven west European nations agree to levy sanctions against South Africa, 1985.

Born Today—Physician Thomas Sydenham, 1624; publisher Isaac K. Funk, 1839; physicist Arthur Compton, 1892; golfer Arnold Palmer, 1929; broadcast journalist Charles Kuralt, 1934; singer Jose Feliciano, 1945.

Today's Quotation—"We have met the enemy and they are ours."— *Commodore Oliver H. Perry, September 10, 1813*

Our Enemy

It was just after the outbreak of World War I when the War Ministry sent messages to all the outposts which read, "War declared. Arrest all enemy aliens in your area." Back to headquarters came this reply: "We have arrested ten Germans, six Belgians, four Frenchmen, two Italians, three Austrians, and an American. Please advise immediately who we are at war with."

How true it is that much of the time we fail simply because we spend most of our energies fighting the battle and not enough focusing on the enemy. Let us be sure that we are directing all of our efforts and resources toward fighting Satan and the forces of evil and not toward fighting fellow saints.

Prayer Suggestion—Help us to keep our sights on attacking our enemy Satan, and not upon fellow children of God.

SEPTEMBER

11

Today in History—Henry Hudson discovers Manhattan Island, 1609; British defeat General Washington's forces in American Revolutionary War, 1777; Battle of Plattsburgh, N.Y., in War of 1812, major U.S. victory, 1814; Turkish Army ousts prime minister in bloodless coup, 1980; baseball's Pete Rose strikes 4,192nd career hit and breaks Ty Cobb's record, 1985.

Born Today—Writer O. Henry (William Porter), 1862; scientist James Jeans, 1877; former Philippine leader Ferdinand Marcos, 1917; football coach Tom Landry, 1924; author Alfred Slote, 1926; director Brian De-Palma, 1940.

Today's Quotation—"There never was a good war or a bad peace."—*Benjamin Franklin, September 11, 1783*

At Peace

It has been said that any nation that could enforce peace could control the world. Returning from a meeting with European leaders, former President Dwight Eisenhower observed, "All the world wants peace," and this is still true today. Mankind is looking for peace and stability in a world racked by war and terrorism. It is against this backdrop that the Antichrist will appear as the great peacemaker, though with his "peace" only evil will triumph. This satanic superman will have such astounding powers and will so overwhelm the world that no nation will seek to make war with him. Slowly but surely, Satan is tightening his grip on the people of this world. It is happening so subtly and silently that few even pause to notice. Only the believer who has the Holy Spirit of God within is able to fully recognize Satan's diabolical plot. That is why we need to warn all those around us of this world's impending doom and that only God can save mankind from certain disaster.

Prayer Suggestion—Don't let Satan gain the victory in your life. Confess your sins and declare peace with Christ today.

SEPTEMBER

12

Romans 6:14–23

Today in History—Old Defenders Day commemorates defense of Baltimore in War of 1812 at Battle of Fort McHenry, 1814; Nikita Khrushchev becomes first secretary of Communist Party of U.S.S.R., 1953; Ethiopia's Haile Selassie ousted by military after fifty-eight years, 1974; National Academy of Sciences urges limitations on usage of fluorocarbon gases, 1976; in worst-ever storm to hit Alabama, Hurricane Frederick whips one hundred m.p.h. winds through Mobile area, 1979.

Born Today—Newspaperman Charles Warner, 1829; lexicographer H. L. Mencken, 1880; publisher Alfred A. Knopf, 1892; scientist Irene Joliot-Curie, 1897; runner Jesse Owens, 1913; baseball player Mickey Lolich, 1940.

Today's Quotation—"Justice, sir, is the great interest of man on earth. It is the ligament which holds civilized beings and civilized nations together."—*Daniel Webster, September 12, 1845*

God's Justice

A number of states have enacted "Good Samaritan" laws in order to protect well-intentioned citizens when assisting victims in an emergency. A young girl reaching into a cage at the zoo cried out in terror as a huge lion grabbed her arm in its teeth. A nearby watchman, seeing the emergency, drew his weapon and promptly shot and killed the lion. The force of the lion's fall apparently knocked both the girl and the guard to the ground which triggered another random shot, striking the girl in the leg. Some time later the girl's parents filed suit against the zoo, the guard, and the government agency which owned the zoo. The jury, hearing testimony in the case, denied all damages except those against the zoo for not having the cage properly guarded. It denied damages against the guard on the ground that he was being a "Good Samaritan" and therefore should not be held legally liable for harm inflicted upon the girl in the effort to rescue her.

We can be thankful for God's justice which transcends that of mankind.

Prayer Suggestion—Thank God that he doesn't administer justice (what we deserve) for our sins, but instead, mercy and grace.

SEPTEMBER

13

Today in History—March 4, 1789, set as the start of government under new U.S. Constitution, 1788; four-day revolt at prison in Attica, New York, ends with loss of thirty-seven lives, 1971; Lynchburg Baptist College opens, 1971; California legislature adopts first "Right to Die" law to avoid life-prolonging treatment, 1976; General William Westmoreland sues CBS for $120 million over Vietnam broadcast, 1982; French President Mitterand looks on as *Arian III* rocket explodes following launch in French Guiana, 1985.

Born Today—Bacteriologist Walter Reed, 1851; General John Pershing, 1860; writer J. B. Priestley, 1894; singer Mel Torme, 1925; educator Ernest Boyer, 1928; producer Fred Silverman, 1937.

Today's Quotation—"Never mind when they lie about you. The time to worry is when they begin to tell the truth."—*General Joseph W. (Vinegar Joe) Stilwell, September 13, 1943*

Being Truthful

Some years ago a study was conducted to determine what qualities American and Canadian church people looked for in their pastors. As reported by *Christianity Today,* the study of more than five thousand persons revealed that congregations most wanted honesty, humility, and Christian example in their spiritual leaders.

It is not surprising that churches expect their pastors to be truthful above all else. Doing so is increasingly difficult in this age of joking and truth-stretching which so often occurs as a form of entertainment. Yet, in God's eyes, an intentional half-truth is just as sinful as a major crime.

Prayer Suggestion—May God instill in us a sensitivity to, and awareness of, the great need for truth in all our transactions.

SEPTEMBER

14

Today in History—Words of "Star Spangled Banner" written by Francis Scott Key during bombardment of Fort McHenry, Md., 1814; Vice President Theodore Roosevelt succeeds William McKinley as president when McKinley dies, 1901; Bob Jones University opens, 1927; ground is broken for United Nations headquarters in New York City, 1948; knife-wielding vandal attacks Rembrandt painting in Amsterdam, 1975; Lebanon's president-elect is killed when bomb shatters party headquarters, 1982.

Born Today—Scientist Alexander von Humboldt, 1769; scientist Ivan Pavlov, 1849; statesman Jan Masaryk, 1886; author Allan Bloom, 1930; sculptor Kate Millett, 1934; actress Joey Heatherton, 1944.

Today's Quotation—"While there is a lower class I am in it; while there is a criminal element, I am of it; while there is a soul in prison, I am not free."—*Eugene V. Debs, September 14, 1918*

In Prison

Few people today know that evangelist Billy Graham preached his first sermon in jail! Graham, just out of high school, and his friend, Grady Wilson, were spending the summer as Fuller Brush salesmen when an evangelist invited them to attend his jail service. During the service, Billy was asked to give his testimony, a talk that launched a world-wide preaching ministry to millions of people. It all began on a warm afternoon when a young salesman gave his testimony in prison.

Where have you shared with others what God has done in your life?

Prayer Suggestion—For those held in prisons and jails; that they would be used by God as the prison visitor, Billy Graham, has been.

SEPTEMBER

15

Ephesians 4:26–32

Today in History—Nazi Germany enacts anti-Jewish Nuremberg Laws, 1933; British Royal Air Force, at peak of Battle of Britain, downs seventy-eight German planes, 1940; two White House aides plead "not guilty" to Watergate break-in charges, 1972; Pope John Paul II meets with PLO leader Yasar Arafat, outraging Israelis, 1982; U.S. Senate unanimously condemns Soviet attack on Korean Air Lines jet resulting in deaths of sixty-one Americans among the 269 fatalities, 1983.

Born Today—Writer James Fenimore Cooper, 1789; President William Howard Taft, 1857; conductor Bruno Walter, 1876; writer Robert Benchley, 1889; educator Milton Eisenhower, 1899; actor Jackie Cooper, 1922.

Today's Quotation—"Government is not a warfare of interests. We shall not gain our ends by heat and bitterness, which make it impossible to think either calmly or fairly. . . ."—*Woodrow Wilson, September 15, 1910*

Bitterness

Are you friendly when you meet others or do you suspect strangers' motives and treat them with bitterness? Dwight L. Moody once told the story of an eagle that was jealous of another bird who could outfly him. Time went by and the eagle finally spotted a hunter whom he asked to shoot down his enemy. The hunter replied that he could only bring down the bird if he had some feathers for his arrows. The bitter eagle, determined to eliminate his rival, began to pull feathers from his own wings for the arrows. The hunter tried again and again to shoot down the bird but the bird was able to soar into the sky out of range of the arrows. Finally, the futile effort had used all the eagle's feathers and so, unable to fly, he was shot by the impatient hunter. Do you harbor bitterness against another? As Moody put it, "You can only hurt yourself" by hating others.

Prayer Suggestion—May God cleanse any feelings of jealousy or bitterness we may have, especially against a fellow child of God.

SEPTEMBER

16

Ephesians 2:11-22

Today in History—Pilgrims sail from Plymouth, England, for the New World, 1620; Shawmut changes its name to Boston, Mass., 1630; Battle of Harlem Heights gives General Washington first major victory of American Revolutionary War, 1776; beginning of Mexico's revolution against Spain, 1810; Oklahoma territory opens to settlement, 1893; President Ford announces pardon for former President Nixon and offers immunity from prosecution to Vietnam era draft-evaders, 1974; for the first time since 1914, the U.S. becomes a debtor nation, 1985.

Born Today—Banker Nathan Rothschild, 1777; historian Francis Parkman, 1823; railroad builder James Hill, 1838; poet Alfred Noyes, 1880; producer Allen Funt, 1914; musician Charlie Byrd, 1925; baseball player Robin Yount, 1955.

Today's Quotation—"Mushrooms scramble up in a night; but diamonds, you know, lie a long while ripening in the bed."—*Charles Lamb, September 16, 1801*

Diamonds

Diamonds are lackluster and unattractive in their natural state. It is only after they are subjected to repeated abrasion and cutting that they become the sparkling gems so sought after for their radiant beauty. Only diamonds have the hardness to wear down other diamonds, and so the abrasives used to polish diamonds are themselves quite expensive.

In the diamond we can glimpse how God sees mankind. In the Master's hand, the surrendered soul becomes a new being. Through the rough and tumble events of life, the believer's life is polished to the point where he becomes a radiant reflector of God's brilliant glory. Surrender your will to God and become a shining gem under his loving hand.

Prayer Suggestion—Have patience to realize that life's abrasions are, for the believer, a way to become more polished for God.

SEPTEMBER

17

Today in History—U.S.S.R. invades Poland in World War II, 1939; Allied paratroopers dropped behind German lines trigger one of the bitterest battles of World War II, 1944; former Nicaraguan leader Somoza is killed in Paraguay, 1980; Vanessa Williams is first black to be crowned Miss America, 1983.

Born Today—General Frederich von Steuben, 1730; writer William Carlos Williams, 1883; former Supreme Court Chief Justice Warren Burger, 1907; actress Anne Bancroft, 1931; football player Anthony Carter, 1960.

Today's Quotation—"Wickedness is always easier than virtue, for it takes a short cut at everything."—*Samuel Johnson, September 17, 1773*

Virtue

This is an age in which society is looking for moral guidance. Never before has ethics been such a visible focus of the business world. Executives pay hundreds of dollars to attend seminars for guidance in what is right and wrong. While the Bible clearly spells out the absolutes, there are other areas of conviction and preference which, in themselves, may be neither clearly right or wrong unless they cause others to stumble. Dr. H. A. Ironsides used to tell the story of the thrifty Scotsman who wore the same shirt several days a week to save laundry expenses. One day, preparing to attend a very special occasion, the man held a shirt up to the light to determine its cleanliness. At this point his wife entered the room, and noticing his indecision, said, "Remember, Sandy, if it's doubtful, it's dirty."

How true that is of life's temptations. If they're doubtful, you can safely assume God views them as dirty.

Prayer Suggestion—May God guide us in virtuous living so that we will not be swayed by the enticing temptations of life.

SEPTEMBER

18

2 Timothy 2:1–21

Today in History—President George Washington lays cornerstone of Capitol in Washington, D.C., 1793; CBS launches radio network of sixteen stations, 1927; U.S. Air Force becomes separate military service (from the Army), 1947; Patty Hearst, held captive nineteen months, found in San Francisco, 1975; funeral conducted for Chinese leader Mao Tse Tung, 1976; President Carter, Egyptian President Sadat, and Israeli Prime Minister Begin end Camp David summit with historic peace agreement, 1978; Rev. Benjamin Weir returns safely to U.S. after having been released from sixteen months captivity in Lebanon, 1985; Philippine President Corazon Aquino addresses U.S. Congress, 1986.

Born Today—Lexicographer Samuel Johnson, 1709; Supreme Court Justice Joseph Story, 1779; Canadian leader John Diefenbaker, 1895; actress Greta Garbo, 1905; singer Frankie Avalon, 1940.

Today's Quotation—"No race that has anything to contribute to the markets of the world is long or in any degree ostracized." —*Booker T. Washington, September 18, 1893*

Contributions to Mankind

Many Christians have greatly contributed to the well-being of mankind as well as to the kingdom of God. One such individual was pro baseball player, evangelist, and reformer Billy Sunday. Sunday's fiery sermons were well known for their attacks on sin. Here is a typical quote: "I am against sin. I'll kick it as long as I have a foot, and I'll fight it as long as I've got a fist. I'll butt it as long as I've got a head. I'll bite it as long as I've got a tooth. Then when I'm old and fistless and footless and toothless, I'll gum it till I go home to glory and it goes home to perdition." May we be as well known for our hatred of sin as the late Billy Sunday!

Prayer Suggestion—Ask God to direct you in such a way that you will contribute to the good of mankind as did Billy Sunday.

SEPTEMBER

19

Today in History—President Washington's farewell address published, 1796; Germans begin siege of Paris in Franco-Prussian War, 1870; President Garfield dies of July 2nd gunshot wound and is succeeded by Vice President Chester Arthur, 1881; widow Jacqueline Kennedy Onassis agrees to $20 million settlement of her late husband Aristole Onassis' estate, 1977; series of earthquakes kill nearly ten thousand in Mexico City and cause estimated $1 billion in damage, 1985; Pope John Paul II ends ten-day visit to U.S., 1987.

Born Today—Author Rachel Field, 1894; revolutionary hero Lajos Kossuth, 1802; former Supreme Court Justice Lewis Powell, 1907; journalist Clifton Daniel, 1912; actor Adam West, 1928; author Mike Royko, 1932.

Today's Quotation—"I am fully alive to the fact that every nation that has ever engaged in war has always involved the sacred name of honor. Many a crime has been committed in its name; there are some being committed now. All the same, national honor is a reality, and any nation that disregards it is doomed."—*David Lloyd George, September 19, 1914*

Sacred Honor

Years ago the *Covenant Companion* carried the story of a man who wished to teach his young daughter the meaning of consecration and trust in the face of hardship. One day he asked the youngster if she loved her daddy enough to give up her prized glass beads. She replied, "Yes," and sorrowfully surrendered them. Several weeks later on her birthday, her father called the little girl over to him and handed her a small box. The girl lifted the lid to see an exquisite string of genuine pearls! Proudly she put them around her neck and told her smiling father, "Oh, Daddy, I did not understand, but now I do." She learned the value of implicit trust in a loving father whom she wished to honor and obey.

Do we trust our heavenly Father as much as this little girl did her daddy?

Prayer Suggestion—We are to come to God as little children. Do we instantly obey God's command as did the girl in this story?

SEPTEMBER

20

Today in History—Explorer Ferdinand Magellan launches voyage around the world, 1519; Civil War Battle of Chickamauga near Chattanooga, Tenn., ends, 1863; Italian troops enter Rome to complete nation's unification, 1870; ten thousand die as Hurricane FiFi hits Honduras, 1974; car bomb kills twenty-three, including two Americans, at U.S. embassy in Beirut, 1984.

Born Today—Nurse Elizabeth Kenny, 1886; writer Upton Sinclair, 1878; basketball coach Arnold "Red" Auerbach, 1917; actress Anne Meara, 1924; author Donald Hall, 1928; actress Sophia Loren, 1934.

Today's Quotation—"There is but one blasphemy, and that is injustice."—*Robert G. Ingersoll, September 20, 1880*

Blasphemy

Though the son of a clergyman, agnostic Robert Ingersoll was well-known for his disbelief and blasphemy of God. M. R. DeHaan describes a lesser-known scoffer who once blasphemed God at a street-corner rally: "If there is a God, let him strike me dead in five minutes," he cried. The minutes ticked slowly by as the crowd waited in stunned silence. "See, there is no God or he would have killed me," the atheist taunted. Then an old lady approached the sneering skeptic. "Do you have any children?" she asked. "Why yes," he replied. "I have a son." "If your son gave you a knife and asked you to kill him, would you do it?" she asked. "No!" he replied. "And why not?" was her next question. "Because I love him too much!" the skeptic exclaimed. As the woman walked away she said, "Yes, and God loves you too; more than enough to accept your foolish challenge. He wants to see you saved, not lost."

We must learn to respect God early in life so that it will become second nature to us later on.

Prayer Suggestion—Help us never to be guilty of treating the things of God lightly but always to hold his name in awe and reverence.

SEPTEMBER

21

Today in History—France abolishes monarchy in favor of a republic, 1792; West Germany established, 1949; Chile's armed forces kill President Salvador Allende in bloody coup, 1973; brother of slain Lebanese president-elect is elected by nearly unanimous vote, 1982.

Born Today—Writer H. G. Wells, 1866; actor Larry Hagman, 1931; songwriter Leonard Cohen, 1934; newscaster Bill Kurtis, 1940; comedian Bill Murray, 1950; basketball player Sidney Moncrief, 1957.

Today's Quotation—"Women work primarily to earn money."— *Roger Freeman, September 21, 1962*

Hard Work

Did you realize that you can glorify God through hard work? Have you ever considered your job as a ministry? For every believer his occupation is his ministry.

A man was hired to do a carving when he suddenly took ill. Knowing that the job must be completed on time, his employers brought in a young sculptor to complete the job. Although he could refer to a drawing, the young man had no idea what the carving was for, but he did his very best work anyway. Week after week he chiseled the stone until at last the job was finished and the carving was shipped away. Time went by and one day the young sculptor found himself walking through a beautiful new building. As he glanced around his eyes focused on a splendid marble pillar. Glancing up to the top he saw the beautiful piece he had carved. He was so overcome with emotion that he removed his cap and said reverently, "Thank God I did that job well."

Yes, work is a ministry—a holy calling that God has provided for us to do. Do your best for him no matter what your occupation may be.

Prayer Suggestion—Acknowledge all work as glorifying to God. Thank him for the ministry he has given you.

SEPTEMBER

22

Philippians 4:12-19

Today in History—Nathan Hale hanged as spy by British, 1776; U.S. Post Office established, 1789; Joseph Smith says the Golden Plates of the Book of Mormon revealed to him, 1827; U.S.S.R. tests its first atom bomb, 1949; commercial television permitted in England, 1955; President Ford escapes injury as, for the second time in seventeen days, an armed female threatens to kill him, 1975; shipyard workers in Gdansk, Poland, create Solidarity union with Lech Walesa as head, 1980.

Born Today—Writer Lord Chesterfield, 1694; scientist Michael Faraday, 1791; actor John Houseman, 1902; baseball manager Tom Lasorda, 1917; singer Debbie Boone, 1956; actor Scott Baio, 1961.

Today's Quotation—"A poor man has no honor."—*Samuel Johnson, September 22, 1777*

Poverty

While Samuel Johnson may feel the poor have no honor, that is not the attitude of God. Of all American presidents, the one most often associated with humble roots is Abraham Lincoln. It was Lincoln who said, "The Lord must love the common people, he has made so many of them."

What is less known, perhaps, is why the face of Lincoln was selected to appear on the penny. It seems sculptor David Brenner, himself a humble immigrant, was responsible for that decision. He recognized that there would be more pennies minted than any other coin and that more of them would be found in the pockets of the common people. The humble face of Lincoln seemed a natural for the penny.

No matter how few of this world's goods we may own, as believers, we may be certain we are truly "children of the (heavenly) king."

Prayer Suggestion—Recognize that as a child of God, your heavenly Father owns the universe and, in him, you will never be poor again!

SEPTEMBER

23

Matthew 7:20–27

Today in History—First U.S. commencement ceremony held at Harvard College, 1642; Lewis and Clark expedition completes its exploration of the West, 1806; time capsule buried at New York World's Fair, 1938; Juan Peron returns to power in Argentina, following ouster in a 1955 military coup, 1973; baseball's Lou Brock steals record 938th base; earlier he scored his 3,000th hit of the season, 1979; Senator Joseph Biden withdraws from Democratic presidential race following stories alleging possible plagiarism in law school, 1987.

Born Today—Educator William McGuffey, 1800; columnist Walter Lippmann, 1889; actor Mickey Rooney, 1920; composer Ray Charles, 1930; writer Mary Kay Place, 1947; singer Bruce Springsteen, 1949.

Today's Quotation—" . . . good resolutions are easier made than executed."—*Benjamin Franklin, September 23, 1770*

Plan Ahead

It was the French surgeon Nelaton who said that given four minutes in which to conduct surgery to save a life he would take one minute to plan how to do it. How many times do we get in trouble because we fail to plan (, or run) ahead of God's plan for our lives? We need to be in step with God each and every day through reading his Word and prayer.

A woman had to be confined to a rest home in her later years. However she always seemed to be happy and to have a radiant testimony for the Lord. Time went by and she lay dying. She told the chaplain her last request: that they sing her favorite hymn at her funeral. Later, the chaplain recalled, "I never will forget that day as a soloist sang, 'I'm a Child of the King' over the humble pine box." By planning ahead and accepting Christ as her Savior she had moved from the lowly poor house to God's great mansion in the sky. How far have you planned ahead?

Prayer Suggestion—Remember, God cannot complete the portrait he is painting of your life until you first surrender the brush to him.

SEPTEMBER

24

Matthew 7:12-19

Today in History—"Black Friday" causes financial panic after Jay Gold and Jim Fisk try to corner the U.S. gold market, 1869; President Eisenhower suffers a heart attack, 1955; President Eisenhower sends U.S. troops to Little Rock, Ark., to enforce school integration, 1957; trial of "Chicago Eight" begins in Chicago, 1969; second *Skylab* crew returns safely from fifty-seven day space mission, 1973; speaking before the United Nations, President Reagan calls for greater cooperation from the Soviets and issues a new arms control plan, 1984.

Born Today—Supreme Court Chief Justice John Marshall, 1755; novelist F. Scott Fitzgerald, 1896; scientist Howard Florey, 1898; sportscaster Jim McKay, 1921; actress Sheila MacRae, 1923; puppeteer Jim Henson, 1936.

Today's Quotation—"I certainly intend some time in my life to see Paris, and equally certainly intend never to learn the language."—*Charles Lamb, September 24, 1802*

Learning the Language

Sometimes we are better off not knowing the language, if it is the language of the world. A certain man had a sparrow he wanted to teach to sing, so he found a canary with a sweet song and placed their cages together. Day after day the birds lived side by side but instead of the sparrow learning to sing like the canary, the canary began to chirp like the lowly sparrow. Yes, the language had been learned but it was the wrong language!

In the same way, Christians living too close to the world begin to take on the language and habits of those who are the enemies of Christ. It might be said they grow accustomed to the dark of sin. What language do you speak?

Prayer Suggestion—May the world see Christ when hearing you speak and in watching how you live.

SEPTEMBER

25

Today in History—Balboa discovers the Pacific Ocean, 1513; Bill of Rights ratified, 1789; Twelfth Amendment, establishing separate Electoral College voting for president and vice president, ratified, 1804; *Journal of Science* reports aerosol gases believed to be destroying Earth's ozone layer; freon-using firms dispute the report, 1974; at least 150 are known dead in the collision of a 727 jetliner with a small private plane over San Diego, 1978.

Born Today—Writer William Faulkner, 1897; composer Dimitri Shostakovich, 1906; broadcast journalist Barbara Walters, 1931; pianist Glenn Gould, 1932; actor Mark Hamill, 1951; actor Christopher Reeve, 1952.

Today's Quotation—"There is one thing that the American people always rise to and extend their hand to, and that is the truth of justice and of liberty and of peace."—*Woodrow Wilson, September 25, 1919*

Truth of Justice

The Bible records a number of instances of poetic justice in which the treatment given to others later comes back to haunt the giver. Remember how Jacob cheated Esau out of his birthright? Later he was cheated by Laban, who substituted Leah for Rachel. King David stole Uriah's wife, then lived to see his son Absalom go in to David's wives. Then there was Haman, who was hanged on gallows he built for Mordecai. Clearly justice triumphed in these cases.

How thankful we should be that God does not give us justice (what we deserve) but mercy and grace instead.

Prayer Suggestion—God is so loving he keeps us from getting what we deserve, but instead treats us as he would treat Christ.

SEPTEMBER

26

Today in History—Former Marine bandmaster John Philip Sousa leads first performance of Sousa's Band, 1892; New Zealand attains dominion status, 1907; first Kennedy—Nixon televised presidential campaign debate, 1960; President Lyndon Johnson confers with West German officials on the costs of defending Europe, 1966.

Born Today—John Chapman (Johnny Appleseed), 1774; poet-playwright T. S. Eliot, 1888; composer George Gershwin, 1898; singer Julie London, 1926; actor Patrick O'Neal, 1927; singer Olivia Newton-John, 1948.

Today's Quotation—"Beware of asking for time! Misfortune never grants it!"—*Count Mirabeau, September 26, 1789*

Good Use of Time

Wishing to be surrounded by fresh blooms throughout the day, noted botanist Linnaeus once planted a "clock of flowers." It was so named because the blooms would each open at a set time of day, providing a continually blooming array.

How many of us have so structured our lives that they reflect God's work and blessing all throughout the day? Do we make productive use of our time, or do we live as if this is just another day we have to get through? Some day we will be called upon to give an account for how we have served the Lord. What will we have to say for the way we have served him?

Prayer Suggestion—May we plan our activities so that God would be pleased with *all* we do and the accomplishments we make each day.

SEPTEMBER

27

Today in History—Warsaw surrenders to Nazi Germany, 1939; first World War II liberty ship launched, 1941; Warren Commission, investigating assassination of President Kennedy, says Lee Harvey Oswald acted alone in the murder, 1964; parents ask court to allow turning off life support systems to Karen Ann Quinlan after five months in a coma, 1975; opponents of Iran's Ayatollah Khomeini battle government guards in Teheran, 1981.

Born Today—Patriot Samuel Adams, 1722; writer Alfred Mahan, 1758; cartoonist Thomas Nast, 1840; actor William Conrad, 1920; director Arthur Penn, 1922; baseball player Mike Schmidt, 1949.

Today's Quotation—"We seem to be approaching an age of gross."—*Spiro T. Agnew, September 27, 1969*

Gross Sin

The worst kind of sin we call "gross"—that which is totally outside the bounds of acceptable human behavior. But God has a different definition. There is a story told of a church service where several hundred people gathered to confess their sins. For several hours the confessions continued: repentance for sins of drinking, dancing, immorality, dishonesty, and more. At last a man said, "I have been guilty of all these sins, but the worst thing I have done in my life was to reject the love of Jesus Christ. I did not love or serve him, nor was I surrendered to him until early this morning when I fully committed my life to him." In God's eyes that is the most gross sin of all. The rejection of Christ's death on the cross as payment in full for your sins is the only sin which alone will send you to hell.

Have you confessed this sin of which every human being is guilty? When you stand before God and he asks why he should allow you into his perfect heaven, what will your answer be? Make sure you have repented and confessed your sins to God.

Prayer Suggestion—Confess all your sins to God so that he can remember them no more and re-establish fellowship with you.

SEPTEMBER

28

Ephesians 5:25-32

Today in History—Eight members of Chicago White Sox indicted for "throwing" 1919 World Series to Cincinnati in "Black Sox" scandal, 1920; *Sword of the Lord* begins publishing, 1934; Nazi Germany and U.S.S.R. partition Poland, 1939; Cambodian leader Pol Pot arrives in Peking for talks with Chinese leaders, 1977; President Reagan holds White House meeting with Soviet ambassador Gromyko to discuss better U.S.—Soviet relations, 1984.

Born Today—Educator Frances Willard, 1839; statesman George Clemenceau, 1841; broadcast executive William Paley, 1901; entertainer Ed Sullivan, 1902; actor Marcello Mastroianni, 1924.

Today's Quotation—"At least we didn't shoot each other."—*Nikita Khrushchev, after interview by Eleanor Roosevelt, September 28, 1957*

Working Together

Getting along with others is one of the most basic and most important skills we can develop because we never can tell who may be watching. A country preacher was once nailing up a fallen vine when he noticed a young lad watching him with great interest. "Looking for some hints on gardening?" the preacher asked. "Oh, no," said the boy. "I'm just waiting to see what you say when you hit your thumb!"

Sometimes we become so concerned with the externals we forget what is really important. M. R. DeHaan tells of a legend in which "doubting" Thomas was again troubled with misgivings concerning the Lord's resurrection. As the story goes, Thomas went to one apostle and then another to voice his doubts, but all were too busy to meet with him. Finally Thomas realized that maybe the reason they had no doubts about the resurrection was that they were all busy serving the Lord. So he began busying himself by teaching the gospel and was freed of his doubts.

If you have trusted Christ, rejoice, then get on with the work he has for you to do.

Prayer Suggestion—Pray that God will keep you so busy serving him that you will soon forget about lesser things.

SEPTEMBER

29

Ephesians 6:10-20

Today in History—U.S. Army established with seven hundred men, 1789; Scotland Yard police headquarters in London established, 1829; British Prime Minister Chamberlain, French Premier Daladier, Italian Premier Mussolini, and German Reichsfuhrer Hitler meet in Munich and agree to give part of Czechoslovakia to Nazi Germany, 1938; President Reagan says $1 trillion debt is U.S.'s main problem, 1981; Henry Ford II, grandson of Ford Motor Company founder, dies, 1987.

Born Today—Naval hero Horatio Nelson, 1758; nuclear physicist Enrico Fermi, 1901; actor Gene Autry, 1907; actress Greer Garson, 1908; actress Madeline Kahn, 1942; TV host Bryant Gumbel, 1948.

Today's Quotation—"Not by speeches and majority decisions will the greatest problems of our time be decided . . . but by iron and blood."—*Otto von Bismarck, September 29, 1862*

Warriors

The professor in Bible college gave his students two subjects to write about on their examination paper. He asked them to write for a half hour each on the Holy Spirit and Satan. One hard-working student wrote furiously for an hour on the Holy Spirit, then when papers were being collected, scrawled across the bottom of the test booklet, "I had no time for the devil."

The Bible tells of a time when people will so long for peace they will willingly make an agreement with the Antichrist to get it. Someone who could enforce peace today would have the power to control the world. It will be in an atmosphere of increased turmoil that the Antichrist will be able to skillfully "weave his net around the world." He will so have society in his grasp that the world will ask, "Who is able to make war with him?" Though it will appear that Satan has the world in his grasp, God is still in control and will be victorious after all.

Prayer Suggestion—Christians know how the story ends—Satan is defeated and God wins. Look forward to Christ's return.

SEPTEMBER

30

Today in History—Ether first used as dental anesthetic, 1846; first round-the-world air passenger race begins at Lakehurst, N.J., 1936; Munich Pact partitioning Czechoslovakia announced to shocked world, 1938; International War Crimes Tribunal finds twenty-two Nazis guilty, 1946; British Bechuanaland becomes free nation of Botswana, 1966; Italian police pick up dozens of Mafiosi in one of the largest raids yet on organized crime, 1984.

Born Today—Actress Deborah Kerr, 1921; writer Truman Capote, 1924; actress Angie Dickinson, 1931; singer Johnny Mathis, 1935; politician James Sasser, 1936; songwriter Deborah Allen, 1953.

Today's Quotation—"This is the second time in our history that there has come back from Germany to Downing Street peace with honor. I believe it is peace for our time."—*Prime Minister Neville Chamberlain, September 30, 1938*

Perfect Peace

Evangelist Charles H. Spurgeon used to tell the story of the dying woman who was visited by her Welsh minister. "Are you sinking?" he asked with concern. "Why no," she struggled to say. If I had been standing in the sand I might sink, but I am standing on the Rock of Ages and there is no sinking there."

Once God forgives, he forgets all that we have confessed to him. A kindly country doctor had died and a judge was going through his accounts. Across many of them he had written, "Forgiven—too poor to pay." The doctor's widow asked whether or not the accounts could still be collected, as some of the patients now could pay. "No indeed," said the judge. There's no court in the land that could order a collection of funds where the account has been marked "forgiven."

There is true peace where God has marked the debt of sin "Forgiven—paid in full!" That truth is the hope of peace in our time. "Stand on Christ, the solid rock; all other ground is sinking sand."

Prayer Suggestion—Troubled soul, realize that an unchanging God has rest for your soul today as well as assurance of a heavenly home.

OCTOBER

1

Today in History—Henry Ford introduces the Model T automobile, 1908; Nazi Germany begins occupying Czechoslovakia's Sudetenland, 1938; Pennsylvania Turnpike (America's pioneer toll highway) opens, 1940; U.S. troops capture Naples, Italy, in World War II, 1943; communists set up People's Republic of China, 1949; Roger Maris sets major league baseball record with sixty-first home run of the season, 1961; Christian Broadcasting Network (CBN) begins broadcasting, 1961; U.S. and Soviets agree on joint guidelines to ensure the rights of Palestinians in the Middle East, 1977; six die and 100 are hospitalized as earthquake rocks Los Angeles, 1987.

Born Today—Naval hero James Lawrence, 1781; pianist Vladimir Horowitz, 1904; actor Walter Matthau, 1920; former President Jimmy Carter, 1924; Supreme Court Chief Justice William Rehnquist, 1924; actress Julie Andrews, 1935.

Today's Quotation—"I cannot forecast to you the action of Russia. It is a riddle wrapped in a mystery inside an enigma."—*Winston Churchill, October 1, 1939*

Riddles

Everyone loves a good riddle. Here's an ancient one: "What animal goes on four legs in the morning, on two at noonday, and on three in the evening?" The answer—man! He crawls on all fours as an infant, walks upright on two legs as an adult, then uses a cane in old age.

The Bible speaks of the great mystery of how we will all be changed into new beings at the rapture. While the details remain a mystery to us on this side of eternity, God knows the answer to this mystery. While no one fully understands everything about God (or they would be equal with God), there is no mystery about how man can have eternal life: through repentance and confession of sin and belief in God.

Prayer Suggestion—Trusting God to solve life's great mysteries, we put our faith in him and strive to serve him in all we do.

OCTOBER

2

James 1:12–16

Today in History—British major executed as spy by Continental Army for dealings with Benedict Arnold, 1780; Rome votes to join Italy, 1870; "Lost Battalion" of U.S. Army holds out against Germans until rescued on October 8, 1918; "Peanuts" comic strip first published, 1950; Guinea gains independence from France, 1958; gold rush in Brazil nets over $50 million since February, 1980; actor Rock Hudson dies from AIDS complications at age 59, 1985.

Born Today—India's Mahatma Gandhi, 1869; statesman Cordell Hull, 1871; comedian Groucho Marx, 1895; writer Graham Greene, 1904; publisher Clay Felker, 1928; critic Rex Reed, 1939.

Today's Quotation—"Courts and camps are the only places to learn the world in."—*Lord Chesterfield, October 2, 1747*

Worldliness

According to William Law, "The world is now a greater enemy to the Christian than it was in apostolic times. It is a greater enemy because it has greater power over Christians by its favors, riches, honors, rewards, and protection than it had by the more obvious dangers of fire and fury of its persecutors." As quoted by Robert H. Lauer, Law cautioned that by losing its evil appearance, "worldliness today is no longer viewed as an enemy. Thus people are easily influenced by it. Don't let Satan trick you into going along with the world. Accept no substitutes for God's amazing grace."

While Christians remain *in* the world they are not to be *of* the world.

Prayer Suggestion—That God would grant the discernment and discipline to reject the attractive lures of the world.

OCTOBER

3

Matthew 5:3–16

Today in History—President Lincoln designates the last Thursday in November as Thanksgiving Day, 1863; Rebecca Felton of Georgia becomes first woman U.S. Senator, 1922; President Nixon in critical condition following surgery to remove blood clot from his thigh, 1974; State Department criticizes growing right-wing violence in El Salvador's "death squads," 1983.

Born Today—Historian George Bancroft, 1800; army physician William Gorgas, 1854; actress Eleanora Duse, 1859; writer Thomas Wolfe, 1900; playwright Gore Vidal, 1925; baseball player Dave Winfield, 1951.

Today's Quotation—"We have only laid the foundations of peace. The superstructure is not even begun."—*Neville Chamberlain, October 3, 1938*

Foundations of Peace

Have you ever noticed how much easier it is to make rules for other people to follow? Winston Churchill is credited with telling this parable of peace: "Long ago all the zoo animals decided to disarm, so they arranged 'peace talks' to work out the details. The rhinoceros asked for a strict ban against the use of teeth in war. The stag and porcupine agreed, but the lion and the tiger defended teeth and even claws as being honorable weapons. The bear, however, wanted both teeth and horns to be banned and suggested that all animals be allowed to give each other a good hug when they quarreled. This only served to offend all the other animals and so they never could agree."

Sometimes we are so protective of our own interests that we cannot see the legitimate concerns of others.

Prayer Suggestion—Help us to sacrifice our selfish interests for the overall good of mankind.

OCTOBER

4

Psalm 32:1–11

Today in History—"Dick Tracy" comic strip first published, 1931; U.S.S.R. orbits first *Sputnik* satellite and launches Space Age, 1957; first jet airplane service across the Atlantic begins, 1958; Pope Paul VI becomes first pontiff to visit U.S., 1965; Lesotho gains independence from Great Britain, 1966; pianist Glenn Gould dies at age 50, 1982.

Born Today—Artist Jean Millet, 1814; President Rutherford B. Hayes, 1822; physicist Michael I. Pupin, 1858; artist Frederick Remington, 1861; writer Damon Runyan, 1884; actor Charlton Heston, 1922; author Alvin Toffler, 1928.

Today's Quotation—"Along with responsible newspapers we must have responsible readers."—*Arthur Hays Sulzberger, October 4, 1955*

Responsibility

Responsibility for the Christian involves putting God first in all things. C. E. McCartney recalls how a former president of Princeton University, Dr. McCosh, always made it a point to pray with the seniors before they left campus to make their mark in the world. When he asked one graduate to pray with him, the young man refused, extending his hand instead to bid the president farewell. Years went by and one day a man and his wife appeared in the president's study. "You don't remember me," he began, "but I was the young man who refused to pray with you. But all along my godly mother was praying on my behalf. Her prayers have won out and I am back to enter the seminary. Before I go, I want you to kneel down with me and offer that long-postponed prayer."

Prayer Suggestion—If God has spoken to you about a spiritual need, commit it to him. Don't put off praying for that all-important decision.

OCTOBER

5

2 Corinthians 5:10–21

Today in History—Portugal becomes a republic, 1910; Harry Truman first president to broadcast TV address from the White House, 1947; British trade commissioner in Quebec, James Cross, kidnapped by separatist terrorists as hostage for release of twenty-three political prisoners. He is released two months later, 1970; following eighth case of product tampering, makers of Tylenol remove capsules from store shelves in massive recall, 1982; spacecraft *Challenger* lifts off with seven astronauts: largest crew in space history, 1984.

Born Today—Theologian Jonathan Edwards, 1703; President Chester A. Arthur, 1830; rocket engine pioneer Robert Goddard, 1882; playwright Joshua Logan, 1908; actress Glynis Johns, 1923; actor Bill Dana, 1924.

Today's Quotation—"Condemn virtue that's thrust upon us."—*Charles Lamb, October 5, 1800*

Virtuous Living

Sin is so subtle in its destruction that without warning it can quickly overwhelm its victims and bring them down to disaster. Dr. Bob Jones, Sr. told of the preacher who for many years had been carrying on a secret affair with a soloist in the choir. Eventually the double lifestyle was discovered and the pastor, in a desperate move to save his ministry, killed the soloist. Imagine the amazement of his congregation as they read of their spiritual leader being imprisoned on murder charges! It has been said, "Though I am not what I ought to be, nor what I wish to be, nor yet what I hope to be, I can truly say I am not what I once was: a slave to sin and Satan."

Can you too say this? Thanks to Calvary I don't do that anymore.

Prayer Suggestion—Reflect upon what God has done in your life and how that "all things are become new" as a result of Christ.

OCTOBER

6

2 Corinthians 12:6–10

Today in History—Edison shows first motion pictures, 1889; Al Jolson speaks in *The Jazz Singer,* the first talking feature picture, 1927; Eduard Benes resigns as president of Czechoslovakia, 1938; New York Mets, New York's "Cinderella" baseball team, become National League champions, 1969; Egypt and Syria launch surprise attack on Israel, 1973; Iraq expels Iran's Ayatollah Khomeini. France agrees to provide refuge for exiled religious leader, 1978; Pope John Paul II is first pontiff to visit White House, 1979; Egyptian President Anwar Sadat is murdered at Cairo parade, 1981.

Born Today—Singer Jenny Lind, 1820; inventor George Westinghouse, 1846; architect Le Corbusier, 1887; explorer Thor Heyerdahl, 1914; author Shana Alexander, 1925; actor Fred Travalena, 1942.

Today's Quotation—"I am in perpetual Anxiety lest . . . an accidental Quarrel, a personal Insult, an imprudent Order . . . make a Breach that can never afterward be healed."—*Benjamin Franklin, October 6, 1774*

Healing the Harried

God heals our hurts today, just as he always has. Sometimes he works through our own families to show us his power. Henry Bosch tells of a man who was struggling under a heavy workload that seemed to require more than the usual exercise of his faith. About this time his little girl, a paralytic, begged to carry his package in to her mother. "How could you possibly carry it?" he asked. "Oh, Daddy!" she exclaimed, "If you give me the package, I can hold it while you carry me." Then he saw the lesson God had for him—that despite his emotional hurts and handicaps, his heavenly Father was there to carry him through the difficult challenges of life.

Are you trusting God to see you through life's crises?

Prayer Suggestion—Recognize that he will carry you through the crises of life when you have not the strength to "go it alone."

OCTOBER

7

Today in History—Spanish-Venetian fleet routs Turks, 1571; first U.S. railroad begins operating at Quincy, Mass., 1826; Denmark's King Christian X defies Nazi occupiers of his nation by attending services in Copenhagen synagogue, 1942; Carter-Ford presidential debate marked by Gerald Ford erroneously stating, "There is no Soviet domination in Eastern Europe," 1976; crowd of 100,000 demonstrators protest recent terrorist bomb attack on Paris synagogue, 1980.

Born Today—Poet James Whitcomb Riley, 1849; former Vice President Henry Wallace, 1888; actress June Allyson, 1917; singer Al Martino, 1927; psychiatrist R. D. Laing, 1927; Marine Lt. Col. Oliver North, 1943.

Today's Quotation—"As sure as man is mortal, and to err is human, justice deferred enhances the price at which you must purchase safety and peace."—*Lord Brougham, October 7, 1831*

Mortal Man

As mortals, all humans are fallible, that is, capable of making mistakes. One way to realize your mortality is to try to find your way to an unfamiliar location. You stop to ask directions and proceed from there in a wandering path toward what you hope leads to your destination. How much better it would be (and how many fewer mistakes you would make) if someone was willing to *lead* you to your goal.

In the same way, there is a difference between *telling* someone how to live the Christian life and *showing* them how. Most states have passed mandatory seat belt laws. It has been interesting to notice that when the driver of the car buckles up, everyone else in the car silently follows suit. People tend to copy what they see more than the advice they hear. Make sure people watching you are seeing you do the right thing!

Prayer Suggestion—Determine that, with God's help, you will be a "show-er" and not just a "tell-er" about God.

OCTOBER

8

Today in History—The great Chicago fire begins (supposedly when a cow kicked over a lantern), 1871; Sgt. Alvin C. York kills twenty-five German soldiers and captures 132 in 1918; Don Larsen of the New York Yankees pitches a no-hit, no-run baseball game against Brooklyn Dodgers in World Series, 1956.

Born Today—Diplomat John Hay, 1838; aviator Eddie Rickenbacker, 1890; Argentine leader Juan Peron, 1895; columnist Rona Barrett, 1936; politician Jesse Jackson, 1941; comedian Chevy Chase, 1943.

Today's Quotation—"I am for the people of the whole nation doing just as they please in all matters which concern the whole nation . . . and for each individual doing just as he chooses in all matters which concern nobody else."—*Abraham Lincoln, October 8, 1858*

Doing Your "Thing"

Some people insist on "doing their thing" despite the risks. This may involve seeing just how closely they can court disaster without it "getting" them. A tourist was once riding up a winding mountain pass aboard a rickety old bus. To the left rose the sheer face of the mountainside. To the right—with no guardrail in between—lay an awesome precipice plunging hundreds of feet to the canyon floor below. The guide, wanting to show off to his rider, boasted, "I can drive right at the edge of the cliff. Want to see how close I can get?" The shocked visitor replied, "No, no, that's okay. Let's see how far away from the edge we can stay. I just want to arrive in one piece."

There's something about grave danger that, for most of us, stifles our independent spirit and makes us want to stay with that which is certain and secure. When spiritual problems threaten to plunge you over the precipice, cling to God and he will carry you safely through.

Prayer Suggestion—Recognize that God controls your life and that you have no need for an independent spirit.

OCTOBER

9

Ephesians 4:25–32

Today in History—Yale University chartered, 1701; assassin kills King Alexander of Yugoslavia and French Foreign Minister Jean-Louis Barthou in Marseilles, France, 1934; Uganda gains freedom from British Commonwealth, 1962; Egyptian President Hosni Mubarak arrives in Amman, Jordan, for first visit to an Arab nation since the Israel peace accord, 1984.

Born Today—Composer Camille Saint-Saens, 1835; singer John Lennon, 1940; France's Captain Alfred Dreyfus, 1859; editor Edward Bok, 1863; writer Gamaliel Bradford, 1863; drama critic Martin Gottfried, 1933; football player Mike Singletary, 1958.

Today's Quotation—"An injury is much sooner forgotten than an insult."—*Lord Chesterfield, October 9, 1746*

Forgiving Insults

How do you react when someone has gossip to share? M.R. DeHaan used to tell the story of the beehive in his yard. It seems that one time when he was out walking with his boys a bee took after one of the lads and stung him above the eye. The insect then went on to chase the younger boy who ran yelling and screaming for help. Gently DeHaan picked up the little lad and told him that there was nothing to fear; the bee had lost its stinger. By being stung, his brother took the sting away.

How do we act when we overhear stinging gossip about a fellow saint? Let us be willing to "take the sting away" by absorbing it ourselves, then re-directing the conversation toward positive things.

Prayer Suggestion—For patience and love to be willing to protect the reputation and interests of others.

OCTOBER

10

Today in History—First settlement in Oklahoma, 1802; classes begin at U.S. Naval Academy, Annapolis, Md., 1845; first tuxedo dinner jacket worn, 1886; Chinese "Double Ten" marks establishment of Chinese Republic on tenth day of tenth month, 1911; Fiji becomes independent of Great Britain, 1970; rally in Bonn draws 250,000 demonstrators to protest deployment of missiles in Western Europe, 1981; actor Yul Brynner dies at age 65, 1985; federal agents seize over two tons of cocaine, worth $41 million, in biggest drug bust to date, 1985.

Born Today—Composer Giuseppi Verdi, 1813; actress Helen Hayes, 1900; dramatist Harold Pinter, 1930; astronaut William Anders, 1933; actor Ben Vereen, 1946; tennis player Martina Navratilova, 1956.

Today's Quotation—"Fear is a psychological factor. But it has very practical results."—*Josef Stalin, October 10, 1944*

Fear

What do you fear? Is it those things which may cause physical harm but which cannot touch your soul, or the things which can affect your eternal soul forever? A father and his little girl were returning to an empty home after burying their wife and mother. Nothing seemed the same. The youngster was tucked into bed as usual but could not go to sleep. For a while all was quiet, then the little girl asked, "Daddy, you can love through the dark can't you?" Choking back the tears, the father replied, "Yes, dear, you can." His daughter, reassured of her mother's love, soon drifted off to sleep. The man then silently thanked God for the lesson of how love conquers fear.

Yes, friend, you can trust God's nearness to permeate the darkness of your fear and reassure you of his constant love.

Prayer Suggestion—God's love is with us through the darkest night. Praise him for his loving care that sees us safely to the other side.

300

OCTOBER

11

Today in History—Pulaski Memorial Day marks death of Brigadier General Casimir Pulaski in American Revolutionary War, 1779; Daughters of American Revolution founded, 1890; in Japan, former Premier Tanaka is judged guilty of accepting $2.1 million in bribes from American aircraft firm, 1983.

Born Today—Former First Lady Eleanor Roosevelt, 1884; former Supreme Court Chief Justice Harland Stone, 1872; General Nathan Twining, 1897; journalist Joseph Alsop, Jr., 1910; physician Robert Gale, 1945.

Today's Quotation—"It is pleasanter to eat one's own peas out of one's garden, than to buy them by the peck at Covent Garden."—*Charles Lamb, October 11, 1802*

No Place Like Home

At the peak of her popularity opera singer Jenny Lind was singing to a strangely indifferent audience of twenty thousand in New York. But when she began the strains of "Home, Sweet Home," tears began to flow among many in the crowded hall. At the conclusion she was greeted with thunderous applause in response to the emotional appeal of home.

Sometimes what we own determines where we live. A wealthy man once spent a lot of money on a famous painting of Christ. However, when he brought it home, he was unable to find an appropriate spot to display it. Finally he called in an architect who carefully looked over the situation and concluded, "You cannot fit this picture into your home. You must make a home to fit it!"

What truth is proclaimed in those wonderful words. We must make our home life fit around Christ and not expect him to adapt to us. How well does Christ fit into your home?

Prayer Suggestion—Dedicate your home and family fully to the Lord, then begin to watch God work in your family anew!

301

OCTOBER

12

Psalm 127:1-5

Today in History—America is discovered by Christopher Columbus, 1492; George Washington lays cornerstone for the White House (oldest building in Washington, D.C.), 1792; Lions International founded in Dallas, Texas, 1917; U.S.S.R. launches first space capsule to carry more than one person, 1964; Vice President Spiro Agnew resigns from office after pleading "no contest" to charges of failing to report income while serving as governor of Maryland; Gerald Ford is nominated to succeed Agnew as vice president, 1973; British Prime Minister Margaret Thatcher narrowly escapes injury in Brighton, England, bomb blast, 1984; producer Orson Welles dies in Las Vegas at age 70, 1985.

Born Today—Composer Ralph Vaughan Williams, 1872; Weight Watchers founder Jean Nidetch, 1923; comedian Dick Gregory, 1932; opera singer Luciano Pavarotti, 1935; sportscaster Tony Kubek, 1936; physicist Ronald McNair, 1950.

Today's Quotation—"Patriotism is not enough."—*Edith Cavell, October 12, 1915*

Beyond Patriotism

In whom do you trust? Abraham Lincoln once said, "Faith in our God is indispensible to successful statesmanship," but more than just patriotism is needed for mankind to survive in today's society. Those who truly love their nation should first love their God, who determines the rise and fall of a people and its leaders. Never be satisfied with mere patriotism toward nations on earth when you can declare your citizenship in God's eternal kingdom and be adopted into his heavenly family.

A flea-bitten kitten once came to the door of a country farmhouse, and the children pleaded with their mother to let them adopt the pitiful thing. They fed it warm milk and it soon became part of the family—they couldn't have gotten it to leave if they had wanted to. In the same way God adopts us poor, shopworn sinners into his eternal family. Once we are adopted into God's family, we become joint heirs with his son Jesus Christ, and we have his promise that he will never leave or forsake us!

Prayer Suggestion—Determine you are a citizen of heaven and pledge your allegiance first to God, then to the kingdoms of earth.

OCTOBER

13

Mark 16:15–18

Today in History—U.S. Navy established, 1775; Jewish fraternal group, B'nai B'rith, founded in New York City, 1843; Finland mobilizes for military action, 1939; President Nixon promises not to be affected by Vietnam War protests, 1969; oil industry chided by President Carter for not accepting energy plan, 1977; William Clark named to succeed controversial figure James Watt as interior secretary, 1983; physicists hope atom smasher started up today will regain U.S. leadership in high energy physics, 1985.

Born Today—Heroine Molly Pitcher, 1754; author Arna Bontemps, 1902; cartoonist Herblock, 1909; actor Yves Montand, 1921; British leader Margaret Thatcher, 1925; singer Art Garfunkel, 1942; singer Marie Osmond, 1959.

Today's Quotation—"Were I to indulge my own theory, I should wish them [American states] to practise neither commerce nor navigation, but to stand, with respect to Europe, precisely on the footing of China. We should thus avoid wars, and all our citizens would be husbandmen."—*Thomas Jefferson, October 13, 1785*

Chinese Citizens

It has been estimated that by the year 2000, one in every three people on earth will be Chinese. Already the Chinese population exceeds eight hundred million, about four times that of the U.S., in the same land area! On top of this, an estimated twenty-two million Chinese live outside the country itself in such nations as the Philippines, Taiwan, Malaysia, Thailand, Indonesia, and Singapore. Some have predicted that the development of oil fields in China will soon make that nation a major economic force in the world. For the foreseeable future, more of the world's people will claim Chinese citizenship than any other country.

While national citizenship is important, how much more important is our eternal citizenship. Where will you spend eternity?

Prayer Suggestion—Pray for all of the world's citizens, especially those who do not yet know Christ as Savior. May we be faithful in proclaiming the gospel of Christ to all nations.

OCTOBER

14

Today in History—William the Conqueror claims England for the Normans at the Battle of Hastings, 1066; pilot Chuck Yeager makes first faster-than-sound flight, 1947; East Germany becomes communist satellite state of the Russians, 1949; Peace Corps established by President Kennedy, 1960; world's first live television broadcast made from an orbiting space ship *(Apollo 7)*, 1968; singer Bing Crosby dies in Madrid at age 73, 1977; National Council of Churches introduces new Bible translation which blurs or omits gender references to God, 1983.

Born Today—Colonial founder William Penn, 1644; President Dwight D. Eisenhower, 1890; author Lois Lenski, 1893; former U.S. Surgeon General C. Everett Koop, 1916; actor Roger Moore, 1928, lawyer John Dean, 1938.

Today's Quotation—"In regard to the moral character generally of our ancestors, the settlers of New England, my opinion is that they possessed all the Christian virtues but charity; and they seem never to have doubted that they possessed that also."—*Daniel Webster, October 14, 1826*

Charity

In his book, *Love as a Lubricant*, Dr. C. H. Parkhurst recalled the story of a commuter. Every day, while riding the train, he noticed the door squeaked as it was pushed open. And so one day he reached inside his pocket, retrieved a small oil can and squirted a few drops on the squeaky part. Returning to his seat, he was heard to say, "I always carry an oil can in my pocket, for there are so many squeaky things a drop of oil will correct."

Love acts as a "lubricant" in life, making relationships in the home and community harmonious. Are you prepared to contribute a dose of love to help smooth over the rough spots of those you meet?

Prayer Suggestion—May God use our love as a soothing lubricant to help other people live together in peace and harmony.

OCTOBER

15

Today in History—New York's La Guardia Airport opens, 1939; premier of Vichy France, Pierre Laval, shot for treason by a French firing squad, 1945; Nazi leader Hermann Goering commits suicide in prison cell in Nuremberg, Germany, 1946; Nikita Khrushchev deposed as head of U.S.S.R., 1964; federal troops requested by Massachusetts to quell racial violence in Boston schools, 1974; El Salvador's leaders meet with rebels for first time, 1979.

Born Today—Writer P. G. Wodehouse, 1881; economist John Kenneth Galbraith, 1908; business executive Lee Iacocca, 1924; actress Penny Marshall, 1942; sportscaster Jim Palmer, 1945; Britain's Duchess of York, Sarah Ferguson, 1959.

Today's Quotation—"It appears to me, that an American, coming to Europe for education, loses in his knowledge, in his morals, in his health, in his habits, and in his happiness."—*Thomas Jefferson, October 15, 1785*

All Around Loser

There was once a successful farmer whose crops and herds grew and increased. But he resisted all attempts to discuss spiritual things. In fact, the man often replied, "I must make my fortune first, then I shall attend to those matters." One day he took suddenly ill and had to be rushed home. As he lay dying he was visited by a man who had often spoken to him in the past about spiritual things. The farmer cried out in bitter remorse, "I am a loser! At last—I have gained the world, but have lost my soul."

What a tragedy to possess all the world's goods but die a loser— eternally lost and separated from God!

Prayer Suggestion—May God help us to communicate his love to all those we meet before it is forever too late!

OCTOBER

16

Psalm 35:4–28

Today in History—Queen Marie Antoinette of France sent to guillotine, 1793; John Brown raids Harper's Ferry, Va., 1859; first public birth control clinic opens in Brooklyn, N.Y., 1916; ten former Nazi leaders, convicted by War Crimes Tribunal, hanged at Nuremberg, Germany, 1946; New York Mets win first world series over Baltimore Orioles, 1969; Israeli statesman Moshe Dayan dies at age 66, 1981; fifty-seven-hour ordeal ends for baby Jessica McClure as she is rescued from a narrow oil well shaft where she had been trapped for more than two days, 1987.

Born Today—Lexicographer Noah Webster, 1758; writer Oscar Wilde, 1854; playwright Eugene O'Neill, 1888; Supreme Court Justice W. O. Douglas, 1898; actress Angela Lansbury, 1925; author Charles Colson, 1931.

Today's Quotation—"Do as you would be done by is the surest method that I know of pleasing."—*Lord Chesterfield, October 16, 1747*

The Golden Rule

A chaplain was assisting injured troops on the battlefield when he came across a young man who had just been wounded. The chaplain inquired if the man would like him to read from the Bible. The soldier replied, "I'm so thirsty, could I have a drink of cold water instead?" The chaplain obliged and drew a cold drink for the injured youth. Later, the kindly minister arranged a pillow for the lad and even covered the boy with his coat when he was cold. The wounded man thanked the chaplain sincerely, then added feebly: "If there's anything in that book in your hand that makes a man do for another what you have done for me, please read it to me."

The chaplain knew the importance of the Golden Rule in helping the hurting. How about you? Do you "do unto others as you would have them do unto you?"

Prayer Suggestion—Make me sensitive to the needs and hurts of others and help me to be especially kind to those who need it most.

OCTOBER

17

Proverbs 22:7–29

Today in History—British General Burgoyne surrenders to American General Horatio Gates at Saratoga, N.Y., in American Revolutionary War, 1777; Albert Einstein comes to U.S. as refugee from Nazi Germany, 1933; body of kidnapped Quebec Labor Minister Pierre Laporte found in a car trunk in Montreal, 1970; Congress passes law prohibiting the hiring of aliens, 1986.

Born Today—Actress Jean Arthur, 1908; dramatist Arthur Miller, 1915; astronaut William Anders, 1933; stuntman Evel Knievel, 1938; actress Margot Kidder, 1948.

Today's Quotation—"The lady bearer of this letter says she has two sons who want to work. Set them at it if possible. Wanting to work is so rare a want that it should be encouraged."—*Abraham Lincoln, October 17, 1861*

Wanting to Work

The great preacher H. A. Ironside told of a welder for the trolley lines who was one of the greatest workers he had ever seen. After laboring on his knees all week welding steel rails together, the man spent his Saturdays calling on shut-ins in hospitals and jails. For those families who were desperately poor, he would leave a cash gift. When Sunday rolled around, he would say, "My, I was worn out Friday, but I had a wonderful time yesterday, and now I am all rested up!" He wanted to work—to keep busy in the work of the Lord.

Prayer Suggestion—May God help us to be about his business, working to further the cause of Christ wherever he would lead.

OCTOBER

18

Today in History—Mason-Dixon Line established as border be-tween Maryland and Pennsylvania, 1767; transfer of Alaska from Russia to U.S., 1867; Mata Hari shot as spy by French firing squad in Paris in World War I, 1917; no one is injured as West German commandos free eighty-six hostages aboard Lufthansa plane minutes before terrorists say it will explode, 1977; U.N. group reports food shortages and possible star-vation face twenty-two African countries, 1983.

Born Today—Journalist A. J. Liebling, 1904; Canadian Prime Minister Pierre Trudeau, 1919; conservative leader Jesse Helms, 1921; actor George C. Scott, 1927; football coach Mike Ditka, 1939; boxer Tommy Hearns, 1958.

Today's Quotation—"The society of excess profits for some and small returns for others, the society in which a few prey upon the many, the society in which a few took great advantage and many took great disadvantage, must pass."—*Wendell L. Willkie, October 18, 1940*

Taking Advantage

Have you ever been tempted to take advantage of a situation where no one would know the difference? A story is told of two shepherds years ago, one of whom had recently accepted Christ as Savior. He went to his neighbor to tell about his conversion and the fact that he wished to re-turn four sheep that didn't belong to him. He explained that the sheep had wandered away from the neighbor's flock some years ago and he had branded them as his. By now the neighbor was getting agitated, not knowing how to understand the change made in his associate. "Please," he said, "keep the sheep and go away." "No, I must return them," implored the convert. "How much do I owe you?" Peeling off a series of bills (paying several times what the sheep were worth), the convert strolled away leav-ing his associate under deep conviction.

When we make it a point to right a wrong we have committed and not take advantage of a situation, we will make a powerful statement to the world looking in!

Prayer Suggestion—May God give us a love for our fellow man so that we will not take unfair advantage of him.

OCTOBER

19

John 14:1-14

Today in History—Spanish monarchs who would later back explorer Christopher Columbus (Ferdinand of Aragon and Isabella of Castile) are married, 1469; surrender of Lord Cornwallis at Yorktown, Va., ends American Revolutionary War, 1781; U.S. embargoes most exports to Fidel Castro's Cuba, 1960; 27-year-old Anatoly Karpov retains world chess championship by defeating Soviet defector Viktor Korchnoi, 1978; U.S. Navy has disabled three Iranian oil rigs in retaliation for repeated ship attacks by Iran in the Persian Gulf, 1987.

Born Today—Actress LaWanda Page, 1920; columnist Jack Anderson, 1922; author John Le Carre, 1931; actor Robert Reed, 1932; designer Peter Max, 1937; Amy Carter, daughter of former President Jimmy Carter, 1967.

Today's Quotation—"I pity the poor in bondage that have none to help them; that is why I am here; not to gratify any personal animosity, revenge, or vindictive spirit."—*John Brown, October 19, 1859*

Poor But Not Needy

John R. Rice tells of the times as a dirt-poor farm boy that he rode to the general store at a small cowtown in Texas. Often when the family had no money he would tell the grocer what he needed and ask him to "charge it to Will Rice," who would settle up later. Rice's father had given him authority to charge on his account. He asked in his father's name and got what he needed.

This is how it is when believers come before God as poor, needy children. We have nothing to offer him, nor do we even know what we need. "But," Rice says, "when I find out what Jesus wants and ask it of my heavenly Father, I can honestly ask for it in Jesus' name and expectantly wait to receive it." What needs do you have? When you pray for it in Jesus' name, and in God's will, things begin to happen!

Prayer Suggestion—We can pray in Jesus' name for those things that we need and if they are in God's will, he will grant them to us.

OCTOBER

20

Ephesians 5:1-21

Today in History—Greece gains independence following Battle of Navarino, 1827; U.S. forces return to Philippines in World War II, 1944; president's widow, Jacqueline Kennedy, marries Aristotle Onassis, 1968; Supreme Court ruling permits spanking in public schools, 1975; ship collision in Mississippi River, north of New Orleans, claims seventy-eight lives, 1976; in worst trading day ever on Wall Street, market loses over 22 percent of its value in one day, 1987.

Born Today—Architect Sir Christopher Wren, 1632; philosopher John Dewey, 1859; actress Arlene Francis, 1908; columnist Art Buchwald, 1925; psychologist Joyce Brothers, 1928; baseball player Mickey Mantle, 1931; baseball player Keith Hernandez, 1953.

Today's Quotation—"Of all the animosities which have existed among mankind, those which are caused by a difference of sentiments in religion appear to be the most inveterate and distressing, and ought to be deprecated."—*George Washington, October 20, 1792*

Animosities

Maxwell Drake tells of an Englishman who was touring the western U.S. when he came upon a desert gas station. Posted above the door was a sign: "Joe Bevins, two hundred percent American." The visitor was intrigued by the sign and asked the surly, scowling owner just what it meant. "Well," said the owner, "you've heard of one hundred percent Americans. I reckon they hate all other nationalities. Me, well I'm two hundred percent. I hate *everybody!*"

May we never be known for how we hate. Rather, as Christians, you and I are told that "they shall know we are Christians by our love." How are you known to others?

Prayer Suggestion—Pray that we would always be known for who and what we are *for* and not who and what we are *against*.

OCTOBER

21

Psalm 37:1-9

Today in History—Boston mob attacks abolitionist editor William Lloyd Garrison, 1835; incandescent electric lamp invented by Thomas Edison, 1879; Reserve Officers Training Corps begins first college R.O.T.C. units, 1916; for the first time in ninety-eight years, Philadelphia Phillies win the World Series, 1980.

Born Today—Writer Samuel Coleridge, 1772, inventor Alfred Nobel, 1833; musician Dizzy Gillespie, 1917; baseball's Whitey Ford, 1928; author Frances Fitzgerald, 1940; musician Elvin Bishop, 1942.

Today's Quotation—"I do not complain of any tactics that are effective of good, whether one wields the quill or the sword . . ."—*Henry David Thoreau, October 21, 1859*

Misguided Tactics

Have you ever taken a short cut which you thought would save time or money, only to discover that just the opposite was true? In the days of the Wild West a young man planned to take a journey on a stagecoach. He noticed that he could save substantially by purchasing a third class ticket rather than a first or second class fare. Reasoning that all the seats were alike, the man went ahead and bought the lowest-priced ticket. All went well for a while and the young man prided himself on making a thrifty investment. That ended however, when the coach neared the foot of a very steep hill. At that point the driver stopped the coach and shouted, "All second class passengers, get out and walk; third class passengers, get out and push; first class passengers may keep your seats."

How many people have prided themselves on their good tactics only to later discover how foolish they were in light of eternity's values? God doesn't make mistakes; his way is always best no matter what the short-term costs and considerations may be.

Prayer Suggestion—Trust the One who sees beyond today and who has promised to guide our steps when we fully trust in him.

OCTOBER

22

Today in History—Princeton University chartered, 1746; first Metropolitan Opera House opens in New York City, 1883; President Kennedy orders Cuban naval blockade, 1962; the man who called history "God revealing himself" to man, scholar and historian Arthur Toynbee, is dead at age 86, 1975; Shah of Iran arrives in New York for medical tests, 1979; day-long concert marks 100th birthday of the "Met" (New York's Metropolitan Opera), 1983.

Born Today—Composer Franz Liszt, 1811; actress Annette Funicello, 1942; artist Robert Rauschenberg, 1925; actor Christopher Lloyd, 1938; actor Derek Jacobi, 1938; actor Jeff Goldblum, 1952.

Today's Quotation—"We were challenged with a peacetime choice between the American system of rugged individualism and a European philosophy of diametrically opposed doctrines . . . of paternalism and state socialism."—*Herbert Hoover, October 22, 1928*

Socialism

Dr. Jerry Falwell's definition for socialism, "Mutually shared poverty," would seem to be borne out in the following story. The late Baron de Rothschild's personal valet was pursuing an interest in socialism. Time went on and the baron noticed his assistant was no longer taking part in socialist gatherings. Puzzled, he inquired why the young man had lost interest in the philosophy he had sought so diligently for before. "Sir," the young man replied, "it has been determined that if the national wealth was equally divided among all the citizens, each would have 2,000 francs." "So what!" the Baron exclaimed. "Well," said the youth, "you see I now have 5,000 francs!"

Be thankful for the unlimited future provided all citizens when they can live and work under a system of free enterprise.

Prayer Suggestion—Thank God for a free country in which there are no limits to our success and where we may keep what we earn.

OCTOBER

23

Psalm 40:1–17

Today in History—General Montgomery's British forces stop German-Italian sweep in North Africa in War II, 1942; "Saturday night Massacre," in which both the attorney general and deputy attorney general resign or are fired for refusing President Nixon's request to fire Watergate special prosecutor Archibald Cox, 1973; widow of Chinese leader Mao Tse Tung jailed for plotting a coup while millions of Chinese demonstrate support for her arrest, 1976; 216 Marines killed in terrorist explosion at Marine barracks in Beirut, 1983; Senate rejects Robert Bork nomination to Supreme Court by a record 58–42 vote, 1987.

Born Today—Inventor Nicolas Appert, 1752; entertainer Johnny Carson, 1925; actress Diana Dors, 1931; soccer player Pele, 1940; football player Doug Flutie, 1962; football player Mike Tomczak, 1962.

Today's Quotation—*"Out with the Russians!"—Cry of Hungarian Revolutionists, October 23, 1956*

Invaders

In his sixteen years in Africa, missionary David Livingstone had never encountered such a threat as now. Angry Africans from the heart of the continent had completely surrounded Livingstone's position. His very life was threatened. Later, he wrote in his diary: "I read that Jesus said, 'I am with you always, even unto the end of the world.' Should such a man as I flee? Nay, verily I feel quite calm now, thank God!" The Lord protected him against the marauding invaders.

When you feel hemmed in by threatening events or circumstances, remember your strength comes from God. If you feel fearful or despondent, remember you are the King of kings' "kid"! Rest secure in his love, knowing that there is nothing that can injure you when you are doing God's will.

Prayer Suggestion—Rejoice that, as a child of God, nothing can happen to you which God does not allow. Rest in his secure embrace.

OCTOBER

24

\

Today in History—Austro-German forces rout Italians in World War I, 1917; George Washington Bridge linking New York City and New Jersey opens, 1931; nylon stockings first go on sale, 1939; Zambia (formerly Northern Rhodesia), becomes free nation in British Commonwealth, 1964; Chinese leader Hua Kuo-Feng proclaimed new head of Chinese Communist Party, 1976; Philippine panel rejects "lone-gunman" theory in shooting death of Benigno Aquino two months ago, instead favoring the view of a high-level plot within the military, 1983; in historic operation in California, a baboon's heart is transplanted into a fifteen-day-old infant, 1984.

Born Today—Scientist Anton van Leeuwenhoek, 1632; writer Sarah Josepha Hale, 1788; actor David Nelson, 1936; football player Y. A. Tittle, 1926; musician Bill Wyman, 1941.

Today's Quotation—"The journey of a thousand leagues, we say, begins with a single step. So we must never neglect any work of peace that is within our reach, however small."—*Adlai E. Stevenson, October 24, 1963*

The Journey Within

While much has been written about the outward accomplishments of mankind, have you considered the phenomenal automatic performances taking place within every human adult? For example, scientists tell us that within the next twenty-four hours your heart will beat 103,680 times pushing your bloodstream some forty-three million miles. You will inhale 438 cubic feet of air in twenty-three thousand breaths. Three and one-fourth pounds of food will be digested along with a half gallon of liquid. Two pounds of water will evaporate through perspiration while your body generates 450 tons of energy!

Who keeps watch over this system to be sure it operates properly? Could it be the omnipotent God who created mankind? Who else but God could accomplish it?

Prayer Suggestion—Praise God that you are wonderfully made. Take care of your bodily temple today and every day.

OCTOBER

25

Today in History—Charge of the Light Brigade, 1854; U.S. routs Japanese in naval battle of Solomon Islands, 1942; U.S. naval and aviation forces crush Japanese fleet in Battle of the Philippine Sea, 1944; United Nations General Assembly votes to admit Red China and expel Nationalist China, 1971; two thousand U.S. Marines and Army Rangers invade Caribbean island of Grenada following an earlier coup which made it a "Soviet-Cuban colony," 1983.

Born Today—Writer Thomas Macaulay, 1800; composer Georges Bizet, 1838; artist Pablo Picasso, 1881; explorer Richard Byrd, 1888; naval avaitor Floyd Bennett, 1890; actor Anthony Franciosa, 1928; entertainer Minnie Pearl, 1936; singer Helen Reddy, 1942.

Today's Quotation—"I know, and you know, that a revolution has begun. I know, and all the world knows, that revolutions never go backward."—*William H. Seward, October 25, 1858*

Revolutionary

God's Word is revolutionary in the changes it makes in the life of one who has confessed Christ as Savior and Lord. Henry Bosch tells of a traveling salesman. For some time he had been stealing money from his company and he was growing increasingly concerned about being caught. As a result he became a workaholic to avoid his nagging conscience. One morning in a Chicago hotel, as he was stropping his old-fashioned razor, he sought a piece of paper to wipe the blade. Finding none, he reached for the nearby Gideon Bible and tore a page from it. Smoothing out the page he saw, "The wages of sin is death; but the gift of God is eternal life through Jesus Christ our Lord." The startled salesman began reading the Bible in earnest and before long had accepted Christ as his Savior. Later, when he told his employer of his theft, he was allowed to make full restitution through deductions from his salary and was not prosecuted. God's Word revolutionized his life and led him to the Savior.

Have you been revolutionized by him? Trust him today.

Prayer Suggestion—Trust in the Lord as your eternal Savior and your life will never again be the same!

OCTOBER

26

Today in History—Erie Canal between Hudson River and Lake Erie opens in New York State, 1825; Torrey-Gray Hall dedicated at Moody Bible Institute, 1924; South Vietnam becomes a republic, 1955; *Lanibird* (Pacific communications satellite) orbited, 1966; Henry Kissinger says peace is at hand in Vietnam, 1972; President Reagan presents Medal of Freedom to singer Kate Smith, 1982; Polish parliament outlaws Solidarity union, 1982.

Born Today—Publisher John Knight, 1894; gospel singer Mahalia Jackson, 1911; French politician Francois Mitterand, 1916; actress Jaclyn Smith, 1948; football player Chuck Forman, 1950.

Today's Quotation—"A radical is a man with both feet firmly planted in the air."—*Franklin D. Roosevelt, October 26, 1939*

Radical for God

The *Gospel Herald* tells of pastor Martin Niemoeller, who was released after six years in a Nazi prison camp. Reporters rushed to cover the story and heard a stirring gospel message. One disappointed reporter was heard to say, "Imagine all those years in prison and all he can talk about is Jesus Christ."

What a testimony to God's power in a life. In the same vein, evangelist D. L. Moody once described the memorial he would like to have when he died, saying: "The only monument I want when I'm gone is one with two legs going about the world—a saved sinner telling about the salvation of Jesus Christ." How radical for God are you? If arrested for being a Christian, would there be enough evidence to convict you, or are you an "undercover" Christian?

Prayer Suggestion—Ask for God's help to have you speak out boldly for him everywhere you go.

OCTOBER

27

Colossians 3:23—4:6

Today in History—William Marcy "Boss" Tweed, Democratic leader of Tammany Hall, arrested for corruption, 1871; Benito Mussolini begins Fascist "march on Rome" (launching Fascism as a world force), 1922; U.S. monitors atomic blast; suspects South Africa of having the atom bomb, 1979; South Korean President Park Chung Hee killed in what appears to be pre-meditated murder, 1979; famine relief to Ethiopia is increased following TV coverage, 1984; kidnapped daughter of El Salvador's Napoleon Duarte is returned unharmed after forty-four days, 1985.

Born Today—Violinist Nicolo Paganini, 1782; President Theodore Roosevelt, 1858; producer Fred De Cordova, 1910; writer Dylan Thomas, 1914; actress Nanette Fabray, 1920; musician Floyd Cramer, 1933.

Today's Quotation—"If you are idle, be not solitary; if you are solitary, be not idle."—*Samuel Johnson, October 27, 1779*

Be Not Idle

It has been said, "Satan finds work for idle hands." But there are some prolific workers: Sir Walter Scott rose at four o'clock each morning and completed a book every two months; violinist Fritz Kreisler who, despite his native talent and ability, spent eight to ten hours a day in practice. Then there is Wesley who preached three sermons a day for fifty-four years, wrote more than eighty works, and traveled 290,000 miles on horseback and carriage to complete his task.

Be not idle, rather "always abounding in the work of the Lord for as much as ye know that your labor is not in vain in the Lord" (1 Cor. 15:58).

Prayer Suggestion—God keep us busy in going about the work of his kingdom!

OCTOBER

28

Ecclesiastes 9:7-10

Today in History—Statue of Liberty dedicated in New York Harbor, 1886; Volstead Act to enforce 18th Amendment (Prohibition) passed by Congress (over President Wilson's veto), 1919; Italy invades Greece, 1940; Pope Paul VI formally issues five decrees of Vatican Council, including statement denying collective guilt of Jews for crucifixion of Jesus Christ, 1965; Ford Motors reports record $595 million loss in third quarter (highest loss ever for any U.S. firm), 1980; cult leader Shree Rajneesh, who ran a commune of 1,500 residents in Oregon, arrested on charges of violating immigration laws, 1985.

Born Today—Explorer James Cook, 1728; scientist Jonas Salk, 1914; former baseball commissioner Bowie Kuhn, 1926; actress Jane Alexander, 1939; singer Telma Hopkins, 1948; sportscaster Bruce Jenner, 1949.

Today's Quotation—". . . I agree with you that there is a natural aristocracy among men. The grounds of this are virtue and talents."— *Thomas Jefferson, October 28, 1813*

Talents

A pastor decided to put the parable of the talents to a modern-day test. He told his congregation that each member could take ten dollars from church funds, providing they returned it in two months with money they had earned. Some members were skeptical that the church would even get the $3,500 back, but when the offering was taken at the end of the period, it totalled $10,207.24—nearly three times the original amount.

In the parable of the talents we are reminded of the priority God gives to being good stewards of the possessions he has given us. But when and where do we learn good stewardship? God considers a person to be a steward—good or bad—when he becomes a Christian. Because all we own belongs to God (and believers are just his managers, or stewards), we have been commissioned by Christ to manage those affairs for him. We must account for how well we have done with them. How good a steward are you?

Prayer Suggestion—Give us your wisdom, Lord. Help us to be a good steward of the resources you have given us to manage.

318

OCTOBER

29

Today in History—Sir Walter Raleigh executed in London, 1618; stock market prices collapse signaling terrible economic depression, 1929; first draft lottery for armed services begins, 1940; billions of dollars pledged at Arab League Summit to assist Arab nations who have fought Israel, 1974; Socialist landslide in Spain elects Felipe Gonzalez, youngest prime minister in Europe, 1982.

Born Today—Biographer James Boswell, 1740; writer John Keats, 1795; cartoonist Bill Mauldin, 1921; singer Melba Moore, 1945; actor Richard Dreyfus, 1947; actress Kate Jackson, 1948; football player J. T. Smith, 1955.

Today's Quotation—"Few rich men own their own property. The property owns them."—*Robert G. Ingersoll, October 29, 1896*

Ownership

Who owns your possessions? For the believer, the answer is God; we are merely stewards or managers of what God has entrusted to us. When we have this relationship clearly in mind, it removes a great burden from us. If it is God's to begin with, why worry when things go wrong?

There was a time when Dr. F. B. Meyer came to feel that his ministry was no longer fruitful and that he was lacking spiritual power. Dr. Meyer says it was as if Christ was suddenly standing beside him saying, "Let me have the keys to your life." Convinced, Meyer actually got out his key ring. The Lord then asked, "Are all the keys here?" Meyer responded by saying, "Yes, Lord, all except the key to one small room in my life." Christ replied, "Well, if you cannot trust me to have access to every room in your life then I cannot accept any of the keys." Dr. Meyer reports he became overwhelmed by the feeling that God was leaving his life, and he cried out, "Come back, Lord. Here are the keys to all the rooms of my life."

Who holds the keys to your life, you or God?

Prayer Suggestion—I surrender my life to you, Lord, fully, completely and unconditionally to do with as you please.

OCTOBER

30

Today in History—Orson Welles' radio dramatization of H.G. Wells' *War of the Worlds* triggers fear of invading Martians, 1938; U.S. Navy destroyer *Reuben James* torpedoed and sunk by Nazi Germany in Atlantic, although U.S. was not yet in World War II, 1941; Dr. Mary Leakey announces discovery of human remains she says date back 3.75 million years, 1975; pro-Solidarity union priest found slain near Warsaw, 1984.

Born Today—President John Adams, 1735; writer Richard Sheridan, 1751; poet Ezra Pound, 1885; broadcast executive Fred Friendly, 1915; baseball's Ted Williams, 1918; actor Henry Winkler, 1945.

Today's Quotation—"Had the doors of Palestine been kept open, hundreds of thousands of Jews, now dead, might have been alive today."—*Stephen S. Wise and Abba Hillel Silver, October 30, 1945*

Open Doors

Like Samuel's cry of "Here am I, Lord," we need to be ready to respond to God's call instantly. Henry Bosch tells of an experience by Paul Rader, who had witnessed to a New York banker on many occasions without any response. One day Rader sensed an urgent need to go visit this man again, so he hurried to the bank. When he got there he found the banker standing in the doorway waiting for him. "Rader," he cried, "I was just going to send you a telegram begging you to come." "That's okay," said the preacher, "I got the message on heaven's 'telegraph.'" He then talked to the man at length, stressing the urgency of making a decision right away. Impressed by Rader's timely visit and under deep conviction, the banker got matters right with the Lord. In a matter of minutes the man suddenly gave a strange sound and fell dead into the evangelist's arms. What would have happened if Rader had been too busy or had put off making the visit until a more convenient time?

Christians are to be ready at *all* times to give a reason for the hope within them.

Prayer Suggestion—Lord, lead me to some soul today. Help me see the open doors all around for sharing your great gospel.

OCTOBER

31

2 Timothy 4:2–8

Today in History—Martin Luther posts his Ninety-five Theses on church door in Wittenberg, Germany, 1517; Nevada admitted to U.S. as 36th state, 1864; President Lyndon B. Johnson orders end of U.S. bombing of North Vietnam, 1968; India's only four-term premier, Indira Ghandi, killed by personal security guards, 1984.

Born Today—Girl Scout founder Juliette Gordon Low, 1860; China's Generalissimo Chiang Kai-shek, 1887; actress Dale Evans, 1912; astronaut Michael Collins, 1931; broadcast journalist Dan Rather, 1931; broadcast journalist Jane Pauley, 1950.

Today's Quotation—"Liberalism is a force truly of the spirit proceeding from the deep realization that economic freedom cannot be sacrificed if political freedom is to be preserved."—*Herbert Hoover, October 31, 1932*

Liberalism

The spread of spiritual liberalism, which seemed to be on a growth curve in the 1950s and 60s, now appears to be in decline. Elmer Towns reports that the ten fastest growing churches in America are not only conservative, but are boldly fundamentalist in their doctrine. He noted eight recurring traits in the fastest growing churches: strong doctrinal commitment (in contrast to liberalism), effective pastoral leadership, use of mass media as an outreach, active Sunday School bus ministry, heavy Sunday School promotion (advertising and contests common), massive auditoriums rather than sanctuaries, for old-fashioned preaching, strong church loyalty (good meeting attendance, tithing, volunteer workers), special "Big" days (homecomings and other major events to excite a big crowd). In many of the mainline denominations these days, attendance has dwindled to the point where churches must often merge to survive.

How much better to simply accept the Bible for what it says it is, the inerrant, infallible Word of God!

Prayer Suggestion—Thank God for his Word, which helps us to know and love him more every day.

NOVEMBER

1

Today in History—U.S. Weather Bureau begins weather observations, 1870; Puerto Rican nationalists try to assassinate President Truman, 1950; test explosion begins H-bomb era for U.S., 1952; Algeria begins revolution against French rule, 1954.

Born Today—Sculptor Benvenuto Cellini, 1500; writer Stephen Crane, 1871; journalist James Kilpatrick, 1920; actress Betsy Palmer, 1926; golfer Gary Player, 1935; baseball player Fernando Valenzuela, 1960.

Today's Quotation—"One on God's side is a majority. . . ."—*Wendell Phillips, November 1, 1859*

A Majority

The Bible tells us that often the people whom the world considers the lowliest are greatest in God's eyes. A. J. Gordon used to tell of a man in his congregation who could speak most eloquently of the Scriptures, quoting the Bible from cover to cover. And yet, when asked to tell what the Lord was doing in his life, he was speechless. It seems the man was involved in worldly habits and pursuits which had destroyed his character and testimony.

However, there was another man in the same congregation who worked in the coal mines. Often he would have to hurry to arrive in time for the mid-week service after work and he frequently appeared unkempt and dirty. Yet when he spoke of the Lord, the congregation paid attention. He lived faithfully for the Lord and served him every day. Often he would witness to others on the job and was a shining beacon of God's love at work. Christ was real in his life. Though humble by the world's standards, the coal miner was a majority leader in the Lord's harvest field.

Prayer Suggestion—Give God the praise for saving you and putting you in his majority as you serve him day by day.

NOVEMBER

2

Today in History—North and South Dakota admitted to U.S. as thirty-ninth and fortieth states, 1889; British Foreign Secretary Arthur Balfour gives approval, in what becomes known as the Balfour Declaration, to "the establishment in Palestine of a national home for the Jewish people," 1917; station KDKA, Pittsburgh, first radio station to begin regularly scheduled broadcasting (with Harding-Cox election returns), 1920.

Born Today—Pioneer Daniel Boone, 1734, France's Queen Marie Antoinette, 1755, President James Polk, 1795; President Warren Harding, 1865; Chinese revolutionary Sun Yat-sen, 1866; actor Burt Lancaster, 1913.

Today's Quotation—"I have endured a great deal of ridicule without much malice; and have received a great deal of kindness, not quite free from ridicule."—*Abraham Lincoln, November 2, 1863*

Ridicule

One of the more popular television programs of years past was the celebrity "roast" in which friends of the individual gathered together and collectively ridiculed the guest. Today, cutting down others still seems to be a popular pastime, even though it can be quite painful to the recipient.

Perhaps the most tragic event in U.S. history was the surprise attack on the naval base at Pearl Harbor. Ironically, there was ample warning of the attack, but those who suggested the approaching aircraft might be enemy planes were either ridiculed or ignored altogether. The results of their indifference resulted in the loss of countless lives and millions in property. It changed the course of history because America was drawn into World War II.

Before criticizing or making fun of someone else, pause to consider what they are saying. Give them the benefit of the doubt. If they sincerely believe in what they say, it should warrant your respect, at least until proven otherwise.

Prayer Suggestion—Ask God to guard your tongue so that it would never be guilty of hurting someone else in its unfounded comments.

NOVEMBER

3

Today in History—Continental Army discharged by Congress at end of American Revolutionary War, 1783; Panama Independence Day marks proclamation of freedom from Colombia, 1903; U. Thant elected Acting Secretary General of the United Nations, 1961; Lyndon B. Johnson won U.S. presidential election over Barry Goldwater by largest popular vote plurality in history, 1964.

Born Today—Texas pioneer Stephen Austin, 1793; newspaperman William Cullen Bryant, 1794; publisher Karl Baedeker, 1801; writer Andre Malraux, 1901; newspaperman James Reston, 1909; politician Michael Dukakis, 1933.

Today's Quotation—"I have sworn eternal opposition to slavery and by the blessing of God I will never turn back."—*Elijah P. Lovejoy, November 3, 1837*

Slavery

In the twentieth century, removed by one-hundred years from the horrors of slavery, it is hard to imagine how fiercely it was once fought for. A young Swiss boy, Abraham Bininger, came to America on the same vessel that transported John Wesley. The boy's parents both became deathly ill on the voyage, died, and were buried at sea, and he faced a new land all alone. Later, as an adult, Bininger was sent to the island of St. Thomas to minister to the slaves. However, when he reached the island he learned that only slaves were allowed to minister to fellow slaves. Not long afterward, the governor of St. Thomas received a letter from Bininger asking to become a slave so that he could proclaim the gospel. The governor sent it on to the king of Denmark, who sent back word that Bininger could proclaim the gospel story anywhere he chose, whether to black or white, bond or free. So from the slavery of sin he was able to reach many with the gospel of God's saving grace.

Prayer Suggestion—Thank God that we are freed from sin's bonds and are now able to tell everyone of what God has done in our lives.

NOVEMBER

4

Matthew 12:33–37

Today in History—Mary Todd marries Abraham Lincoln, 1842; United Nations Educational, Scientific and Cultural Organization (UNESCO) established, 1946; U.S.S.R. troops take over Hungary, crushing revolt against communist regime, 1956; four killed and eighteen injured in Greensboro, N.C., when two carloads of white men fired on a group of demonstrators opposed to the Ku Klux Klan, 1979; five hundred Iranian students seize the U.S. embassy in Teheran, holding fifty-two Americans hostage for 444 days, 1979; Ronald Reagan, 69, elected fortieth president of the U.S., 1980; senior KGB official Vitaly Yurchenko returns to Russian custody after defecting to the U.S., 1985.

Born Today—Poet Eden Philpotts, 1862; humorist Will Rogers, 1879; newscaster Walter Cronkite, 1916; actor Cameron Mitchell, 1918; actor Art Carney, 1918; actor Martin Balsam, 1919.

Today's Quotation—"Back in 1910 . . . I had a particularly disagreeable opponent, and he called me names . . . and I answered him in kind. And the names that I called him were worse than the names that he called me. So we had a very joyous campaign."—*Franklin D. Roosevelt, November 4, 1944*

Slander

Scientists say the sound waves begun by our voices carry on into the vastness of space and that, having sufficiently sensitive instruments, we might be able to find them again and re-create the words we once spoke.

How careful we should be then to choose our words wisely, for they may go on forever. Even if they don't live on, God hears what we say. The Bible reminds us, "For every idle word men may speak, they will give account of it in the day of judgment" (Matthew 12:36). How much will you have to account for on Judgment Day?

Prayer Suggestion—May God help us to realize every time we speak that we must some day justify every idle word that we've ever spoken.

NOVEMBER

5

Today in History—Guy Fawkes attempts to blow up British Parliament, 1605; first U.S. automobile patent granted to George B. Selden, 1895; Franklin D. Roosevelt smashes precedent by winning election to third term as president of U.S., 1940; British and French forces land at Suez, Egypt, while Israel occupies Sinai peninsula, 1956.

Born Today—Socialist leader Eugene Debs, 1855; writer Ida Tarbell, 1857; historian Will Durant, 1885; actor Roy Rogers, 1912; lawyer Arthur Liman, 1932; singer Paul Simon, 1942.

Today's Quotation—"The Old World and the New will ever live in harmonious accord as long as we do not try to jump over their fences and they do not try to jump over ours."—*Carl Schurz, November 5, 1881*

Boundaries

It would be interesting to learn how many wars had been fought in disputes over boundaries. People always seem to want something that does not belong to them, whether it is land or other property.

Years ago the War Department received a letter from a veteran of World War I. In the letter, the man said that he had stolen equipment and clothing worth about fifty dollars, adding, "God has wonderfully saved me and I am now seeking to make everything right that I can."

He enclosed a check for fifty dollars with the added thought that "I hope nothing of its kind (stealing) will ever have to be repeated."

Have you overstepped someone else's boundaries? It needn't be a major crime to be sin in God's eyes. Confess your sin to God, then take steps now to make things right with those you have offended, returning that which does not belong to you to its rightful owner.

Prayer Suggestion—Help us to realize that the only things we own are what God has given to us, and not the things we may have obtained deceitfully from others.

NOVEMBER

6

Today in History—Abraham Lincoln elected president, 1860; first intercollegiate football games played by Princeton and Rutgers at New Brunswick, N.J. (Rutgers won 6–4), 1869; Italian Prime Minister Benito Mussolini bans all opposition, 1926.

Born Today—Composer John Philip Sousa, 1854; pianist Ignace Paderewski, 1860; basketball's inventor James Naismith, 1861; band leader Ray Conniff, 1916; writer James Jones, 1921; director Mike Nichols, 1931.

Today's Quotation—"I knew once a very covetous, sordid fellow, who used to say, 'Take care of the pence, for the pounds will take care of themselves.'"—*Earl of Chesterfield, November 6, 1747*

Taking Care

It is not always God's will for full-time Christian service to involve the ordained ministry. God has called each one of us into various avenues of service—all equally important in doing his will. A man once hired two laborers but noticed they were not out working on the job. After searching for some time he found one of them, Joe, fast asleep. Soon he found the other one loafing nearby. The boss asked the second laborer what he had been doing. "Why I've been helping out Joe," was his reply.

Too many Christians are content to just "help out Joe" by warming a pew and not becoming actively involved in the work of the Lord. Taking care of God's business is everybody's job. Seek out your pastor and ask where you might be of service. There is work for everyone to do!

Prayer Suggestion—May we know God's will and do it gladly.

NOVEMBER

7

Today in History—Abolitionist editor Elijah P. Lovejoy murdered by a mob while trying to defend his newspaper, 1837; Jeannette Rankin of Montana became first woman elected to U.S. House of Representatives, 1916; Bolshevik Revolution against provisional democractic government of Russia led to establishment of communist dictatorship, 1917; Museum of Modern Art opened in New York City, 1929; Marine Corps Women's Reserve established, 1942; President Franklin D. Roosevelt elected to fourth term, 1944; act establishing Corporation for Public Broadcasting signed by President Lyndon B. Johnson, 1967.

Born Today—Scientist Marie Curie, 1867; writer Albert Camus, 1913; evangelist Billy Graham, 1918; trumpeter Al Hirt, 1922; opera singer Joan Sutherland, 1929; songwriter Joni Mitchell, 1943.

Today's Quotation—"Here is my first principle of foreign policy: good government at home."—*William E. Gladstone, November 7, 1879*

At Home

An increasing emphasis of both business and government is keeping their employee's home life in the proper perspective. Douglas MacArthur II, an extremely hard-working man, served for a time in the State Department under the equally ambitious John Foster Dulles. On one occasion, Dulles called the MacArthur residence seeking MacArthur. Mrs. MacArthur, who answered the call, thought Dulles was an aide and shouted, "MacArthur is where MacArthur always is, weekdays, Saturdays, Sundays and nights—in that office!" Immediately Dulles called MacArthur at the office and instructed him, "Go home at once, boy. Your home front is crumbling."

A nation is built on a solid home life. If that area fails, the very life of the nation is threatened.

Prayer Suggestion—Thank God for Christian homes. Seek his help in keeping your family in the proper place, before your job.

NOVEMBER

8

Isaiah 40:21–31

Today in History—The Louvre opened to the public, 1793; Montana admitted to U.S. as forty-first state, 1889; "Beer hall putsch" (by Adolf Hitler and his Nazi followers against Germany's Weimar Republic) began today and ended in total failure the next. Hitler, jailed, wrote *Mein Kampf* in prison, 1923; Moody Memorial Church dedicated, 1925; U.S. and British forces landed in French North Africa to join battle with Axis forces in World War II, 1942.

Born Today—Astronomer Edmund Halley, 1656; author Margaret Mitchell, 1900; actress Katherine Hepburn, 1909; pioneer heart surgeon Christiaan Barnard, 1922; singer Patti Page, 1927; newscaster Morley Safer, 1931.

Today's Quotation—"It is so much pleasanter and wholesomer to be warmed by the sun when you can, than by fire."—*Henry David Thoreau, November 8, 1850*

Warmed by the Sun

A story is told of an old violinist whose music always impressed the audience with its soothing, mellow sound. His music always received a warm response from all those who heard it. When asked to define the secret of his music, the old man pointed to his instrument and said, "A great deal of sunshine must have gone into this wood. What has gone in comes out."

E. Townley Lord asks, "How much of God's sunshine has entered your life? How much time have you spent in the radiance of his presence?"

Contemplate God's wonder in quietness and awe. It has been said that "silence characterizes the highest in art, and the deepest in nature. The surest spiritual search is made in silence." Are you waiting upon the Lord's sunshine and reflecting it on the people you know?

Prayer Suggestion—Give us the patience to wait upon God for his guidance and blessing.

NOVEMBER

9

Titus 1:1-9

Today in History—President Theodore Roosevelt sails on a U.S. battleship for the Panama Canal Zone and becomes first U.S. president to leave U.S. while in office, 1906; Germany's Kaiser Wilhelm abdicates and flees to sanctuary in the Netherlands; Germany proclaims itself a republic, 1918; Cambodia declares its independence of France, 1953; electric power failure blacks out New York and most of northeast U.S., 1965.

Born Today—Newspaperman Elijah Lovejoy, 1802; scientist Florence Sabin, 1871; former Vice President Spiro Agnew, 1918; astronomer Carl Sagan, 1934; golfer Tom Weiskopf, 1942; actor Lou Ferrigno, 1951.

Today's Quotation—"The maxim of the British people is 'Business as usual.'"—*Winston Churchill, November 9, 1914*

Business as Usual

Having a holy boldness can greatly enhance our witness. One of the first concerns of a new pastor was to confront the city administration for their obvious corruption. Seeking God's face in meditation and prayer, the pastor made an appointment to meet with the mayor. As J. E. Conant tells the story, the pastor congratulated the mayor on being selected to the office, then added, "There is a far greater honor awaiting you— something much bigger than the office of mayor of a city like this. You ought to be a servant of Jesus Christ." The mayor was astonished, saying, "No one ever spoke to me like this before." It wasn't long before the pastor received a phone call from the mayor. "I must see you," he said. Within two weeks the pastor welcomed into his church not only the mayor, but the fire and police chiefs and five aldermen. The harvest was rich because the pastor was not content to carry on "business as usual."

Prayer Suggestion—Make us ever faithful in communicating the gospel to friend and foe alike.

330

NOVEMBER

10

John 6:40–48

Today in History—After brief Dutch rule, British retake possession of New York, 1674; U.S. Marine Corps established by Continental Congress, 1775; Henry M. Stanley finds Dr. David Livingstone in Central Africa, 1871.

Born Today—Protestant reformer Martin Luther, 1483; artist William Hogarth, 1697; writer Oliver Goldsmith, 1728; sculptor Jacob Epstein, 1880; actor Richard Burton, 1925; civil rights activist Russell Means, 1940; singer Donna Fargo, 1949.

Today's Quotation—"This is not the end. It is not even the beginning of the end. But it is, perhaps, the end of the beginning."—*Winston Churchill, November 10, 1942*

Everlasting Life

It is nearly impossible for the human mind to comprehend the scope of life eternal, yet even scientists have found reasons to believe in life after death. Dr. Wernher von Braun, known for his contributions to the space program, says, "Science has found nothing that can disappear without a trace. Nature does not know extinction. All it knows is transformation. If God applies the fundamental principle to the most minute and insignificant parts of the universe, doesn't it make sense to assume that he applies it to the masterpiece of his creation—the human soul? I think it does."

In God's eyes this life is only the "end of the beginning."

Prayer Suggestion—Thanks be to God for his unspeakable gift; the gift of life eternal to all those who believe.

NOVEMBER

11

Today in History—Washington admitted to U.S. as forty-second state, 1889; armistice ends World War I, 1918; Nazi Germany takes control of France in World War II, 1942; U.S. and British invasion forces gain control of French North Africa after three days of fighting, 1942; Rhodesia declares its independence from Great Britain, 1965; ship carrying 2,517 Vietnamese refugees remains in South China sea after being rejected by Malaysia and Indonesia, 1978; Catholic bishops call for spending fund to create new jobs instead of weapons, 1984.

Born Today—Author Fyodor Dostoevsky, 1821; actress Maude Adams, 1872; General George Patton, 1885; preacher R. G. Lee, 1886; actor Pat O'Brien, 1899; author Kurt Vonnegut, Jr., 1922; comedian Jonathan Winters, 1925.

Today's Quotation—"May God save the country, for it is evident that the people will not."—*Millard Fillmore, November 11, 1844*

Preserving the Nation

America's affluence is well known, but only God can save the nation. Quoted in *Christianity Today,* Henry S. Leiper illustrates the wealth of our nation: "Imagine that we could compress the world's population into one town of one thousand people. In this town there would only be sixty Americans who would receive half the income for the entire town! They would have an average life expectancy of seventy-two years in contrast to less than forty years for all the others. The sixty Americans would own fifteen times as much per person as all their neighbors and would eat 72 percent more than the maximum food requirements (while many of the others go hungry). The lowest income group among the Americans would be far better off than the average of the other townsmen."

How much do Americans owe to God for creating and preserving our nation? How important it is that we freely share with others what God has so richly given us!

Prayer Suggestion—Express our gratitude to God for his love and sustaining power for America.

NOVEMBER

12

Today in History—Communist Party expells Leon Trotsky, leaving Josef Stalin as sole dictator of U.S.S.R., 1927; Japan's World War II premier, Hedeki Tojo, sentenced to death by international war crimes tribunal in Japan, 1948; U.N. votes to suspend South Africa from current session because of apartheid, 1974; Supreme Court Justice William Douglas resigns after longest term ever (over 36 years), 1975; former KGB chief Yuri Andropov named new leader of U.S.S.R., 1982.

Born Today—Elizabeth Cady Stanton, 1815; sculptor Auguste Rodin, 1840; Supreme Court Justice Harry Blackmun, 1908; actress Kim Hunter, 1922; Princess Grace of Monaco, 1929; gymnast Nadia Comaneci, 1961.

Today's Quotation—"You must creep before you can run; you must run before you can fly."—*Henry David Thoreau, November 12, 1851*

Growing Up At Home

Studies have shown that more accidents occur at home than anywhere else. Perhaps it is because at home we tend to be off guard—not watching for those things which would trip us up.

Bishop Charles Slattery tells of a new pastor who stopped to visit a certain family. When the husband came home that night, his wife said, "The new pastor called today." "What did he say?" the husband wanted to know. "He asked, 'Does Christ live here?' and I didn't know what to say." The man became flustered, "Didn't you tell him we were respectable people?" "No," she replied, "he didn't want to know that." "Didn't you tell him we read our Bible and say our prayers, and that we were always at church?" "No," she responded, "he didn't ask that. All he asked was, 'Does Christ live here?'" The couple thought about the pastor's question for some time and, after a while, chose to put Christ first in their lives. Then, indeed, they could testify that "Christ does live here."

It is said, the best way to avoid spiritual accidents in your home is to have the great Physician residing there.

Prayer Suggestion—Pray God's protection upon your family both physically and spiritually so that there would be no spiritual casualties.

NOVEMBER

13

Today in History—Holland Tunnel (first automobile passage under Hudson River) opens between New York and New Jersey, 1927; first known sit-down strike occurs at Hormel Packing Company, 1933; Vietnam Moratorium demonstrations begin, 1969; PLO leader Yasir Arafat addresses U.N., calling for a Palestinian state to welcome Moslems, Christians, and Jews, 1974; Navy Admiral Hyman Rickover, 81, Father of the Nuclear Navy, is ordered by President Reagan to resign as head of the Navy's nuclear program, 1981.

Born Today—Physicist James Maxwell, 1831; actor Edwin Booth, 1833; writer Robert Louis Stevenson, 1850; former Supreme Court Justice Louis Brandeis, 1856; producer Gary Marshall, 1934.

Today's Quotation—"The tree of liberty must be refreshed from time to time with the blood of patriots and tyrants."—*Thomas Jefferson, November 13, 1787*

Keeping Liberty

Have you heard the expression "Freedom is not free"? Christians must ever be on the lookout for an erosion of our freedoms or soon we will be held captive to the will of others. It reminds me of the story of two baby eagles, abandoned in infancy, who were taken in by an old gentleman who raised them with great care. However, one day when they had fully grown, the door to their cage was left open and they escaped. One eagle roosted in the low branches of a tree, as it had never learned to fly. Soon it was killed by the blast from a passing hunter. Later, the other eagle, which also could not fly, fell into a river and drowned. Both met an untimely death because they had missed God's plan by being taken captive. Eagles were created to soar in high mountain peaks, not flounder in the confines of a tiny cage, no matter how good their care. In order to be all that God intended, we need to keep vigilant, making sure that no one ever takes away our freedoms.

Prayer Suggestion—Thank God for your freedoms. Be ever vigilant so that no one ever takes them away from you.

NOVEMBER

14

Today in History—First recorded blood transfusion, made between two dogs, 1666; Nellie Bly sets off on an around the world trip, 1889; Captain Eddie Rickenbacker and seven others rescued after twenty-three days on a life raft following Pacific air crash, 1942; Britain's Princess Anne marries Captain Mark Phillips in London, 1973; Solidarity leader Lech Walesa freed after nearly a year in Polish jail, 1982; two volcanoes erupt in Colombia killing twenty thousand persons, 1985.

Born Today—Inventor Robert Fulton, 1765; artist Claude Monet, 1840; Indian leader Jawaharlal Nehru, 1889; composer Aaron Copland, 1900; actor Brian Keith, 1921; Jordan's King Hussein, 1935; Britain's Prince Charles, 1948.

Today's Quotation—"Call me Ishmael. . . . I love to sail forbidden seas, and land on barbarous coasts."—*Herman Melville in* Moby Dick, *November 14, 1851*

Forbidden Territory

There is something about that which we are forbidden to do that makes it almost irresistible. However strong the temptation may be, it is encouraging to learn of others who have experienced similar lures without giving in.

Christian Herald once wrote of a man who had responsibility for large sums of money in a major organization. Knowing it would be some time before an audit was made, he was tempted to temporarily transfer some of the funds to his personal account. He overcame the temptation but felt he must talk with someone about it. So he called the man who had held the position before to share his experience. To his relief, the man was not shocked or disgusted, but shared how he had faced and rejected similar temptations while he held the position.

As believers, we are not alone in suffering temptation. Being tempted is no sin, but surrendering to sin is always wrong. The Bible reminds us that the Son of God himself "was in all points tempted like as we are, yet without sin" (Heb. 4:15).

Prayer Suggestion—Realize that, with God's help, you can overcome temptation, regardless of how overpowering it may seem to be.

NOVEMBER

15

Psalm 37:28–40

Today in History—Brazil Republic Day marks end of monarchy, 1889; National Broadcasting Company goes on the air over twenty-four stations, 1926; U.S. calls up seventy-five thousand men to armed forces duty in first peacetime draft, 1940; anthropologist Margaret Mead dies of cancer at age 76, 1978; Chilean army and air force troops round up thousands of people for questioning about recent leftist demonstrations, 1984.

Born Today—Hymnwriter William Cowper, 1731; artist Georgia O'Keefe, 1887; former Senator Howard Baker, Jr., 1925; singer Petula Clark, 1932; TV weatherman John Coleman, 1935; conductor Daniel Barenboim, 1942.

Today's Quotation—"That's all there is; there isn't any more."—*Ethel Barrymore, November 15, 1904*

All There Is

A popular song in the 1960s dealt with the apparent insignificance of life, asking the question, "Is that all there is?" Mankind needs hope in order to survive the pressures of the world today.

Many years ago a submarine was rammed by another ship and quickly sank off the Massachusetts coast. Although rescue was impossible at that depth, a diver was dispatched to determine if there was still life aboard the disabled vessel. The diver placed his helmeted ear against the sub's hull and heard a faint tapping sound. Carefully he made note of the dots and dashes and decoded the following question: "Is . . . there . . . any . . . hope?" With great remorse he slowly signaled back: "Hope . . . in . . . God . . . alone."

God's Word reminds us that Christ is the hope of the world; indeed Christ is the basis of all human existence. In what do you place your hope?

Prayer Suggestion—Commit your life to Christ and he will give you a reason to live!

NOVEMBER

16

Romans 6:14–23

Today in History—President John Adams is the first to occupy the new Executive Mansion (the White House), in Washington, D.C., 1800; General William T. Sherman's Union Army begins march from Atlanta to the sea in the Civil War, 1864; Oklahoma admitted to U.S. as forty-sixth state, 1907; twelve Federal Reserve Banks open, 1914; U.S. establishes diplomatic relations with U.S.S.R., 1933; Leonid Brezhnev worries about food shortages in Russia, 1981.

Born Today—Composer Paul Hindemith, 1895; songwriter W. C. Handy, 1873; actor Burgess Meredith, 1909; singer Bob Gibson, 1931; baseball player Dwight Gooden, 1964; actress Lisa Bonet, 1967.

Today's Quotation—"It is beginning to be hinted that we are a nation of amateurs."—*Lord Rosebery, November 16, 1900*

Amateurs

While salvation comes by faith alone, becoming an effective Christian takes work; it is no job for amateurs.

A group of college students in Chicago banded together to form an amateur rescue team to save victims from drowning in Lake Michigan. Early one November day, the group was summoned to rescue the crew of a shipwrecked vessel not far off shore. One student, Ed Spencer, showed unusual bravery. Swimming out to the wrecked ship repeatedly, Spencer rescued ten people before stopping to warm by the fire. But as he stood there, he saw more men, women, and children waiting to be rescued. Ignoring the pleas of those on shore, Spencer dove in and rescued six more victims. Spencer finally stopped to rest, but his only thought was of those he couldn't rescue. He may have been an amateur rescuer but he was a full-fledged hero to those he had saved.

While it is true that God hasn't called everyone into full-time Christian service, all believers are called to be full-time Christians. Child of God, don't settle for amateur status when God asks you to give your best to him.

Prayer Suggestion—Accept God's free gift of salvation, then ask God to help you share the eternal hope of this message with others today.

NOVEMBER

17

Today in History—Queen Elizabeth I succeeds to throne of England, 1558; John Zenger, printer and journalist, arrested for libel against the colonial governor (his acquittal was important step in establishing freedom of the press), 1734; Congress meets for its first Washington, D.C., session, 1800; Suez Canal opens, 1869; U.S. and U.S.S.R. launch talks on strategic arms limitation, 1969.

Born Today—Astronomer August Mobius, 1790; artist Titian Peale, 1799; General Bernard Montgomery, 1887; track athlete Bob Mathias, 1930; singer Gordon Lightfoot, 1939; actor Danny DeVito, 1944.

Today's Quotation—"There is no time now for anything but fighting and working to win."—*Franklin D. Roosevelt, November 17, 1942*

Winning

It is amazing to see how effective a bit of encouragement can be to those who are most in need of hope. The mother of a severely crippled boy was helping him learn to walk. His spindly legs were nearly covered by heavy metal braces that caused him to hobble along one step at a time. While he was straining to move, his mother was there to encourage each improvement no matter how small. With every word of encouragement, the little lad would try still harder. Finally, his confidence increased and he told his mother, "Watch me, I'm going to run." He did well for a few steps but then his brace caught on his leg. He would have tumbled to the ground if his mother had not caught him at the last moment. She wrapped the discouraged boy up in her arms, kissed him, and said, "You did fine! And I know you will do even better next time!"

Our heavenly Father is like that—ready to lift us up when we've fallen, there with support and encouragement when we are ready to quit. God has said, "We are more than conquerors, through him who loved us" (Rom. 8:37).

Prayer Suggestion—Recognize that if you aren't using God's strength and help, you aren't using *all* of your power.

NOVEMBER

18

Today in History—Antarctica discovered by U.S. Navy Captain Nathaniel Palmer, 1820; Soviets recover spacecraft after successful flight around the moon, 1968; insider trading scandal sweeps Wall Street, 1986; Senate and House panels say President Reagan is "ultimately responsible" for Iran arms sale controversy, 1987.

Born Today—Inventor Louis Daguerre, 1789; songwriter William Gilbert, 1836; pollster George Gallup, 1901; astronaut Alan Shepard, 1923; actor Marcello Mastroianni, 1925; singer Dorothy Collins, 1926.

Today's Quotation—"Necessity is the plea for every infringement of human freedom. It is the argument of tyrants; it is the creed of slaves."—*William Pitt, the Younger, November 18, 1783*

Necessity

As believers we are under a barrage today unlike any seen before in history. Satan knows his time is short and has greatly increased his attacks on those who are children of God. As Christians, we need to resolve to do whatever must be done to be faithful to our Lord.

In the tragic destruction of Pompeii, many persons were buried alive in the volcanic eruption of Mount Vesuvius. The victims were all frozen in time. Particularly significant was the excavator's discovery of the remains of a Roman sentry. They found the guard standing outside the gate still grasping his weapon—at the same location as he had been placed by his captain centuries before! Despite the choking ash and terrifying roar of the volcano, the guard remained steadfast at his post, faithful to his cause.

When our lives are inspected by God in the hereafter, will he find us faithful, doing his will? May we be found "steadfast, immovable, always abounding in the work of the Lord." (1 Cor. 15:58).

Prayer Suggestion—Help us to be found faithful in doing the work of God as he has called us to do it.

339

NOVEMBER

19

John 20:24–31

Today in History—The *Mayflower* arrives off Cape Cod, Mass., 1620; Lincoln's Gettysburg Address, 1863; U.S. Senate rejects Versailles Treaty and idea of League of Nations, 1919; U.S. Steel agrees to buy Marathon Oil for $6.3 billion, 1981; five hundred killed in gas explosion in Mexican warehouse, 1984; President Reagan denies Israeli involvement in Iran arms sale, 1986.

Born Today—President James Garfield, 1831; evangelist Billy Sunday, 1862; ambassador Jeanne Kirkpatrick, 1926; business executive John Welch, Jr., 1935; communications executive Ted Turner, 1938; broadcast journalist Garrick Utley, 1939.

Today's Quotation—"Be wiser than other people if you can, but do not tell them so."—*Earl of Chesterfield, November 19, 1745*

Wisdom

We may acquire all the wisdom of the ages but if we have not "seen" Christ, we are indeed ignorant.

The German sculptor Dannecker labored several years to fashion a figure of Christ in stone. He wanted to ensure that it closely resembled the Savior so, summoning a little girl to his studio, he asked her to identify the person represented by the sculpture. "A great man," was her reply. Dannecker was crushed. Sensing his failure to properly portray Christ, he returned to his studio and worked six more years. Again he invited a little girl to his studio and, pointing to the statue, inquired, "Who is that?" Suddenly the girl began to sniffle and said, "Suffer the little children to come unto me." His goal was achieved; he had fashioned a likeness of Christ so real that even a small youngster could see him. Then he confessed that in his hours of discouragement, he had personally turned to Christ as Savior. In so doing, Dannecker was able to carve into marble the vision of Christ he had already "seen."

Prayer Suggestion—Praise God that, through faith, you can know him without ever having "seen" him in this life.

NOVEMBER

20

Matthew 25:1–30

Today in History—Peregrine White was first child born to Pilgrims in New World (aboard the Mayflower), 1620; U.S. forces land on Japanese-held Pacific island of Tarawa, 1943; International War Crimes Tribunal opens trial of Nazi leaders, 1945; Great Britain's Princess (later Queen) Elizabeth marries Prince Philip, 1947; Senate Committee says CIA utilized by U.S. officials in plots to kill various foreign leaders, 1975.

Born Today—Poet Thomas Chatterton, 1752; journalist Alistair Cooke, 1908; politician Robert Byrd, 1917; pianist Ruth Laredo, 1937; comedian Dick Smothers, 1938; broadcast journalist Judy Woodruff, 1946.

Today's Quotation—"I should be glad if I could flatter myself that I came as near to the central idea of the occasion in two hours, as you did in two minutes."—*Edward Everett to Abraham Lincoln, November 20, 1863*

Winning Words

Those who have been faithful in witnessing can attest to the power of the Word of God in leading a skeptic to the Savior. That is what occurred one day to a Swiss physician en route to Paris. Along the way, he struck up a conversation with a fellow passenger on the subject of Christianity. The man had many doubts and questions concerning Christianity, but each was carefully answered with a quotation from Scripture. The skeptic grew more agitated with each response, saying, "I don't believe your Bible. Why do you keep quoting it to me?" The doctor responded with yet another verse, "If ye believe not that I am he, ye shall die in your sins." Years later the physician received a letter from the former skeptic saying that now he was a Christian. Referring to their spirited discussion on the way to Paris, the man said that by quoting Scripture, "You made me feel as if I was not fighting you, but God." The physician had been faithful in planting God's winning words, which years later bore the intended fruit.

Prayer Suggestion—Give us a persistent spirit to be faithful in sharing the winning Word of God with everyone we meet.

NOVEMBER

21

Luke 7:41–50

Today in History—Pilgrims sign the Mayflower Compact, 1620; first manned free balloon flight, 1783; North Carolina becomes the twelfth state to ratify the U.S. Constitution, 1789; Verrazano-Narrows Bridge opens in New York Harbor, 1964; in historic address before the Israeli Knesset, Egyptian President Anwar Sadat pledges "no more war" with Israel, 1977; President Reagan and Soviet leader Mikhail Gorbachev meet in Geneva and hold longest summit conference yet between Russian and American leaders, 1985.

Born Today—Author Jean Voltaire, 1694; surgeon William Beaumont, 1785; financier Hetty Green, 1835; baseball's Stan Musial, 1920; actress Marlo Thomas, 1938; actress Lorna Luft, 1952.

Today's Quotation—"Every sunset inspires me with the desire to go to a West as distant and fair as that into which the sun goes down."—*Henry David Thoreau, November 21, 1850*

Forgiveness

One of the most reassuring passages of Scripture is Psalm 103:12, which reminds us that our sins have been removed "as far as the east is from the west"—an incalculable distance away. When missionaries first called upon the Eskimos, there was no word in their language for forgiveness. After considering a number of possibilities, a new word was coined—one with an unmistakable meaning. The new word, a tongue-twister, means, "Not-being-able-to-think-about-it-anymore." What an apt description of what God has done in our lives!

It was Martin Niemoller who said, "It took me a long time to learn that God is not the enemy of his enemies!" God loves his enemies and sent his only Son to die in their place. Have you trusted Christ as Savior? If not, do so today.

Prayer Suggestion—Thank God for his forgiveness that takes away all of your sin and remembers it no more.

342

NOVEMBER

22

Today in History—President John F. Kennedy assassinated in Dallas, Tex., and Lee Harvey Oswald arrested for the murder, 1963; Spain's Prince Juan Carlos crowned king upon death of dictator Francisco Franco, 1975; cigar and pipe smoking banned on all U.S. airliners, 1977; in Spain, Basques call strike to protest the killing of their leader, 1984; over one thousand Cuban inmates facing deportation take over detention center in Oakdale, La., 1987.

Born Today—Former First Lady Abigail Adams, 1744; author George Eliot, 1819; French leader Charles de Gaulle, 1890; aviator Wiley Post, 1898; songwriter Hoagie Carmichael, 1899; composer Benjamin Britten, 1913; actor Robert Vaughan, 1932.

Today's Quotation—"What the imagination seizes as Beauty must be truth—whether it existed before or not."—*John Keats, November 22, 1817*

Beauty

God's concern for detail can be realized in even the smallest things of life. One of the world's smallest plants is the minuscule Cyclococcolithus leptoporus. It is said that five hundred such plants could be placed on the head of a pin! Each plant has an elaborate outer shell of patterned scales. However, the smallest of all known plants is the Coccolithophoridae, a type of plankton which is startlingly beautiful and which has an elaborate outer armor made of a substance like chalk. These nearly invisible plants are as beautiful in their own way as the huge California redwood.

The same God that created these beauties, big and small, also created you in your unique complexity. What an awesome God we have!

Prayer Suggestion—Praise God for the beauty of his creation!

NOVEMBER

23

Today in History—Civil War Battle of Lookout Mountain, 1863; Enrico Caruso makes his New York debut at the Metropolitan Opera in *Rigoletto,* 1903; SPARS (women's unit of U.S. Coast Guard) authorized, 1942; China expands private sector by allowing private businesses to hire more workers, 1981; Miami elects Xavier Suarez as first Cuban mayor, 1985.

Born Today—President Franklin Pierce, 1804; actor Boris Karloff, 1887; author Maurice Zolotow, 1913; actress Ellen Drew, 1915; composer Jerry Bock, 1928.

Today's Quotation—"In this country, if someone dislikes you or accuses you, he must come up in front. He cannot hide behind the shadows, he cannot assassinate you or your character from behind without suffering the penalties of outraged citizenry will inflict."—*Dwight D. Eisenhower, November 23, 1954*

Mutual Dislike

You can never tell what others may be thinking of you. Evangelist H. A. Ironside used to tell the story of the bishop who was bound for Europe aboard an ocean liner. Upon boarding, he met the man who was to share his room. He immediately made a visit to the ship's purser to deposit his valuables. The bishop explained that ordinarily he'd have no concerns about the safety of his belongings, but after meeting his roommate, he felt it best that he deposit his valuables for safekeeping. The purser replied, "Why, that's quite okay. You see, your roommate has just been here and left his for the same reason!"

One can never tell the extent to which others will go to be sure they are safe from us! Be aware of the impression you leave with others.

Prayer Suggestion—May others see Jesus reflected in your life.

NOVEMBER

24

Today in History—Patent for barbed wire granted to Joseph Glidden, 1874; U.S. wins Battle of Tarawa in Pacific, 1943; Lee Harvey Oswald, accused assassin of President Kennedy, shot and killed on live television in Dallas, 1963; President Ford and Soviet leader Brezhnev reach tentative agreement to limit strategic nuclear arms, 1974; three thousand die in earthquake in eastern Turkey, 1976; in deal between Israel and the Palestinian Liberation Organization (PLO), six Israeli soldiers are traded for five thousand Palestinians, 1983.

Born Today—President Zachary Taylor, 1784; artist Henri de Toulouse-Lautrec, 1864; motivator Dale Carnegie, 1888; pastor Lee Roberson, 1909; columnist William Buckley, 1925; composer Al Cohn, 1925; opera singer Alfredo Kraus, 1927.

Today's Quotation—"What is our task? To make Britain a fit country for heroes to live in."—*David Lloyd George, November 24, 1918*

Heroes

Have you noticed how many of today's heroes credit God for their success? Whether it is a football receiver praying in the end zone after catching the scoring pass, or entertainers openly espousing their faith in God, it is refreshing to see.

It is not a new phenomenon. The "Father of our Nation," General George Washington, found peace and assurance from regularly addressing God in prayer. Some time ago the *Sunday School Times* told of a farmer who saw Washington on his knees in prayer at Valley Forge and told his wife, "The Americans will gain their independence." "Oh, what makes you so sure?" she asked. "I heard him praying out in the woods today, and the Lord will surely hear his prayer," predicted the farmer.

Isn't it interesting to see how God makes heroes out of those who honor him?

Prayer Suggestion—May your life always honor God and make others want to know him better as a result of seeing you.

NOVEMBER

25

Today in History—British forces leave New York following end of American Revolutionary War, 1783; in a free election, Russians choose a constituent assembly in which the communists hold less than a third of the deputies, 1917; President Nixon orders gas stations closed on Sundays and reduction from the seventy-mile-per-hour speed limit to cut energy consumption, 1973; world's second artificial heart implant performed in Louisville, Ky., 1984.

Born Today—Industrialist Andrew Carnegie, 1835; composer Virgil Thomson, 1896; baseball player Joe DiMaggio, 1914; actor Ricardo Montalban, 1920; actress Kathryn Crosby, 1933; football player Bernie Kosar, 1963.

Today's Quotation—"The characteristic of the present age is craving credulity."—*Benjamin Disraeli, November 25, 1864*

Credulity

We might define credulity as "unquestioned trust." Normally this would be considered a liability, but there are times when credulity is quite appropriate.

A man dressed in overalls and boots visited a new car dealership one day and told the salesman he wanted to buy sixteen cars. "Get lost," was the salesman's response. The man left the dealership and walked across the street to another new car showroom where he got a warmer reception and his sixteen cars, which he paid for in cash! The casually dressed man was a crew member aboard a fishing ship that had just brought in a record catch. Each crewman decided to buy a new car with his earnings, and they decided to purchase them all at once for cash to get the best discount. The first salesman lost this record sale because he did not exercise credulity (blind faith) at the right time.

In spiritual matters, we need to be very cautious who we trust because there are many false religions. That is why it is so important that we compare our faith to that of the Bible. Only if it agrees with God's Word can we be certain our faith is well founded.

Prayer Suggestion—Thank God for his Word which gives us the standard by which we may validate our faith.

NOVEMBER

26

Today in History—First lion to be seen in America is exhibited in Boston, 1716; first college social fraternity, Kappa Alpha, formed at Union College, 1825; Red China enters Korean War, 1950; President Nixon's secretary, Rose Mary Woods, says she caused eighteen-minute erasure on key White House tape, 1973; U.S. Steel says it will close fifteen plants leaving thirteen thousand workers unemployed, 1979; Yasuhiro Nakasone is elected seventy-first Japanese prime minister, 1982.

Born Today—Physician Mary Walker, 1832; author Eugene Ionesco, 1912; TV commentator Eric Sevareid, 1912; cartoonist Charles Schulz, 1922, singer Robert Goulet, 1933; impressionist Rich Little, 1938.

Today's Quotation—"We suppose that the rupture of the present negotiations does not necessarily mean war between Japan and the United States."—*Ambassadors Nomura and Kurusu, November 26, 1941*

War Talks

If tried sincerely, peace will many times prevail where war will not succeed. A missionary once needed to cross over a mountain pass which was held by cannibals. And so, calmly, peacefully, he climbed the mountain and proceeded to the other side. Later he met a military leader who was amazed that he had passed through the area unscathed and who asked how he did it. The missionary replied, "You attempted to cross as men of war. I made the trip as a man of peace."

But the Bible reminds us to be cautious, for "when they shall say, Peace and safety; then sudden destruction cometh upon them . . ." (1 Thess. 5:3). History bears this out. While Japanese ambassadors were in Washington talking peace, their military forces were preparing for their attack on Pearl Harbor. That is why, while being a peace-loving people, we must also be ever on the alert, "wise as serpents, and harmless as doves" (Matt. 10:16).

Prayer Suggestion—May we be ever alert to Satan's attempts at war while proclaiming God's message of love and peace.

NOVEMBER

27

Matthew 6:24-34

Today in History—Army War College in Washington, D.C., established, 1901; Joint Distribution Committee (for relief of Jews all over world) organized, 1914; French Navy scuttles its ships in Toulon Harbor rather than have Nazis capture them in World War II, 1942; San Francisco Mayor George Moscone and supervisor Harvey Milk are shot and killed by former supervisor Dan White, 1978.

Born Today—Historian Charles Beard, 1874; Israeli statesman Chaim Weizman, 1874; producer David Merrick, 1912; entertainer Buffalo Bob Smith, 1917; author Gail Sheehy, 1937; actress Robin Givens, 1964.

Today's Quotation—"Civilization and profits go hand in hand."— *Calvin Coolidge, November 27, 1920*

Profits

While there's nothing wrong with making an honest profit from honest effort, the Bible cautions, "For what shall it profit a man, if he shall gain the whole world, and lose his own soul?" (Mark 8:36).

The Upper Room once told of a pioneer western preacher who had temporarily abandoned the pulpit to join the prospectors in panning for gold. Soon, however, he realized how much time his prospecting was taking him from the pulpit and decided to re-evaluate his priorities. He opened the handkerchief that contained the precious gold he had so laboriously retrieved and shook the contents out in the wind. That early preacher had seen how he was letting the drive for financial profit get in the way of everlasting spiritual gains. He was letting the desire for wealth overtake his spiritual priorities.

As Dr. Jerry Falwell has said, "It is okay to own things as long as things don't own you!" Be sure that the love of money has not overtaken you.

Prayer Suggestion—God help us to realize that the only thing we can take into eternity are the souls we lead to the Lord. *All* else will pass away.

NOVEMBER

28

Today in History—Lady Astor becomes first woman elected to British Parliament, 1919; Rhodesia said to be ready to give full voting rights to black majority, 1977; Senator Robert Dole of Kansas elected senate majority leader, 1984.

Born Today—Clergyman John Bunyan, 1628; poet William Blake, 1757; writer Brooks Atkinson, 1894; actress Hope Lange, 1933; politician Gary Hart, 1936; musician Paul Shaffer, 1949; basketball player Roy Tarpley, 1964.

Today's Quotation—"It is a melancholy law of human societies to be compelled sometimes to choose a great evil in order to ward off a greater [one]."—*Thomas Jefferson, November 28, 1814*

Great Evil

How easy it is for a small sin to rapidly grow into a great evil that soon takes over and consumes our life.

E. Gorhma Clark tells of a circus trainer who had long worked with a twenty-five-foot boa constrictor. He had bought it when it was but a few days old and for over twenty years had handled it daily. It seemed perfectly harmless and under the trainer's control. The trainer worked with many animals, but he always reserved the boa constrictor act for the grand finale. And so it was this time. The trainer, dressed as a hunter, was making his way through a wooded setting when he was confronted by the mammoth serpent. On a cue from the trainer, the snake began to coil around its master. Relentlessly, the snake coiled higher and higher around the helpless trainer, until finally the serpent raised its ugly head above the man and the crowd applauded. Then suddenly, for no apparent reason, the serpent lapsed into its deadly nature. The man uttered a helpless cry, bones cracked and broke, and his very life was squeezed from him. What a picture of the dread power of sin; it seems so comfortable, and then comes sudden destruction!

Prayer Suggestion—May we never underestimate the subtlety of sin as it silently, gradually strangles the very moral life from us.

NOVEMBER

29

Today in History—Richard E. Byrd heads crew of airplane making first flight over the South Pole, 1929; President Johnson names commission to investigate the assassination of President Kennedy, 1963; actress Natalie Wood, 43, drowns in apparent accident off California coast, 1981; powerfully addictive concentrated form of cocaine, "crack," is beginning to appear on New York City streets, 1985.

Born Today—Colonial historian Charles Thomson, 1729; reform leader Wendell Phillips, 1811; author Louisa May Alcott, 1832; sportscaster Vin Scully, 1927; politician Jacques Chirac, 1932; trumpeter Chuck Mangione, 1940.

Today's Quotation—"From the commencement of the titanic struggle in America, the working men of Europe felt instinctively that the "Star Spangled Banner" carried the destiny of their class."—*Karl Marx, November 29, 1865*

Victory Banner

The Bible tells the believer to be a "light unto the world," being an example wherever we go. A story is told of an Army officer who, having been saved, resolved to fly the banner of Christianity. So he bought a large Bible and laid it open on his nightstand. Although ridiculed by his companions, the officer eventually gained their respect. He put the matter into the proper perspective as he prayed, "Lord, help me to please you and still please my colonel." Satan constantly tries to entice us with attractive short cuts to keep us from our spiritual purpose. The Bible says, "There is a way that seemeth right to a man, but the ends thereof are the ends of death" (Prov. 14:12). That is why it is essential to devote part of each day to consulting God's road map, the Bible. With so many "banners" in the world today, all claiming to be right, which one are you following?

Prayer Suggestion—Ask the Lord to show you the importance of following his map by daily reading the Bible and praying.

NOVEMBER

30

Today in History—United Nations votes to partition Palestine into Arab and Jewish states, 1947; gasoline prices expected to rise to fifty cents per gallon on most expensive grades in wake of oil embargo, 1973; actor Cary Grant dies at age 80, 1986; President Reagan faces stiff questioning about possible arms for hostage deals with Iran, 1986.

Born Today—Writer Jonathan Swift, 1667; merchant Cyrus W. Field, 1819; writer Mark Twain (Samuel Clemens), 1835; former British Prime Minister Winston Churchill, 1874; actor Efrem Zimbalist, Jr., 1923; former Congresswoman Shirley Chisholm, 1924; entertainer Dick Clark, 1929.

Today's Quotation—"I have never accepted what many people have kindly said, namely that I inspired the nation. It was the nation . . . that had the lion heart. I had the luck to be called upon to give the roar."— *Winston Churchill, November 30, 1954*

Determination

The Sunday school teacher, trying to teach the importance of determination, was having his students read from the book of Daniel. He called on a lad to read Daniel 6:3, which says of Daniel, "because an excellent spirit was in him. . . ." The youth mistakenly read it "because an excellent spine was in him." While his reading was incorrect, his theology was right on target. To succeed in life we must be purposefully striving toward a goal.

C. E. McCartney has pointed out the truth of this in the field of transportation. When compared with all other forms of locomotion, only airplanes must continue on a forward course. Since the airplane has no "reverse" on its engine, it cannot back up. If it loses its momentum and forward thrust, it quickly crashes. The life of the Christian should be like the airplane's flight, constantly driving forward toward the goal. To stall is to crash and be destroyed. Satan's detours, no matter how compelling, must be ignored if we are going to be successful in completing our God-given task in life and reach our final goal.

Prayer Suggestion—May God help us ever keep our attention fixed upon his goals for us, not on the lures of the tempter.

DECEMBER

1

Psalm 28:1–9

Today in History—Civil Air Patrol Day founded as auxiliary aviation group, 1941; Britisher Sir William Beveridge proposes plan for "cradle to grave" social security, 1942; Cuban leader Fidel Castro publicly declares himself a Marxist, 1961; Israel's first premier David Ben Gurion dies in Tell Aviv at age 87, 1973; Chinese open first high-level talks with western nations in over thirty years, 1988.

Born Today—Writer Rex Stout, 1886; actor Cyril Ritchard, 1898; baseball's Walter Alston, 1911; actress Mary Martin, 1914; producer Woody Allen, 1935; actor Lou Rawls, 1935; golfer Lee Trevino, 1939.

Today's Quotation—"Conquest gives no right to the conqueror to be a tyrant."—*Charles James Fox, December 1, 1783*

Conquest

The crucial battle of Dunkirk marked a turning point in history, as Britain seemed about to be conquered by invading forces. Forty-seven ships had been sunk in the sea off Norway and the Royal Air Force was diminished by 40 percent. It was Britain's darkest hour. Yet despite the discouragement, Winston Churchill challenged his countrymen to resist by saying, "We shall fight on the beaches, we shall fight in the fields, we shall fight in the streets. . . . we shall never surrender!"

This should also be true in our Christian walk. Either declare war on the lures of the world, or the enemy of God will have conquest over your life.

Prayer Suggestion—Ask God's help to withstand the sinful temptations of this life. Stand up and be counted, not conquered.

DECEMBER

2

Today in History—First savings bank opens (in Philadelphia), 1816; President Monroe proclaims Monroe Doctrine as U.S. policy, 1823; first self-sustaining nuclear reaction achieved at University of Chicago, 1942; U.S. Senate votes to censure Senator Joseph McCarthy, 1954; patient fitted with first permanent artificial heart, 1982; investment firm Shearson Lehman Brothers announces plans to buy E. F. Hutton for one billion dollars, 1987.

Born Today—Artist Georges Seurat, 1859; composer Adolph Green, 1915; musician Charlie Ventura, 1916; opera singer Maria Callas, 1923; politician Alexander Haig, 1924; actress Julie Harris, 1925.

Today's Quotation—"I, John Brown, am now quite certain that the crimes of this guilty land will never be purged away, but with Blood. . . ."—*John Brown, on the day of his hanging, December 2, 1859*

Blood

Over the years criticism has been leveled at certain beloved hymns because they sing of the blood shed by Christ. Yet, it is through Christ's blood that we are able to be saved.

Some years ago a large rally was being held on the west coast. The speaker, though eloquent, was directing skepticism against the saving blood of Christ. The crowd appeared unmoved until a godly, frail, elderly woman stood on her feet and sang softly the familiar words by William Cowper: "There is a fountain filled with blood/Drawn from Emmanuel's veins/And sinners, plunged beneath that flood,/Lose all their guilty stains." Slowly others in that massive audience stood to join her on the final verse: "Dear dying Lamb, Thy precious blood shall never lose its power, till all the ransomed church of God be saved to sin no more." It was the example of that one saintly believer and the truths of the hymn that had a greater influence on the audience than that of the renowned speaker.

Prayer Suggestion—Acknowledge the saving power of Christ's death on the cross and the blood he shed for your salvation.

DECEMBER

3

Today in History—Illinois admitted to U.S. as twenty-first state, 1818; first low-cost public housing project dedicated in New York City, 1935; first human heart transplant performed by Dr. Christiaan Barnard in Capetown, South Africa, 1967; British official James R. Cross, kidnapped two months earlier by Quebec separatists, released, 1970; since fall of Saigon (in 1975), 165,000 Indochina refugees have entered the U.S., 1977; thousands die in accidental leak of toxic gas at chemical plant in Bhopal, India, 1984.

Born Today—Artist Gilbert Stuart, 1755; General George McClellan, 1826; writer Joseph Conrad, 1857; singer Andy Williams, 1930; singer Jaye P. Morgan, 1932; racer Rick Mears, 1951.

Today's Quotation—"We desire the peace which comes as of right to the just man armed; not the peace granted on terms of ignominy to the craven and the weakling."—*Theodore Roosevelt, December 3, 1901*

A Strong Defense

Many times people are led into sin because they have neither anticipated the temptations they would encounter, nor armed themselves accordingly. A wealthy banker's rebellious son left home to join the military. There the boy had the same problems obeying the orders of the officers as he had while at home. Finally, his commanding officer took him aside to remind him that, while the service was not able to force him to do anything, they could certainly make him wish he had obeyed.

In the same way, when the believer has no strong defense against evil, Satan will, sooner or later, make him wish he had followed God. Those people known for their great character have often had a written statement in which they commit to keep themselves from those things which would cause their moral defeat. How are you defending yourself?

Prayer Suggestion—Dedicate your life to God to do that which is right. Call upon God's strength as your only sure defense.

DECEMBER

4

Today in History—America's first Thanksgiving Day celebrated at Berkeley Plantation, Virginia, 1619; National Grange founded in Washington, D.C., 1867; Thomas Alva Edison's first phonograph completed, 1877; Free University of Berlin founded in West Berlin during Communist blockade, 1948; Bernadette Dorn, formerly associated with radical group the "Weathermen," turns herself in to Chicago authorities, 1980; Cuban inmates end eleven-day siege in Atlanta Federal Prison, 1987.

Born Today—Writer Thomas Carlyle, 1795; actress Lillian Russell, 1861; nurse Edith Cavell, 1865; actress Deanna Durbin, 1921; producer Max Baer, Jr., 1937; actor Jeff Bridges, 1949.

Today's Quotation—"Every rich man reaches a time in his career when he comes to a turning point and starts to give it away."—*Will Rogers, December 4, 1924*

Generosity

A young boy was given two cookies and asked to share with his sister with the words "remember to be generous." Unconvinced, he asked his mom if she wouldn't please give his sister the cookies, "so she could be generous." Many of us like generosity when it is someone else who's being generous.

George Peabody was once asked which he enjoyed more, making money or giving it away. "After I saw the happiness and joy of those who lived in the new housing I built for the poor . . . I can truly say that as much as I have enjoyed making money, I now enjoy giving it away a great deal better."

Evangelist D. L. Moody told of a very wealthy man who was dying. His little girl asked, "Daddy, are you going away?" He replied, "Yes, dear, and I won't be returning either." "Have you got a nice home and lots of friends there?" she continued. Then this great man of wealth saw the point. Although he had amassed a sizeable fortune in his lifetime, he was totally unprepared for the life to come. He would be a pauper in eternity.

Friend, what are you doing for Jesus' sake?

Prayer Suggestion—What are you giving to God, who has given his all for you? Will you be as generous with God as he is with you?

355

DECEMBER

5

Luke 6:27-38

Today in History—First college fraternity, Phi Beta Kappa, founded at William and Mary College, 1776; repeal of Prohibition becomes effective, 1933; missionaries John and Betty Stam beheaded by Chinese communists, 1934; disastrous four-day fog cover hits London leaving more than four thousand dead, 1953; American Federation of Labor and Congress of Industrial Organization merge as AFL-CIO, 1955; Dow Jones average sets a new record high of fifteen hundred, 1985.

Born Today—President Martin Van Buren, 1782; cartoonist Walt Disney, 1901; politician Strom Thurmond, 1902; director Otto Preminger, 1906; singer Chad Mitchell, 1936; actress Morgan Brittany, 1950.

Today's Quotation—"I love best to have each thing in its season only, and enjoy doing without it at all other times. It is the greatest of all advantages to enjoy no advantage at all."—*Henry David Thoreau, December 5, 1856*

An Advantage

Have you noticed how that the more you give to God, the more he gives back to you? This might be called the "believer's advantage." A well-to-do farmer was converted and vowed to do all he could to assist a poor family who had lost everything in a fire. He promised not only money, but a large ham from his smoke house. On the way to get the ham, though, the tempter spoke up and encouraged him to give the smallest ham he had. The man listened a moment, but then called upon God's strength to overcome the temptation. He told Satan, "If you don't keep still, I'll give that poor man *every* ham in my smoke house."

No doubt he recognized the spiritual advantage he would receive simply by sharing his blessings. But we can be certain that God will return multiplied material blessings as well.

Prayer Suggestion—Recognizing that all we have is owned by God, we will look for ways to share his blessings with those in need.

DECEMBER

6

Today in History—Coal mine explosions kill three hundred fifty men in Monngah, W.Va., 1907; Finland Independence Day marks declaration of independence from Russia, 1917; munitions ship collision in Halifax Harbor, Nova Scotia, causes blast that kills sixteen hundred and injured four thousand, 1917; "Democracy Wall" torn down in Peking after being papered with anti-communist slogans, 1979; gunman who shot six police officers gives himself up in New York City, 1987.

Born Today—Lyricist Ira Gershwin, 1896; photographer Alfred Eisenstaedt, 1898; poet Joyce Kilmer, 1898; actress Eleanor Holm, 1913; pianist Dave Brubeck, 1920; football coach Walter Perkins, 1941.

Today's Quotation—"The one ultimate unforgivable crime is to despair of the republic. . . . In every era for a century and a half it has been doomed to death by gloomy young theorists and by tired and hopeless elders."—*Thomas E. Dewey, December 6, 1939*

Despair

How often have you felt defeated and full of despair because of the events of life? The great dome of St. Paul's Cathedral in London has a vast staircase of over six hundred steps leading to the base of the dome. Then, in order to climb to the very peak, visitors are required to pass downward through a small corridor and climb up yet another staircase. In life, as in the dome, we sometimes have to go down to go up!

Edward Judson said, "Success and suffering are vitally and organically linked. If you succeed without suffering, it is because someone else has suffered before you; if you suffer without succeeding, it is that someone else may succeed after you."

When it seems as if life has dealt us a harsh blow, we must recognize our need to depend upon God for strength to carry us through the temporary crisis to a point where we will be able to again look up.

Prayer Suggestion—Tomorrows are always bright for believers who have God's strength to carry them through.

DECEMBER

7

Today in History—Delaware first state to ratify U.S. Constitution, 1787; Japanese attack on Pearl Harbor, Hawaii, bringing U.S. into World War II, 1941; Kurt Waldheim nominated for second five-year term as U.N. secretary general, 1976; U.S. Court of Appeals orders U.S. military to accept homosexuals into military service unless there is "some explanation" for exclusion, 1978; Soviet Premier Gorbachev tells U.N. that Soviets will unilaterally reduce their armed forces by five hundred thousand troops, 1988; twenty-five thousand die as earthquakes strike Soviet Armenia, 1988.

Born Today—Museum creator Marie Tussaud, 1761; writer Willa Cather, 1873; actor Eli Wallach, 1915; business executive Victor Kiam, II, 1926; baseball player Johnny Bench, 1947; basketball player Larry Bird, 1956.

Today's Quotation—"Praise the Lord and pass the ammunition."— *Reverend Howell M. Forgy, December 7, 1941*

Praising the Lord

Despite life's hardships, we always need to praise the Lord. There was an elderly woman who rejoiced in praising her Lord, especially during sermons at her church. Eventually, this got to her pastor, who lost his train of thought each time she shouted out the Lord's praise. In exasperation, the pastor offered the poor woman several warm blankets, which she desperately needed because she was very poor, if she would simply refrain from shouting out her praise in the service. She got the blankets and did her best to earn them. She did well for several weeks until a guest speaker visited the church, preaching on the forgiveness of sins. As he preached, the woman found she was less and less able to restrain herself. Finally she could not restrain herself and cried, "Blankets or no blankets, praise the Lord!"

Prayer Suggestion—Praise God for his forgiveness which makes us rejoice!

DECEMBER

8

Today in History—American Federation of Labor founded, 1886; Congress passes Declaration of War against Japan, 1941; Chinese Nationalist government under Chiang Kai-shek moves to Formosa, 1949; Israel's first woman prime minister, Golda Meir, dies at age 80, 1978; singer John Lennon killed by gunman outside his New York City apartment, 1980; French government gives in to student demonstrators demanding reforms to university system, 1986.

Born Today—Inventor Eli Whitney, 1765; composer Jan Sibelius, 1865; writer James Thurber, 1894; entertainer Sammy Davis, Jr., 1925; actor Maximilian Schell, 1930; comedian Flip Wilson, 1933.

Today's Quotation—"I am not a bit afraid of anything I have said in a long political life."—*Winston Churchill, December 8, 1944*

No Regrets

How many people wish they had the opportunity to go back and change history? A public speaker often experiences this feeling. Earl Derby once said a speech cost him two nights' sleep—the night before, thinking what he should say, and the night afterward, thinking of how he wished he had said it differently.

An Indiana youth, Richard Marquard, was signed as a pitcher by the New York Giants for the fantastic sum (in 1908) of eleven thousand dollars. He tried hard in his first two seasons, but his efforts just couldn't match the glowing predictions made about his performance. Fans soon referred to him as "the eleven thousand dollar lemon." However, in his third season, he lived up to his billing, pitching nineteen consecutive winning games. It seems safe to say that after that year's performance, he had no regrets about staying with the team despite the lean years.

Prayer Suggestion—Rejoice that God stays with us in the bad times as well as the good times.

DECEMBER

9

2 Timothy 4:1–8

Today in History—After centuries of Moslem rule, Jerusalem is surrendered to the British by the Turkish troops in World War I, 1917; John Birch Society founded, 1958; Tanganyika gains independence, later to become self-governing Tanzania, 1961; five Argentinians are convicted on charges of being junta leaders during 1970s, 1985.

Born Today—Poet John Milton, 1608; writer Joel Chandler Harris, 1848; theologian G. Campbell Morgan, 1863; actor Lee J. Cobb, 1911; actor Kirk Douglas, 1916; former football player Dick Butkus, 1942; singer Donny Osmond, 1958.

Today's Quotation—"My guiding principle is 'No peace without victory.'"—*Winston Churchill, December 9, 1944*

Victory

President Woodrow Wilson said of victory, "I would rather fail in a cause that someday will triumph, than triumph in a cause that someday will fail." Spiritual failure seems so prevalent these days. The following example might show why. Two soldiers were facing one another in combat. The first said to the other, "My, how well-trained and equipped you are. Your gun looks so powerful, but I can't believe it is real." The other soldier said, "Well if you don't think it is real I might as well throw it away," and he did. What happened next? Suddenly the enemy soldier grabbed him and carried him off into captivity.

You can expect Satan, too, to flatter you and talk you into letting down your guard so that he may gain the victory. Be prepared. Know what your response will be when someone asks, "You don't really believe the Bible, do you?" You must give him a taste of what Christ did to Satan. Claim victory by using the sword of the Spirit (the Word of God) to send Satan and his followers on the run. How much Scripture have you committed to memory and stored in your arsenal?

Prayer Suggestion—May God use his Word to defeat Satan's lures and allow us to cross life's finish line victoriously.

DECEMBER

10

Today in History—Mississippi admitted to U.S. as twentieth state, 1817; Treaty of Paris formally ends Spanish-American War, 1898; wife of Nobel Prize winner, dissident Andrei Sakharov, accepts prize for him, 1975; angry farmers converge on Washington protesting low prices and tough farm conditions, 1977; Egyptian President Anwar Sadat and Israel's Menachem Begin are joint winners of Nobel prize, 1978; Mother Theresa in Calcutta named Nobel prizewinner, 1979; Solidarity's Lech Walesa wins Nobel peace prize, 1983; survivor of Nazi death camp, Elie Wiesel, 58, wins Nobel prize, 1986; President Reagan and Soviet leader Gorbachev sign first joint agreement to reduce number of nuclear arms, 1987.

Born Today—Educator Thomas Gallaudet, 1787; composer Cesar Franck, 1822; poet Emily Dickinson, 1830; musician Morton Gould, 1913; actress Dorothy Lamour, 1914; actor Harold Gould, 1923.

Today's Quotation—"All human beings are born free and equal in dignity and rights. . . . Everyone has the right to freedom of thought. . . . Everyone has the right to freedom of opinion and expression."—*United Nations Declaration of Human Rights, December 10, 1948*

Free Expression

How easy it is for our tongue to get us into trouble, often before we realize what we have done. A young man once went to Socrates to learn how to speak. Noting his tendency to talk incessantly, Socrates asked for double his usual fees. Not surprisingly, the youth objected, "Why charge me two fees?" Socrates replied, "Because I have to teach you two skills; how to hold your tongue and how to speak. The first is more difficult, but if you are not proficient at it, you will suffer greatly and create trouble without end." It is one thing to have the right to free expression and another to use the opportunity wisely.

Prayer Suggestion—May God direct us to those who need the Savior so that we might be faithful in reaching them with the gospel.

DECEMBER

11

John 13:34—14:6

Today in History—Indiana admitted to U.S. as nineteenth state, 1816; England's King Edward VIII abdicates the British crown to marry Mrs. Wallis Simpson, 1936; John D. Rockefeller, Jr., donates New York City site for U.N. headquarters, 1946; UNICEF (United Nations International Children's Emergency Fund) established, 1946; Judge Anthony Kennedy nominated by President Reagan to U.S. Supreme Court, 1987.

Born Today—Composer Hector Berlioz, 1803; scientist Robert Koch, 1843; politician Fiorello La Guardia, 1882; evangelist John R. Rice, 1895; writer Aleksander Solzhenitsyn, 1918; actress Rita Moreno, 1931; singer Brenda Lee, 1944.

Today's Quotation—"I have found it impossible to carry the heavy burden of responsibility and to discharge my duties as King as I would wish to without the help and support of the woman I love."—*Edward VIII, December 11, 1936*

Love

The Christian marriage in which a man shows love for his wife is a parallel of Christ's love for the church. John R. Rice tells that when he was in college, he was very poor and had to forego much to live. Yet when his fiancée wanted candy that cost $1.50 per pound, in the days of the nickel candy bar, he made sure she had it. When they separated, he wrote every day. He recalls, "No work was hard if she were pleased with it, and no road was too long if she were at the end of it. . . . I never thanked God for a blessing without pouring out to her my joys."

This is how God loves sinners, with an all-encompassing love, even if he is not loved in return. We will never be able to fathom the greatness of God's love.

Prayer Suggestion—Since God is love, pledge to love others as he has first loved us.

DECEMBER

12

1 John 3:13–24

Today in History—Pennsylvania becomes second state to ratify U.S. Constitution, 1787; U.S. gunboat *Panay* shelled and sunk by Japanese on Yangtze River in China; Japan apologizes and pays indemnity, 1937; U.S. announces plans to withdraw from UNESCO because of poor management and other concerns, 1984; chartered plane crash in Newfoundland kills 250 persons (mostly U.S. servicemen returning to Ft. Campbell, Ky., from duty in Europe), 1985; President Reagan signs Gramm-Rudman bill designed to force balancing of the federal budget, 1985.

Born Today—Statesman John Jay, 1745; writer Gustave Flaubert, 1821; singer Frank Sinatra, 1915; TV host Bob Barker, 1923; politician Edward Koch, 1924; singer Connie Francis, 1938; singer Dionne Warwick, 1941.

Today's Quotation—"We disaffiliate."—*John L. Lewis, December 12, 1947*

Severing Ties

The thread of life is so fragile within us that, when severed by death, the forces of destruction rapidly take over. Doctors tell us that for any human body parts to be utilized for transplants, they must be removed within minutes of death. A surgeon describes the process this way: "The human body is filled with 'invaders' who are held in check by life. When death comes, these invaders sweep out to destroy the body. Within two hours their damage has become so extensive that nothing may be salvaged for a living human being."

That describes our spiritual condition. With Adam's sin, Satan's invaders moved out and permeated the race so that they left nothing good to restore spiritual life or growth. It is only through Christ's death, burial, and resurrection, which conquered sin, that we have any hope at all of eternal life. Friend, don't disaffiliate from God. Accept his prescription for eternal life and be saved today.

Prayer Suggestion—Accept Christ's forgiveness for your sins today. Then tell others of his saving power.

DECEMBER

13

Today in History—New Zealand discovered, 1642; Dartmouth College chartered, 1769; George Gershwin's "An American in Paris" premieres, 1928; thousands flee Bhopal, India, following word that the plant would be started up again; death toll is now estimated at twenty-one hundred, with many others injured or blinded by the toxic fumes which spread over the nearby community ten days earlier due to a faulty valve, 1984.

Born Today—Writer Heinrich Heine, 1797; clergyman Phillips Brooks, 1835; war hero Alvin York, 1887; government official George Shultz, 1920; actor Dick Van Dyke, 1925; actor Tim Conway, 1933; entertainer John Davidson, 1941.

Today's Quotation—"It is well that war is so terrible—we should grow too fond of it."—*Robert E. Lee, December 13, 1862*

Fond of War

It is sometimes amazing what "war fever" will do to some people. During the skirmishes leading up to World War I, an enterprising New York newspaper reporter, restricted by budget to staying at home, invented a fictitious "general" who kept winning battles wherever he went. Competing papers, not wanting to be upstaged, sent their reporters overseas to the scene of the "battles" in search of the elusive general. Just as they were closing in, the enterprising reporter "killed off" his general in a final blaze of glory. The reporter's fondness of war drove him to dishonesty as he tried to capture the headlines.

As serious as armed warfare is here on earth, how much more significant is the spiritual battle for men's souls, the battle between good and evil, which is growing more fierce all the time.

Prayer Suggestion—Help us to declare war on Satan and sin, and to always strive to work for God, who is on the winning side.

DECEMBER

14

Today in History—George Washington dies at Mount Vernon, Va., 1799; Alabama admitted to U.S. as twenty-second state, 1819; explorer Roald Amundsen first to reach the South Pole, 1911; United Nations selects New York City as permanent headquarters, 1946; NATO nations warn Soviets not to interfere in Poland's internal affairs, 1980.

Born Today—Astronomer Tycho Brahe, 1546; English preacher George Whitefield, 1714; aviator James Doolittle, 1896; politician Margaret Chase Smith, 1897; actor Morey Amsterdam, 1914; producer Don Hewitt, 1922; actress Lee Remick, 1935.

Today's Quotation—"In my judgment woman suffrage has nothing but mischief in it. . . . For it revolutionizes the opinions of those among us who believe that the legitimate and proper sphere of woman is the family circle as wife and mother and not as politician and voter."—*Senator George G. Vest, December 14, 1882*

Women's Rights

The TV quiz show host asked the woman contestant the secret of happiness in her marriage. "My husband is boss," she said. "And who made the decision that he was to be the boss?" the host persisted. "Why, naturally, I did," she exclaimed.

How should husband and wife respond to the trials of life? An excellent starting point is for the couple to share a time of Bible reading and prayer together each day. It is in this time together that the normal abrasions of married life can be healed. Each spouse should ask the other what it is they are doing that displeases the other. Likewise each should ask their partner what matters they would like mentioned in prayer. The truly happy couple will discover that the closer they draw to God, the closer they will be to each other, and the stronger their marriage will be. "Draw nigh to God, and he will draw nigh to you" (James 4:8) applies as much to couples and families as it does to individuals.

Prayer Suggestion—Help me to so uplift my spouse that he or she will become more Christ-like each and every day because of me.

DECEMBER

15

Today in History—Bill of Rights, the first ten amendments to U.S. Constitution, ratified, 1791; Sitting Bull killed by Indian police in South Dakota, 1890; Shah of Iran leaves U.S. for Panama following medical treatment in New York City, 1979; running for president of the Philippines, Corazon Aquino vows to put President Ferdinand Marcos on trial for his part in the murder of her husband, opposition leader Benigno Aquino, 1985.

Born Today—Roman Emperor Nero, 37 A.D.; playwright Maxwell Anderson, 1888; oil executive J. Paul Getty, 1892; scientist Willard Libby, 1908; actor Don Johnson, 1949; football player Daryl Turner, 1961.

Today's Quotation—"Congress shall make no law respecting an establishment of religion, or prohibiting the free exercise thereof; or abridging the freedom of speech, or of the press, or the right of the people peaceably to assemble, and to petition the Government for a redress of grievances."—*First Amendment, ratified December 15, 1791*

Freedom to Worship

Every week each citizen, consciously or not, votes on the issue of religious freedom. By attending church, they are voting for the opportunity to worship as they please. Likewise, by staying away, they are casting a negative vote. Which way will you vote this week?

When asked why he attended church, the board chairman of Sun Oil Company, J. Howard Pew, was quoted as saying, "I go to church to hear heralded the mind of Christ, not the mind of man. I want to hear expounded the timeless truth contained in the Scriptures, the kind of preaching that gets its power from, 'Thus saith the Lord.' Such preaching is hard to find these days."

If you've found a good gospel-preaching church, be sure to cast your vote this week—be there every time the doors are open. If you haven't yet found such a church, ask God to direct you to one near you.

Prayer Suggestion—Thank God for the freedom to worship in peace. Then take advantage of the opportunity by worshipping him each week.

DECEMBER

16

Today in History—Boston Tea Party, 1773; Anton Dvorak's *New World Symphony* premieres, 1893; Battle of the Bulge, German counter-attack in Belgium launched against U.S. troops, 1944; two airliners collide over Staten Island, New York, killing 134, 1960; O. J. Simpson sets new rushing record of over two thousand yards in one football season, 1973; Cleveland, Ohio, becomes first city since the Depression to default, 1978; Libya becomes fifth OPEC nation to raise oil prices in the past week, 1979; Senator Gary Hart says he's back in the Democratic presidential race as he leads in current polls, 1987.

Born Today—Composer Ludwig van Beethoven, 1770; writer Jane Austen, 1775; actor Noel Coward, 1899; anthropologist Margaret Mead, 1901; actress Liv Ullmann, 1939; broadcast journalist Lesley Stahl, 1941.

Today's Quotation—"It is honorable for us, to have produced the first legislature who had the courage to declare, that the reason of man may be trusted with the formation of his own opinions . . ."—*Thomas Jefferson, December 16, 1786*

Free Thinking

Americans are fortunate to be able to think independently of the dictates of government. However, not just free thinking but spiritual thinking is the greatest need today. President Woodrow Wilson once said, "Our civilization cannot survive materially unless it be redeemed spiritually. It can be saved only by becoming permeated with the spirit of Christ and being made free and happy by the practices which sprang out of the Spirit. Only thus can discontent be driven out and all the shadows lifted from the road ahead." While we can thank God for our freedoms, we must never become free of his guiding hand.

Prayer Suggestion—Praise God for his Word, which serves as our road map to direct us upon life's way.

DECEMBER

17

Today in History—First powered airplane flight, by Orville and Wilbur Wright, 1903; German battleship *Graf Spee* scuttled by its crew to avoid British in World War II, 1939; Nazi troopers gunned down 80 U.S. prisoners of war during Battle of Bulge in World War II, 1944; two women, guilty of attempted assassination of President Ford, both sentenced to life in prison, 1975; seven Poles killed while resisting imposition of martial law, 1981.

Born Today—Poet John Greenleaf Whittier, 1807; conductor Arthur Fiedler, 1894; TV host Gene Rayburn, 1917; author William Safire, 1929; actor Tommy Steele, 1936; basketball player Albert King, 1959.

Today's Quotation—"He is indeed a semi-Solomon. He half-knows everything."—*Thomas Babington Macaulay, December 17, 1830*

A Little Knowledge

This has been called the "information age"—an era of unprecedented increase in human knowledge. Yet it is still true that "a little knowledge is a dangerous thing"; that is, just enough knowledge to get into trouble without doing it right.

Because of the knowledge explosion, this is an era of increased specialization in learning. Not many years ago, a leading university offered just one psychology class, and it was in the philosophy department. Today that same school offers a full-blown psychology program with specializations in clinical, experimental, or educational psychology. In addition, there are numerous sub-disciplines such as learning theory, physiological, and social psychology. Other areas of knowledge are also rapidly expanding.

The Bible predicts a vast increase of knowledge in the time before Christ returns for believers in the rapture. Although few humans will ever master great knowledge of the universe, anyone can have knowledge of the One whom to know is life eternal. Do you have personal knowledge of God's Son who died for you?

Prayer Suggestion—Get to know God better by reading and meditating upon his Word.

DECEMBER

18

Today in History—New Jersey becomes third state to ratify U.S. Constitution, 1787; ratification of Thirteenth Amendment abolishes slavery, 1865; first U.S. commercial nuclear power plant begins supplying electricity, 1957; Soviets announce plans to resume nuclear testing, which had been stopped since last year, 1986; inside stock trader Ivan Boesky sentenced to three years in jail, 1987.

Born Today—Clergyman Charles Wesley, 1707; composer Carl Maria Von Weber, 1786; baseball's Ty Cobb, 1886; inventor Edwin Armstrong, 1890; General Benjamin Davis, 1912; dramatist Ossie Davis, 1917; director Steven Spielberg, 1947.

Today's Quotation—"Politics is not an exact science."—*Otto von Bismarck, December 18, 1863*

Imprecise

Although politics may not be an exact science, prayer always brings definite results. Sometimes we may wonder why our prayers apparently go unanswered. It could be because our prayers are imprecise; maybe God doesn't grant our request simply because it is not clear what we seek.

As a teenager, John R. Rice learned the lesson of precise prayer. It was in a rally in west Texas, when a country preacher asked Rice to join him in a time of specific prayer for the crusade. After reading Scripture the two agreed that the Lord was encouraging them to pray for five souls to be saved that night. At the end of that service, five people did come forward. The next day, the pair prayed that three souls would be saved. That evening, exactly three people acknowledged Christ as Savior. Encouraged by God's answers to specific prayer, they began to pray for people by name. Again God responded to the faithful prayers of his children. As the famed evangelist said, "In those few days it dawned on me that God wants Christians to pray for definite objectives—to be explicit in their requests."

Prayer Suggestion—May God give specific answers to our specific requests to him each day.

DECEMBER

19

Today in History—Thomas Paine publishes first "American Crisis" essay, 1776; General George Washington leads Continental Army into winter encampment, 1777; communists begin war against French rule of Indochina, 1946; General Dwight D. Eisenhower appointed as military commander of NATO (the North Atlantic Treaty Organization), 1950; U.S. Apollo moon program ends with splashdown of *Apollo 17* in the Pacific; two of the astronauts spent a total of seventy-five hours walking on the moon's surface, 1972; pianist Arthur Rubinstein dies at age 95 in Geneva, 1982.

Born Today—Explorer William Parry, 1790; physicist Albert Michelson, 1852; pastor W. A. Criswell, 1909; actress Cicely Tyson, 1939; anthropologist Richard Leakey, 1944; basketball player Kevin McHale, 1957.

Today's Quotation—"These are the times that try men's souls."—
Thomas Paine, December 19, 1776

Trying Times

God sometimes uses sharp setbacks to get our attention focused on him and to redirect our life. A man once walked down a windswept street in a small northeastern town, unaware that ahead lay the end of a high voltage wire which had been blown from its pole. A witness, seeing what was about to happen, tried to yell at the man, but he was unable to get his attention over the howling wind. So he decided upon more drastic measures. He spotted a nearby rock and hurled it directly at the chest of the man approaching the wire. Stunned, the man looked up just in time to see the wire and avoid certain tragedy.

Has God seemed to deal you a low blow? Perhaps he is hoping to draw your attention to some need not now being addressed in your life. Look for God's leading in all things.

Prayer Suggestion—Seek God's will in all matters affecting your life, whether they seem to be blessings or hardships at the time.

DECEMBER
20

Today in History—Louisiana Territory formally transferred to U.S., 1803; South Carolina becomes first state to secede from the Union, 1860; Thomas Alva Edison demonstrates the incandescent electric light, 1879; U.S.S.R. (Union of Soviet Socialist Republics) forms, 1922; Far East Broadcasting Company founded, 1945; Senate passes 1.5 billion dollar federal loan guarantee for Chrysler Corporation, 1979.

Born Today—Industrialist Harvey Firestone, 1868; philosopher Susanne Langer, 1895; columnist Max Lerner, 1902; director George Hill, 1922; artist David Levine, 1926.

Today's Quotation—"I am not a friend to a very energetic government. It is always oppressive. It places the governors indeed more at their ease, at the expense of the people."—*Thomas Jefferson, December 20, 1787*

Energetic

While Jefferson was worried about a government being too active, most adults have the opposite ailment, namely, a lack of energy.

Not long ago a power company in the Philippines became suspicious of a consistently low light bill encountered by one of their customers. They were even more troubled when they learned that this man earned over one thousand dollars per month and thus could afford all the power he needed. The firm sent investigators to check out the situation and were totally amazed to find that this relatively wealthy man had only two light bulbs and no electric appliances in his home and thus he had limited his power consumption to just one dollar per month!

I wonder if there aren't some Christians who act as if God's power will soon run out in their lives. The Bibles makes clear, "for whomsoever much is given, of him shall much be required" (Luke 12:48). Are you tapping into God's unlimited energy resource?

Prayer Suggestion—God, I want more of your power to flow through me. Remove all of the sin which insulates me from fully relying on your energy.

DECEMBER

21

Today in History—Forefathers Day marks landing of Pilgrims at Plymouth, Mass., 1620; Pierre and Marie Curie discover radium, 1898; comedian Jack Benny dies at age 80, 1974; only one minor injury, but considerable damage, reported as fire bomb explodes at Harrod's department store in London, 1974; Rhodesia's civil war ends after seven years, 1979; Nicaragua frees downed American airman Eugene Hasenfus, 1986; Pan Am jet explodes over Scotland, killing all 259 passengers aboard, 1988.

Born Today—Statesman Benjamin Disraeli, 1804; Soviet Premier Josef Stalin, 1879; statesman Kurt Waldheim, 1918; ventriloquist Paul Winchell, 1922; TV host Phil Donahue, 1935; tennis player Chris Evert Lloyd, 1954.

Today's Quotation—"Governments exist to protect the rights of minorities. The loved and the rich need no protection—they have many friends and few enemies."—*Wendell Phillips, December 21, 1860*

God's Help

A United Nations worker witnessed an unusual sight recently in Java. There he saw countless workers caked with mud, hauling dirt out of a deep pit. They had to carry their load up a swaying bamboo ladder to the top. The U.N. worker suggested to another observer that they bring in bulldozers and other heavy equipment to assist. He was warned not to interfere with the project: "Understand this is their canal. For the first time they will have something of their own for which they owe no one. Once they learn to believe in themselves maybe they can believe in the help we can give them."

Sometimes God must sit back and let us try to work it out so that when we ask his assistance we will better understand the miracle he performs for us.

Prayer Suggestion—Turn your burdens over to the Lord and leave them there. Then watch him work on your behalf.

DECEMBER

22

Today in History—French Army Captain Alfred Dreyfus found guilty of treason (vindicated years later), 1894; Lincoln Tunnel linking New York and New Jersey opens, 1937; Wake Island falls to Japanese, 1941; "Nuts," replied Maj. Gen. Anthony McAuliffe to German demand for surrender of encircled U.S. 101st Airborne Division at Bastogne, Belgium, in World War II, 1944; patient takes first steps after surgery to implant artificial Jarvik 7 heart, 1982; four black youths shot on New York City subway by white gunman, 1984; fifty thousand Chinese students demonstrate on behalf of domestic reforms, 1986.

Born Today—Composer Giacomo Puccini, 1858; poet Edwin Robinson, 1869; former First Lady Ladybird Johnson, 1912; actress Barbara Billingsley, 1922; baseball player Steve Carlton, 1944; broadcast journalist Dianne Sawyer, 1946.

Today's Quotation—"Age does not endow all things with strength and virtue, nor are all new things to be despised."—*Henry W. Grady, December 22, 1886*

Despising the New

Someone has said, "If it's new, it isn't true, and if it's true, it isn't new." We do need to be cautious in accepting new beliefs (especially in the spiritual area), measuring them all against the truths of God's Word. One good idea which seems especially appropriate in this age of travel has to do with the distribution of Bibles. The Belgian Bible Society has converted a vending machine from selling candy to distributing Bibles in various languages. The machine, placed outside the society's offices at a busy bus stop, was reported to be selling about one hundred copies of the books per month. While this could never be the sole means of distributing Bibles, it works well for people on the go in Brussels.

Prayer Suggestion—Help us to be flexible in the *means* but not the *message* of God's saving grace to this lost and dying world.

DECEMBER

23

Today in History—First loan floated by an American government (by the Massachusetts Bay Colony), 1690; Federal Reserve System established, 1913; John Bardeen, Walter H. Brattain, and William Shickley invent the transistor, 1947; in North Korea, twenty-one Americans held as prisoners of war embrace communism and refuse to return to U.S., 1953; North Korea releases crew of U.S. Navy intelligence ship *Pueblo* after U.S. "apology," 1968; President Reagan signs a record fifty-two billion dollar, three-year farm bill said to favor large farm producers, 1985; Soviet physicist Andrei Sakharov and his wife return from exile to address scientific seminar, 1986.

Born Today—Author Samuel Smiles, 1812; baseball's Connie Mack, 1862; photographer Yousuf Karsh, 1908; actress Ruth Roman, 1923; newscaster Floyd Kalber, 1924; author Robert Bly, 1926.

Today's Quotation—"To play is for a man to do what he pleases, or to do nothing—to go about soothing his particular fancies."—*Charles Lamb, December 23, 1822*

Doing Nothing

One of the most welcome sounds for a tired foot soldier at the end of a long hike is the command "At Rest." While the command "At Ease" signifies only temporary relief, "At Rest" calls for a time of extended refreshment—"doing nothing" at the completion of the day's activities.

This reminds me of the story of the little girl who had been raised to believe that Christians were to go around with a dreary, tired expression. She once visited a stable where she quickly became excited by a young horse. She got so caught up that she was overheard to exclaim, "Oh, Horsey, you must be a Christian for you have such a long face!"

What kind of feeling do others, including your family, have when they see you coming? Are they happier to see you coming or going? If you love Christ, then enjoy life in the world God made for his children!

Prayer Suggestion—Help me to be an encourager to those around me who need to see God's love reflected through my life.

DECEMBER

24

Today in History—"Silent Night" composed by Franz Gruber in Oberndorff, Germany, with words by Josef Mohr, sung for first time Christmas Day, 1818; Enrico Caruso's last U.S. performance, 1920; Admiral Jean-Francois Darlan, administrator of French North Africa for Nazi-occupied France, assassinated, 1942; Libya Independence Day marks nation's gaining freedom after United Nations trusteeship, 1951; Richard Rutan and Jeanna Yeager fly non-stop around the world in nine days, three minutes and forty-four seconds, 1986.

Born Today—Physician-patriot Benjamin Rush, 1745; frontiersman Kit Carson, 1809; financier Howard Hughes, 1905; actress Ava Gardner, 1922; physician Anthony Fauci, 1940; director Nicholas Meyer, 1945.

Today's Quotation—" 'Twas the night before Christmas and all through the house, not a creature was stirring—not even a mouse."— *Clement C. Moore, December 24, 1822*

The Night Before Christmas

What was the scene like in Bethlehem the night before Christ's birth? No doubt the inn was filling up with visitors from distant places, coming to their hometown to register. For the shepherds, it was probably a night like so many others in that pre-electric era of darkness with everyone seated around flickering campfires. It is no wonder, with such all-encompassing darkness, that the shepherds were frightened by the angels' heavenly appearance.

An interesting question deals with why shepherds were chosen to receive the angelic announcement. Perhaps the fact that the shepherds were outdoors at night where they would be most likely to see the herald angels was a reason. Also, who could be more fitting witnesses to the birth of the Good Shepherd than men who were, themselves, shepherds? What amazement they must have had to realize that here, in a humble feeding trough, lay the Savior of all mankind. Have you any room for Jesus?

Prayer Suggestion—May we be surrendered to God and open to his salvation and will for our lives.

DECEMBER

25

Today in History—Christ was born to Mary in Bethlehem stable; William the Conqueror becomes first monarch to Britain to be crowned in Westminster Abbey, 1066; General George Washington leads his troops across the Delaware River for a surprise attack, 1776; Hirohito becomes Emperor of Japan, 1926; HCJB missionary radio begins, 1931.

Born Today—Jesus Christ; scientist Isaac Newton, 1642; nurse-philanthropist Clara Barton, 1821; hotelman Conrad Hilton, 1887; writer Rod Serling, 1924; singer Barbara Mandrell, 1948.

Today's Quotation—"Behold I bring you good tidings of great joy . . . for unto you is born this day . . . a Savior which is Christ the Lord."—*Angel of the Lord, Christmas Night*

Delight

"God so loved the world that he sent his only begotten son that whosoever believeth in Him should not perish but hath everlasting life" (John 3:16)—not because he had to but because he loved mankind so much. One of the most fascinating characters related to the Christmas story is the godly priest Simeon, who had waited years for Christ's arrival. We can scarcely underestimate his joy at seeing the fulfillment of years of anticipation with the birth of the Messiah. Other than the first Christmas celebration, historians note it was not until A.D. 98 that Christmas was celebrated and another forty years before Christians officially adopted the observance. The December 25 date was not settled on until about the fifth century with Christmas observed in April, December, and January (most often) before that time. The Pilgrims did not observe Christmas (nor any other church festival) but instead built the first house in the Plymouth settlement, Christmas Day 1620. Over the years a number of kings have been crowned on Christmas Day but no great battles have ever been fought that day, as it is widely recognized as a day for cessation of battles in honor of the Prince of Peace.

Prayer Suggestion—"O Come to my heart, Lord Jesus, there is room in my heart for thee."

DECEMBER

26

Today in History—General George Washington defeats British Hessians at Battle of Trenton, 1776; encircled U.S. 101st Airborne Division at the Battle of Bastogne, Belgium, in World War II, relieved by other U.S. units, 1944; former President Harry Truman dies at age 88, 1972; Russians airlift five thousand troops into Afganistan, 1979; study shows it costs New York City $40,000 to house and feed one prisoner for one year, 1984.

Born Today—Admiral George Dewey, 1837; actor Richard Widmark, 1914; entertainer Steve Allen, 1921; comedian Alan King, 1927; producer Phil Spector, 1940; baseball player Carlton Fisk, 1947.

Today's Quotation—"I am a child of the House of Commons. I was brought up in my father's house to believe in democracy; trust the people, that was his message."—*Winston Churchill, December 26, 1941*

Brought Up Right

Some people seem to think their children will grow up to be godly, productive adults, simply by leaving them alone. What could be further from the truth?

Coleridge was once talking with a man about raising children. The man said he didn't see any need to direct his children spiritually, preferring to "let them grow up and decide for themselves which way is right." Coleridge then beckoned the man to come and look at his garden. "Why, it is just a patch of weeds!" exclaimed the visitor. "Quite true," responded the philosopher. "But I decided some time ago to simply let the garden grow its own way. You see, I didn't want to influence how it would turn out."

Does this sound familiar? Never let it be said of you that you let the children grow up on their own. Give them spiritual instruction and encouragement because, after all, our families are the only earthly things we can ever take with us to heaven!

Prayer Suggestion—May I be a worthy parent or teacher to the young people God has entrusted to me.

DECEMBER

27

Psalm 126:1–6

Today in History—Cornerstone of Episcopal Cathedral of St. John the Divine laid in New York City, 1892; Radio City Music Hall opens, 1932; World Bank begins its existence, 1945; one thousand guerillas attack government forces in El Salvador (nine thousand now dead as a result of fighting since 1979), 1980; Pope John Paul II meets with Ali Agca, his would-be assassin, 1983; President Reagan takes responsibility for lack of security in Beirut, allowing terrorists to kill 241 Marines, 1983.

Born Today—Astronomer Johann Kepler, 1571; aviator George Cayley, 1773; scientist Louis Pasteur, 1822; physician William Masters, 1915; psychologist Lee Salk, 1926; designer Bernard Lanvin, 1935.

Today's Quotation—"We are bounded by the law of God and men to do good unto all men and evil to no one."—*Remonstrance to Peter Stuyvesant, December 27, 1657*

Doing Good to All Men

Don't put off doing acts of kindness as the opportunities arise, because "you may never pass this way again." An unknown poet has expressed that idea so well in this poem, entitled "Say It Now":

> If you have a tender message, or a loving word to say;
> Don't wait till you forget it, but whisper it today!

> The tender words unspoken, The letter never sent,
> The long-forgotten messages, the wealth of love unspent.

> For these some hearts are breaking, for these some loved ones wait,
> Then give them what they're needing, before it is too late!

Look for someone who needs your help and encouragement today!

Prayer Suggestion—Lord, lay someone upon my heart today, and help me to love them as you do.

DECEMBER

28

Today in History—Iowa admitted to U.S. as twenty-ninth state, 1846; U.S. Navy Construction Battalions (Seabees) established in World War II, 1941; Jozsef Cardinal Mindszenty, leader of Hungary's Roman Catholics, arrested by communist government there, 1948; left-wing rebels kill three and take twenty others hostage in attack in Managua, Nicaragua, 1974; Australia wins over Sweden in Davis Cup tennis match, 1986.

Born Today—President Woodrow Wilson, 1856; author Carol Brink, 1895; actor Lou Jacobi, 1913; business executive John Akers, 1934; actress Maggie Smith, 1934; politician David Peterson, 1943.

Today's Quotation—"Give me a log hut, with only a simple bench, Mark Hopkins [professor of moral philosophy and rhetoric] on one end and I on the other, and you may have all the buildings, apparatus, and libraries without him."—*James A. Garfield, December 28, 1871*

Knowledge

Garfield's observation describes the basics of how learning takes place— the communication of knowledge. But how much does mankind really know? As it turns out, very little, especially in light of an all-knowing God.

It was prolific inventor Thomas Alva Edison who said of mankind, "We do not know one-millionth part of one per cent about anything. We do not know what water is. We do not know what light is. We do not know what electricity is. We do not know what gravity is. We don't know anything about magnetism. We have a lot of hypotheses, but that is all." A man credited with superior knowledge in many areas, Albert Einstein, said, "We know nothing about [the world] at all. Our knowledge is but the knowledge of school children."

Our God has all knowledge and keeps the universe constantly under his control—yet has time enough to hear the prayers of you and me! What a mighty God we serve!

Prayer Suggestion—Praise God for his knowledge and power; thank him for all he's done for you this year and today!

DECEMBER

29

Today in History—Republic of Texas joins U.S. as twenty-eighth state, 1845; Gregory Rasputin, the monk who was power behind the Czar's throne in imperial Russia, assassinated, 1916; Professor Harold C. Urey announces the identification of heavy water, 1931; bomb explosion in locker at La Guardia airport kills fourteen, 1975; millions of Iranians demonstrate against the Shah, 1978; Rajiv Gandhi elected Indian prime minister in landslide race, 1984.

Born Today—Inventor Charles Goodyear, 1800; President Andrew Johnson, 1808; statesman William Gladstone, 1809; President Woodrow Wilson, 1856; politician Tom Bradley, 1917; broadcast journalist Tom Jarriel, 1934; actress Mary Tyler Moore, 1936; actor Jon Voight, 1938.

Today's Quotation—"Those marriages generally abound most with love and constancy that are preceded by a long courtship."—*Joseph Addison, December 29, 1711*

Continuing Courtship

Marriage counselors say that one way to ensure a strong marriage is for both spouses to commit to a regular time of togetherness. For some this may mean leaving the kids with a baby sitter for a special "date" or it could be something as basic as reading Scripture and praying together. Historically, couples have acknowledged their love in unusual ways.

A Paris artist, Marcel de Leclure, set the world's record for love letters, according to Robert Ripley. In 1875, Leclure sent his true love, Magdalene, a letter containing only three words, "I Love You," repeated 1,875,000 times. But the story doesn't end there, for Leclure individually repeated (and had repeated back to him by his scribe) the phrase, a total of 5,625,000 times saying "I Love You" in speech and writing. Ripley says, "Never was love made manifest by as great an expenditure of time and effort."

Prayer Suggestion—Thank God that he first loved us and has given us others to love and to love us in return.

DECEMBER

30

Today in History—U.S. agrees to purchase southern portion of Arizona and New Mexico from Mexico for ten million dollars, 1853; six hundred die in Iroquois Theatre fire in Chicago, 1903; first Liberty Ship of World World II, the *Patrick Henry,* is delivered at Baltimore, Md., 1941; House committee concludes there is likelihood of conspiracy in the murder of Martin Luther King, Jr., 1978; composer Richard Rogers dies at age 77, 1979.

Born Today—Writer Rudyard Kipling, 1865; philanthropist Simon Guggenheim, 1867; actor Bert Parks, 1914; sportscaster Sandy Koufax, 1935; actress Tracey Ullman, 1959; sprinter Ben Johnson, 1961.

Today's Quotation—"In short, in matters vegetable, animal, and mineral, I am the very model of a modern Major-General."—*W. S. Gilbert, December 30, 1879*

A Good Role Model

Have you ever heard the statement "You are the only Bible some will ever read"? What do others "read" of Christ in your life? Are you a good Christian role model for others?

An article in *The Christian Herald* illustrates how people learn from what they see. A senior executive in one of New York's largest banks recalled how he got his start in banking. It began shortly after he was hired as an office boy many years before. One day the bank president called the youth to his office and told him he wanted him to work with him each day. The lad protested that he knew nothing of banking. The president told him, "Never mind, you will learn a lot faster if you just stay by my side and keep your eyes and ears open." The young boy did just that and later recalled, "Being with that man made me just like him. I began to do things the way he did, and that accounts for what I am today."

Prayer Suggestion—May others see Jesus fully reflected in my life.

DECEMBER

31

Today in History—First public demonstration of Thomas A. Edison's incandescent electric lamp, 1879; President Harry Truman officially proclaims end of World War II, 1946; U.S. energy department directs standby gas rationing plan, 1973; President Carter accuses Soviet leader Brezhnev of not telling the truth about Afganistan invasion, 1979.

Born Today—Artist Henri Matisse, 1869; statesman George Marshall, 1880; musician Odetta, 1930; singer John Denver, 1943; actor Ben Kingsley, 1943; designer Diane von Furstenberg, 1946; singer Donna Summer, 1948.

Today's Quotation—"Education belongs pre-eminently to the church . . . neutral or lay schools from which religion is excluded are contrary to the fundamental principles of education."—*Pope Pius XI, December 31, 1929*

Christian Education

"Train up a child in the way he should go: and when he is old, he will not depart from it" (Prov. 22:6). These words from God form the basis of all Christian education. No parent would expect his child to compete physically against professional athletes every day and yet this is, in effect, what occurs educationally when children attend non-Christian schools staffed by non-Christian professionals. It is doubtful if, after twelve years in such an atmosphere, they can emerge with their original beliefs and faith intact.

Listen to these words from the early 1940s: "Day after day young people are subjected to the bombardment of naturalism with all of its animosity toward Christianity. In the formative years of their lives . . . they must listen to and absorb these ideas of man, the world and religion. With these facts before them, why do (believers) wonder that Christianity has so little influence over their young people!" Who made this observation? It was none other than long-time New York newspaper columnist Walter Lippman!

Prayer Suggestion—Since children are God's greatest gift on earth, resolve to ensure they are trained to know and love God.

Dear Reader:

Thank you for reading this book. I hope it has given you a new appreciation for the history and traditions which have blessed our nation and the world over the years.

What a privilege it would be to meet you and hear all about your memorable days! I hope we can, if not in this life, then in the life to come. You ask, "How can I know for certain where I will spend eternity?" God has given us his Word, the Bible, which tells us without a doubt our eternal destiny. You see, God loved you so much that he sent his sinless son, Jesus Christ, to earth in human form, to adopt you into God's family. Although God loves all of his creation, we are not all God's children, for the Bible says, "all have sinned, and come short of the glory of God" (Rom. 3:23). A perfect God cannot look upon sin. But the story doesn't end there, because a loving God has provided forgiveness for our sins. "For God so loved the world, that he gave his only begotten Son, that whosoever believeth in him should not perish, but have everlasting life" (John 3:16).

You say, "God could never forgive me for what I have done!" God says, "He that cometh unto me I will in no wise cast out." Do not delay, for God does not promise us tomorrow, but rather says, "Today is the day of Salvation." If you would like to talk with someone who can show you, from God's Word, how you can experience Christ's forgiveness and know positively that you are part of God's eternal, heavenly family, please call 1-800-LIFE-AID (543-3243) or (804) 847-9000 any time day or night, to speak in confidence with a trained counselor who wants to help *you* –

There could be no greater tribute paid to an author than that his book introduced you to the Creator of all history. In believing in God and trusting Christ for your salvation, today could be the greatest of all the days of your life, your spiritual birthday—the day God adopted you into his eternal family!

So if our paths don't cross here on earth, be sure to look me up when we get to heaven. We'll have forever to talk about the day you met Jesus and claimed him as your Savior and Lord.

May all your days be blessed by God as you trust in him!

Your friend,

Carl Windsor
Forest, Virginia
April 1989